Da Capo Press Series in
ARCHITECTURE AND DECORATIVE ART

General Editor: ADOLF K. PLACZEK
Avery Librarian, Columbia University

Volume 35

THE ARTS AND CRAFTS
IN NEW YORK
1726–1776

THE ARTS AND CRAFTS
IN NEW YORK
1726–1776

ADVERTISEMENTS AND NEWS ITEMS
FROM NEW YORK CITY
NEWSPAPERS

Compiled by Rita S. Gottesman

DA CAPO PRESS · NEW YORK · 1970

A Da Capo Press Reprint Edition

This Da Capo Press edition of
The Arts and Crafts in New York, 1726-1776,
is an unabridged republication of the first
edition published in New York in 1938 as the
Collections of The New York Historical Society for the Year 1936.

Library of Congress Catalog Card Number 70-127254

SBN 306-71129-X

Published by Da Capo Press
A Division of Plenum Publishing Corporation
227 West 17th Street
New York, N. Y. 10011

COLLECTIONS OF

THE NEW YORK HISTORICAL SOCIETY

FOR THE YEAR 1936

THE JOHN WATTS DePEYSTER
PUBLICATION FUND SERIES

LXIX

THE ARTS AND CRAFTS
IN NEW YORK

1726–1776

ADVERTISEMENTS AND NEWS ITEMS
FROM NEW YORK CITY
NEWSPAPERS

NEW YORK
PRINTED FOR THE NEW YORK HISTORICAL SOCIETY
1938

PRINTED IN THE UNITED STATES OF AMERICA
BY J. J. LITTLE AND IVES COMPANY, NEW YORK

OFFICERS OF THE SOCIETY

Until January 21, 1941

PREFACE

This source book on *The Arts and Crafts in New York* has been compiled by Mrs. Rita Susswein Gottesman from advertisements and news items gleaned from all the New York City newspapers for the years 1726 through 1776. It constitutes the sixty-ninth volume of the John Watts DePeyster Publication Fund Series, and is distributed to shareholders in that series as the *Collections of The New York Historical Society for the Year 1936*.

As this volume has wide appeal to specialists in many fields, the Committee on Publications decided to make it available to others than shareholders, who may be interested. For that purpose, four hundred additional copies have been printed, bound differently from the *Collections*, and these are for sale by the Society.

The analytical index is the work of Miss Dorothy C. Barck, Head of the Society's Reference Department.

ALEXANDER J. WALL,
Director

CONTENTS

INTRODUCTION

Advertisements by craftsmen were conspicuously absent from New York City newspapers before 1750. The newspaper columns were devoted for the most part to European news and only comparatively small sections contained local news and advertisements. Such advertisements as did appear dealt largely with runaway slaves, counterfeiting, sailings of vessels, real estate, and sales of merchandise.

There were undoubtedly craftsmen at the time other than the few who advertised. Reference to them is found in recorded wills, Minutes of the Common Council, lists of Freemen and other documents, and mention of them was made from time to time in runaway slave notices, real estate advertisements and the like. The explanation for the lack of advertisements by craftsmen may lie in the fact that New York was hardly more than a village at the time. It was not essential to advertise since each person knew about the affairs and occupation of his fellows.

The early New York artisan had apparently not yet won the confidence of his community, for most articles offered for sale in New York were imported. Even repairs were made abroad. James Foddy, one of the first craftsmen to advertise in New York papers, complained bitterly that he had not received "suitable encouragement."

The kind and number of craftsmen who advertised or were mentioned before 1750 are shown in the following table:

Joiners and carpenters............................ 12
Silversmiths 9
Clockmakers 7

There was also a miscellaneous group of craftsmen of whom notices or advertisements appeared sporadically.

That a comparatively large number of silversmiths should have advertised was to be expected, for silverware was commonly the repository of an individual's wealth. Having no place to store their money and being in constant fear of having it stolen, many people had their silver melted into useful pieces of ware. The silver was then less likely to be stolen since each piece had its characteristic design and marks.

Of the early craftsmen who did advertise many laid stress on business activities other than their crafts. This was especially true among watchmakers. One sold bags of new hops, another a patent medicine and still another Cheshire cheese. John Miller, who mended looking glasses, was more interested in the garden seeds he had to sell. A tooth powder notice was emphasized in a goldsmith's advertisement.

After 1750 there was a marked increase in the number and scope of advertisements largely as a result of the natural growth of the city and the constant effort to encourage home manufactures. "They are equal if not superior in quality to any imported from Europe," "No Duties Here," "To be sold as cheap as can be imported," "Preference to what is American Made" and similar statements indicated a dawning American consciousness.

Although the advertisements contained nothing of the modern arresting technique, they clearly expressed the humor, honesty and competitive spirit of the artisans. Rhymes, letters and anecdotes often formed part of an advertisement. The absence of house numbers often necessitated a long description of the location of the craftsman. Sometimes the major portion of an advertisement was given over to a description of where the craftsman could be found. The lack of guilds, membership in which would automatically have given prestige and status, made it important for the craftsman to keep his reputation unspoiled. Entire notices were sometimes devoted to long and eloquent defenses against malicious attacks on the character or skill of a craftsman.[1] Our modern price wars seem quite mild when compared to some of those reflected in these pre-revolutionary advertisements. "None of your cents, but GOODS given away Gratis" was the climax of a price war among a group of importers in 1771.

Other Compilations of Newspaper Notices

This compilation of advertisements from New York City newspapers will serve the same purpose as source material for New York as the reader will find for other states in the following compilations: George Francis Dow, *The Arts and Crafts in New England, 1704-1775* (Topsfield, Mass., 1927); Lyman Horace Weeks and Edwin M. Bacon, *An Historical Digest of the Provincial Press, Massachusetts Series, 1704-1707* (Society for Americana, Inc., Boston, 1911); Alfred Coxe Prime, *The Arts and Crafts in Philadelphia, Maryland and South Carolina, 1721-1785, 1786-1800* (The Walpole Society, 1929, 1932); *Colonial Craftsmen of Pennsylvania: Reproductions of early newspaper advertisements from the private collection of Alfred Coxe Prime* (Pennsylvania Museum and School of Industrial Art, Philadelphia, July, 1925); and newspaper extracts relating to

[1] For instance, many advertisements were inserted in the *New-York Gazette or the Weekly Post-Boy* of 1764 by Benjamin Halsted, silversmith, in an attempt to discredit the accusations of customer Andrew Bowne. *See pages 45-46.*

New Jersey, 1704-1782, in eleven volumes of the First
Series of *New Jersey Archives,* and in *New Jersey
Archives,* Second Series, volumes I-V.

New York City Newspapers, 1726-1776

The following are the newspapers, published in New
York City, through which I made a careful search, and
from which the advertisements and news items printed
in this volume have been gleaned:

> *The American Chronicle,* 1762
> *The New-York Chronicle,* 1769-1770
> *The Constitutional Gazette,* 1775-1776
> *The New-York Evening Post,* 1744-1752
> *The New-York Gazette,* 1726-1744
> *The New-York Gazette, or the Weekly Post-Boy,*
>   1747-1773
> *The New-York Gazette.* (Weyman's), 1759-1767
> *The New-York Gazette, and the Weekly Mercury,*
>   1768-1783
> *The New-York Journal, or, the General Advertiser,*
>   1766-1776
> *The New-York Mercury,* 1752-1768
> *The New-York Packet And the American Advertiser,*
>   1776
> *The New-York Pacquet,* 1763
> *Rivington's New-York Gazetteer,* 1773-1775
> *The New-York Weekly Journal,* 1733-1751
> *The New-York Weekly Post-Boy,* 1743-1747

In selecting and classifying advertisements found in
the above New York City newspapers from 1726 through
1776, I have adopted the following procedure:
1. Only the first notice of a craftsman and those subsequent notices which gave additional information have
been used. If the craftsman advertised over a period of
years without adding anything of importance to his
advertisements, I have not included the subsequent
advertisements but have merely referred to them in a

footnote. This complete chronology of advertisements has been adhered to for major crafts, such as silver, cabinetmaking, pewter, watchmaking, painting, etc. The years of continued advertising by lesser craftsmen has, in most instances, not been noted.

2. When a name of a craftsman appeared in print without any mention of his craft, I have not included the notice, unless it clearly indicated that he worked at such craft.[2]

3. The phonetic spelling and typographical errors appearing in the advertisements have been exactly reproduced without notation. I have, however, indicated where proper names have been misspelled. Paragraphs, italics and capitalization of an entire word or group of words were used by the early printers for emphasis. To copy each advertisement as it originally appeared in print would require a great deal of unnecessary space. I have, therefore, eliminated capitalization of entire words and italics in the body of the advertisements. Dashes and paragraphs have been retained only when their omission would fail to make the advertisement clear.

4. Although the original wording has been copied in most advertisements, I have in a few instances inserted summary statements. These can be readily recognized.

5. Where I have supplied the caption of an advertisement it is followed with a period and a dash; a caption appearing as part of the original advertisement is followed either by a comma or by no punctuation at all depending upon how it appeared in the newspaper.

6. Prior to 1752, when England discarded the Julian Calendar and adopted the new-style Gregorian Calendar

[2] For instance, notices concerning the following known silversmiths appeared without mention of their craft: Jeremiah Wool advertised for a runaway apprentice, *The New-York Gazette and the Weekly Mercury*, June 20, 1774; Jeremiah Wool and Cary Dunn were assignees in a notice which appeared in *The Weekly Mercury*, July 20, 1767; Elias Pelletreau sold tar and pitch, *The New-York Gazette Revived in the Weekly Post-Boy*, December 16, 1751; Jacob C. Ten Eyck was mentioned as Judge of the Inferior Court of Common Pleas, of the City of Albany, *The Weekly Mercury*, November 2, 1767; Richard Van Dyck sold imported goods, *The New-York Gazette or the Weekly Post-Boy*, May 27, 1754.

used by other European countries, the New York newspapers from January to March 24th, usually carried the date-years of both systems (as 1748/1749), the first representing the Julian year ending in March, and the second the year beginning in January. In citing such a date, I have given only the second figure, for the year beginning in January, according to the new style.

7. I have included all craftsmen who advertised in New York City newspapers whether or not they worked or resided in New York.

8. I have included among the advertisements some news items which refer definitely to artisans and craftsmen. Such items have been specified as news in my citations. When the newspaper indicates that the news came from another city than New York, that city is always mentioned.

9. The chapter on "Miscellaneous Crafts" includes only a representative group of craftsmen.

RITA SUSSWEIN GOTTESMAN

THE ARTS AND CRAFTS IN NEW YORK

1726–1776

PAINTING AND ENGRAVING

PAINTERS

ABRAHAM DELANOY, jun. just arrived from London: Takes this Opportunity to inform the Public, That he is now settled at Mr. Turner's, in New-Dutch Church Street, near the Colonel Robinson's; Where he intends to carry on Portrait Painting; Ladies and Gentlemen that Please to employ him, may depend on all the Justice in his Power, and he doubts not, but he shall give satisfaction.—*The New-York Journal or the General Advertiser*, May 28, 1767.

ABRAHAM DELANOY, Junior, Takes this Opportunity to inform those Ladies and Gentlemen that have proposed to favour him with their commands, that he intends for the West-Indies in the Spring; it is therefore necessary that they apply speedily; He expresses his Acknowledgement to those that have employed him hitherto. He continues to paint Portraits at his Room in New Dutch-Church-street, near Col. Robinson's. His name over the Door.—*The New-York Mercury*, January 18, 1768.

ABRAHAM DELANOY.—Likenesses Painted for a reasonable Price, by A. Delanoy, Jun. who has been Taught by the celebrated Mr. Benjamin West, in London. N.B. Is to be spoke with opposite Mr. Dirck Schuyler's, at his Fathers.—*The New-York Gazette and the Weekly Mercury*, January 7, 1771.

JOHN DURAND.—The Subscriber having from his Infancy endeavoured to qualify himself in the Art of historical Painting, humbly hopes for the Encouragement from the Gentlemen and Ladies of this City and Prov-

1

ince, that so elegant and entertaining an Art, has always obtain'd from People of the most improved Minds, and best Taste and Judgement, in all polite Nations in every Age. And tho' he is sensible, that to excel (in this Branch of Painting especially) requires a more ample Fund of universal and accurate Knowledge than he can pretend to, in Geometry, Geography, Perspective, Anatomy, Expression of Passions, ancient and modern History, &c. &c. Yet he hopes, from the good Nature and Indulgence of the Gentlemen and Ladies who employ him that his humble Attempts, in which his best Endeavours will not be wanting, will meet with Acceptance, and give Satisfaction; and he proposes to work at as cheap Rates as any Person in America.

To such Gentlemen and Ladies as have thought but little upon this Subject, and might only regard painting as a superfluous Ornament, I would just observe, that History-painting, besides being extremely ornamental, has many important uses. It presents to our View, some of the most interesting Scenes recorded in ancient or modern History; gives us more lively and perfect Ideas of the Things represented, than we could receive from an historical account of them; and frequently recals to our Memory, a long Train of Events, with which those Representations were connected. They shew us a proper Expression of the Passions excited by every Event, and have an Effect, the very same in Kind, (but stronger) than a fine historical Description of the same Passage would have upon a judicious Reader. Men who have distinguished themselves for the good of their Country and Mankind, may be set before our Eyes as Examples, and to give us their silent Lessons, and besides, every judicious Friend and Visitant shares with us in the Advantage and Improvement, and increases its Value to ourselves.

John Durand,
near the City-Hall, Broad-street.

The New-York Gazette or the Weekly Post-Boy, April **11, 1768.**

Du Simitiere.—Mr. Du Simitiere, Miniature Painter, Intending shortly to leave this City, and it being uncertain whether he will return again, if any Gentlemen or Ladies should incline to employ him, he is to be found at his lodgings, in the House of Mrs. Ferrara, in Maiden Lane.—*The New-York Gazette and the Weekly Mercury,* July 31, 1769.

Stephen Dwight, Begs leave to acquaint the Publick, that he continues Portrait and History Painting, as usual; and begs such Gentlemen and Ladies who incline to employ him in the Portrait way, that they would be speedy in their Application, as the present Season is most suitable for that work. He likewise intends the ensuing Week to open a school for the Instruction of Youth in the several Branches of Drawing; the Hours of Drawing at School will be from 1 to 2, and from 5 to 6 in the Afternoon, at 6 Shillings per Week; if it should suit any Persons he will attend from 5 to 6 in the Morning, he proposes not to take above 6 or 8 Scholars.

N.B. Said Dwight also continues to Carve all Sorts of House, Ship and cabinet Work in the best Manner.—*The New-York Mercury,* May 2, 1763.

Lawrence Kilburn, Limner, just arrived from London with Capt. Miller, hereby acquaints all Gentlemen and Ladies inclined to favour him in having their Pictures drawn, that he don't doubt of pleasing them in taking a true Likeness, and finishing the Drapery in a proper Manner, as also in the Choice of Attitudes, suitable to each Person's Age and Sex, and giving agreeable Satisfaction, as he has heretofore done to Gentlemen and Ladies in London. He may at present be apply'd to at his Lodgings, at Mr. Bogart's, near the New Printing-Office in Beaver-Street.—*The New-York Gazette and the Weekly Post-Boy,* May 13, 1754.

LAWRENCE KILBURN,[1] Limner, from London, who lately advertised in this paper; hereby acquaints all Gentlemen and Ladies, that are mindful to see some of his Performances.

That he has now several Pieces taken from the Life, finished in his Room; as also sundry other curious Pieces, scarcely to be met with at any other Place in this City, and hopes that Gentlemen and Ladies who have a Taste that Way, will favour him with their Companies; and doubts not but a View of his Performances will engage them to incourage him in this Branch of Business, as at present there is no other in Town who pretends thereto.

N.B. He lodges at Mr. Bogart's next Door to the late Domini Boel's near the New-Printing-Office in Beaver-Street.—*The New-York Gazette or the Weekly Post-Boy,* September 30, 1754.

LAWRENCE KILBURN, Limner, from London. Intends during the Winter Season, to instruct Gentlemen in the Art of drawing Landskips, Faces, Flowers, &c. on very reasonable Terms, and at such Hours as will be most suitable to those Gentlemen.

N.B. He lodges at Mr. Schuyler's, next Door to Mr. Henry Holland's near Coenties Market.—*The New-York Gazette or the Weekly Post-Boy,* October 13, 1755.

LAWRENCE KILBURNN, Limner from London Continues, as usual, to draw to the life. Ladies and gentlemen that have not as yet seen many of his performances, may now have an opportunity of viewing sundry pieces together, which he has drawn to the entire satisfaction of the persons for whom they were designed. He may be applied to at his lodgings, at the house of Mr. Peter Rosevelt, in Bayard's-street. He draws also in miniature. —*The New-York Mercury,* September 26, 1757.

LAWRENCE KILBRUNN.—As my Business calls me up to Albany in about three Weeks Time, I desire therefore

[1] Name is spelled various ways: Kilbrun, Kilbrunn, Killbrun, Kilburn, Kilburnn.

all who are indebted to me, to settle with me; and all who hath any Demands one me, to send in their Accounts that they may be settled. And as my Affairs may Keep me in Albany all next Summer, I shall therefore be glad that if any Gentlemen or Ladies who might incline to have their Pictures drawn by me, to apply speedily, at my lodgings in Bayard-Street, at Mr. John Lansing's. LAWRENCE KILBRUNN.—*The New-York Mercury,* March 30, 1761.

LAWRENCE KILBURN, Intending to remove into the country, all persons having any demands on him, are desired to bring them in, and receive payment; and all who are indebted to him either on book, note, or bond, to discharge the same, within three months from the above date, to prevent trouble. As at present there is no other Portrait painter in thie city but himself; whoever inclines to have anything done of that kind, are desired to apply in time, as it may be long before they have another opportunity.
N.B. He hath yet some white lead, ground to dispose of.—*The New-York Gazette or the Weekly Post-Boy,* August 22, 1765.

LAWRENCE KILBURN.—Sells paints and painter's materials; . . . . Portrait Painter's Colours; Canvas, Hair and Fitch Pencils, Tools, and gilt carv'd Frames for Portraits, Leaf-Gold, and Silver, Ditto, &c.—*The New-York Gazette and the Weekly Post-Boy,* April 26, 1764.

LAWRENCE KILBURN.—All persons indebted to the estate of Lawrence Killbrun, late of this city, deceased, are hereby requested to pay the same speedily to Judith Killbrun, or Abm. H. Van Vleck, Merchant, who are to be spoke with at the store of Henry Van Vleck and Son at which place is for sale the remaining assortment of all kinds of painters colours, and different sizes of glass, which will be sold low for cash only. And likewise to be let and entered upon immediately, the pleasant situated

and convenient house which the said Killbrun occupied.—*The New-York Gazette and the Weekly Mercury,*
July 17, 1775.

THOMAS MILWORTH, Portrait Painter, Has removed to
the House of Mr. Samuel Deall, in Broad-street, opposite
to Beaver-street, His first Sett of Pictures are now
finished: and as this is the most proper Season for Painting, he desires Gentlemen and Ladies that incline to any
Thing done in his way, to be speedy in their application.
—*The New-York Gazette and the Weekly Post-Boy,*
August 21, 1758.

WILLIAM BIRCHALL TATLEY, from London, Begs leave
to acquaint the public, that he has taken a commodious
house the Corner of Beaver-Street, and facing General
Haldimand's, where he purposes Painting portraits in oil,
or in a miniature for the bracelet, or so small as to be set
in a ring. Those Ladies and Gentlemen who please to
favour him with their commands, may depend on having
them done in the best manner, and with the greatest
expedition.—*The New-York Gazette and Weekly Mercury,* August 8, 1774.

WILLIAM BIRCHALL TETLEY.[2]—Dancing, Taught at
Home and Abroad by Wm. Birchall Tetley. Late
apprentice to Monsieur Gherarde, of London; He teaches
on the usual terms the minuet, cottilions, Allemande,
English Country dances; single double, and treble hornpipes, &c. &c. as they are now danced at London and
Paris, which last place he has lately visited. Those
Gentlemen and Ladies who please to favour him with
their commands, at the corner of Beaver-street, shall be
duly attended. An Evening School at home, three times
a week.
Continues painting Portraits in oyl or miniature, as
usual, Teaches Ladies and Gentlemen drawing and

---

[2] Another form of spelling for Tatley.

painting in crayons or water colours.—*The New-York Gazette and the Weekly Mercury*, November 14, 1774.

WILLIAM WILLIAMS, Painter, at Rembrandt's Head, in Batteaux-street, Undertakes painting in general, viz. History, Portraiture, landskip, sign painting, lettering, gilding, and stewing smalt. N.B. He cleans, repairs, and varnishes, any old pictures of value, and teaches the art of drawing. Those ladies or gentlemen who may be pleased to employ him, may depend on care and dispatch. —*The New-York Gazette and the Weekly Mercury*, May 8, 1769.

PAINTINGS

PAINTING ON GLASS.—By a Person lately arrived in this Town. Painting upon Glass (commonly call'd burning upon Glass) is performed in a neat and curious Manner so as never to change its Colour; Perspective Views neatly colour'd for the Camera Obscura. N.B. Young Gentlemen and Ladies are instructed in either of the above, so as to be capable to perform it themselves in a little Time, at a reasonable Rate. By the same Person, Land survey'd designs for Buildings, Plans and Maps neatly drawn. Enquire at Mr. John Ditcher's, Tallow-Chandler and Soap-Boiler in the Sloat.—*The New-York Gazette or the Weekly Post-Boy*, July 9, 1753.

PAINTINGS.—Twenty-four fruit and flower pieces, elegantly done by Jones, just imported, and to be sold, by John Wetherhead, at his store in King-street . . . . . —*The New-York Mercury*, December 24, 1764.

PICTURES.—For Sale, at Garrat Noel's, next Door to the Merchant's Coffee-House, a Great Variety of the most elegant Pictures, framed and glazed in America, which in Neatness of Workmanship, equal any imported from England, and will be Sold at a much lower Price.— *The New-York Gazette or the Weekly Post-Boy*, June 5, 1769 (*Supplement*).

ENGRAVERS

——ADEMS.—. . . N.B. Any Persons may have their Coats of Arms, or Names, to paste on the Inside of the Covers of Books; Shop Bills, with proper Figures and Designs, or any other engraving work, neatly executed by Adems, Schoolmaster and Engraver, on Golden Hill.— *The New-York Gazette or the Weekly Post-Boy*, June 23, 1763 (*Supplement*).

DUNLAP ADEMS, writing master, Has lately open'd school, in Queen-street, near the Fly, at half a guinea per month. Hours of teaching is from 10 to 12 in the forenoon. Those who can't spare time in the day time, may be taught at night.—*New-York Mercury*, January 10, 1763.

JOHN ANTHONY BEAU.—To The Public, John Anthony Beau, Engraver and chaser, Proposes to teach any Ladies or Gentlemen that incline to learn, the Art of Drawing, in all its Branches. He engraves and does all sorts of chasing Work, at the most reasonable Rates. Whoever will favour him with their Commands, are desired to apply to Mr. Lewis Fueter, Gold and Silver Smith, opposite the Coffee House.—*New-York Journal or General Advertiser*, December 20, 1770.

ISAAC CLEMENS, Engraver, (who lately arrived with his Majesty's Fleet from Boston in New-England.) Informs the Gentlemen of the Navy and Army, and Public in general, that he now carries on the Engraving Business, at his Shop, near the French Church, in King-street, New-York.—*The New-York Gazette and the Weekly Mercury*, October 21, 1776.

HENRY DAWKINS, engraver, who lately lived with Mr. Anthony Lamb, has now set up his business in the shop late Mr. Paiba's, opposite the Merchants Coffee-House, in New York, where he engraves in all sorts of mettals.

Gentlemen that will favour him with their work, may depend on having it done in the best manner, with expedition, and on the most reasonable terms.—*The New-York Mercury*, October 20, 1755.

MICHAEL DE BRULS.—Curious Chasing or other Raised Work, in general on Gold and Silver Watch-Cases, Snuff Boxes, &c. Engraving, Crests and Coats of Arms, &c. on Gold, Silver and Copperplate; Also, Engraving of Seals on Gold, Silver or Steel Done. By Michael De Bruss,[3] At the House of Mr. Frederick Beckers, in Maiden-Lane, near the Fly-Market. N.B. He also doth draw Plans of Fortifications, &c.—*The New-York Gazette or the Weekly Post-Boy*, December 19, 1757.

MICHAEL DE BRULS.—By the Advice and Encouragement of several Gentlemen of this City, is published by Subscription, and curiously engraved on two large Copper Plates, by Michael De Bruls, Engraver and Inhabitant of this City, A plan of the Landing, Encampment and Attack against Fort Niagara, on Lake Ontario, reduced with the adjacent Country, by his Majesty's Forces under the Command of Sir William Johnson, Baronet; the Place of Engagement where the French Reinforcement was defeated. Also a Plan of Fort Niagara, on a large Scale, shewing its advantageous Situation and Harbour, its extraordinary Strength, fortified both by Art and Nature, with the required References, the whole laid down by an experienced Engineer.

Conditions of Subscription, viz.

I. This Plan, with Part of Lake Ontario, and the opposite Shore, over that River, which proceeds from over Niagara Falls, into said Lake, is beautifully engraved on two large Copper-Plates, as abovementioned, and almost ready for Printing; they are to be printed on the largest and best Paper, said Work will form a

[3] In the next issue of the same newspaper the name is spelled De Bruls.

handsome Print of two Feet eleven Inches, by one Foot one Inch, exclusive of the Margin.

II. Each Subscriber is desired to give in his Name and Place of Abode.

III. This Plan shall be delivered on, or before the last Day of June next ensuing, to the several Subscribers at their Places of Abode, at Eight Shillings, New-York Currency, one Half to be paid on Subscribing, the other Half on Delivery of the Plans.

IV. The Subscription will be closed on the 26th of June next, after which none will be sold for less than 16 Shillings New-York Currency, each Plan.

To deliver these Plans immediately after being printed, Notice shall be given by the New-York News-Papers on and from the 28th of June next ensuing.

Subscriptions are taken in by Messrs. Parker and Company, Mr. W. Weyman, and Samuel Farley, Printers in New-York, also by Michael De Bruhls, [*sic*] Engraver of the above Plan, in the Road beyond the New-Goal on the Hill, where the above engraved Plates may be seen.

Such Gentlemen and others, as shall please to encourage this Undertaking will great oblige their most obedient and obliging Servant, M. de Bruls.—*The American Chronicle*, April 19, 1762.

MICHAEL DE BRULS.—For publishing by Subscription, Two different water views, and two different land views, of this flourishing city of New-York. The editor and engraver, has taken great pains, and been very exact in laying down these four beautiful prospects, with which the city presents itself to the eye of every judicious Beholder. He hopes to meet with encouragement from all Gentlemen and Ladies, &c. especially, as nothing of this Kind ever has been undertaken before by any body in this part of the world.

Conditions of Subscription.

1. These above-mentioned four different views, with the respective references, in English, High Dutch and

Low Dutch, will be curiously engraved on a copper plate, of 21 by 12 inches each, and printed on best large paper.

2. A plan of the streets, &c. of this city, with their respective names, will also be neatly engraved on another copper plate, and printed on best large paper.

3. Each subscriber to sign his name, and give his quality and place of abode.

4. These four prints will be delivered on or before the last day of May next, to be several subscribers at their place of abode, at Twenty Shillings, New-York currency; one half to be paid on subscribing, the other half on the delivery of the five prints.

5. The subscription will be closed on the 28th day of May next, after which none will be sold or disposed of.

6. A separate Pamphlet will be published along with the prints, giving an exact account of the wholesome climate, pleasant situations, products, &c. of this province, for the benefit of the subscribers, which they may chuse, either in English, High Dutch, or Low Dutch.

7. The above plates are partly finished engraving. The editor and publisher has settled a correspondence in the most noted cities and towns in New-York government, New-England, the Jersies, and Pennsylvania, for to deliver the prints immediately after publication, whereof notice will be given in the public News-Papers in New-York, Boston, Philadelphia, &c.

Subscriptions are taken in by W. Weyman, Printer in Broad-street, Hugh Gaine, in Hanover-Square, John Holt at Burling's Slip, and Michael De Bruls, publisher and engraver of the above plates, at the lower end of New-Street, next door to Col. Thody.

P. S. The reason why these above-mentioned four views, with the plans of this city, have not been finished and delivered according to Advertisement, is, 1st. a great many Gentlemen and Ladies, having as yet only promised to subscribe; this my undertaking being of a very extraordinary charge to me. 2d. I find a great deal more land laid in lots additional to this city, than what I was acquainted with, consequently requires more expence and

time to complete the same; particularly as I am desirous
to give Satisfaction to all those that have, and may
encourage the above undertaking, as well as for my
recommendation and credit; therefore, all Gentlemen,
and others are requested to be expeditious in subscribing,
and giving in their names and places of abode as they are
intended to be printed, and prefixed to the pamphlet.

And in complying with this request, they will greatly
oblige their most obliged humble servant, MICHAEL DE
BRULS.—*The New-York Gazette*, March 7, 1763.

ELISHA GALLAUDET, Engraver, is removed from the
house where he lately lived in Smith-Street, to the house
wherein Mr. Moran lived, in the Broad-Way near the
Bowling-Green, where he carries on his business as usual.
—*The New-York Journal or General Advertiser*, August
1, 1771.

JOHN HUTT, From London, Engraver and Copper plate
Printer Engraves Coats of Arms, Crests and Cyphers on
Plate, Seals, &c. Likewise Bills on Parcels, Shop Bills,
Card Plates, Bills of Exchange, Bills of Loading, Maps,
Portraits, &c. All other Engraving and Printing per-
formed in the neatest and most elegant taste.

Specimens of his Work to be seen at Mr. Rivington's.—
Rivington's New-York Gazetteer, June 24, 1773.

JOHN HUTT from London, Engraver in general, and
copperplate Printer at Mr. Sickles's, next door to the
Merchant's Coffee-House, New-York:

Engraves all Architecture,	Maps,
sorts of Coats of arms,	Portraits,
Crests,	Frontispieces,
Seals and Cyphers,	Door Plates,
Shop Bills,	Compliment Cards,
Bills of Exchange,	Spoons & all sorts of plate
Bills of Lading,	marked and cypher'd,
Bills of Parcels,	Dogs collars,
Card Plates &c.	Stamps, &c. &c.

Said John Hutt returns his most sincere thanks to his friends, for the favours already conferred on him, and assures the Public, that he intends carrying on the Engraving and Printing business in the most elegant manner, and with the greatest dispatch.—*Rivington's New-York Gazetteer*, January 20, 1774 (*Supplement*).

JOHN HUTT, Engraver in General, And Copper Plate Printer, Directly opposite the coffee house, in Water-street, New-York. Performs every article in the different branches of engraving, with the utmost neatness and dispatch. N.B. Stamps cut for the news paper on the shortest notice; arms neatly painted on vellum.—*The New-York Journal or the General Advertiser*, September 15, 1774.

JOHN LAMB.—Engraving in gold, silver and copper and other metals by John Lamb, at Sir Isaac Newton's head on Hunter's-Key, New-York.—*New-York Mercury*, March 15, 1756.

HENRY PURCELL, Engraver, Begs leave to acquaint his friends in particular, and the public in general, that he has opened a shop in Broad-Way, nearly opposite Mr. Hull's Tavern, where he carries on the engraving business in different branches, and hopes he can give satisfaction to all gentlemen that may be pleased to favour him with their commands, as they may depend upon the greatest care and dispatch.—*Rivington's New-York Gazetteer*, September 15, 1774.

JOSEPH SIMONS, Seal-Cutter and Engraver, from Berlin, next Door to Mr. Edward Leight, Leather-Dresser, in the Fly, Cuts all sorts of Coats of Arms, Cyphers, & etc. in Stone, Steel, Silver, or any other Metal. Also engraves Coats of Arms, Crests, Cyphers, on the Plate, &c. Those Gentlemen and Ladies that please to send their Escutcheons, may depend upon having them done after the Manner of the Herald's office, and as neat as in any Part of England. N.B. He will wait on any Gentlemen or Ladies, on Notice being sent to him.—*The New-York Gazette*, May 9, 1763.

ENGRAVINGS

VIEW OF THE CITY OF ALBANY.—This is to give Notice, there is in Hand a view of the City of Albany which Design, (if a sufficient number of Subscribers come in) to engrave it on Copper, and print it on fine Paper, all Gentlemen that are willing to forward it, are Desired to Subscribe at Matthias Cregeer on the Dock, in New-York, and at Mr. Waters in Albany. (The price is three Shillings per Print).—*The New-York Gazette*, July 18-25, 1736.

PRINTS AND MAPS.—To be sold cheap by the Printer hereof, viz. A Map of the whole World; a Map of each Quarter of the World; a Map of England, a Plan of the City of London; a View of the City of New-York;—A View of the Battle of Culloden; a View of Captain Phillips's retaking the Solebay; two large Prints of Horses, one the Duke of Bolton's, the other the Earl of Portmore's; a beautiful small Print of Sir Philip Sidney; and several other small Prints.—*The New-York Gazette Revived in the Post-Boy*, April 24, 1749.

MR. STRANGE'S PRINTS.—To the Curious. Lately published in England, and to be sold by Garrat Noel and Company, near the Meal-Market, the celebrated Mr. Strange's Twelve very elegant Prints, consisting of, Le Retour du Marche, a Cupid, a Magdalane, a Cleopatra, a Headpiece from the Painting of Guido Rheni, a Virgin Mary from ditto, Liberality and Modesty from ditto, Apollo rewarding Merit and punishing Arrogance, Caesar putting away Pompey, and receiving his Wife; the finding of the Romulus and Remus, Belisarius, Charles Prince of Wales, James Duke of York, and Princess Mary, Children of King Charles 1st. These surprizing

pieces are bound up in Boards to preserve them, but may
be taken out to put into Frames. Likewise, the Heads
of illustrious persons of Great Britain, on 180 Copper-
Plates, engraved by Houbraken and Mr. Virtue, with
their Lives and Characters, by Thomas Birch, D. D.
Secretary to the Royal society. Done upon Imperial
Paper, and curiously bound. N.B. Gentlemen of Taste
that are willing to purchase either of these much
esteemed Curiosities, are desired to apply in Time, as
there are but very few Copies to dispose of.—*The New-
York Mercury*, March 26, 1759.

VIEW OF NIAGARA.—Engraving, A View of the Cataract
of Niagara, which will be published in June next. From
this Representation of one of the most wonderful Aspects
of Nature, designed as a Specimen of what the Publisher
intends to do with many other great and stupendous
Scenes throughout America, he has some Reason to hope,
that a Work of such Elegance and Beauty, will meet with
the Aid and Countenance, as may enable him to give
these amazing Subjects every Help that Art can with
Propriety bestow of, which this his first Essay he flatters
himself will be judged a very striking Instance. After
the Subscription shall be closed the Price will be raised.
Proposals to be seen at Mr. Rivington's, Mr. Noel's, Mr.
Dyckinck's, where Subscriptions are taken in.—*The New-
York Gazette and the Weekly Mercury*, February 8, 1773.

CHURCH-MUSIC, Ready for engraving, and to be published by subscriptions, . . .—*Rivington's New-York
Gazetteer*, June 24, 1773.

AMERICAN MAGAZINE. Those gentlemen and ladies
who incline to encourage the publication of the Royal
American Magazine, are hereby informed, that the subscription papers will be returned to the intended publisher in a few days, in order that he may ascertain the
number subscribed for. Subscriptions are taken in by
Hugh Gaine. N.B. The introduction to the Royal

American Magazine (or No. I to be ornamented with two elegant copper-plate prints) will be published on the first day of January next.—*The New-York Gazette and the Weekly Mercury,* November 15, 1773.

MEZZOTINT OF DOCTOR OGILVIE.—A Mezzotinto Print of the Revd Doctor Ogilvie, (taken from an extraordinary likeness) is now in hand, and will be finished in a few weeks; the size of the plate is 15 inches by 11. As the Subscriber has done it solely at his own risque, and was the first person in this city, who proposed it, and was even promised the portrait, which is now to be sent to England, to take a sketch from: He is in hopes that all those who are inclined to promote arts and ingenuity in America, will make it a point to encourage the undertaking. Anthony Lamb.—*The New-York Journal or the General Advertiser,* January 26, 1775.

MEZZOTINT OF JOHN HANCOCK.—It Is Proposed, To print in about Ten days, A Neat Mezzotinto Print, of the Hon. John Hancock, Esq; President of the Continental Congress. Subscriptions are taken in by H. Gaine, and R. Sauce, in New-York; and by Mr. Nicholas Brooks, in Philadelphia. Price, 3s. 9d. or in double-carv'd gilt frames, at 7s. 6d.—*The New-York Gazette and the Weekly Mercury,* October 9, 1775.

ENGRAVINGS & MEZZOTINTS.—Minshull's Looking Glass Store, Removed from Smith street to Hanover-square (opposite Mr. Goelet's the sign of the Golden Key,) has for sale, Engravings. By Strange, Wollet, Vivare's & other eminent masters. A pleasing variety of mezzotintos well chosen and beautifully coloured . . .—*The New-York Journal or General Advertiser,* March 15, 1775.

MAPS AND CHARTS

MAP OF THE FIVE GREAT LAKES.—There is now in the Press, and will shortly be Published, The History of the

Five Indian Nations depending on the Province of New-York, giving an Account of their Wars both with the Indians and Christians, from the first Settling of Canada and New York, as also their Treaties of Peace with several Governments in North America.

There is also a Map of the five great Lakes, Rivers and Indian Countries, shewing the Scituation of the several Indian Nations, from Canada to the Branches of Misissippi and the Upper Lake. Both printed and Sold by William Bradford in New-York.—*The New-York Gazette,* February 20-27, 1727.

MERCATOR CHART.—This is to give Notice, That the Mercator Chart Drawn by Philip Cockrem, extending from the Lat. of 9 Degrees to the Lat. of 43 Degrees North; Easterly to the Island of Barbados, Westerly to the Entrance of Massisippi; is now entirely finished and printed on fine Royal Paper, and are to be seen and sold at the House of Philip Cockrem in Princes Street, near Smith Street, in New-York; the Price being Twenty Shillings each, New-York Money.—*The New-York Gazette,* September 21-28, 1730.

PLAN OF NEW YORK CITY.—Just Published, A Plan of the City of New-York, from an actual Survey made by James Lyne, being curiously, engraved on a Copper Plate and printed on a sheet of demy Royal Paper, wherein is laid down the situation of his Majesty's Fort and Chappel, all the Churches and Meeting-Houses, City-Hall, Custom-house, Weigh-house, Exchange, Market-houses & other Remarkable Places, shewing also the Names and Boundaries of the six Wards in said City, with all the Streets, Lanes and Allyes therein. The Names of the streets are as follow, viz.

Kings Street, Queens Street, Prince Street, Duke-Street, Hanover Square, Little Queen street, Broad street, Broad way, Dock-street, White-hall street, Pearl-street, Bridge-street, Market street, Mill street, Stone street, Wall street, Cherry street, Rutgers street, Garden

street, Nassau street, John street, Anne street, Beekmans
street, Gold street, Kips street, William street, Beaver
street, Vandercliff street, Smiths street, Frankford street,
Fair street, George street, Clfits street, Flatten barrack
street, New street, Maiden Lane, Wind-Mill Lane,
Hunters Key, Burnets Key, etc. Printed and Sold by
William Bradford, Price 4s. 6d.—*The New-York Gazette,*
August 30-September 6, 1731.

CHART OF THE NEW ENGLAND COAST.—There is now
Published, and to be Sold, The New-England Coasting
Pilot, from Sandy-Point of New-York unto Cape Canso
in Nova-Scotia, and part of the Island Breton; with
Courses and Distances from Place to Place, and Towns
on the sea-board; The harbours, Bays, Islands, Roads
Rocks and Sands; The Setting and Flowing of Tydes
and Currents, with Directions of great Advantage to this
part of Navigation in North-America. As also, the
Soundings, Sands, Rocks and Harbours, with Distance
of Places from New-York (between Long-Island the
Main) to Rhode-Island, by Capt. Cyprian Southack.
Which work being Presented to the King, and his
Majesty taking into his gracious Consideration the Use-
fulness of the said Performance, was pleased to order
the sum of Fifty Pounds to be paid to Capt. Southack
for buying him a Gold Chain and Medal, as a mark of
his Majesty's Royal Favour for his Labour and Palns
[*sic*] in so useful a Work. To be Sold by William Bradford in the City of New-York.—*The New-York Gazette,*
June 24-July 1, 1734.

MAP OF NEW YORK HARBOR.—There is now Published
a new Map of the Harbour of New-York, from a late
Survey, containing the Soundings and setting of the
Tydes, and the bearings of the most remarkable Places,
with the Proper Places for Anchoring. To be Sold by
the Printer hereof.—*The New-York Gazette,* March
24-31, 1735.

MAP OF THE FIVE NATIONS OF INDIANS.—On Monday next will be published [4] a Map of the five Nations of Indians, with the Road from Albany to Oswego and the Situation of the Lakes.—*The New-York Gazette*, August 18-25, 1735.

PLAN OF LOUISBOURG.—Just published at Boston (Price 20 s. Old Tenor) A Plan of the City and Fortress of Louisbourg; with a small Plan of the Harbour: Done in Metzotinto on Royal Paper, from the Original Drawing of Richard Gridley, Esq; Commander of the Train of Artillery at the Siege of Louisbourg. Sold by J. Smibert, in Queen-Street, Boston.—*The New-York Weekly Post-Boy*, October 6, 1746.

MAPS OF PENNSYLVANIA &c.—Just published (in Philadelphia) the Second Edition of a Map of Pennsilvania, New-Jersey, New York and the Three Lower Counties on Delware, By Lewis Evans.

The Determination of the Bounds of Pennsilvania and Maryland, by a Decree in Chancery; a new Purchase made of the Indians and the Erecting four new Counties in Pennsilvania, since the first Publication of the Map,[5] have made this Edition necessary. And Care has been taken to supply the Omissions, and to rectify the Errors which have escaped in the former Impression; and the South Side of Lake Ontario is now added.

The several Provinces and Countries are distinguished in the plain Maps by Division of Lines, and in the Colour'd Ones, by different Colours.

Besides what are Common to other Maps, as the Sea-Coast, Rivers, Creeks, Mountains, Roads, intermediate Distances of Places, and the Situation of Cities, Towns, Villages &c. there are inserted in this, how far the Tide runs up the Rivers, and the Time of the High-Water, full and Change, of the greatest Use in Commerce: the

---

[4] The notice of the map's publication is to be found in next issue of the newspaper.

[5] The map was first proposed for publication by subscription in 1749.

Variation of the Needle, by several accurate Observations, and the Rate of its Decrease, of Use in adjusting old Surveys of Land; the greatest Length of Days and Nights, a Table of the Distances between the most considerable Towns, besides Barometrical and Thermometrical Observations, Accounts of the Weather in this Climate, the Production of Lighting and Fogs accounted for: with several other Articles recommended by the Curious to the Enquiry of the Travellers.

The Smallness of this Map has been very often objected to the Author; but if Gentlemen would consider, that they seldom have seen Maps of any Parts of Europe to a larger Scale, and that there is not a City, Town, or even a Village of six Houses within the Compass of the Map, that are not inserted in it, and that Pensilvania, as far as tolerably settled, which is between Delaware River, the Lower Counties, Mariland, and the Kittatinny Mountains, tho' now divided into eight Counties, is not of Extent equal to Yorkshire in South-Britain, they would be induced to think a larger Map impertinent; if they did not expect it for other Uses then Geography, Physics, History and Commerce.

The Price of the Plain Maps is One Spanish Dollar; of the colour'd Ones, on superfine Writing paper, Two Dollars; and there are a few on fine Calico, at a Dollar and a Half each.

In Justice to the Buyers of the former Impression, their colour'd Maps, tho' torn or defaced will be exchanged for the new Edition [6] at Five Shillings, and their plain Ones at two Shillings and Six-pence.

To be sold or exchanged by the Author in Philadelphia, and by the Printer hereof.—*The New-York Gazette Revived in the Weekly Post-Boy*, August 24, 1752.

CITY OF PHILADELPHIA.—Proposals for publishing by Subscription, A Prospect of the City of Philadelphia. Taken from the East, By George Heap. Conditions.

[6] Still another edition is mentioned in *The New-York Gazette and the Weekly Post-Boy*, of August 27, 1753.

That the Print shall be seven Feet four Inches in Length, taking in the Extent of near a Mile and a Half.

That in order to have the Work executed in the best Manner, the Plates shall be engraved in England, and well printed, on fine white and strong Paper.

That the Price of each Prospect be Twenty Shillings, Money of Pensilvania; one Half to be paid at the Time of Subscribing, the other on Delivery of the Prints.

That if a sufficient Number are not subscribed for before the first of December next, the Subscription shall be void, and the Money returned to the Subscribers again.

Subscriptions are taken in by Mr. Nicholas Scull, and the Author in Philadelphia, and by the Printer hereof . . . —*The New-York Gazette Revived in the Weekly Post-Boy*, November 20, 1752.

PLAN OF NEW YORK CITY.—To be sold by G. Duyckinck, The Plan of the City of New-York, shewing the several Wards, Streets, Lanes and Allies, Churches, Meeting Houses, Markets, Sugar and Distilling-Houses, Water Lots, with the additional New Lots &c. &c. to this present Year. Done from actual Survey. Also Window Glass, Oil and Painters Colours, Pictures of all sorts made and sold at a reasonable Price.—*The New-York Gazette or the Weekly Post Boy*, February 24, 1755.

MAP OF THE MIDDLE BRITISH COLONIES.—Proposals For publishing by Subscription, a general Map of the Middle British Colonies in America, &c. . . .—*The New-York Gazette or the Weekly Post-Boy*, July 28, 1755.

MAP OF THE MIDDLE BRITISH COLONIES.—Just published, a General Map of the Middle British Colonies in America, viz. Virginia, Maryland, Delaware, Pennsilvania, New-Jersey, New-York, Connecticut, and Rhode-Island; of the Country of the Confederate Indians; of the Lakes Erie, Ontario, and Champlain, and of the Port of New-France. By Lewis Evans. This Map includes the Ohio, and all the present Places of Action of the British, French, and Indians; and was composed with a particular View to the Connection our Colonies have with Canada, the Lakes, Ohio, and the Countries of the adjacent Indians.

The Price of the colour'd Maps, on superfine Writing-Paper, Two Pieces of Eight; and of the plain Ones, on printing Paper, One Piece of Eight each. With each colour'd Map is given a Pamphlet of four Large Sheets and a Half, containing an Analysis of the Map; a Discription of the Face of the Country. the Boundaries of the Confederate Indians, whereon the British Rights are founded, and the Maritime and Inland Navigation of the several Rivers and Lakes contained therein. To be Sold, in Philadelphia, by the Author [7] in Arch-Street; at Carlisle, Trenton, Brunswick, New-York, New-Haven, New-London, Providence, and Boston Post-Offices: In Burlington, by Mr. Pere, and also in New-York, by Mr. Garrat Noel, Bookseller, in Dock-Street, near Coenties Market.

N.B. At the same Places are also sold, a few Copies of the Pamphlets separately; Price one Quarter of a Piece of Eight each.—*The New-York Gazette or the Weekly Post-Boy*, November 23, 1755.

PLAN OF PHILADELPHIA.—Just published, and to be sold by Garret Noel, Bookseller, in Dock Street, A large, and very curious Plan of the City of Philadelphia, taken by George Heap, from the Jersey-Shore, under the direction of Nicholas Scull, surveyor general of the Province of Pennsylvania. This fine perspective contains four sheets, of imperial paper, price Three Dollars, in sheets. —*The New-York Mercury*, March 17, 1755.

PLAN OF THE BATTLE NEAR LAKE-GEORGE.—To be sold at the Bible and Crown, in Queen-street, Price, Four Shillings, A prospective Plan of the Battle near Lake-

---

[7] Evans's map of the middle British Colonies is discussed in a letter from a gentleman in New York to his friend in Philadelphia.—*The New-York Mercury*, January 5, 1756.

George, on the 8th Day of September, 1755. With an Explanation thereof, containing a full, tho' short, History of that Affair, By Samuel Blodget, occasionally at the Camp when the Battle was fought.—*The New-York Mercury*, March 8, 1756.

MAP OF PENNSYLVANIA.—Just Published, And to be sold at the Printing-Office, at the Bible and Crown, in Hanover Square, Price 12 Shillings; A Map of the improved Part of the Province of Pennsylvania, wherein are laid down all the principal Rivers, Creeks, Mountains, Highways, Churches, Meeting-houses, Merchant-Mills, Gentlemen's Seats, Houses of Entertainment, Situation of Iron Works, such as Furnaces, Forges, &c. all taken by actual Surveys, made by the Author, The Names of the Townships are also inserted nearly in the Places where they lie. There is also a Pamphlet given gratis with each Map, containing the Distances from Philadelphia, of all Places of Note within the Province, which makes this Work of real Use, not only to the People of Pennsylvania, but to the neighbouring Governments.— *The New-York Mercury*, July 9, 1759.

MAP OF NOVA-SCOTIA.—Just published, and Sold at the Printing-Office in Beaver-Street. The second Edition (with very large Additions, Corrections and Improvements) of a Map of Nova-Scotia and Parts adjacent; wherein is accurately described, Part of New-England (from Boston Northeastward) Nova-Scotia, its true Extent, Boundaries, and Fishing Banks; the Islands of Cape-Breton, St. John's Anticosti, and New-foundland; the great River of Canada, or St. Lawrence, with Orleans, Coudre, and other Islands that lie in it. Shewing also, all the various Communications, by Means of the River Ristigochi, St. John's, Penobscot, Kenebeck, Chaudiere, &c. between Quebec, and other Places situate on St. Lawrence River, on the North, across the Lands with the Gulph of St. Lawrence on the East, the Bay of Fundy and the Atlantic Ocean on the South. The English Fort and Settlements, and the Seats of the (pretended Neutral) French Inhabitants in Nova-Scotia; with every thing else worthy of Notice, or that may serve to give a true Idea of the Situation, and connection of the several parts of that Country, and of the Advances and Operations of his Majesty's Troops that have been, or now are employed in those Parts. Also in a vacant Part of the Plate are inserted the following (more particular) Draughts of the principal Places, that are situate within the Bounds of this Map, viz. 1st the Situation of Halifax, Draught of Chebucto Harbour, &c. 2d. A Plan of the Town of Halifax. 3d. A Plan of Quebec. 4th a Plan of the Port and Fortress of Louisbourgh, with the English Works raised against it in 1745. 5th a neat View of the Town of Boston.

Price Half a Dollar plain, or a whole Dollar colour'd. Note, The Western Part of this Map contains the same Places that are contained in the Eastern Part of A general Map of the Middle British Colonies, published by the late ingenious and accurate Mr. Lewis Evans, and as this Map begins with the Eastern Limits of that, and proceeds Eastward from it, as far as to include the Streights of Belle Isle, it may serve a Supplement thereto; and those two Maps together afford an entire View of all the Places on this Continent, that have been, or now are the Objects, or Scenes of any millitary Operations.—*The New-York Gazette or the Weekly Post-Boy,* January 14, 1760.

A MAP OF NEW YORK.—A New Map of the Province of New-York and New Jersey, with Part of Pennsylvania, and the Government of Trois Rivieres and Montreal, drawn by Capt. Holland, engraved by Thomas Jefferies, Geographer to his Majesty; four and a half Feet high, Breadth 21 Inches: Also the Map of the Globe, and the four Quarters, in four Sheets, two sheets, and one Sheet— in Sheets or on Canvis and Rollers. Maps and Charts of different Sorts and Sizes. Variety of large and small Metzitinto and engraved Prints, Jappaners do. drawing and Copy Books, oil and Water Colours in Shells, Limners and Black Lead Pencils, red and black Chalk, and Variety of Limners and Jappaners Articles, with Varnish of all kinds, too tedious to mention; Sold by G. Duyckinck, at the Universal Store, at the Corner of the Old Slip-Market.—*The New-York Journal or the General Advertiser*, May 5, 1768.

MAP OF NORTH AMERICA.—Death Notice of Dr. Mitchell, maker of the map of North-America.—A news item from London, February 25, in *The New-York Gazette or the Weekly Post-Boy*, April 25, 1768.

PROPOSED DRAUGHTS.—Jonathan Carver, formerly a Captain in the Provincial Troops of the Massachusetts Bay, during the War in North-America, and lately employ'd as a Surveyor and Draughtsman, in exploring the interior and upper Parts of the Continent, adjoining to, and beyond the Lake Superior, and a Thousand Miles upwards, and Westward of the great River Missisippi; offers the following Proposals to the Public, viz. To publish, as soon as a proper Number of Subscribers encourage him in the Design, the exact and minute Journal of His Proceedings, and Remarks on the Nations and Countries he passed through, together with Draughts and Plans annexed, of these Countries, and of his recent Discoveries. Each Subscriber to pay the Sum of two Spanish Dollars, for every Copy of the proposed Work, and as soon as a sufficient Number have subscribed, (in order to indemnify the Expence of the Press, and Engraving) the Publication will immediately ensue. Subscriptions are taken in by Jonathan Carver, at Mr. Burns's, in the Broad-Way, and by the Printer hereof.—*The New-York Gazette and the Weekly Mercury*, August 15, 1768.

PLAN OF NEW YORK CITY.—Just published, and to be sold by H. Gaine, (Price 16s. coloured, and 8s. plain) A Plan of the City of New-York, Dedicated to his Excellency Sir Henry Moore, Bart.

The above Plan is done on a Sheet of Imperial Paper, and Streets laid down very exact, with the Names of each, the Wards, Wharfs and all the publick Buildings in and about the City properly distinguished, and the whole carried considerably farther than Corlear's Hook.—*The New-York Gazette and the Weekly Mercury*, August 21, 1769.

MAP OF VIRGINIA.—A Most accurate and excellent map of the colony of Virginia, taken from actual surveys, finely engraved and beautifully printed on 4 sheets of royal paper, price 30s. Virginia currency, each, (equal to 5 dollars) may be had on application to the printer, where one of the maps may be seen.—*The New-York Journal or the General Advertiser*, September 13, 1770.

A PLAN OF NEW YORK CITY.—To be sold by the Printer hereof, A Plan of the City of New York, and its Invirons, surveyed and laid down in the years 1766, and 1767, with a South Prospect of the same, taken from the Governor's Island. In this Plan is taken in Powlis-Hook, Red-Hook, the Long Island Shore, and the Islands in our Bay &c. &c.—*The New-York Gazette and the Weekly Mercury*, October 15, 1770.

MAPS OF THE NEW CEDED COUNTRIES.—Three very elegant geographical maps of the new ceded countries, being by far the most extensive and accurate work of this nature that has yet been attempted in America, are offer'd for publication by subscription. Proposals to be seen, and subscriptions taken in, by the printer hereof.

The author offers himself for the establishing of any important lines in any part of America, either in the common or astronomical way, or for the survey of any estate, country, or province, that might want accuracy and neatness. He flatters himself that this work in any of the above branches will sufficiently recommend itself. He may be heard of at the printer's, or at the widow

Blau's, near the exchange.—*The New-York Gazette and the Weekly Mercury,* July 5, 1773.

BERNARD ROMANS.—Mr. Bernard Romans begs leave to inform the public, that his maps are now ready for publication, and the copper-plates being all done, and the paper which he was obliged to get manufactured on purpose, is likewise finished, but not yet received from Philadelphia, or else at least a great part would have been delivered before now: The subscribers may rest assured of receiving the copies within the time prescribed, which is the first day of January next.

As his edition is small, it is requested that such Gentlemen who incline to have copies may subscribe, as after publication none will be to be had for less than 16 Dollars.—*Rivington's New-York Gazetteer,* November 10, 1774.

ROMAN'S MAP OF BOSTON, Is just printed, published, and to sold by Richard Sause, at his Store near the Fly-Market, Little Dock Street, Where Subscriptions are taken in for any number, This Map of Boston, &c. is one of the most correct that has ever been published. The draught was taken by the most skilful Draughtsman in all America, and who was on the spot at the engagements of Lexington and Bunker's-Hill. Every Well-wisher to this country cannot but delight in seeing a plan of the ground on which our brave American Army conquered the British ministerial forces. Price plain 5s. coloured 6s. and 6d. Pennsylvania currency.—*The New-York Gazette and the Weekly Mercury,* September 11, 1775.

COPPER PLATE PRINTING

CHRISTMAS PIECES.—Blank Copper-Plate Christmas Pieces for School-Boys, whole-sale or retail, to be Sold by the Printer hereof.—*The New-York Gazette Revived in the Weekly Post-Boy,* November 20, 1752.

JOHN DAVIS, Copper Plate Printer, lately from London; Neatly prints off Silver, Copper, Brass, or Pewter Plates; on Paper, Parchment, Vellum, Silk or Linen, in the neatest Manner, at Mr. William Post's Painter, at Burling's Slip, New-York.—*The New-York Gazette or the Weekly Post-Boy*, June 23, 1763 (*Supplement*).

JOHN HUTT.— . . . Copper Plate Printing. Said Hutt having lately for the better accomodation of his customers, and the public in general, erected a press for that purpose, by which means he will be enabled to execute every piece of engraving he is favoured with, in a neater more expeditious, and reasonable manner than heretofore could be done, the printing branch being attended with great difficulty, and an expence rather extravagant.—*The New-York Journal or the General Advertiser*, September 15, 1774.

SILVER AND JEWELRY

SILVERSMITHS

JOHN ARCHIE.—Henry Clopper, Sadler, Is removed from the Corner of the Meal-Market, to the House where Mr. John Archie, Silver-Smith, formerly lived, in Dock-Street, opposite to Mr. Garrit Van Horne's, where he sells Sadles, Bridles, Whips, and all Sorts of Sadlery Ware, cheap, wholesale or retail.—*The New-York Mercury*, June 4, 1759 (*Supplement*).

A. B.—This is to give Notice, That there is a Silver Spoon stopt on suspicion of being stolen; Silversmith's Stamp (A.B.) (A. B.). Whoever owns the said Spoon may apply to Samuel Sands, living in Ulster County, near New-Windsor, before whom they most prove their property and pay the Costs.—*The New-York Gazette*, July 23, 1764.

E. B.—Stolen last Wednesday a Silver Tankard, containing a Quart, the Tankard hath a new Lid lately put on, the Handle thereof is mark'd with Letters following, (to Wit)   E V B
　　　　　　E V B
　　　　　　M B
The Stamp of the Silver-smith or Maker is with the letters E. B. Upon the Front of the Tankard is engraved a Coat of Arms. Whosoever shall bring the said Silver Tankard to the Printer hereof, (if found in the Country) shall have Forty Shillings, and if in this City, Thirty Shillings as a Reward for their Pains, and no Questions asked, how they came thereby.—*The New-York Gazette*, February 8-15, 1732.

I. B.—Stolen out of the House of the Subscriber, in Horse Neck, on the Morning of the 15th of this Instant April, a large Silver Tankard, that will contain three Pints, markt with the Letters C. I. B. and stampt I. B. or P. G. Whoever will bring said Tankard to me in Horse Neck, or to Alexander Montgomery, Tavern Keeper, near the Ship Yards in New-York, or will apprehend the Thief or Thieves, so that he or they may be Convicted, shall have a Reward of Five Dollars, and all reasonable Charges paid by Matthew Mead.—*The New-York Journal or the General Advertiser*, April 20, 1769.

T. B.—Tuesday last, was stole out of a House in
T
Maiden-Lane; two Silver Table Spoons, marked I S. the Maker's Mark TB in one. If offer'd to be pawn'd or sold please to stop them, and give Notice to the Printing-Office in Beaver-street. A reasonable Reward, with Thanks will be given.—*The New-York Gazette or the Weekly Post-Boy*, January 15, 1759.

ADRIAEN BANCKER.[1] To Be Sold, By Flores Bancker, (At the House of Adriaen Bancker, Gold and Silver-Smith, in Bridge-Street, near the Exchange;) wholesale and retale; Sundry dry goods. . . . —*The New-York Journal or the General Advertiser*, October 23, 1766.

THAUVET BESLY, Gold-Smith, on Golden-hill in New-York, has at his House Peter Lorin, a Jeweller, from London who setts after the neatest & Newest Fashions, all sorts of Jewels, Rings, Ear-Rings, Solitairs, Lockets, Aigrettes, Stay-Hooks, Seals, as also Diamonds, Rubies, Emeralds, Saphires, or any other kind of stone to the best advantage, at very reasonable Rates.—*The New-York Weekly Post Boy*, November 10, 1746.

THAUVET BESLY.—All Persons that have any Demands on the Estate of Mary Carter, late of this City deceased,

[1] Also spelled Adrian Bancker.

are desired to bring their Account to Thauvet Besly, Gold smith on Golden-Hill, in order to their being satisfied; and all those indebted to the said Estate are desired to discharge it forthwith, that the legacies may be paid; and prevent more trouble from Thauvet Besly, Executor. —*The New-York Gazette Revived in the Weekly Post-Boy*, January 30, 1749.

JACOB BOELEN.—Stole at Flatbush on Long-Island, One Silver Tankerd, a piece of Money in the Led of King Charles II, and the Led all engraved, a Coat of Arms, before (in it Man on a Waggon with two Horses) mark'd on the Handle, L P A. One Silver Tankerd plain, with a Piece of Money in the Led, mark'd on the Handle A P or A L. One Cup with two twisted Ears chas'd with Skutchens, marked L P A. One Tumbler marked L P A. One Dutch Beker weighs about 28 Ounces, Engraved all around, marked L P A. All the above were made by Mr. Jacob Boele, [*sic*] Stamp'd IB. One large Cup with two cast Ears, with Heads upon them and a Coat of Arms, Engraved thereon, One Cup with two Ears, a small hole in the Bottom, One Pair of leather Women Gloves. One black Girdle lined with blue Callico. And two Pair Shoe Clasps new cleaned. Whoever can inform Peter Lefferts of Flatbush or Long-Island, or Abraham Lefferts in New-York, so that it may be had again, shall have Fifteen Pounds Reward and no Question asked.—*The New-York Gazette*, October 1-8, 1733.

EPHRAIM BRASHER.—Stolen. On the nineteenth instant, out of Mr. John Tuttle's, near Powles Hook Ferry, New-York. A Silver mounted Hanger, with a Dog's Head, and green ivory grip, the grip rather small, the swell of which designed for the underside, is above; the Scabbard a little damaged, and cut through in one place. On one side of the Plate of the Scabbard, is engraved E—m. Brashier, New-York, Maker; and on the other side Issac Morrison. Whoever secures said Sword, and Thief, so that the Owner may get the one, and the other be brought to justice, shall have for the Sword, three Dollars, and for the Sword and Thief, Seven Pounds Ten Shillings. New-York Currency, paid by John Tuttle.— *The New-York Journal or the General Advertiser*, February 22, 1776.

JOHN BREVOORT.—Stolen on Sunday Night the 21st of September last, out of the House of Nicholas Burger, living in Queen-street, in this City, One Silver Tea Pot, and one Cream Pot, and six Silver Table Spoons, a Silver Sugar Tongs, and six Tea Spoons, Made by Mr. John Brevoort, stampt with his Stamp thus, I B V, in a Circle, and mark'd on the Bottom of the Tea Pot and

Cream Pot thus, N $\overset{B}{}$ I and on the Handles of the Table $\overset{}{V}$

Spoons the same; and on .the Tea Spoons I D. Whoever will give any Information about the said Things, so that they may be had again, or the Thief apprehended, shall have Five Pounds Reward, paid by Nicholas Burger.

N.B. If offer'd to be pawn'd, or sold, pray stop the same, and the Person who offers it.—*The New-York Gazette*, October 6, 1760.

CHARLES OLIVER BRUFF, Goldsmith and jeweller, at the sign of the Tea-pot and tankard, in Maiden-Lane, near the Fly-market, Having employed a jeweller from London, who understands making or mending any kind of diamond or enamel'd work in the jewellery way. Also makes and mends all manner of stone buckles, stone rings, ear-rings, broaches seals, solitairs, hair jewels, lockets, enamel'd. Makes all manner of sleeve buttons, mourning rings of all sorts, trinkets for Ladies, plats hair in a curious manner in true lovers knots, for buttons, rings or lockets, plain or enamel'd; gold necklaces or stone of all sorts. Said Bruff makes all sorts of silver smiths work, mends old work in that way, and has put himself to a great expence in sending to London for diamonds and all manner of precious stones, and he hopes for the encouragement of the gentlemen and ladies of this City, as he will study to use them well.—*The New-York Mercury*, January 3, 1763.

CHARLES OLIVER BRUFF, Goldsmith and Jeweller, at the Sign of the tea pot, and tankard, opposite the Fly-Market, next door to Mr. Laffar's, Is provided with jeweller's, one from London and another from France, . . . —*The New-York Gazette or the Weekly Post-Boy*, June 9, 1763.

CHARLES OLIVER BRUFF.— . . . Whereas the said Bruff, has had his work undervalued by three different Silver-smiths of this city, by one I lost three pounds for workmanship, out of eleven pounds five shillings, workmanship; and by another I lost six shillings, on making a set of table-spoons; and the third tried to undervalue a piece of work of two pounds eight shillings, to one pound fifteen shillings, whereby I have hurted myself by keeping up the prices, which I know no reason I should hurt myself for others. He hopes for the encouragement of the Gentlemen and Ladies of this city and country, as he will study to use them well. Since those Gentlemen of the trade has brought the prices so low, I therefore give notice, that I will work for the following prices, viz.

For making silver tankard 3 s. per ounce. For making a silver tea-pot, £ 4. For making a Sugar-pot, 35 s. For making a milk-pot, 24 s. For making a Soop-spoon 20 s. For making six table-spoons 21 s. For making six tea-spoons 10 s. For making tea-tongs, bows or others, 10 s. For making a pair of carved silver buckles, 8 s. I design to put the stamp of my name, in full, on all my works; and will work as cheap as any in the city. —*The New-York Mercury*, April 20, 1767.

CHARLES OLIVER BRUFF, Goldsmith and Jeweller, at the sign of the Teapot, Tankard, and Ear-ring, has removed to the upper end of Maiden-Lane, near the

Broadway, and near the Oswego Market, Where he makes
or mends any kind of diamond or enamel'd work in the
jewellery way; also all manner of stone buckles, stone
rings, ear-rings, broaches, seals, solataires, hair jewels,
lockets, plain and enamel'd sleeve buttons, mourning
rings of all sorts, trinkets for Ladies, gold neck-laces or
stone of all sorts.   Likewise makes all sorts of silver-
smiths work, and mends old work in that way; Ladies
fans mended in the neatest manner and at the lowest
price; watch glasses put in for one shilling a piece.   To
all gentlemen merchants that travel the country, or
pedlars, that please to favour me with their custom, may
depend on being used well, and will make any kind of
work cheaper than they can get it in the city elsewhere;
I have finished some of the neatest dies for making sleeve
buttons, with the neatest gold custs on them to stamp
all sorts of gold buttons, silver, pinchbeck, or brass, and
will sell them cheaper than any in the city.   Said Bruff
has for sale, all sorts of earthen ware, and a few articles
in the dry good way, also all sorts of buckles.—*The New-
York Gazette and the Weekly Mercury,* May 25, 1772.

CHARLES OLIVER BRUFF— . . . He gives the highest
price for old gold, silver, and jewels, rough crystals, paste,
and all sorts of old stones, as he is fitting up a lapidary's
mill, and is just ready to cut any kind of stones, &c.   He
has for sale, diamonds, rubies, emeralds, emathist, onyx
and saphires, garnets of different sizes; also a neat onyx
top, bottom and sides of a snuff box, and one of mother
of pearl, fit to be set in gold; likewise stones and paste of
all sizes, colours and sorts.   Country jewellers can be
supplied cheaper than at any other place in the city; and
he makes it a point with those that bring him jobs from
the country, to dispatch them with expedition.—*The
New-York Gazette and the Weekly Mercury,* January
24, 1774.

CHARLES OLIVER BRUFF.— . . . N.B.   I Have Engaged
a Stone Seal Engraver, who engraves arms, crests,

cyphers, figures, heads and fancies, in the neatest manner
and with the greatest expedition, with the heads of
Shakespear, Milton, Newton, Pope, Homer, Socrates,
Hannible, Mark Anthony, Caesar, Plato, Jupiter, Apollo,
Neptune, Mars, Cleopatria, Diana, Flora, Venus, Marcel-
lany, with the figures of most of the above, and others
too tedious to mention. He makes it a point with those
who bring him jobs from the country, to dispatch them
with expedition. All country jewellers may have stone
seals engraved in the neatest manner. Just bought some
Egyptian pebbles, very curious for snuff boxes and seals.
—*The New-York Gazette and the Weekly Mercury*, July
18, 1774.

√ CHARLES OLIVER BRUFF.—Those Gentlemen who are
forming themselves into Companies, in Defence of their
Liberties, and others, that are not provided with Swords,
May be suited therewith by applying to Charles Oliver
Bruff, in Maiden-Lane, near the Fly-Market. Small
Swords Silver mounted, Cut-and-thrust and Cutteau De
Chase, mounted with beautiful green Grips; and, Broad
Swords with the Heads of Lord Chatham, and John
Wilkes, Esq; with Shells pierced and ornamented with
Mottoes,—for Pitt's Head, Magna Charta and Freedom,
—for Wilkes's Head, Wilkes and Liberty; or mounted in
whatever Form Gentlemen may fancy, being a Collection
of the most elegant Swords ever made in America, all
manufactured by said Bruff. N.B. Best Small Arm and
Pistol Oyl Flints.—*The New-York Gazette and the
Weekly Mercury*, June 19, 1775.

√ CHARLES OLIVER BRUFF.— . . . Scabbards made for
Swords, at the shortest Notice, at different Prices, Gun
Screw Drivers and double Worms fit to draw a Ball, at
2s. All the Gentlemen of the American Army who are
not supplied, may have them at the above shop.

N. B. Best Sword Belts, with or without Swivels.
Wants to hire Silversmiths, a Cutler, Chape Forger,
Filers, and Whitesmiths; if any in the Army good Wages

will be given. Ready Money given for old Gold and
Silver, Ivory and Sword Blades.—*The New-York Gazette
and the Weekly Mercury*, July 8, 1776.

I. C.—Stolen, on the 21st of March last, at Night, out
of the House of Jacob J. Lansing, of Albany, a Silver
Tankard, weight 34 oz. and some Pennyweight, marked
H
I   L the Maker's Mark I.C. Whoever secures the Tankard, that the Owner may get the same again, shall have
Forty Shillings Reward, and all reasonable Charges paid
by Jacob Jacob Lansing.—*The New-York Mercury*, April
24, 1758.

——CARROL.—We hear from Shrewsbury, that about a
Fortnight ago, one Carroll, of that Place, a Silver-Smith,
was committed to Goal and still remains there, for de-
bauching his own Daughter, a Girl not fifteen Years of
Age, who has sworn that she is with Child by him, and
that this detestable Commerce has subsisted for about
two Years.—News item in *The New-York Gazette and
the Weekly Mercury*, September 4, 1769.

SIMEON AND WILLIAM COLEY.—Notice is hereby given,
that the partnerships between Simeon and William
Coley, silver-smiths in New York, is now dissolv'd and
ended, and all persons indebted to the said partnership,
are hereby requested to make immediate payment to the
same; and all persons having any demands are desired
to bring in their accounts, that they may be satisfied, to
Simeon Coley, at this house near the coffee-house, where
he carries on the said business as usual, and takes this
opportunity of returning his hearty Thanks to those gentlemen and ladies, who have been pleased to honour him
with their commands, and hopes for a continuance of
their favours, as he shall always make it his principal
study to merit the same. He has now for sale, just
imported a fresh and curious assortment of Jewellery,
viz. garnet necklaces and ear rings, paste ditto, curious

sets of paste buckles, corals and coral necklaces, for children, and various other articles.—*The New-York Gazette or the Weekly Post-Boy*, September 11, 1766.

SIMEON COLEY, Gold-Smith, and Jeweller, from London, Has made several very neat Fancy-Rings, to be worn on the above happy occasion,[2] which may be had at his Shop near the Merchants Coffee-House. Said Coley, makes all Sorts of large and small Plate, Mourning Rings, &c. &c.—*The New-York Gazette*, March 16-23, 1767.

SIMEON COLEY.—Just imported in the ships Edward and Hope, from London, and to be sold cheap by Simeon Coley, Silver-smith, near the Merchant's Coffee house;
A Large assortment of jewellery, diamond, garnet, and other rings; the neatest paste & stone buckels, garnet and paste necklaces, ear rings, egrets and solatiers, ditto neat etwe cases, silver-handle knives and forks in cases, ivory ditto, neat small swords, and cutteau de chase, and sword belts, great variety of pocket books for gentlemen and ladies, silver and other watches, ditto chains, neat clocks in mahogany cases, best gilt and other buckels, masons broaches and jewels, gold buttons and seals, silver ditto, neat tortise-shell snuff-boxes and smelling bottles, plated bits, and stirrups, best violins, german and common flutes, fifes, aeolus harps, hand organs, and a variety of other articles.—*The New-York Mercury*, October 5, 1767.

SIMEON COOLEY.[3]—The Conduct of Simeon Cooley, in his daring Infractions of the Non-importation Agreement; his insolent and futile Defence of those inglorious Measures; with his avowed Resolution obstinately to persevere in counteracting the legal Efforts of a brave and free People in support of their inestimable Rights "alarmed and insenced" the Inhabitants of this City, who dreading the destructive Consequence that might have

[2] The "happy occasion" was the celebration of the repeal of the Stamp Act, held in the house of Edward Bardin.
[3] Different spelling of Simeon Coley.

ensued from so dangerous an Example, determined, at a
General Meeting held on Friday Evening last, to call the
said Cooley to Account; and prevail on him, If Possible,
to desist from his vile Practices, and endeavour to bring
him to such Concessions as should to them appear best
calculated to attone for his repeated and unprecedented
offences.   Two Gentlemen were appointed to inform him
of the Sentiments of the Inhabitants, who required his
immediate Attendance at their Place of Meeting, and to
assure him that no injury should be offered to his Person;
(to prevent which, every imaginable Precaution was
taken) but Cooley, (influenced perhaps by some ill-
disposed and Stupid Adviser) refused to attend the Place
appointed, and alledged in Excuse for his Non-attend-
ance, "that he did not think it consistent with his per-
sonal Safety to meet them There", at the same Time
he expressed a Willingness to make the Concessions
required, from his Parlour Window.   When the Inhabitants received this disagreeable Intelligence, they
immediately proceeded towards his House; but Cooley,
apprized of their coming, thought proper to decamp,
accompanied by a Military Gentleman, (who covered his
Retreat) sought for a Sanctuary within the Fort Walls,
which could afford him but an indifferent Protection
against the keen Reproaches of a guilty Conscience, the
only Punishment he had to dread.   Whilst the Inhabitants were assembled in the Fields, M—r P—r ordered
a File of Soldiers to guard his (Cooley's) House, who
were accordingly drawn up before his Door, with their
Musquets loaded, &c.   Whether the Author of this un-
warrantable Step, designed a compliment to the Magistracy and Inhabitants of this City, or to recommend
himself to his Superiors by his officious and blundering
Zeal, is unknown: but 'tis more than probable, that his
precipitate Conduct was disapproved of by the latter, . . .

On Saturday Morning, Cooley consented to meet the
Inhabitants; and Four in the Afternoon being the Time
appointed, and the Merchants's Coffee-House the Place,
they assembled in Expectation of this Important Event;

but the Majority thinking it a very unsuitable Place for the Purpose, required his appearance in the Fields, where he attended, and publickly acknowledged his Crimes; implored the Pardon of his Fellow Citizens; engaged to store an equivalent to the Goods he had sold, together with all that he had in Possession that were imported contrary to Agreement; and so to conduct for the future as not to render himself obnoxious to the Contempt and just Resentment of an injured People.—News item in *The New-York Gazette and the Weekly Mercury,* July 24, 1769.[4]

SIMEON COLEY, Silversmith and Jeweller Begs leave to inform the Public, that he intends to leave this City this Month, with his Family; humbly intreats all that stand indebted to him to settle their accounts directly; all those that have any Demands upon him are desired to call, and they shall be paid.—*The New-York Gazette and the Weekly Mercury,* September 4, 1769.

P. D.—Stolen on Friday Night, the 14th Instant, from me the subscriber in Sussex County, One Gold Chain of four Strings with a Locket marked E. G. Four Silver Spoons marked M. G. the Silversmith's mark P D. One ditto with the name Hannah Burges on the Handle; One ditto marked I $\underset{\text{L}}{\overset{\text{B}}{}}$. One ditto the Handle broke off marked S $\underset{\text{C.}}{\overset{\text{K}}{}}$ One Child's Spoon marked M. G. One round Silver Salver with a round Foot; One Set of Woman's Breast Jewels for a Stomacher set in Silver wash'd with Gold, consisting of six different Pieces, the Uppermost and Largest with a large Chrystal Stone in the Middle, set round with small Stones of different Colours, the lowermost or Girdle Hook being set round with Emeralds and Pearl; a Silver Scissars Chain marked

---

[4] Other papers which printed similar accounts of Simeon Coley were: *The New-York Journal or the General Advertiser,* July 20-27, 1769 and *The New-York Chronicle,* July 12-20, 1769 (in which Simeon Coley is mentioned as a haberdasher, jeweller, and silversmith).

on a Heart M G. a Silver Watch Chain and Pincushion
Chain . . . Shepard Kollock.—*The New-York Journal,*
August 31, 1741.

JOHN DAWSON, Gold-Smith and Jeweler, Has open'd
shop on Rotten-Row, where he carries on the said Business in their several branches, after the best Manner.
Gentlemen and Ladies may have any piece of diamond
work made in the genteelest taste, or repair'd in the best
manner, at reasonable rates: He makes all sorts of
curious enamel'd, mourning, fancy, or plain lockets;
mourning or fancy enamel'd rings, cluster or fancy stone
rings of all kinds; All other articles in the Jeweler's way
likewise He also plaits hair in the neatest manner to any
size or shape, for rings or lockets, and forms it (after
the new taste) to resemble Mocco. Also he makes and
sells all sorts of silver work. As he is a stranger, and a
young Beginner, can hope for encouragement only from
the goodness of his work, and the reasonableness of his
prices, which he hopes will entitle him to the favour and
encouragement of the public. Said Dawson takes this
opportunity to return his grateful thanks to those Gentlemen and Ladies who have been pleased to employ him
since his arrival here; and from his desire to please, hopes
for a continuance of their custom.—*The New-York Mercury,* May 4, 1767.

CARY DUNN.—Stopt last Week, a Gold Watch Case
and one large Silver Spoon; Any Person proving their
Property, paying Charges for the same, may have them
by applying to the subscriber, Silver-Smith, living between the New Dutch Church and Fly-Market, Cary
Dunn.—*The New-York Gazette or the Weekly Post-Boy,*
March 19, 1770.

CARY DUNN.—Whereas one hundred and twenty four
persons have lately arrived in this city, from the North
of Scotland, in the brigantine Nancy, Capt. Smith,
master consisting of men, women and children, with and

without trades; they take this method to inform their benefactors, and all others, ladies and gentlemen, that want to employ any of the said persons, that they may be informed where to find them by applying to Mr. Cary Dunn, Gold and Silver Smith, near the New-Dutch Church, who has in his custody, a true list of their names, ages, and places of residence.—*Rivington's New-York Gazetteer*, January 27, 1774.

DANIEL DUPUY.—To be Sold, A Very good Plantation in the County of Orange . . . Enquire of Mrs. Ann Dupuy in New-York, or Mr. Daniel Dupuy, Gold-Smith in Philadelphia.—*The New-York Weekly Post-Boy*, March 31, 1746.

——FIELDING.—Robert M'Alpine, Book-Binder, who lately lived in Hanover-Square is removed into the house where Mr. Fielding Gold-Smith, formerly lived, at the corner of Broad and Princes Streets, . . .—*The New-York Gazette or the Weekly Post-Boy*, November 17, 1755.

DANIEL FUETER, Gold and Silver-Smith, Lately arrived in the Snow Irene, Capt. Garrison from London, living back of Mr. Hendrick Van De Waters, Gun-Smith, near the Brew-House of the late Harmanus Rutgers, deceased, makes all sorts of Gold and Silver work, after the newest and neatest Fashion; He also gilds Silver and Metal, and refines Gold and Silver after the best Manner, and makes Essays on all sorts of Metal and Oar; all at a reasonable Rate. N.B. he buys old Gold and Silver Lace, and Gold-Smith's Sweeps.—*The New-York Gazette or the Weekly Post-Boy*, May 27, 1754.

DANIEL FUETER, Silver Smith and Jeweller, next Door to Mr. Peter Curtenius, facing the Oswego Market, Has lately imported: A Beautiful Assortment of Jewellery, which for Elegance and Taste is greatly superior to any Thing hitherto brought to this Place; Consisting of a great Variety of Rings, set knot Fashion, Entourage, Cluster, &c. Viz. Brilliant Diamonds and Rose Diamonds of all Sizes, Rubies, Topazes, Emeralds, Saphirs, and all Kinds of Precious Stones, warranted. Ear-rings of all Sizes, Fashions and Prices; Paste Shoe and knee Buckles, fine Twezer Cases, and Snuff Boxes of curious Workmanship. Also a genteel Parcel of Silver Work, tea Pots, Milk Pots, Sauce Boats, Shoe and knee Buckles, and other Articles too numerous to mention, all extremely Cheap.

N.B. The said Daniel Fueter, importer of the above Goods, who was bred a Jeweller and Goldsmith, will give full Satisfaction to those Gentlemen and Ladies who will honour him with their Custom: and will undertake to execute on the shortest Notice, and as Cheap as may be done in London, any Orders he receives in the several Branches of Jewellery, and Gold or Silver Smith's Work; being furnished with the best of Workmen, and all Requisites for the purpose.

Also he will make exact Assays of all Sorts of Ores and Metals; and will perform Refining and Gilding in the neatest Manner. He gives ready money for old Gold and Silver.—*The New-York Gazette or the Weekly Post-Boy*, March 10, 1763.

DANIEL FUETER, imports Blackwood's true cordial elixir, at 5s. per bottle, for all cold, coughs, sore throats, . . .—*The New-York Gazette or the Weekly Post-Boy*, September 6, 1764.

DANIEL FUETER, Silversmith, from London, Begs Leave to acquaint the Public, that he is removed into the House of Mrs. Pinto, between Mr Sherbroke's, and Mr. M'Cartney's, in Bayard Street, where he continues to follow the Silversmith's Business, and Jewellery in all its Branches; also Gilding, assaying of Ores, and refining in the exactest Manner; and all at the most reasonable Prices. He also informs the Public that Mr. John

Anthony Beau,[5] Chaiser, from Geneva, works with him; where Chaising in general, viz. Snuff Boxes, Watch Cases, &c. &c. is done in the best and cheapest Manner . . . —*The New-York Gazette and the Weekly Mercury*, July 31, 1769.

DANIEL & LEWIS FUETER.—This serves to inform the Public, and our former kind Customers, that we the Subscribers, are return'd to this City, in the House we remov'd out, in Dock-Street, next to Mr. G. Dyckinck's, and purpose to carry on the Business of Gold, Silversmith's and Jewelery Work, in all its Branches, as also gilding, assaying oar, refining, &c. at the most reasonable rates; and we return Thanks to our former Customers, and assure them and the Public that will be pleased to employ us, that they shall be serv'd with punctuality, and Honour, by their Very oblig'd and humble Servants, Daniel and Lewis Feuter.—*The New York Gazette and the Weekly Mercury*, January 30, 1769.

LEWIS FUETER, son of Mr. Daniel Fueter, late of Bayard-Street; Begs leave to inform the publick, that he is removed to the small house next door to Mr. Isaac Heron's Watch-maker, at the Coffee-House Bridge, where he makes and mends all kinds of work in the jewellers and goldsmith's business, as neat and cheap as can be done (he flatters himself) by any man in this City. He likewise tries ores of any kind, assaying, refining and guilding in all its branches, perform'd with the utmost accuracy and dispatch. He thinks himself obliged, in the name of his father, as well as for himself, to return thanks to the respectable publick for the many favours done, and to assure those who shall honour him with their commands, that he will make it his utmost endeavour to deserve their countenance and encouragement. —*The New-York Gazette and the Weekly Mercury*, May 21, 1770.

[5] J. A. Beau was also employed by Lewis Fueter, according to *The New-York Journal or General Advertiser*, December 20, 1770.

LEWIS FUETER, Gold and Silver-Smith, Has removed his shop from the Coffee-House Bridge, to the house in Queen-street, lately occupied by Mr. Judah, Silver Smith, and opposite Robert G. Livingston, Esq; where he carries on his business as usual in all its branches, and hopes for the continuance of those gentlemen and ladies who have been so obliging as to favour with their custom: he will make it his constant study to merit their approbation. N.B. He gives the highest price for old gold and silver.—*Rivington's New-York Gazetteer*, May 12, 1774.

——GILBERT.—Tuesday Night last some Villains broke into the Shop of Mr. Gilbert, Silver-Smith in the Broad Way, and robb'd the same of near two Hundred Pounds, in Plate, &c. Diligent Search has been made after the Thieves, but we have not heard of any Discovery being made.—News item in *The New-York Gazette or Weekly Post-Boy*, August 27, 1770.

J. H.—Whereas on Tuesday the 29th of August last, a chest was broke open at my house, by persons unknown, out of which was taken four silver table spoons, marked M. C. M. maker's name J. H. in a heart; seven or eight silver tea spoons, the same mark and stamp, and one pair of silver tea tongs. If the same should be offered for sale, or pawned to any person or persons, they are desired to stop the same, and to secure the theif for which they shall have Four Dollars reward, paid by Mosses Clement. Queensbury, Orange-county.—*The New-York Gazette and the Weekly Mercury*, October 2, 1775.

T. H.—On Wednesday Evening last, about 6 o'Clock, a Silver Tankard was taken out of the Box of a Chaise standing at the Sign of the Dove, opposite to the Gate that opens to John Boss's House, in the Outward of this City. The Makers Mark T H, with a Cypher of the Letters J B on the Fore-Part of the Tankard. Whoever brings it to the Printer hereof, shall have Three Pounds

Reward, and no Questions asked: If offer'd to be pawn'd or sold, pray stop it, and the same Reward will be given. —*The New-York Gazette,* October 31, 1763.

BENJAMIN HALSTED.—A Premonition to those Gentlemen that may hereafter have an Occasion to employ a Silver-Smith, to beware of that Villain Benjamin Halsted; lest they be bit by him, as I have been. Andrew Bowne.—*The New-York Gazette or the Weekly Post-Boy,* August 16, 1764.

BENJAMIN HALSTED.—Having been informed that a defamatory Advertisement, against me signed by one Andrew Bowne, of Shrewsbury, was intended to be published in the Thursday's Gazette; This is to desire the Public not to suffer themselves to be seduced by the Malice of the said Andrew Bowne, but to suspend their Judgement, until, either the Truth, or the Calumny of his Assertion, be properly determined by a due Course of Law; for I am resolved to sue him immediately for Scandal. Benjamin Halsted.—*The New-York Gazette or the Weekly Post Boy,* August 23, 1764.

BENJAMIN HALSTED.—The Subscriber finds himself obliged, with infinite Reluctance, to address the Public on Account of a surrilous Advertisement in the New-York Gazette of Thursday last Week, signed by one Andrew Bowne. The Character and Reputation of a Man in Trade, being of the most delicate and tender Nature, any Attempts to stigmatize it, not founded on Facts, or supported by Evidence, will never, I flatter myself, influence the impartial Part of Mankind, before the Truth has been scrutinized in a legal Manner. But, some Time must elapse before this can be done: And as the Audaciousness of the Advertisement may make impressions to my Prejudice, I shall endeavour to remove them, by laying all my Transactions with Bowne, open to the Public; where by it may easily be perceived the

Means by which his Brain was so violently heated as to overcome his Reason.

Andrew Bowne, of Shrewsbury, called on me last Summer, telling me Joseph Holmes, of this City, had recommended me to him as an honest Silversmith. He then bespoke a Set of Silver Buttons for a Suit of Clothes. They were made exactly to his Directions; and when he came to fetch them he seemed perfectly pleased with them. Three Weeks afterwards he called on me, and desired I would take them back. I represented to him how unsaleable Things made after another's Whim were; and that before I found a Person of his Taste, Years might elapse. He then offered me a Dollar; which I refusing he grew passionate, and went away in the greatest Anger. On his Return Home, he wrote me the Annexed Letter (No. 1) which I despised, and returned no answer to. Last May he wrote me another (No. 2) in both which he has been very lavish of Names that no honest Man can well brook. I returned him an Answer (No. 3) with a View to pass the Affair into Ridicule; but it had a contrary Effect; and the Advertisement in Question was produced by it.[6]

Private Affairs, of a trival and insignificant Nature, are unworthy the Attention of the Public. But when malicious Defamation is allowed to blast Characters in a public Newspaper, a justifaction in the same public Manner becomes necessary; This Apology, I hope, will plead my Excuse. Benjamin Halsted.—*The New-York Gazette or the Weekly Post-Boy*, September 6, 1764.

BENJAMIN & MATTHIAS HALSTED, Gold and Silver-Smiths, Take this method to acquaint the public, that they have now set up their business in Elizabeth-Town (nearly opposite to Mr. Joseph Jelf's Merchant) where they propose to carry it on in all its branches, as the said Benjamin Halsted, has followed the business some

[6] Letters No. 1, 2, and 3 were published below the statement of Halsted. In the same paper the printer of the paper published a notice stating that the notices were published with the consent and desire of the persons affected.

time in New-York, to the satisfaction of his employers, he hopes his former customers there and in the country will not forget him, as he will now obey all orders for work from them and other gentlemen and ladies of the city or country, at the shortest notice and most reasonable prices, with the greatest care and exactness to their intire satisfaction; as we purpose to make work of all qualities (prices accordingly) we hope our employers will not expect the best of work for the meanest prices.

Any orders for work being left at Mr. Thomas Star Tredwell's, at Burling's-slip, New-York, will come safe to hand; or any gentlemen or ladies wanting work done, that are desirous to see one of us to deliver their orders to, if they will please to leave word at the above Mr. Tredwell's, one or the other will wait on them at a very short notice.

√ Said Matthias Halsted has for sale, a few silver-smiths tools, which he will sell cheap for cash, viz. Forging, planishing, hollowing and bouge hammers, piercing, riffling and common files, fine Turkey oil stone slips, and Bohemia polishing stones, double aqua fortis, corn, half-corn and flour emery, borax and sandever. The above tools, &c. may be had of the above Mr. Tredwell, and likewise a few best steel top thimbles.—*The New-York Gazette or the Weekly Post-Boy*, September 25, 1766.

CHARLES HAMBELTON.—Run Away from his Bail, the 4th of this instant Charles Hambelton, by Trade a Silver Smith . . .—*The New-York Gazette*, January 7, 1760.

√ ——HAMILTON.—We hear from Poughkeepsie, that about a Fortnight since, one Hamilton, a Silversmith, was committed to Goal there on Suspicion of making Spanish milled Dollars; but in a few Days after he was put in, to save any further Trouble, he hang'd himself with his own Handkerchief, by making it fast to a Spike that was drove into the Goal Wall.—News item in *The New-York Mercury*, July 13, 1761.

THOMAS HAMMERSLEY.—Run away, on friday the
20th inst. August, from Thomas Hammersley of the city
of New-York, goldsmith, a negro fellow named Duke
. . .—*The New-York Mercury*, August 30, 1756.

THOMAS HAMMERSLEY,[7] Gold-Smith, who lately lived
near the Change in Dock Street has removed his Shop
into Hanover-Square, next Door to Mr. John Waters,
Merchant. Where he continues to carry on his Business,
with the usual Expedition; and trusts he shall afford the
same general Satisfaction as heretofore. N.B. Any Person well acquainted with the Gold Smith's Business, may
meet with good Encouragement, by applying to the said
Hamersley.—*The New-York Gazette or the Weekly Post-
Boy*, June 27, 1757.

THOMAS HAMMERSLEY.—Last Wednesday Night two
Silver Spoons were offered to Sale to Thomas Hamersly,
of the City, Goldsmith, which he stop'd, on Suspicion
of their being stole: . . .—*The New-York Mercury*,
January 22, 1759.

THOMAS HAMMERSLEY.—Run-away, the 13th Instant,
from Thomas Hamersly, of this City, Goldsmith, A negro
Man. . . .—*The New-York Gazette or the Weekly Post-
Boy*, February 23, 1764.

JOHN HASTIER.—Thomas Butwell, is parted Partners
from James Munden, and Liveth in the House of Mr.
John Heistier [*sic*] Gold-smith, opposite to Mr. Franks
Merchant in Queen-Street . . .—*The New-York Weekly
Journal*, March 10, 1735.

JOHN HASTIER.—This is to give Notice that I John
Hastier, Gold Smith in this City, have at my House a
Frenchman, who teaches to Read and Write French, as
also Arithmetick in a very short Method. Whoever inclines to learn may apply to the said John Hastier at his

[7] Also spelled Hamersley and Hamersly.

House who will agree on reasonable Terms. . . .—*The New-York Weekly Journal*, June 27, 1737.

JOHN HASTIER.—

N. York, March 5, 1738/9

Mr. Bradford;

You are desired to publish the following account for the benefit of the Publick, as a Caution against Counterfeits.

Yours, &c.

On Saturday the 24th of February ult. Samuel Flud, alias Flood came with one Joseph Steel to the House of John Hastier of this City, Gold-smith and desired to be with him in private, who accordingly went into a Room, and Flud produced to him a Five Shilling Bill of New Hampshire, and asked him if he could engrave a Copper-plate for him like that? who answered, That he could. Flud desired that he would be expeditious about it, and he would reward him handsomly; and said, he would call again on Monday Morning following, and so Flud & Steel departed. Whereupon Mr. Hastier went immediately to a Magistrate and acquainted him of the Case, who desired Hastier to give notice when Flud came to him again, that he might be apprehended. He accordingly came again, with the said Steel, to the Goldsmith on Monday Morning, and said, he was glad that he had met with a Workman for his Turn; He brought a Ten Shilling Rhode-Island Bill, and bespoke a Plate for that also, promising the Gold-smith, that he should be well rewarded, he should have Money enough, and he would supply him with those Bills. But the Goldsmith having given Notice to the Magistrate, that those Men were at his House, they were immediately apprehended; and upon Examination there were found in Steel's Possession eleven Counterfeit Five Pound Rhode Island Bills, and afterwards two more of the same sort were discovered, which Steel had passed & Changed that Morning. . . .
—*The New-York Gazette*, February 27—March 6, 1739.

JOHN HASTIER.—Run away on Monday last, from John Hastier, of this City, Goldsmith, a lusty well-set Negro Man named Jasper . . .—*The New-York Gazette or the Weekly Post-Boy*, May 15, 1758.

JOHN HEATH.—To be Sold. The house on the corner of Van Gelder's alley in the Broadway . . . Any person inclining to purchase the same before the day of sale, may apply to John Heath, goldsmith, in Wall-street.— *The New-York Mercury*, January 3, 1763.

✓ HENRY JENAIN.—To Be Sold. A parcel of very good Duck Trousers by Henry Jenain, Gold Smith; Enquire for him at the House of Capt. Britton, at the Corner of Stone Street near Fort George in New-York.—*The New-York Journal*, January 23, 1750.

JACOB JENNINGS.—Broke open on Wednesday the 6th Instant April, at Night, a Gold-smith's, joining the Thacher's mills, in Norwalk, and carried of the following Ware, a Cream Pot, large Spoons stampt I I, Shoe and Knee-Buckles flower'd and plain, some of them were without Flukes, Teaspoons and Tongs, Stone Buttons of different Sorts, Gold and Silver Sleeve Buttons, and several other Things of Value. Whoever takes up the Thief or Thieves, and secures the said Ware, so that the Owner may have them again, shall be well rewarded, and all reasonable Charges paid by the Subscriber. Jacob Jennings. All Silversmiths are desired to stop the said Ware if offer'd for Sale.—*The New-York Gazette*, April 18, 1763.

WILLIAM KUMBEL, Clock and Watch-Maker, at the sign of the Dial, Near the Coenties Market, Begs leave to inform the public, that he carries on said business in all its branches; likewise the gold and silver smiths business. Any gentlemen or ladies who favours him with their work, may depend on its being done in the neatest manner, and at the most reasonable rate, with the quickest dispatch.—*The New-York Gazette and the Weekly Mercury*, July 24, 1775.

B. L. R.—Stolen out of the House of Mr. Jacob Franks, some Time last Sunday Night, two Pair of Silver Candlesticks, with the Cypher of J. A. F. on the Foot and the Mark B. L. R. the Makers Names stampt on the bottom, Weight of each Candlestick about 20 Ounces, a large chaced Salver wt. about 49 oz. one scollopt plain ditto, about 38 oz. a round plain Waiter, with the Arms of the late Sir Peter Warren, engraved in the middle wt. about 16 oz. a chaced Coffee-Pot wt. about 20 oz. All these are Sterling Plate, have a Lion Stampt on the Bottom . . .—*The New-York Gazette*, January 31, 1757.

JOHN BURT LYNG.—To be sold, at private Sale, the House wherein John Burt Lying, Silver-Smith, now lives, in the Broad-Way, adjoining the House of Mr. George Harrison, and directly opposite the Lutheran Church. For further Particulars apply to said Lying, on the Premises. Good security will be taken for one Half. N.B. The Gold and Silver-Smith Business is carried on as usual, by the Public's very humble Servant, John Burt Lying.—*The New-York Gazette or the Weekly Post-Boy*, January 5, 1764.

JOHN BURT LYNG.—To be Sold, A Smart Wench about 23 years old; the reason for parting with her is, she does not understand country work: She can be as well recommended as any Black that ever was sold. For farther particulars enquire of John Burt Lyng, Goldsmith, living in Great-George-Street.—*Rivington's New-York Gazetteer*, May 12, 1774 (*Supplement*).

CHARLES LE ROUX.—Stolen early this Morning out of the House of Judah Hayes, in Broadstreet, the following Plate, viz. One plain Quart Silver Coffee Pot, made by Charles Le Roux; One large Soop Ladle; One Table Spoon; Three Tea ditto; One chased Milk Pot, English

make; One Punch Strainer; One Small Silver Sauspan and Cover; And one Pepper Caster; all marked, except
H
the Coffee Pot, thus I R.—It is desired that they may be stopped if offer'd to be pawn'd or sold, and Notice given to the Subscriber; if the Things are recovered, Ten Pounds Reward will be given by Judah Hayes.—*The New-York Gazette,* August 16, 1762.

M. M.—Whereas the Dwelling House of Isaac Seixas, nigh the New Dutch Church, was last Night broke open, and sundry Things stolen therefrom; among which were two large Silver Table Spoons, mark'd with the Cypher I R S. Maker's Name M M; six Tea Spoons, mark'd R L. and Sugar Tongs; a Silver Pepper Box, and a Salt-Celler with the same Mark; a Pewter Ring Stand, two French Silver Candlesticks, and a Pair of Boys Silver Buckles . . .—*The New-York Gazette or the Weekly Post-Boy,* March 18, 1754.

SAMSON MEARS, Goldsmith, Has open'd his Shop in Pearl-street, in the house Mr. Andrew Breasted, formerly lived, where he intends to carry on the gold and silver-smith's business, after the newest and neatest Fashion; and all Commands he is favoured with, will be executed with the most thankful Dispatch.—*The New-York Mercury,* November 29, 1762.

EDMOND MILNE.—Run away from Edmond Milne, Goldsmith, . . . indented servant man . . . James Samuel Gordon, by trade a jeweller . . . Philadelphia.— *The New-York Gazette and the Weekly Mercury,* April 8, 1771.

JOHN M'INTOSH.—Deserted from His Majesty's 17th Regiment of Foot . . . John M'Intosh, aged 25 Years, 5 Feet 8 Inches and an half high, he was born near Fort George, in Scotland, by Trade a Silver Smith, short neck'd, fresh complexion, large Eyes, well set, has a small stoop in his Shoulders and speaks Irse [*sic*] and English equally well . . .—*The New-York Mercury,* December 22, 1760 (*Supplement*).

MYERS & HALSTED, Gold Smiths, Have removed to the lower End of King-Street, at the House of Mr. John Bell, Where they continue to make, all kinds of work, in gold and silver, and have to sell, a neat assortment of ready made plate, chased and plain; diamond rings, garnet hoops, and broaches in gold, crystal buttons and earrings, in ditto, silver, ivory, and wood etwees, tooth pick cases, and smelling bottles; cases of silver handled knives and forks, best spare blades for ditto, glasses for silver salts, cut cruets for table equipages, and an assortment of tools, for watch and clock makers.—*The New-York Gazette or the Weekly Post-Boy,* November 10, 1763.

MYERS & HALSTED, Gold Smiths, have removed to the Store House of Mr. Elias Desbroses, where Messrs. Phenix and Brown lately kept Store, being the next Corner to Mr. Henry Cuyler. . . .—*The New-York Gazette or the Weekly Post-Boy,* July 5, 1764.

MYER MYERS.—Run away . . . an English Servant Man, named Lewis Meares . . . a jeweller by Trade, and can engrave. Had on when he went away, a turn'd blue Cloth Coat with black Buttons half trim'd, small round Cuffs without Buttons, an old blue lapell'd Waistcoat with Brass Buttons, the Lappels lin'd with black Velvet, a Pair of black Leather Breeches with solid Silver Buttons, an old Hat and brown cut Wig; took with him four new Check Shirts, a new white one, and an old one mark'd M. M. Whoever takes up said Servant, and secures him, so that his Master may have him again, shall have Three Pounds Reward, and all reasonable Charges paid, by Myer Myers.—*The New-York Gazette or the Weekly Post-Boy,* April 9, 1753.

MYER MYERS, is removed from his shop at the Meal-Market to the house in King-street, belonging to the

widow of old Doctor Dupuy, opposite Mr. Lawrence
Reade's; where he continues to follow the Goldsmith's
business in all its branches.—*The New-York Mercury,*
August 12, 1754.

MYER MYERS.—New-York, March 27, 1767. Ten
Pounds, Reward. Whereas the House of Mrs. Rebecca
Hays, of this City was, last Thursday Night robbed of
the following pieces of Plate and Money, viz.

1 Two-Quart Silver Tankard, marked I, H, R.
1 Large Silver Punch Bowl, with two Handles.
3 Silver Porringers, marked M, M, K.
1 Silver Sugar Castor, marked M, M, K.
2 Pair of Round Silver Salts, with Feet, marked I, H, R. And one
   odd do. marked in the same Manner.
1 Small Silver Salver, without any Mark.
6 Table Spoons, marked B, H. Maker's Name Myers.
1 Pair of Diamond Rings, with Drops.
1 Silver Coffee-Pot, no Mark, Maker's Name I, P.
And a Silver Tea-Pot. . . .

'Tis Possible more of the Plate is marked, than what is
mentioned above. Whoever takes up and secures any
Person or Persons concerned in the above Robbery, so
that they may be brought to Justice, shall have the above
Reward, paid by me. Moses M. Hays.—*The New-York
Gazette,* April 6-13, 1767.

MYER MYERS.—On Monday the third day of June
next, between the hours of twelve and two, will be sold
at public vendue, on the premises, a house and lot of
ground, in Elbow-Street, Montgomery Ward; the buildings have seven fire-places; the lot in front and rear
twenty two feet, length on the north side ninety six feet
three inches, and on the fourth ninety three feet six
inches. The conditions of sale will be made known on
the day of the sale, and a sufficient title given to the
purchaser, by Myer Myers.—*The New-York Gazette and
the Weekly Mercury,* May 20, 1771.

MYER MYERS.—To Be Sold, A House and lot of ground
in King-Street, thirty four feet front and rear, and
seventy eight feet deep, containing every convenience

necessary to a family, for conditions of sale apply to
Myer Myers.—*Rivington's New-York Gazetteer*, August
26, 1773.

E. P.—Taken out of a House about the Twenty-third
of September last, in the Out ward, A Quart Silver
Tankard, almost new; weight thirty three ounces,
marked with the initial letters E. B. of the owner's name
in a cypher, the makers name E. P. . . .—*The New-York
Gazette and the Weekly Mercury*, August 26, 1776.

OTTO PARISIEN, Gold-Smith, from Berlin, Makes all
Sorts of Plate Work, both plain and chas'd, in the neatest
and most expeditious Manner; Likewise undertakes
chasing any Piece of old Plate, at his House, the lower
End of Batto Street.—*The New-York Gazette*, March
14, 1763.

OTTO PARISIEN.—Five Pounds Reward. Stolen out of
the Shop of Otto Parisien, Goldsmith, in Smith-street,
on Friday last the 17th of May, in the Afternoon; A
small four-square black Shagreen Box, containing the
following Rings, viz. One Diamond Ring, middle Stone
Shape of a Heart, set round with Sparks, one ditto with
brown Stone, with a Roman Head cut on, set round with
Sparks; one ditto, a Garnet Eight-square, one Spark each
Side; one ditto, an Emerald, four-square, one Spark on
each Side; one ditto set in the Form of a Flower-pot, the
Middle a Diamond, two Sparks, three Rubies above, and
an Emerald and a Topaz on each Side; one ditto, a
Saphio, in the Shape of a Heart, with an Emerald and
two Sparks above in the Form of a Crown; one ditto, a
Moco the Middle, Garnets all round; one ditto, a Garnet,
the Middle in Form of a Heart, very long, two Bristol
Stones each Side; one ditto, four Garnets set across, a
small white Stone in the Middle. Any Person or Persons
that should offer any of the above Rings for Sale, or to
pawn, it is desired they may be stopped, that they may
be brought to Justice, and the above Reward will be

given by Otto Parisien.—*The New-York Mercury,* May 20, 1765.

OTHO [8] PARISIEN, Silver-Smith, Living near Peck's-Slip, opposite to Mr. Vandervoort's, Returns Thanks to his Customers for past Favours, and hopes their Continuance; which he shall endeavour to deserve, by supplying those Gentlemen and Ladies who please to employ him, with all kinds of wrought Plate, either chased or plain, according to any Pattern they shall please to send or direct; and by doing the Work in the best and neatest Manner, and at the cheapest Rates.

N.B. The upper Part of his House to let.—*The New-York Journal or the General Advertiser,* February 9, 1769.

OTTO PARISIEN.—About six o'Clock last Friday Evening, the House of Mr. Otto Parisien, Silversmith, in the Fly, in this City, took Fire by Means of his Furnace. . . .—News item in *The New-York Gazette and the Weekly Mercury,* April 25, 1774.

OTTO PARISIEN, Silversmith, who was reduced by fire, is removed to Dock-street, opposite to Mr. Ward Hunt, Joiner, gives thanks to his former customers for their encouragement, and hopes for their continuance. Those gentlemen and ladies, who will favour him with their employ, will have their work done as reasonable as by any of the trade. He makes all sorts of plate, plain or chassed.—*Rivington's New-York Gazetteer,* May 12, 1774.

ELLIAS PELLETREAU, Takes this method to inform the Merchants and the Public in general, That he has set up at his House on Golden-Hill, at the Sign of the Dish of Fry'd Oysters, a place for cutting of Whale Bone; those that will favour him with their Custom, may depend upon being served with care and expedition.

[8] A different spelling for Otto.

N.B. He has also for Sale, a parcel of Silver Smith's
Tools, which he will sell cheap for cash.—*The New-York
Gazette and the Weekly Mercury*, May 24, 1773.

JOSEPH PINTO.—For Sale, by Joseph Pinto, Silver-
smith, at his Shop in Bayard-Street, Men's Shoe, knee
and Stock Stone Buckles; Women's Shoe and Girdle, do.
Silver Watches, chased Silver Milk Pots, Stone Rings:
Also a healthy and likely Negro Boy, who has had the
Small-Pox, and is suitable for a Merchant or Tradesman.
—*The New-York Mercury*, October 30, 1758.

JOSEPH PINTO.—To be Sold, by Joseph Pinto, Silver-
Smith, in Bayard-Street, A very fine silver chass'd turene,
dish and spoon; chass'd and plain stands, full furnished,
chass'd candlesticks, coffee and tea pots, sugar dishes,
slop bowls and sauce boats, chass'd and plain pint and
half pint mugs, salvers of different sizes, and milk pots,
salts and pepper casters, and marrow spoons, cases with
silver handled knives and forks, silver watches, silver
and plated spurs, chass'd and plain whistles, gold headed
canes, locket buttons set in gold, shoe, knee, and girdle
buckles, and a variety of stone rings.—*The New-York
Mercury*, October 26, 1761.

P. Q.—Stolen, out of the House of Daniel Dunscomb,
of this City, on Saturday last, the first Instant, a Silver
M
Tankard, marked on the Bottom thus D D, containing
a Wine Quart. It had a large bruise on the side, the
hinge pretty much wore, the Maker's Stamp p Q near the
Handle. If it should be offered for Sale, or to be pawn'd,
all Persons are desired to stop the same with the Vender,
and they shall be well rewarded by Daniel Dunscomb.—
The New-York Mercury, September 3, 1764.

PETER QUINTARD.—A Good house and Lot belonging
to the Widdow Bellarow is to be Sold, whereon there is
a good Stable and other out-Buildings, a good pump in

the Yard, and a good Garden; There is also three other
Lots adjoyning the same, which are situated in Queen-
street over against the House of Mr. Benj. Peck. . . .
Whoever inclines to buy the same, may apply to Peter
Quintard, Goldsmith, living near the New Dutch Church
in the City of New-York . . .—*The New-York Gazette,*
July 7-14, 1735.

N. R.—Stolen out of the House of Mr. Andrew
Barclay, of this City, last Thursday Evening a Quart
                                     R
Silver Tankard marked on the handle I C. with a Scratch
from the Bottom of the Letter R. Maker's Mark, on the
Left Side of the Handle N. R. with a Scratch on the
Letter R. also, and a Coat of Arms on the fore part of
the Tankard. Whoever discovers the Thief so that the
Tankard may be had again shall receive Five Pounds
Reward, and no Question asked, Paid by Andrew Barclay.
—*The New-York Gazette and the Weekly Mercury,*
November 4, 1771.

STEPHEN REEVES, Gold and Silver Smith, Living near
the corner of Burling's Slip, in Queen-Street, opposite
Mr. Benjamin Getfield's, Breeches-maker, New-York:
Takes this method to inform his friends and customers,
and the public in general, that he now carries on his
business as usual, such as making and mending all kinds
of gold and silver ware, mounting and mending swords,
and making all sorts of jeweller's work, &c. &c
He returns his sincere thanks for all past favours, and
hopes for a continuance of the same, as he flatters himself
of giving general satisfaction to all who may be pleased
to employ him. N.B. Ready money given for old gold
and silver.—*The New-York Gazette and the Weekly
Mercury,* October 7, 1776.

PAUL REVERE.—Thursday Morning last Mr. Paul
Revere, an Express from Boston, passed through here,
on his way to the Congress at Philadelphia.—News item

in *The New-York Gazette and the Weekly Mercury,*
September 19, 1774.

GEORGE RIDOUT.—Just imported from London, and to
be Sold by George Ridout, Goldsmith, Near the Ferry-
Stairs, Price four Shillings per box: The most fam'd and
long-experience Powder for Preserving the Teeth and
Gumms; which after two or three Times using makes the
foulest Teeth white and beautiful, preserves them from
growing rotten, and in a little Time removes the cause of
an ill scented Breath. He likewise sells fine Hungary and
Lavender Water; Harthshorn, Lavender and salvolatile
Drops: also an Assortment of Diamond Rings and Ear-
rings, Stone Solitairs, Stone Rings, with sundry other
Goods at the most reasonable Rates.—*The New-York
Gazette Revived in the Weekly Post-Boy,* June 10, 1751.

NICHOLAS ROOSEVELT.[9]—To be Let, and enter'd upon
the 1st of May next, The house in which Nicholas Roosevelt now lives, at the lower end of Thames Street, on
the wharf fronting the North-River: The conveniency
and commodiousness of the situation excells any on the
river; it fronts two slips, one of which is near 100 feet
broad, and the greatest part of the year is fill'd with boats
and crafts, from the Jersies and North-River. The house
will suit a merchant or shopkeeper, and great quantities
of rum, sugar, molasses, and salt, with all manner of dry
goods, have a ready sale. Is a roomy and convenient
house, with seven fire-places; a large yard, in which is a
pump and cistern, and a garden and grass-plot. Likewise
a silver-smith's shop to be let, and the tools of the trade
to be sold. Also to be sold by said Roosevelt, a parcel
of ready made silver, large and small, Viz. Silver tea-
pots and tea-spoons, silver hilted swords, sauce-boats,
salts and shovels, soup-spoons both scollep'd and plain,
table spoons, tea-tongs, punch ladles and strainers, milk-

[9] In an advertisement of John Blank mention is made of Nicholas
Roosevelt, deceased.—*New-York Gazette and the Weekly Mercury,*
January 7, 1771.

pots, snuff-boxes, and sundry other small articles, both
gold and silver, as buckles, clasps, buttons, broaches,
rings, and lockets, both plain and set with paste moco,
&c. &c. which he will sell very reasonable, as he intends
declining business, and to move in the Country in the
spring.—*The New-York Gazette and the Weekly Mercury*, January 30, 1769.

S. S.—Lost a Silver Pepper Box, mark'd on the Side
T
R * M and on the Bottom S. S, the Silver Smith's Mark,
and somewhat bruis'd on the Top; Whoever brings it
to the Printer hereof, or to the Cryer, shall receive its
Weight in Silver as a Reward. If offer'd to be Sold or
Pawn'd its desir'd to be stopt.—*The New-York Weekly
Journal*, December 19, 1743.

S. S.—Three Pounds Reward. Whereas on Friday
night last, the house of John Woods, attorney at law at
the upper end of Queen-Street, was broke open, and the
following articles were taken therefrom, viz. One silver
tankard, marked J. W. M. in a cypher, upon the lid
J. W. M. on the handle, maker's two first letters, S. S.,
five silver table spoons, mark'd J. W. M. maker's first two
letters, S. S., one silver porringer marked J. W. M.
makers two first letters, S. S. one silver milk pot, marked
J. W. M. makers mark R. V. D. Whoever apprehends
and secures the thief or thieves, so that they may be
brought to justice, shall have the above reward. N.B.
The Silver Smiths, as also all other persons are desired
if either of the above articles should be offered for sale,
to stop them; and they shall be handsomely reward.—
The New-York Gazette and the Weekly Mercury, May
24, 1773.

ABRAHAM SKINNER.—Charles Morse, Attorney at Law
and Conveyancer, &c. At the House of Mr. Abraham
Skinner Silversmith, on the New-Dock between the Ferry

Stairs and Rotten Row, . . .—*The New-York Gazette,* June 7, 1762.

WILLIAM SMITH, Gold and Silver-smith in Chapel-Street, Makes and mends all sorts of gold, silver and jewellery ware, in the best and neatest manner. N.B. He gives ready money for old gold and silver.—*The New-York Gazette and the Weekly Mercury,* November 5, 1770.

SIMEON SOUMAIN.—This is to give notice to All Gentlemen and others, That a Lottery is to be drawn at Mr. John Stevens, in Perth Amboy, for 501 L. of Silver & Gold Work, wrought by Simeon Soumain of New York, Gold-Smith, all of the newest Fashion. The highest Prize consists of an Eight square Tea-Pot, six Tea-Spoons, Skimmer and Tongs, Valued, at 18£ 3s. 6d. The lowest Prize consists of Twelve Shillings Value. There is 278 Prizes in all and there is only five Blanks to each Prize.

Tickets are given out at Six Shilling York Mony or seven Shillings Jersey Mony for each Ticket, at the house of Mr. John Stevens in Amboy, at Mr. Andrew Bradfords in Philadelphia, at Mr. Lewis Carrees in Allens-Town, at Mr. Jolines in Elizabeth-Town, at Mr. Cortlands at Second River, at Mr. Samuel Clowse in Jamaica on Long-Island, and at Simeon Soumains in the City of N-York, which last place the good are to be seen.—*The New-York Gazette,* April 3-10, 1727.

SIMEON SOUMAINE.—. . . To be Sold By the above said Gerard Beekman, two Lotts of Ground lying on the North-West Side of Beekmans-Swamp, commonly call'd and known by the name of Cripple-Bush, joining the upper Side of Mr. Simeon Soumaine's Garden, . . .—*The New-York Weekly Journal,* April 9, 1744.

TOBIAS STOUTENBURGH.—To be Sold, Two good Dwelling-Houses of two Story each, in the Broad-Way, adjoining to the Lutheran Church; also three others near the French Church, of a Story and a half each, all belonging to the Estate of Tobias Stoutenburgh, late deceased. Enquire of Tobias Stoutenburgh, Gold-Smith, near the Spring Garden, New-York.—*The New York Weekly Post Boy*, October 22, 1744 (*Supplement*).

SAMUEL TINGLEY, Gold and Silver-Smith, Has removed from his Shop in the Fly, to the Rotten-Row, where he continues his Business. The Shop he left is to Let.—*The New-York Mercury*, May 11, 1767.

P. V. B.—Stolen, Out of a House near Ellis's Dock, on Friday Night being the 5th of February, one Diamond Ring with seven Diamonds, 3 large and four small, one Diamond in most the Shape of a Flower Pot, one Ring with four Diamonds and a flat Stone, with a little Hair under; one Diamond Girdle Buckle, with about 30 or 32 Stones; one plain Gold Ring, maker's Name P V B; also twelve Pound in Cash, mostly Jersey Money. If any Person or Persons shall offer any of the above Articles to Sale, stop them and give information to the Printer, who will reward them for their Pains.—*The New-York Mercury*, February 8, 1762.

P. V. D.—Last Saturday Night the House of James Mills in this City, Tavern Keeper, was broke open and rob'd by Persons unknown, of sundry Things of Value, among which were one Silver Pint Mugg, mark'd A. M. Maker's Name P. V. D. one ditto English make old fashion'd; two old fashion'd Spoons, the Ends with Seals, English make; four ditto, mark'd J. M. C. Maker's Name TB. one ditto mark'd T. C. E. Makers Name P. V. D. one ditto mark'd W. T. A. six ditto mark'd B. T. S. Maker's Name P. V. D. one ditto mark'd W. B. S. Silver Marrow Scoup; . . .—*The New-York Gazette or the Weekly Post-Boy*, June 16, 1755.

——VAN DYKE.—Mr. Obadiah Wells living in the Sloat, in New York keeps a Shop of Dry Goods in Han-

over-Square, next Door to Mr. Vandyke's, Gold-Smith.—
*The New-York Gazette Revived in the Weekly Post-
Boy,* March 28, 1748.

W K

B .—Taken out of the House of Mr. Edward Fast-
ham who keeps the Fighting Cocks-Inn, in New-York, a
                                                    E
Silver Quart Tankard, marked on the Handle E S en-
                                          W K
graven, the Silversmiths Mark is B Punch'd, and a
Cypher on the Lid of E S. The Person who is suspected
to have taken it is of midle Stature, wore his own dark
coloured Hair or a natural Wig, and a brown Coat with
a small Cape, very much worn, and out at the Elbows.

Three Pounds as a Reward to any one that shall bring
the said Tankard home, and no Questions asked. If left
in secure Hands, the Reward shall be paid on Receipt of
the Tankard. If offered to be sold or pawn'd pray stop it.
N.B. He passes by the Name of John Coffin.—*The New-
York Weekly Journal,* May 24, 1736.

W K

C .—Lost or Stolen a few Days ago, out of the
House in this City, three Silver Spoons of Common Size,
            VD.   w k
mark'd I.   I. with the Silver smith's mark   c .
Whoever brings the said Spoons to the Printer hereof,
shall have Fifteen Shillings Reward and no Questions
ask'd: And all Persons, to whom they may be offer'd to
be sold or Pawn'd are desired to stop them.—*The New-
York Weekly Post Boy,* November 10, 1746.

JOHN WOOD.—To the Public. The subscriber begs
leave to acquaint the publick in general, and his friends
in particular, that he has taken the shop lately occupied
by Mr. James Bennett, Jeweller, situated in the lower
end of Maiden-lane, near the upper end of the Fly-
Market, where he intends to carry on the gold and silver

smith's work, in its different branches, at the most reasonable rates, and in the neatest manner, and hopes by
the steady application of his business, to give all possible
satisfaction to those who please to favour him with their
commands, I am, Gentlemen and Ladies Your most
obliged Servant, John Wood.—*The New-York Gazette
and the Weekly Mercury,* April 30, 1770.

JEWELLERS

JEREMIAH ANDREWS, Jeweller, from London, Takes
this Method to inform the Public, That he has set up his
Business on Gold-Hill-Street, at the House of Catherine
Hubbs, opposite Mr. Scandaret's Beer and Oyster House.
Ladies and Gentlemen who have not previously engaged
with any Persons of the same Business, may rest assured
they will be served to their Satisfaction, in every Branch
of his Profession.

N.B. Gold and Silversmiths may have their Work
done on reasonable Terms. Mourning Rings made in
the newest Fashion, and with greatest Dispatch.—
Rivington's New-York Gazetteer, September 15, 1774.

JEREMIAH ANDREWS.—Hanover-Square, New-York.
Jeremiah Andrews, Jeweller, Continuing his business still
in the same place, thinks it proper to acquaint shop-
keepers and traders who are under disadvantages by
reason of the non-importation, that he is willing chearfully to bear his part; therefore engages to make every
article for such, pertaining to his branch, as cheap as they
could be imported from London, and materials good.
He returns thanks to his customers for their past, and
hopes a continuance of their future favours, which he
will always gratefully acknowldge. Also informs them
and the public, that he hath a great variety of patterns
of the newest fashions, which he received from London
since his last advertisement.—*Rivington's New-York
Gazetteer,* May 25, 1775.

JEREMIAH ANDREWS, Jeweller in Hanover Square, New-York; Thinks proper to inform the Public, as he hath been absent from the city some time, (and understanding that many things have been called for, in his way, during his absence, that he is now returned to his former place of business; where he will gratefully receive the commands of his kind friends and customers, which shall be performed with faithfulness and dispatch.

N.B. Said Andrews will give a good price for old gold and silver.—*The Constitutional Gazette,* June 8, 1776.

WILLIAM BATEMAN.—Stone Seals neatly engraved, by William Bateman, from London, At the House of Mr. Hopkins, Pilot, in Fair-Street, New-York. Engraves Coats of arms, Crests, Cyphers, figures, heads and fancies in the neatest fashion, arms neatly painted on vellum. N.B. Most money for broken, crack'd, or fould diamonds. —*Rivington's New-York Gazetteer,* October 20, 1774.

WILLIAM BATEMAN, Stone Seal Engraver, Lapidary and Jeweller from London, at the House of Mr. Hopkins, Pilot, in Fair-street, Golden-hill, New-York; Engraves on stone, steel, silver and copper plates, coats of arms, crests, cyphers, figures, heads and fancies in the neatest manner, and on the most reasonable terms. Cuts stones of all sorts, in the best manner for bracelets, pictures, lockets, rings, buckles and seals; makes or mends all kinds of jewellers work in the best manner, coats of arms neatly painted on vellum. He has had the honour to do work for the first nobility and gentry in London to their satisfaction; he flatters himself that he will meet the encouragement of the ladies, gentlemen and public in general, whom he will make his constant study to use in a manner which shall recommend him to their future favours.

N.B. Has a book of heraldry which contains some thousand of names, where gentlemen who want their coat of arms engraved by him, and do not know them, may search the book gratis.—*The New-York Gazette and the Weekly Mercury*, November 7, 1774.

WILLIAM BATEMAN.—A Reward of Eight Dollars will be paid for taking up a servant man named William Bateman, about 25 years old, fair complexion, brown hair tied behind: had on a brown surtout coat, a beaver hat with a large cut in the brim. He was born in England, and came from London to Philadelphia in the ship Minerva, Arthur Hill, master. The said Bateman is a jeweller and Lapidary by trade, has worked in this city with Charles Oliver Bruff, and left this town about three weeks ago, and was heard to say he would go to New-Haven, Rhode-Island or Boston, to try his business.

The above reward and all reasonable charges will be paid to any person that will bring the above servant to Peter Berton.—*The New-York Gazette and the Weekly Mercury*, March 6, 1775.

FREDERICK BECKER.—Fine Indian-Jewels, made and sold by Frederick Becker, opposite to Capt. Thomas Ware, in Beekman street, in New-York, at reasonable Rates.—*The New-York Weekly Journal*, October 18, 1736.

JAMES BENNET, Jeweller, lately arrived from London; Begs leave to acquaint Ladies, Gentlemen, and others, that he has open'd a Shop at the House of Thomas Griggs, Cabinet-Maker, the Bottom of the Fly-market, with an Assortment of all kinds of jewellers Goods of the newest Fashion, also Watches, trinkets, Mettle Buttons and Buckles of various kinds, very neat Fowling Pieces and Pistols, and different Sorts of hard Ware; likewise a very good Assortment of Mens and Womens Leather Gloves, Womens black and white Satten and Brocade Shoes, black Ruffel, do. velvet and silk Clogs, and sundry other Articles too tedious to mention; and is determined to sell as low as possible, for ready Money only. Those Gentlemen and Ladies, &c. that oblige him with their

Comands, may depend on their being compleated in the neatest Manner, by their humble Servant. James Bennett. N.B. Great Allowance will be made to those who take large Quantities to sell again.—*The New-York Gazette and the Weekly Mercury*, October 3, 1768.

JAMES BENNETT, Goldsmith and Jeweller, from London, Begs leave to return thanks to the ladies and gentlemen, (those in particular who have favour'd him with their commands since his commencement of business in this city,) and to the public in general, for the encouragement he has received, and informs them, that he has removed his shop from Mr. Gregs, at the corner of the Fly-Market, to a house at the lower end of Maiden-Lane, a few doors above Mr. Booth's store, where he continues to sell as usual, on the lowest terms, all sorts of goods in the jewellery and goldsmith way; also makes, mends, and changes any kind of goods in the above mentioned ways; as he is determined studiously to observe such commands as he shall be favoured with, hopes to merit a continuance of their custom.—*The New-York Gazette and the Weekly Mercury*, May 8, 1769.

JAMES BENNETT.—All persons indebted to James Bennett, jeweller and goldsmith, of this city, are desired to make speedy payments; and those who have any demands, are requested to bring in their accounts, and receive their money; as he is going to England very soon. —*The New-York Gazette and the Weekly Mercury*, October 8, 1770.

JAMES BENNET.—Brought to the house of Mr. James Bennett, jeweller, by two young men a Silver Spoon. Whoever owns the same may have it by applying to said Bennett, paying charges.—*The New-York Gazette and the Weekly Mercury*, July 5, 1773.

BENNETT & DIXON.—Bennett, and Dixon, Jewellers, Gold-smiths, and Lapidaries from London; At their shop next door but one to the General Post-Office, between the corner of Wall-street, and the Fly-Market, beg leave to inform their friends, and the public in general, they have imported per the last vessels from London, a great variety of jewellery and toys, consisting of necklaces, ear rings, egrets, sprigs, and pins for ladies hair, rings, lockets, and broaches of all sorts, ladies tortoise-shell combs plain and sett, stone paste, garnet and marquisite shoe, knee and stock buckles, silver shoe, knee and stock do. best London and Birmingham pinchbeck do. common brass do. the above will be sold very cheap, wholesale or retail.

Likewise for the better carrying on the jewellery, gold-smith and lapidary business, have engaged some of the best workmen in those branches, that could be had in any part of England, and are determined to work as cheap and good as in the City of London.

N.B. Also may be had all sorts of foill and stones, wholesale or retail, most money for gold, silver and clear crystal.—*The New-York Gazette and the Weekly Mercury*, August 26, 1771.

BENNETT & DIXON.—The Partnership of Bennett and Dixon, Jewellers, Gold-smiths, and Lapidaries,[10] in King-street, near the lower end of Wall-street, being dissolved, all persons having demands on the said partnership, are desired to send in their accounts and receive payment, by Bennet who requests the continuance of the favours of his friends and customers, and is the only real maker in this city of Ladies set shoe buckles, ear-rings, egrets, sprigs and hair pins, seals, necklaces, combs, crosses, and lockets, sleeve buttons and bracelets, &c. Gentlemens set shoe, knee and stock buckles; seals, broaches, buttons and rings, &c. . . .

N.B. Mourning rings, plain or set, with any kind of stone with hair work'd in landskips. . . .—*The New-York Journal or General Advertiser*, August 6, 1772.

[10] A List of jewelry imported by Bennett & Dixon appeared in the same paper on May 21, 1772.

ABEL BUELL.—We can also assure the Public from our own Knowledge, as well as from Testimony of a Gentleman lately from the Westward, that Mr. Abel Buell, of Killingsworth, in Connecticut, Jeweller and Lapidary, has lately, by his own Genius, without any Assistance, made himself Master of the Art of Founding Types at the same Price they are sold at in Great Britain. Some of the Types have actually been exhibited in this Town and Philadelphia.—News item from Newport, R. I., August 21st, in *The New-York Gazette and the Weekly Mercury*, August 28, 1769.

CHARLES DUTENS.—. . . [11] Besides, I have a Business which takes up a great Part of my Time, when Gentlemen and Ladies are pleased to employ me, in making divers Sorts of Rings, as mourning, enamell'd, fancy, motto Rings, &c. Ear-Rings, Solitairs, Stay Hooks, Seals, Lockets. Also, I set Diamond, Rubies, Emeralds, Saphires, or any other Kind of Stone to the best Advantage, and at very reasonable Rates, at my Lodgings, at Mrs. Eastham's, the lower End of Broad Street, near the Long-Bridge. And all Gentlemen and Ladies who have a Mind to send their Children (or others under their Dependency) to learn French, may depend upon my exact Compliance in teaching them properly, and with the greatest Diligence. Charles Dutens.—*The New-York Gazette Revived in the Weekly Post-Boy*, March 4, 1751.

CHARLES DUTENS, Jeweller, continues his Business at Mrs. Eastham's House, near the Long-Bridge in Broad-Street; where all Gentlemen and Ladies who shall please to Honour him with their Custom, may depend upon having all kind of Jeweller's Work done after the most neat, and newest Fashion, as one in London, and at very reasonable Rates.

[11] This advertisement follows a long philosophical discussion, in which Mr. Charles Dutens states that his "Intention is only to encourage Youth to make a good Choice in preferring Wisdom above all other Things."

Note. He has just imported from London, by Capt. Richards, some beautiful DiamondSparks Rubies, Saphires, Emeralds, Amethists Topaz, Granets to set in Hoop-Rings all round, Fancy, Rose Rings, and all sorts of Ear-Rings: He has likewise fine white and black for Mourning Rings, with Death Heads and Skeletons to put under; also Stones fit for Waistcoats and Sleeve Buttons of different Sorts.—*The New-York Gazette Revived in the Weekly Post-Boy*, June 3, 1751.

HENRY HART, Jeweller, from London, Next door to Mr. Thurman's, in Crown-street, at the North-River, Has for sale all kinds of jewellery generally made by those of his profession, which he will dispose of at the most reasonable rates. Mourning rings made in the most elegant manner, and with the utmost dispatch.—*The New-York Gazette and the Weekly Mercury*, November 28, 1774.

HENRY HART, Jeweller, At the Bottom of Crown street, near the North River. Makes and Sells all kinds of Jewelry, viz. Stone Buckles, Bracelets, Lockets, for ladies, Stock shoe, and knee Buckles for gentlemen, Gold Seals, Mourning and Fancy Rings, with every other article of the branch done in the neatest Manner . . .—*The New-York Journal or General Advertiser*, March 9, 1775.

PETER LORIN, Jeweller, is remov'd from Capt. Troup's House in New Street, to Mr. Peck's House in Crown-street; where all Gentlemen and Ladies who shall please to favour him with their Custom may depend on having any kind of Jeweller's Work done after the most neat and newest Fashion, at reasonable Prices.—*The New-York Gazette Revived in the Weekly Post-Boy*, May 13, 1751.

JOHN MECOM, on Rotten Row; A Few very neat Aqua marine white, green, red, black and blue Paste and garnet Earings and Necklaces, in the newest Taste; black and blue enamelled Earings and Necklaces, neat French ditto; French Fancy Rings with Rubies, Saphires, and Emeralds; Hoop, garnet, and Paste Fancy, Rings, Moco with garnet Clusters ditto; Fancy Garnet double Hearted ditto, single Hearted ditto, Garnet and Diamond Fancy Rings, twisted; garnet Rings, very neat Hair Sprigs, Heart Lockets, the most fashionable Paste and Stone Shoe, Knee, Neck and Shirt Buckles; very neat chas'd and plain mettal Watches, Silver and Tortise Shell Watches, Shagreen ditto, Ladies gilt metal and Steel Watch Chains, Hooks and Keys; the most fashionable Cornelian and Christal Fancy Seals, in gilt, metal, and Silver.—*The New-York Mercury,* May 23, 1763.

JOHN MECOM.—To be Sold, By John Mecom, Opposite The Whitehall Tavern, in Albany-street, New-Brunswick . . . gives long list of a general assortment of hardware, sadlery, ironmongery and cutlery . . . Said Mecom makes and sells all sorts of jewelers and goldsmiths ware; those therefore that will favour him with their custom, may depend on being served on the most reasonable terms.— *The New-York Mercury,* April 29, 1765.

JOHN MECOM.—This is to give Notice to the Creditors of John Mecom, Jeweller, who died on Sunday the 30th of September last, That Catharine Mecom, his Widow, declining the Administration, is ready to deliver the Effects and Estate he died possessed of, to the Creditors, or to any one that shall administer on the same; and that she would be glad to hear from them soon. Catharine Mecom. New Brunswick.—*The New-York Gazette or the Weekly Post-Boy,* October 8, 1770.

THOMAS READ.—Run away from the Subscriber, (John Inch) on Sunday the 3d. Instant, a Convict Servant Man, named, Thomas Read, alias Culbert, by Trade, a Jeweller and Motto Ring Engraver; . . .—News item from Annapolis, Maryland, in *The New-York Gazette,* June 18, 1759.

THOMAS RICHARDSON, Jeweller, lately from London having brought with him, and introduced into this City, Jewellery, and materials for his Business, which he exposed to sale and refused to store altho' the Committee of Merchants generously offered to raise a sum of Money for him, adequate to the loss he might sustain by the temporary storage of his goods; he was upon Tuesday last conducted to Liberty Pole, where, upon a Scaffold raised for that purpose, he publickly begged pardon for his misconduct, and agreed to store his Goods, upon which the numerous Company assembled upon that occasion quietly dispersed.—News item in *The New-York Chronicle*, September 14-21, 1769.

THOMAS RICHARDSON, Jeweller and Silver Smith from London, Takes this opportunity to inform the publick in general, that he hath taken a shop of Mr. Gregg, at the Corner of the Fly-Market, in this City, where all sorts of jewellery and silver smith's work are made and sold wholesale and retail, considerable cheaper than hath been sold here; he likewise repairs jeweller and silver smith's work in the neatest manner; gives cash for old gold or silver, diamonds, or any curious stones. Mourning rings made on the shortest notice, and all favours gratefully acknowledged by your most humble Servant, Thomas Richardson.—*The New-York Gazette and the Weekly Mercury*, October 30, 1769.

THOMAS RICHARDSON, Jeweller and Silver-Smith, At the lower End of Wall-street in this City, Takes this opportunity to inform the publick in general, that he is just arrived from London, and has fresh imported a great assortment of all sorts of jewellery, plated buckles and spurs, pinchbeck buckles, great choice of curious snuff boxes, chapes, watch chains, Singleton's Cock spurs, and a great many other articles too tedious to mention, which he will sell wholesale and retail, on the most reasonable terms, Gives ready money for old gold and silver, and beeswax.—*The New-York Gazette and the Weekly Mercury*, November 12, 1770.

JOHN SHAW.—The Subscriber would inform the Public, that he continues to teach the Languages; as also some Branches in the Sciences and Mathematicks; also the English Tongue gramatically; in the House of Mr. John Shaw, Jeweller, in Elbow-Street, on Golden-Hill. . . . Thomas Ustick.—*The New-York Gazette or the Weekly Post-Boy*, March 16, 1772.

JOHN SHAW, Jeweller, Informs the Public in general, he has removed into Nassau-Street, near John-Street, at the Sign of the Crown, where he makes and mends, in the neatest Manner, and at the lowest Rates, all Sorts of Jeweller's Work in its various Branches: He also returns his humble Thanks to his former Customers for their kind Favours, and hopes he will meet with the Encouragement his Merit deserves in his Branch of Business. Likewise, Cyphers in Hair done for Lockets, Rings, &c. &c. &c.—*The New-York Gazette and the Weekly Mercury*, May 20, 1776.

WHITEHOUSE & REEVE, Jewellers from London, Beg leave to inform their friends and the public in general, that they have taken the shop lately kept by Messrs. Robinson and Price, in William-Street, commonly called Horse and Cart-Street, where they intend carrying on the above business in all its branches in the greatest perfection, which we flatter ourselves we shall be capable of doing, as we have had the honour to serve a number of the first families of distinction in London. Any ladies or gentlemen that please to favour them with their commands may depend upon having them punctually obeyed, as it will always be their study to merit the favours of the public.

N.B. We have lately imported from London, some of the most fashionable patterns for ladies paste shoe-buckles, which they may depend upon being made in the

neatest manner. Any work we recommend we will engage
to keep in repair two years free from expence.—*Rivington's New-York Gazetteer,* September 29, 1774.

WHITEHOUSE & REEVE.— . . . have engaged a person
from London, that understands the art of working hair
in sprigs, birds, figures, cyphers, crests of arms, warranted equal to any done in London. Engraving in all
its branches done in the neatest manner.—*The New-York
Gazette and the Weekly Mercury,* January 2, 1775.

WHITEHOUSE & REEVE.—Whereas a verbal agreement
of partnership, has been carried on between John Whitehouse, and Mr. Reevs, [*sic*], jewellers of William Street,
New York, this is to inform the public, that said partnership is dissolved; all persons indebted to said partnership,
are desired to pay the same to John Whitehouse . . . —
The New-York Journal or General Advertiser, May 4,
1775.

MISCELLANEOUS SILVER AND JEWELRY

GIRDLE BUCKLE.—Lately lost a Gold Girdle Buckle,
set round with small diamonds, whoever has found it,
and will bring it to the Printer hereof shall be very well
Rewarded. If it is sold or pawn'd the Money shall be
returned. N.B. One of the Diamonds is lost.—*The New-
York Weekly Journal,* April 15, 1734.

MASONIC EMBLEMS.—Taken Out of the House of Mr.
Todd, a small Silver Square, a Level, a Plumb-Rule, and
Silver Pen, and other Utensils belonging to the Lodge
of Free Masons in New-York, Whoever brings them to
the Printer hereof shall be handsomely rewarded, and no
Questions ask'd.—*The New-York Weekly Journal,* November 14, 1737.

SNUFF BOX.—Lost or Stolen an Oval Snuff Box, with
a Hinge, marked E P, Whoever brings it to the Printer
shall be well rewarded and no Questions ask'd. If offered

to be Sold or Pawn'd pray stop it.—*The New-York Weekly Journal*, January 2, 1738.

SNUFF MILL.—Lost or Mislaid a Silver Snuff Mill whoever brings it to the Printer hereof shall be very well rewarded.—*The New-York Weekly Journal*, April 3, 1738.

BOWL.—Lost, or Taken from the House of Moses Taylor, at the Old-Slip, a few days ago, a Silver quart Bowl marked I. V. B. . . . twenty shillings reward.—*The New-York Gazette Revived in the Weekly Post-Boy*, August 12, 1751.

✓ SENTENCE OF DEATH FOR STEALING SILVER (*Philadelphia*).—Friday last Trial of John Webster Came on, when he was indicted and found guilty of breaking open the Dwelling House of Mr. William Clemm of this City on the 24th of September 1750, in the Night; and taking from thence a Silver Tea-pot and tea-spoon; upon which he received the Sentence of Death.—News item from Philadelphia in *The New-York Gazette Revived in the Weekly Post-Boy*, April 27, 1752.

TANKARDS.—Stolen, between the 24th and 25th inst. May, at Night, from John Pell, Esq; in the Manor of Pellham, in the Country of West-Chester, four Silver Tankards, one being mark'd T. A. P. one I. A. H. and two I. H. P. one Silver Mugg, mark'd I. R. P. one Silver Tea-pot, and one Silver Sword, to the Value of Ninety Pounds . . . Reward of Thirty Pounds paid by John Pell.—*The New-York Gazette or the Weekly Post-Boy*, June 6, 1757.

COFFEE POT.—Stolen out of the Dwelling House of John Tabor Kempe, of this City, Esq; A large Silver Coffee-Pot, holding about a Quart, but [*sic*] a Table Spoon; the Coffee-Pot had no other Mark but the Stamps, and had a Dent on the Back Part of the Lid, where the same had fallen back on the Handle in opening; The Spoon was marked with a Falcon standing on a Wheat-Sheaf; Any Person stopping the same, if offerd for Sale, or apprehending, or discovering the Thief, so that he may be apprehended, shall be well rewarded by J. T. Kempe. N.B. It is imagined the same may be carried in the Country in order to be melted up.—*The New-York Gazette or the Weekly Post-Boy*, January 7, 1760.

TANKARD.—Whereas a Three Pint Silver Tankard, marked on the Handle with the Letters E. L. and T. at Top, and having the Handle of the Lid, by which it is open'd formed in the Figure of a Lion was on Monday last, about Two o'clock in the Afternoon, in Smith-Street, near my Door, opposite to Messrs Lot and Low's Store, taken by Force from a Negro Girl . . . Five Pound York Money Reward by Edward Tittle.—*The New-York Gazette or the Weekly Post-Boy*, November 27, 1760.

HORSE RACE.—To be Run for, on Tuesday the first of June next, at the Beaver Pond, in Jamaica, A Silver Bowl, Value Twenty Pounds, free for any Horse, Mare, or Gelding, the best of Three two Mile Heats, Paying Two Dollars Entrance, or double at the Post. . . . —*The New-York Gazette*, May 31, 1762.

SILVER PLATE (*Philadelphia*).—The Dwelling-House of Thomas Clifford was broke open last Night, from whence was stolen,[12] and taken away, One Silver Tankard, One Ditto Tea Pot, one Ditto Quart Bowl, six Ditto Porringers, one Ditto Sugar Pot and Cover, one Ditto Water, one Ditto Pepper Box, two Ditto Salts, one Ditto Soup Ladle, two Ditto Half-pint Tumbelers, one Ditto Cream Pot, eight Ditto Table Spoons, one Pair Tea
C.
Tongs, and four Tea Spoons; all marked T. A. One large Silver Pint Can, one Table Spoon, six Tea Spoons,

---

[12] The thief was later captured and sentenced to death according to a Philadelphia news item in *The New-York Mercury*, May 14, 1764.

marked E. C. One Silver two handle Caudle Cup, marked
  G.
T. R. One large Cream Pot, no Mark, two Table
  M.
Spoons marked I. R. One Custard Spoon, marked
E. G. One Pair of Mens Silver Shoe Buckles, and one
Pair of Knee Ditto . . . Thomas Clifford.—News item
from Philadelphia, February 28th, in *The New-York
Mercury*, March 5, 1764.

IMPORTED SILVER PLATE.—Just imported by Captain
Jacobson, from London, and to be sold at the House of
Francis Cooley, on Golden-Hill, a Variety of neat chas'd
silver coffee pots with cases; tea cannisters with do.
sugar or tea tongs, and spoons, great choice of silver shoe
and knee and stock buckles; solid buttons, clasp and
watch chains, chas'd corrals, christal shoe, knee and stock
buckles, stay hooks, and buttons, do. gold buttons set
with mocco and garnets, gold seals, shirt buckles, lockets,
mocco and enamel'd sleeve buttons, double gilt do. very
best coat and breast buttons, gilt and plated; great
variety of silver watches, rich chas'd and gilt pinch-beck
do, with tortise and shagreen cases; a variety of cristal,
garnet, and diamond rings, gilt buckles and common do.
plated and steel spurs; neat temple spectacles, paper
boxes, toothpick cases, steel chains and silk strings for
watches; a small parcel of augers, by the best makers in
Birmingham, warranted; watches glased inside, chains
and springs, hands and keys, and enameled dial plates,
a neat eight day clock, a neat japan'd case.—*The New-
York Mercury*, April 29, 1765.

TANKARD.—Stolen out of the House of the Subscriber,
at the Ferry at Brooklyn, on Long-Island, the 9th Inst.
a Three Pint Silver Tankard, with an English Half
Guinea on the Lid. Whoever will return the Tankard,
shall have Three Pounds Reward, and no Questions
asked, paid by Francis Koffler.—*The New-York Mercury*,
January 27, 1766.

SHOOTING CONTEST.—To the Lovers of Shooting. To be shot for at Mr. Miller's, at Corleir's Hook, on Shrove Tuesday next, Three Prizes, Viz. One Half-pint Silver Mug, Value 7 l One Silver Shoe and Knee-buckles at 3 l. and one stone Ring at 2 l. Each Member paying One Dollar at signing his Name, and to have three Shots with Ball. The Articles to be seen at the aforesaid Mr. Miller's.

N.B. For Supper will be provided a Leg of Mutton and Turnips, boiled, out of Curiosity, in a Butter Firkin. To begin shooting exactly at One o'clock.—*The New-York Mercury*, February 3, 1766.

SNUFF BOX.—Lost, or left on one of the Pews in the Presbyterian Meeting House, an oval Silver Snuff-Box, with a Mother-o'pearl Top, mark'd with the Letters G.
T. C. Whoever has found it, and will bring it to the Printer hereof, shall have Five Shillings Reward. Also mist out of a House, a large Family Silver Spoon, M.
marked C. C. The same Reward will be given for it as the Box, by bringing it to the Printer . . . —*The New-York Mercury*, March 3, 1766.

MOURNING RING.—Found in the Broad-Way . . . A Mourning Ring, with a stone in the Top in the Form of a Coffin . . . —*The New-York Mercury*, January 4, 1768.

SEMI-PRECIOUS STONES.—We can assure the public, that Millstones and Grindstones equal if not superior to British, are now to be had among ourselves, in such quantities as will discourage any import of the latter; and that our Lappadaries may soon be supply'd with Berryl's, Topaz, Amethysts, Garnets, Christals, &c. found in New England; Samples of the several sorts in the Rough having been shewn upon Change, and several Rings imbellished with the same sorts cut here, have

been sold to Gentlemen of taste, who esteem them not
inferior to what is imported from England.

The present spirit of the people in the colonies to
invent and promote manufactures, is such, and the late
discoveries so many and important, as may lead into
hope providence intends great things in some future time
for this present distressed and burthened continent.—
News item from Boston in *The New-York Gazette Extraordinary*,[13] February 4, 1768.

SILVER PLATE OF CAPT. JOSEPH RYALL.—To-morrow
Morning, will be sold at Public Vendue, all the House-
hold and Kitchen Furniture, Plate, and China of the late
Capt. Joseph Ryall, deceased, at his House, near the
Merchant's Coffee-House; amongst which are . . . Silver
Tankards, Sugar-cups, Sauce-boats, Candlesticks, Spice-
Box, Chafing-dishes, Castors, Sauce-boats, Spoons, Forks,
Salts, China Tureens, Dishes, Plates, Bowls, Jarrs, Mugs,
Cups and Saucers &c. &c. &c.—*The New-York Gazette
and the Weekly Mercury*, July 11, 1768.

JEWELRY.—Mr. Nicholas Guyon, Native of the Island
of Rhe, near Rochelle, in Old France, proposes to
follow the Business of a Broker, in French, Dutch and
English: He lodges at Mr. Joseph Colley's, at the Edinburgh Castle, on the New-Dock and will transact all
Business in his Way with the greatest Secrecy, Fidelity
and Dispatch. He has to sell, a neat assortment of
Jewellery, consisting of the neatest Pinchbeck Buckles,
and other Buckles of different kinds, Trinkets for Ladies
and Gentlemen, Watches, with Steel Seals, Pinchbeck
Rings wash'd with Gold, of several Sizes, Pinchbeck compass Seals Sleeve Buttons, which will be sold at the
lowest Prices.—*The New-York Gazette and the Weekly
Mercury*, April 12, 1770.

SILVERSMITH'S TOOLS.—A Compleat Set of Silver
Smith's Tools, to be sold by William Ustick, At the Sign

[13] The titles of a few issues of *The New-York Gazette or the Weekly
Post-Boy* were changed to *The New-York Gazette Extraordinary*.

of the Lock and Key, between Burling's and Beekman's Slip.—*The New-York Gazette and the Weekly Mercury*, February 18, 1771.

SEAL.—Dropt in the Street sometime in the Month of December, a Gold Seal, Cornelian Stone, with the two Letters C. A. engraved thereon. There was fasten to it, Part of a Steel Chain, and a Watch Key. Should it have been found by any honest Person it is hoped he will bring it to the Printer hereof, and a Reward of Three Dollars will be given to the Finder.—*The New-York Gazette or the Weekly Post-Boy*, March 25, 1771.

SILVER PLATE.—Stolen, Out of the House of Ennis Graham, One Silver Pint Mug, marked G. E. S. one Silver Porringer marked S. G. E. three Silver Table Spoons, one marked G. E. S. the other two Marks unknown. If any of the above Things are offered for Sale the Person to whom offered are desired to stop them.—*The New-York Gazette or the Weekly Post-Boy*, April 8, 1771.

SILVER PLATED WARE.—Sold very cheap, by Benjamin Davis, in Dock-Street, Consisting of tea kettles, coffee-pots, tankards, and mugs, pillar'd candlesticks, bottle stands, castors, salts, knives and forks, also japaned tea boards, and oval pewter dishes and tureens, and sundry cutlery ware . . . —*The New-York Gazette and the Weekly Mercury*, July 8, 1771.

SNUFF BOX.—Was lost out of a gentlemen's pocket some time ago, a leather japan'd snuff box, with a Scotch peble set in silver on the top. Whoever has found the same, and will deliver it to the printer hereof, shall receive Two Dollars reward, which is more than its value. —*The New-York Gazette and the Weekly Mercury*, July 8, 1771.

PUNCH LADLE.—Stolen On Wednesday the 21st Instant, (August) from Mary Airey, living at the Corner

of King and Smith Streets, three Silver Table Spoons,
and a Silver crooked handled Punch Ladle, the Bowl of
which is in the Form of a Scallop Shell; one of the
Spoons is marked M*W, the other two and the Ladle,
with a Cock having a Sprig in his Bill, on the back of
the Handles. Any Person to whom the said Goods may
be offered to Sale, or who may otherwise see or hear of
them, are desired to stop them, and endeavour to secure
the Thief, giving her Notice, who will make a thankful
and proper Acknowledgment.—*The New-York Journal
or General Advertiser,* August 22, 1771.

HORSE RACE.—To Be Run For, Round the course at
Morris Town, and to be won by the best of three two
mile heats; a Silver Tankard of Twenty Pounds value.
. . . —*The New-York Gazette and the Weekly Mercury,*
October 7, 1771.

MUGS.—Ten Guineas Reward. Stolen from Fort-
George, on Tuesday Evening, two Half Pint Silver Mugs
with Handles, having his Excellency the Governor's Coat
of Arms engraved on each. The above Reward will be
given on recovering them, and conviction of the Offender.
—*The New-York Journal,* June 17, 1773 (*Supplement*).

SILVER PLATE.—Ten Pound Reward. On Thursday the
25th ult. was broke open the house of Samuel Henry, in
Trenton, New-Jersey, and sundry pieces of plate stolen
out of the same, viz. One half gallon tankard, marked
S. H. cypher; one quart do. one pint cann, marked as
above; one tea pot and stand, marked I. P. cypher; two
                                                      R.
salt cellars; one large soup spoon, marked R.   M. one
                                                      H.
punch ladle; and one punch strainer, marked S.   M.
Whoever secures the thief and plate, shall receive the
above reward from the subscriber. Samuel Henry—*The
New-York Gazette and the Weekly Mercury,* January 10,
1774.

TANKARD.—Five Pounds Reward. Taken away from a House in this city, a Silver Tankard, mark'd T. B. on the Handle, on the End of which is engraved the Head of a Man, with a Wig. Whoever will return the Tankard, shall have the above Reward paid by Hugh Gaine.—*The New-York Gazette and the Weekly Mercury*, August 8, 1774.

JEWELLER'S MATERIALS.—John Richardson, At his store in Cortlandt-street opposite Mr. John Leary's, Has just imported in the ship Samson, Capt. Coupar, (which he will dispose of on good terms) a large and neat assortment of jewellery, jeweller's materials, good choice of watch materials, seals, chains, silk strings, keys, an elegant assortment of plated shoe, knee, and stock buckles, on pinchbeck, copper and steel; steel, metal, and pinchbeck stone buckles, good scales and weights in neat japan'd boxes, cases with razors compleat, best shoe and knee chapes, plated snaffle and Pellom's bridle bitts, fine guns mounted with tooth and egg, silver mounted pistols, good choice of common sleeve buttons, steel cork screws, temple spectacles, polished steel spring snuffers, and jobo boxes, with several articles, wholesale and retail.—*The New-York Gazette and the Weekly Mercury*, November 7, 1774.

SWORD.—Lost or Stolen. Some time since, a Silver Hilted Sword with Abraham Livingston's name cut on the blade. Any person that will return it to the Printer, shall receive Twenty Shillings reward.—*The New-York Journal or the General Advertiser*, May 18, 1775.

BUCKLES.—On Sunday July 30th, the house of the subscriber was broken open and robbed of sundry articles, viz. a silver punch ladle with a mahogany handle, marked on the bottom R. C. a large table spoon, mark unknown; a pair of silver shoe buckles, 1 pair marked R. C. and 1 P. C. S., an odd ditto marked J. S., 2 pair of silver carved knee buckles, 6 silver tea spoons, 6 old do. do. one of them marked M. C. a stone box in the form of a prayer book. . . . Richard Cornish.—*The New-York Journal or General Advertiser*, August 3, 1775.

SNUFF BOX.—Lost, Some Day this Week, a Snuff Box, Made of Paper Machee, lined with Tortoishell, had a Female Figure, and two Boys painted on the Lid: the Painting much abused; a neat Circle of pierced Work round the Picture. Whoever will bring it to the Quarter Master, or Assistant Quarter Master General's Office, shall receive Four Dollars for their Trouble.—*The New-York Gazette and the Weekly Mercury*, August 5, 1776.

PORCELAIN, POTTERY AND EARTHENWARE

POTTERS

EDWARD ANNELY.—Any Gentlemen or others, desirous of adorning their Gardens, Tops of their Houses, or Doors &c. with Flower Pots, Incense Pots, Urns, Vases or any other Ornament capable of being made with Clay, may be supplied by Edward Annely, near the Fly-Market, he having set up the Potter's Business, by Means of a Family of Germans he bought, supposed by their Work, to be the most ingenious in that Trade, that ever arrived in America, at his Estate at Whitestone, where he has Clay capable of making eight different sorts of Earthen Ware, a large Quantity of various kinds being already made, fitting to be baked, which will be soon.— *The New-York Gazette, Revived in the Weekly Post-Boy*, May 20, 1751.

JOHN CAMPBELL, Potter, At the upper end of the Broadway, opposite the Negroes Burying-Ground, Has set up the business of making pantile, and will warrant them to be better than any imported from England or Holland, at 2l. 10s. per thousand; also continues making what is called Philadelphia earthen ware of the best quality, and will sell on the lowest terms for Cash, whole-sale and retail. All Merchants and shopkeepers shall have their's delivered without any expence, to any part of the town.—*Rivington's New-York Gazetteer*, May 19, 1774.

JONATHAN DURELL.—Philadelphia Earthern-Ware, Now manufacturing, and to be sold at that well known house, called Keechemet's mead-house, about mid-way between the New city-hall, and the Tea-water pump, on

the left hand side of the road as you go out of the city;
Where city and country store-keepers may be supplied
with any quantity of said ware, at reasonable rates; the
ware is far superior to generality, and equal to the best
of any imported from Philadelphia, or elsewhere, and
consists of butter, water, pickle, oyster and chamber pots,
milk pans of several sizes; jugs of several sizes; quart
and pint mugs, quart, pint and half pint bowls of various
colours; porringers, and smaller cups of different shapes;
striped and clouded dishes of divers colours, pudding and
wash hand basons, with sauce pans, and a variety of
other sorts of ware, too tedious to particularise, by the
manufacturer late from Philadelphia. Jonathan Durell.
The purchaser of twenty shillings or upwards, may depend on having it delivered to any part of this city
without charge.—*The New-York Gazette and the Weekly
Mercury*, March 15, 1773.

SAMUEL HALE.—Run away the 14th Day of June last
from Samuel Hale of the City of Philadelphia, Potter a
Servant man, Edward Pain by trade a potter . . . —*The
New-York Gazette*, June 24-July 1, 1734.

CHRISTOPHER LEFFINGWELL & THOMAS WILLIAMS.—
Wanted at the new earthenware manufactory, in Norwich in Connecticut, New-England, two throwers, or
wheelmen, for which good encouragement will be
given by the proprietors. CHRISTOPHER LEFFINGWELL,
THOMAS WILLIAMS.
Said Leffingwell will also give good encouragement to
one or more young men (paper makers) to work in his
mill in said Norwich.—*The New-York Gazette and the
Weekly Mercury*, June 10, 1771.

POTTER.—Wanted, A Potter. A Sober well behaved
Man, who understands the Potter's Business, may hear
of good Encouragement by applying to the Printer at the
Exchange.—*The New-York Journal or the General Advertiser*, January 15, 1767.

CHINA AND GLASS MENDERS

JAMES BYERS.—Broken China and Glass, Riveted in the very neatest and best Manner, and warranted to hold, at the low Price of Nine-Pence per Rivet, by the Subscriber, living in Wall-street, opposite to Mr. Abraham Lynsen's. James Byers.—*The New-York Gazette and the Weekly Mercury,* January 14, 1771.

JACOB DA COSTA, In Batteau-Street, a little above the Oswego-Market, Gives notice to all Gentlemen and Ladies in this city or country, who have, or may have in their houses any broken China or glass of any sort, that they may have it mended in the neatest manner ever seen in this City, either by riveting or a cement so strong and durable, that it may be used either in heat or cold without separating or loosening the joints. He also mends all sorts of marble or china furniture, such as is used for ornamenting Chimney pieces, chest of drawers, &c. He mends the necks of decanters that have been broken, and some of the pieces lost, cuts them even and makes them fit for use, likewise hoops glass and china mugs that have been cracked, and makes them as strong and useful as ever. He also mends Lady's fans.—*The New-York Journal or General Advertiser,* October 12, 1769.

NATHANIEL LANE.—To the Public in general this Notice is given, That I Nathaniel Lane, at my House in Warren-street, undertake to mend all Kinds of broken china, Delft, Glass, &c. on the most reasonable Terms. It is likewise to be observ'd, that if his Work gives Way, he will as often mend gratis.—*The New-York Gazette,* January 31, 1763.

NATHANIEL LANE.—Broken China & Glass, Mended and riveted in the neatest Manner and on the most reasonable Terms, by Nathaniel Lane, near Major James's. The Price of the Rivets, he finding the Silver is 2s. each if the Silver is found 1s. each Rivet, if Brass, is

1s. if white metal 6d.—*The New-York Journal or the General Advertiser,* July 9, 1767.

JAMES WALKER, from London. To be heard of at the Sign of the Ship aground, near the White Hall Slip. Mends broken China in the neatest and strongest Manner, with Rivets and Cramps, and where Pieces are wanting in broken Bowls, supplies the Defects; and makes Spouts and Handles to Tea-pots, in the same Manner as done in the East-Indies. Likewise he has a new and neat Method of riming and Sewing China; All which he performs at the cheapest Rates.—*The New-York Gazette or the Weekly Post-Boy,* November 20, 1760.

SELLERS OF PORCELAIN, POTTERY AND EARTHENWARE

GEORGE BALL.—Imported . . .

Burnt China.

Tureens with dishes,	Sugar dishes and cream jugs,
Large cups and saucers,	Breakfast plates,
Lesser do. do.	Tea pots, several sizes,
Lesser do. do.	Tea-table sets complete,
Bowls of several sizes,	Flowers jars of several sizes.
Mugs of do. do.	

Blue and white China.

Two quart bowls,	3 sizes of cups and saucers.
Three pint do.	Coffee cups and saucers.
One Quart, pint, and half	Butter tubs and stands
pint mugs of several sizes	Tea pots and spoonboats,
Tea pots large and small,	Salt cellars,
Plates, two sizes,	Pudding dishes,
Sugar dishes and cream jugs,	Sets of jars for flowers,

Pencil'd China.

Sauce boats, two sizes,	Pint mugs,
Cups and saucers, with handles,	Half pint ditto,
Sugar dishes and cream jugs,	Pint basons,
Tea pots, two sizes,	Tea pot stands, with spoon boats,
Butter and cake plates,	Odd cups and saucers,

The New-York Journal or General Advertiser, August 3, 1775.

ANTHONY L. BLEECKER.—To be sold at Anthony L. Bleecker's . . . 1 Table, and 2 tea table set Burnt China. 1 Dozen very handsome caudle cups and saucer, Several large bowls, dishes, plates, and other pieces.—*The New-York Gazette and the Weekly Mercury*, January 13, 1772.

BREESE & HOFFMAN.—Just imported, and to be Sold, by Breese & Hoffman in Wall-Street, India China, enamelled and blue and white Bowls, Caudle Cups, &c. Sets of Table China, blue and white Cups and Saucers, with small Sets of Service China, Nankin China Mugs, Salt Cellars, &c. &c. . . . —*The New-York Journal or General Advertiser*, January 8, 1767.

CHARLES OLIVER BRUFF.—C. O. Bruff, Goldsmith and Jeweller . . . likewise has opened a shop of earthen ware and china, and sells tea, sugar, coffee, pepper, rice, nutmegs, cinnamon, cloves, and mace; his shop is on the right hand side of the door in going into the house; and as there is two shops in the house, I have a board wrote on for a distinction . . . —*The New-York Gazette and the Weekly Mercury*, January 1, 1770.

DAVIES AND MINNITT, at their Glass, China and Earthen-Ware Store, Between Beekman's and Peck's-Slips, formerly kept by Lambert Garrison, sell all sorts of plain and cut glasses; also China of all sorts, and cream colour, stone, delf, Nottingham, black and other earthern-ware, of which they purpose keeping up an assortment, both for city and country consumption, and hope for a continuance of their friends' Custom.

Country orders carefully supplied and well packt up, and also for going abroad, on the lowest terms, for cash or short credit.—*The New-York Journal*, January 2, 1772.

DAVIES AND MINNETT,[1] . . . have imported . . . a great variety of gilt and plain cream colour'd ware, red china

[1] Another form of spelling for Minnitt.

tea pots and flower pots, china bowls and cups and saucers of all sorts, with a usual assortment of cream, aggitt, delf, black and white stone ware, and crates of flat and hollow ware for country consumption . . . —*The New-York Gazette and the Weekly Mercury*, May 11, 1772.

LAMBERT GARRISON.—On Monday Morning about 5 o'Clock, great Quantities of thick black Smoak, were observed to issue violently from the House of Mr. Lambert Garrison, seller of Earthen Ware, on Cromlyn's Dock . . . —News item in *The New-York Gazette or the Weekly Post-Boy*, May 14, 1770.

JAMES GILLILAND.—A most curious and useful Assortment of Stone, Delft and Glass Ware, is just open'd and now selling on the very lowest Terms by James Gilliland, at his Earthen and Glass Ware House, in the Wall Street. N.B. Good Encouragement will be given to those who take large Quantities, and he will take Produce, or Connecticut Bills of Credit, in immediate Payment, or give Time to those who buy to sell again. He has also a few boxes of best Chocolate, and some choice dript Candles, which he will sell very cheap for ready money.[2] —*The New-York Gazette*, April 4, 1763.

GROVES AND STONEHOUSE, at their Store, opposite Mr. Elias Degrushe, near the Ship-Yards, Has for Sale . . . all kinds of Delph and Stone Ware, yellow Dishes by the Crates; Corks, Loaf Sugar, and Lump do . . .—*The New-York Journal or the General Advertiser*, March 24, 1768.

JAMES & ARTHUR JARVIS, at their Glass and Earthen Store . . . sells among other things . . . a compleat assortment of cream colour, stone, Nottingham, delf and other earthen-ware.—*The New-York Gazette and the Weekly Mercury*, January 6, 1772.

[2] A list of James Gilliland's wares is contained in *The New-York Mercury*, April 4, 1763.

KEELING AND MORRIS. . . . Moves and sells stock . . . Table plates and Dishes, both of the oval and round Shape, black Tea-pots, Milk-pots, Mugs and Bowls of all Sizes; Tortois Table Plates and Dishes of the neatest Patterns; green and Tortois Tea-pots, Milk-pots, Bowls, and Cups and Saucers; Venis Flower Faces both green and white; Glass Quart, Pint, and Half-Pint Decanters, Wine Glasses, &c. &c. Enameled Stone Tea-pots, Milk-pots, Mugs, Bowls and Cups and Saucers of all Sizes . . . —*The New-York Gazette,* August 2, 1762.

ANDREW MARSCHALK.—A Few very neat Scripture and Landskip Chimney Tiles. Also Boston ditto, for Oven Floors, and Hearths, to be sold, by Andrèw Marschalk, on Cannon's-Dock.—*The New-York Mercury,* December 17, 1764.

P—— M'DAVITT.—To be sold at P. M'Davitt's Ven-due-House . . . a box of China, pint, quart, and ½ gallon bowls burnt and blue and white; chocolate cups and saucers, sugar dishes with covers, tea cups and saucers . . . —*The New-York Gazette and the Weekly Mercury,* January 27, 1772.

JOHN MORTON.—At his Store in Dock-Street, between Coenties Market, and the Exchange, has just received per the Hope, Capt. Benjamin Davis, from London, a fine Assortment of China, viz. Table Sets of long, octagon, and round Dishes, compleat; very fine Tea-Table Sets, Compleat; half Pint Basons, with Handles and Saucers; Breakfast Cups and Saucers with or without Handles; Tea Pots; Milk Pots; Sugar Dishes; Fruit, Sallad, and Pudding ditto; Quart and Pint Mugs; blue and white and enamel'd Bowls, from half a Pint to 12 Quarts each; Dishes and Plates; Jars and Beckers, &c. &c.—*The New-York Gazette,* September 8, 1766.

EDWARD NICOLL.—To be Sold by Edward Nicoll, on the New-Dock, next Door to Philip Livingston, Esq;

Crates Common yellow Ware both cups and Dishes, Crates white Stone Cups and Saucers, Crates of blue and white, Cups and Saucers, Crates white ware, Crates of blue and white, Crates of black, crates of Tortise Shell, and crates of red Ware, all well sorted; Crates of Pocket-Bottles, Boxes of Glass, consisting of Wine Glasses, Salts, Sugar Dishes, Cream-Pots, and Tumblers, Tierces and Hogsheads of Delph Ware, consisting of Punch Bowls, Plates, Dishes, Tea-Cups, and Saucers, with a large and good Assortment of Earthen Ware and Glasses, and a Parcel of fine white Mosaic Dishes, and Plates, by Retail, Muscovado Sugar, and choice good old Jamaica Rum, by the Hogshead or 5 Gallons, at 5s 6 Per Gallon.—*The New-York Gazette or the Weekly Post-Boy,* February 14, 1757.

JONAS PHILLIPS.—To be sold by Jonas Phillips, in Stone-Street, A Choice parcel of black and red Philadelphia Earthen Ware, sorted in crates fit for town or country shop keepers . . . —*The New-York Gazette and the Weekly Mercury,* September 7, 1772.

RHINELANDER.—To be sold at Rhinelander's Store . . . china ware, blue and white cups and saucers of all sizes; burnt and enamel'd ditto; blue and white sugar dishes & milk pots; burnt and enamel'd ditto; blue and white tea setts compleat; burnt and enamel'd ditto; blue and white table setts ditto; blue and white bowls of different sizes; burnt and enamel'd ditto, from half a pint to two gallons . . . —*Rivington's New York Gazetteer,* January 13, 1774.

HENRY WILMOT.—Ornamental China. The greatest variety of ornamental china, consisting of groups, sets, figures, pairs and jars, just opened, and to be sold at a very low advance, by Henry Wilmot, in Hanover-Square . . . —*The New-York Gazette or the Weekly Post-Boy,* December 3, 1770.

GLASS

Glass Houses

Lodewick Bamper.—All Persons that have Demands on the Company of the Glass-House at New Windsor,[1] are desired to bring in their Accounts to Lodewick Bamper, in New York, as speedy as possible, in order to have them adjusted by the said Company. Said Bamper has also to sell, a Parcel of choice good Molasses, and New-York Rum by the Hogshead.—*The New-York Gazette or the Weekly Post-Boy*, July 7, 1755.

Lodewick Bamper.—Run away from the Owners of the Glass-House at New-Windsor, on Wednesday the 4th Instant. A German Servant Man named Christian Medsher . . . Whoever takes up the said Servant and secures him, or delivers him to the Subscriber, shall have Three Pounds Reward, and all reasonable Charges paid by Lodewick Bamper.—*The New-York Gazette or the Weekly Post-Boy*, July 7, 1755.

Nicholas Bayard & Matthew Ernest.—This is to inform the Publick, That the new erected Glass-House at Newfoundland, within four Miles of this City; is now at Work, and that any Gentlemen may be supply'd with Bottles, Flasks, or any sort of Glass agreeable to their Directions.

N.B. Any Persons that has Oak Wood to dispose of by bringing it to the above-mentioned Place, will receive the New-York Price upon Delivery, by Matthew Ernest. —*The New-York Gazette or the Weekly Post-Boy*, October 30, 1758.

---

[1] Johanes Will, pewterer, advertised that he sold glass ware manufactured at the Glass House in New Windsor.—*The New-York Gazette or the Weekly Post-Boy*, September 27, 1756. See the chapter on "Pewter."

NICHOLAS BAYARD & MATTHEW ERNEST.—To be Sold, the Glass House,[2] Out-Houses, and all the Implements belonging thereto, about four Miles from this City. For further Particulars Enquire of Nicholas Bayard, or Matthew Ernest.—*The New-York Gazette or the Weekly Post-Boy*, July 22, 1762.

BRAINTREE, MASSACHUSETTS.—Tuesday last a Ship arrived here from Holland, with about 300 Germans, Men, Women and Children, some of whom are going to settle at Germantown (a part of Braintree) and the others in the Eastern Parts of this Province. 'Tis said about 40 Children were born during the Passage. Among the Artificers come over in this Ship, there are a Number of Men Skilled in making of Glass; and a House proper for carrying on that useful Manufacture, will be erected at Germantown as soon as possible.—Boston news item in *The New-York Gazette Revived in the Weekly Post-Boy*, October 2, 1752.

THOMAS LEPPER.—Notice is Hereby Given, That there is to be sold by Thomas Lepper,[3] Store-keeper to the Glass House Company, living at their Store on the late Sir Peter Warren's Dock, at the North River, near Mr. Peter Mesiers, all sorts of Bottles from 1 Quart to 3 Gallons and upwards, as also a Variety of other Glass Ware too tedious to mention, all at reasonable Rates; and all Gentlemen that wants Bottles of any size with their Names on them, or any Chymical Glasses, or any

[2] Notice of the opening of the Glass House (also known as Newfoundland), for public entertainment, was given in *The New-York Gazette*, May 23, 1763. John Taylor, New York upholsterer, took over the Glass House for the purpose of opening a tavern (*The New-York Gazette or the Weekly Mercury*, June 13, 1768, *Supplement*), and ran a stage coach to the Glass House for his patrons. (*The New-York Gazette*, August 8, 1768.) In the following years the Glass House was advertised for rent at frequent intervals. See *The New-York Gazette and the Weekly Mercury*, May 10, 1773; *Rivington's New-York Gazetteer*, May 12, 1774; *The New-York Gazette and the Weekly Mercury*, March 20, 1775, *Supplement*.

[3] Thomas Lepper had a tavern opposite the Merchant's Coffee House and at the Ferry House on Staten Island.—*The New-York Gazette Revived in the Weekly Post-Boy*, November 19, 1750.

other sort of Glass Ware, by applying to said Lepper, have them made with all Expedition. N.B. Said Lepper gives ready Money for Ashes, and old Window Glass.— *The New-York Gazette or the Weekly Post-Boy,* October 14, 1754.

GARRIT RAPALJE.—Broken Flint Glass, single or double is wanted, and if brought by any Persons to Garrit Rapalje, shall receive for the same Two Pence per Pound. As it is intended again to be worked up here, at a new Glass-House, it is hoped all Lovers of American Manufacture will encourage what is in their Power, and particularly on this Instance save, collect and send such broken Glass as above directed. N.B. No Duties Here: There is also wanted at said Glass House, a Person that is thoroughly acquainted with the Process of making Red Lead; he will meet with good Encouragement at the said Manufactory.—*The New-York Gazette and the Weekly Mercury,* October 9, 1769.

HENRY WILLIAM STIEGEL.—American Flint Glass, Is now made at the factory in Manheim, in Lancaster County, [Pennsylvania] equal in quality with any imported from Europe, where all merchants, store-keepers and others, may be supplied on very reasonable terms; and as the proprietor of those works well knows the patriotic spirit of the Americans, he flatters himself they will encourage the manufactories of their own country, and hopes to be favoured with their orders for Flint Glass, and begs leave further to assure them, that whatever commands he may receive, shall, with great punctuality and dispatch, be executed. Wholesale dealers may expect proper allowance or abatement, on buying large quantities. Patterns and orders will be received (and forwarded to the manufactory) at Philadelphia, at the London Coffee House, and by Isaac Melchor in Second-street, at Lancaster by Paul Zantzinger, at York Town, by Mr. George Stake, and at Baltimore by Mr. John Little. N: B. A glass-cutter and flowerer, on application, will meet with good encouragement at said manufactory. HENRY WILLIAM STIEGEL.—*The New-York Gazette and the Weekly Mercury,* July 29, 1771.

HENRY WILLIAM STIEGEL.—American Flint Glass Store, Removed from the store kept by Mr. Henry Wm. Stiegel, near the Exchange, to the store of James and Arthur Jarvis, between Burling and Beekman's Slips, in the Fly; who have for sale of the American manufacture, quart, pint, and half pint decanters; pint, half pint, gill, and half gill, flint and common tumblers; carrosts, enamel'd, mason, and common wine glasses; jelly and cillabub glasses, with and without handles; mustard and cream pots, flint and common; salts, salt linings, and crewets, wide-mouth bottles for sweetmeats, rounds and phyals for doctors, wine and water glasses, ink and pocket bottles. Orders taken for all kind of glasses for chymical or other uses, agreeable to patterns. It is expected that all friends to American manufactures will do their utmost in promoting this. They have likewise for sale as usual, a very large and general assortment of earthen, delf, &c. Also a variety of English garden seed of the last year's growth, viz. Early charlton, marrowfat, badmansdwarf, and golden hotspur peas; winsor, scarlet, runners, and large white kidney beans; lettice and cabbage of various kinds, carrot, parsnip, radish, turnip, &c &c. Pepper, coffee, redwood, logwood, &c. &c. Ready money given for broken Flint Glass.—*The New-York Gazette and the Weekly Mercury,* February 8, 1773.

RICHARD WISTAR (*of Philadelphia*).—Made at the Subscriber's Glass-Works, and now on Hand, to be sold at his House in Market-Street, opposite the Meal-Market, either wholesale or retail, between Three and Four Hundred Boxes of Window Glass, consisting of the common Sizes, 10 by 12, 9 by 11, 8 by 10, 7 by 9, 6 by 8, &c. Lamps Glass, or any uncommon Sizes under 16 by 18, are cut upon a short Notice. Where also may be had, most Sorts of Bottles, Gallon, Half Gallon, and Quart, full Measure Half Gallon Case Bottles, Snuff and Mustard, Receivers and Retorts of various Sizes, also electrifying Globes and Tubes, &c. As the abovementioned Glass is of American Manufactory; it is consequently clear of the Duties the Americans so justly complain of, and at present it seems peculiarly the Interest of America to encourage her own Manufactories, more especially those upon which Duties have been imposed, for the sole purpose of raising a Revenue.

N.B. He also continues to make the Philadelphia Brass Buttons, well noted for their Strength, such as were made by his deceased Father, and are warranted for seven Years. RICHARD WISTAR, Philadelphia, August 10.— *The New-York Journal or General Advertiser*, August 17, 1769 (*Supplement*).

GLASSWARE

IMPORTED GLASS.—Richard Smith . . . lately imported, a large Assortment of drinking Glasses, Pint and Quart Decanters, with sundry other sorts of Glasses, &c.—*The New-York Gazette Revived in the Weekly Post-Boy*, June 8, 1747 (*Supplement*).

OPTIC GLASSES.—Notice is hereby given, that the Widow of Balthaser Sommer, late from Amsterdam, now lives next Door to Mr. Laffert's on Pot-Baker's Hill, in Smith-Street, New-York, Grinds all sorts of Optic Glasses to the greatest Perfection, such as Microscope Glasses, Spying Glasses of all Lengths, Spectacles, Reading-Glasses, for near-sighted People or others; Also, Spying-Glasses of three Feet long; which are to set on a common Walking-Cane, and yet be carried as a Pocket-Book; all at the most reasonable Rates.—*The New-York Gazette or the Weekly Post-Boy*, May 21, 1753.

GLOBE LAMPS, to be sold cheap, At Capt. William Mercier's in French Church-Street next Door to Mr.

Benjamin Jervis, Hatter.—*The New-York Gazette or the Weekly Post-Boy*, March 3, 1755.

APOTHECARY'S FURNITURE.—Gerardus Duyckinck at the sign of the Looking-Glass and Druggist-Pot, at the Corner of the Old Slip Market . . . Has for sale among many other things . . . London and Bristol crown window glass of all sizes (Can be cut to any size required) White fine glass ware, plain, ornamented, cut ground and engraved suitable for families and apothecary's furniture. Optick glasses, as telescopes, reading, burning, visual, temple spectacles, and near-sighted glasses . . . —*The New-York Mercury*, October 6, 1766.

PLAIN & FLOWER'D GLASS WARE.—George Ball being obliged to move until the Store in which he now lives, in Bayard-Street, is rebuilt, will sell very low for Cash . . .

Plain Glass Ware

Gallon Decanters,—3 Qu do.	Cruets,—Butter Tubs and Stands,
2 Quart do. 1 do. do.	Punch Glasses with Handles,
Wine and Water Glasses,	Patty Pans, Sugar Dishes,
Wash Hand Glasses with Plates,	Salt Sellers and Linings,
Beer Glasses,	Jelly and Bird Glasses.
Common Wine do.	

Flower'd Glass

Decanters, New Fashion,	Bowls with Covers, 2 Sizes,
Wine and Water and Ale Glasses,	Odd Glasses with Silver Tops, for
Neat Cut Salts,	Cruet Stands,
Do. Cruets,	Cruets Stands from 12s to £3.

The New-York Journal or General Advertiser, May 24, 1770.

LONDON AND BRISTOL GLASS.—George Ball, who has removed into Carman-street, next door to Alderman Gautier, has received by the last London and Bristol Vessels, a general assortment of glass ware, consisting of flower'd and cut pint, half, and quarter pint tumblers; plain pint, half and quarter pint tumblers; flower'd and cut pint and quart decanters; a variety of neat enamel'd cut wine glasses, chamber lamps, bird glasses and salt lining, &c. with an assortment of cheap glass fit for the country.—*The New-York Gazette and the Weekly Mercury*, April 15, 1771.

GLASS WARE.—James and Arthur Jarvis, At their Glass and Earthen Store. Between Burling's and Beekman's Slips, in the Fly. Have just open'd a Variety of Glass, viz. Cut, plain, sprig'd and engrav'd quart decanters, a few plain ½ gallon do. cut enamel'd and plain wine glasses; quart, pint and ½ pint carrosts; root glasses; plain and with loops; blue and white soy crewets and stands, with gilt labels; common do. elegant cut sallad bowls and trifle dishes, elegant cut sweetmeat glasses, glass water cups, a variety of smelling bottles, cut and plain, with and without cases; sprig'd, cut and moulded milk-pot and jelly glasses; ribb'd, cut and scollop'd sullabub glasses and tumblers; a variety of ground shop bottles and phials, for doctors; ink and oyl squares, elegant cut salts, sugar-dishes, and butter tubs; genteel salvers, stands, scroles and baskets; breast pipes; with a variety of common tumblers, wine and drinking glasses . . . —*The New-York Gazette and the Weekly Mercury*, December 6, 1771.

LONDON GLASS WARE.—Davies and Minnett At their glass, china and earthen Ware store . . . imported from London . . . a very large and neat assortment of glass, china and earthen ware of all sorts, for city and country consumption, among which is elegant cut and sprig'd quart, pint, and half pint decanters; neat cut wines of the newest patterns in London, guglets, soy crewets, water cups and tumblers with covers, fine cut salts, sugar dishes and milk pots, and other glass ware; . . . —*The New-York Gazette and the Weekly Mercury*, May 4, 1772.

BRISTOL GLASS WARE.—At Rhinelander's Store . . . A large assortment of Glass Ware, by the Ellen, Capt.

Clarke, from Bristol, Decanters, cut, engraved and plain of all sizes: wine glasses ditto; tumblers of all sizes; quart, pint and half pint cans; caster frames and bottles; plain, engraved, cut and top'd with silver . . . —*Rivington's New-York Gazetteer*, January 13, 1774.

GREEN GLASS.—Imported by George Ball. . . .

Green Glass

Gallon square bottles,	Ink bottles,
Two quart ditto,	Blue, oval and round salt lining,
Pint ditto,	Ditto white ditto
Pint and half pint flasks,	

One penny per pound for broken white flint Glass.— *The New-York Journal or the General Advertiser*, August 3, 1775.

PEWTER

ROBERT BOYLE, Pewterer, At the sign of the Dish, next
Door to Mr. Samuel Pell's; Makes and sells at the most
reasonable rates, all sorts of pewter ware, wholesale or
retail: He also makes worms for stills of all sizes, in a
new and compleat way; likewise, hogshead, barrel or
bottle cranes, with or without cocks; and the infusion
pots, so much made use of in colds; as well as any uncommon thing in pewter, in any shape or form, that may
be ordered; Likewise, all kinds of lead work for ships or
houses, with due care and expedition.—*The New-York
Mercury*, June 17, 1754.

ROBERT BOYLE.—To Be Sold, by Robert Boyle, Pewterer, At the Sign of the Gilt Dish in Dock Street, between the Old-Slip and Coenties's Markets in New-York,
Wholesale or Retail, at the most reasonable Rates, either
in Exchange for old Pewter, or otherwise, all Sorts of
Pewter Ware, viz.

Dishes and Plates of all Sorts, Basons, Tankards, and
Porringers of all Sizes, Quart and Pint Mugs, Tea-Pots
of all Sorts, Cullenders, Bed Pans, and Stool Pans of all
Sizes, Infusion Pots so much approved of in Colds or
Consumptions, Cups and Flaggons for Churches, Half-
pint and jill Tumblers, Wine Measures from a Quart to
a Half-jill, Salts, and Ink Stands, Spoons of all Sorts,
Limbecks and cold Stills, Candle Molds of different Sizes.
Hogshead, Barrel, and Bottle Cranes, Pewter or Block-
Tin Worms of all Sizes, as shall be ordered, Funnels of
all Sizes. Also any Thing relating to the Pewterer's or
Plummer's Business; as leading of Houses or Ships, in
any Way as required: Sash Leads, Deep Sea Leads, and √

Bullets of all Sizes, made for 3s. per Hundred, with the utmost Dispatch. Likewise the highest Prices in Cash, for old Pewter, Copper, Brass and Lead. All those that will favour him with their Custom, may depend on the best of Usage.—*The New-York Gazette or The Weekly Post-Boy*, December 22, 1755.

CORNELIUS BRADFORD.—To be Sold, By Cornelius Bradford, at his Father's House, in Hanover Square, Pig and Bar Iron, by the Ton, or otherwise; Iron Chimney Backs and Cart Boxes; Iron Weights from 56 lb. to 7 lb fixed or unfixed. Pewter, by the wholesale or retail, to be sold at the above House; and ready Money given for old Pewter and Brass.—*The New-York Mercury*, November 13, 1752.

WILLIAM BRADFORD.—To be Sold By William Bradford, Pewterer, in Hanover Square, in New-York; Cannon four Pounders, and Swivel Guns, Cannon Shot of all Sizes, Iron Pots and Kettles of all Sizes, Cart and Waggon Boxes, Backs for Chimneys, Fullers Plates, Pig and Bar Iron, &c. &c. Where may be had Money for old Brass and Pewter.—*The New-York Weekly Post-Boy*, August 13, 1744.

WILLIAM BRADFORD.—All Persons indebted to the Estate of William Bradford, late of this City, Pewterer, deceased, are desired to make immediate Payment; and those that have any Demands against said Estate, are desired to send in their Accounts to William Merceir, at the late Dwelling House of said William Bradford, in Hanover Square.

N.B. To morrow at ten o'Clock will be sold by Vendue at said House, sundry Household furniture.—*The New-York Mercury*, April 21, 1760.

BRADFORD AND MC EUEN, Beg leave to inform the Public in general, and their friends in particular, that they have lately set up the Pewterer's and Plummer's

business, at their shop at Peck's-slip, where they make
and have for sale on the most reasonable terms, all kinds
of pewter ware, viz. Dishes, plates, basons, teapots, quart
and pint mugs, tankards, porrengers, cream pots, sugar
dishes, slop bowls, half pint and gill tumblers, cullenders,
bed pans, chair pans, chamber pots, wine measures, table
spoons and many other articles in the pewterer's way,
Store keepers in town or country, may be supplied with
any quantity of the above articles, on the shortest notice.
They likewise make in the best and neatest manner, block
tin and pewter worms for distilling, of any size; hogshead
and bottle cranes, and candle moulds of different sizes.
In the plummers way they make and fix hawse leads,
and scuppers, or any other lead work necessary for shipping, in the best manner, also leaden trunks or pipes of
any size, for houses, and laying of sheet lead, and solder
the same upon either roofs or gutters. Ready money
given for old pewter, brass, or lead, or the same taken
in payment for work. They flatter themselves that from
their experience in the business, and their having a complete set of tools, and every thing in order for carrying
on the same extensively, it will be in their power to give
satisfaction to those persons who please to employ them
in the above branches.—*The New York Journal or The
General Advertiser*, August 27, 1772.

PETER KARBY.—Just Published, And to be Sold by the
Printer hereof, or at Mr. Peter Karby, Pewterer near the
North River. A Brief Vindication of the Purchasors
against the Proprietors Price 7d.—*The New-York
Weekly Journal*, April 28, 1746.

WILLIAM KIRBY, Pewterer, at the corner of Dock-
street, near the Old Slip Market, and opposite the late
corner-store of Gerardus Duyckinck, has just imported
in the Earl of Dunmore, Capt. Lawrence, a large and
general assortment of London pewter, which he will sell
wholesale and retail, on the most reasonable terms, viz.
Dishes, plates and basons; hard-metal water plates,

tureens, tankards, quart and pint pots, teapots of different sorts and sizes; coffee, sugar, and milk pots; pint, ½ pint and gill porringers; soup, table and teaspoons; round-bowl spoons, soup ladles, quart and pint bowls, wash-hand basons, funnels, large chamber pots, close-stool and bed pans, measures from one gallon to half a gill, dram cups, round and square chest ink-stands, large and small crains.

Said Kirby has likewise just come to hand, a curious and general assortment of English and Dutch toys, which he will sell wholesale and retail, at a low advance, amongst which are, a few large humming tops, japan'd waiters, bread baskets, clothes and shoe brushes, hair brooms, hearth brushes, plated shoe and knee buckles, and a variety of other articles in the toy way, too tedious to mention.

He takes old pewter and bees-wax in exchange for new pewter.—*The New-York Gazette and The Weekly Mercury,* September 26, 1774.

JOSEPH LEDDEL, Pewterer, who for many Years has liv'd at the Sign of the Platter in Dock-Street, opposite to Mr. Franks's, is now removed to the lower End of Wall-Street, near the Meal Market, in the House where Mr. Joseph Sacket lately lived, and has the Same Sign; where his former Customers, or any others, may be supplied with most Sorts of Pewter-Ware, Wholesale or Retail, at reasonable Rates; and gives ready Money for old Pewter and Brass.—*The New-York Weekly Post-Boy,* May 7, 1744.

JOSEPH LEDDEL.—To be Sold by Joseph Leddel, jun. at his House in Smith-Street, opposite to Mrs. Carpenter's, at the most reasonable Rates; all sorts of Pewter-ware by wholesale or retail, and makes Worms for Stills of all Sizes, by a compleat Way at the lowest Prices: Likewise, Makes Hogshead, Barrell, or Bottle Cranes, either with or without Cocks, and makes infusion-Pots, so much approv'd of in Colds, and any uncommon Thing

in Pewter, in any Shape or Form as shall be order'd;
likewise does all sorts of lead-work, either House or
Ship-work.

He also Engraves on Steel, Iron, Gold, Silver, Copper,
Brass, Pewter, Ivory or turtle-Shell in a neat Manner,
and reasonably.—*The New-York Gazette Revived in The
Weekly Post-Boy*, March 23, 1752 (*Supplement*).[1]

JOSEPH LEDDEL.—All Persons who have any demands
on the estate of Mr. Joseph Leddle, [*sic*] jun. late of this
City, pewterer deceas'd, are desired to apply to Abraham
De Lanoy, hatter, in Queen Street, near the Meal Market.
—*The New-York Mercury*, June 24, 1754.

✓ HENRY WILL.—To be Sold, The Glue-House, near
Fresh-Water, with all the Utensils for Glue-making. It
is also very convenient for the Soap and Candle making
Business, which may be conveniently carried on, besides
the Glue making. For further Particulars inquire of
Henry Will, Pewterer, near the Old Slip. Who makes,
sells, and exchanges, all Sorts of Pewter Ware, and gives
Cash, for old Pewter.—*The New-York Journal or The
General Advertiser*, March 15, 1770.

HENRY WILL, Begs leave to acquaint his friends and
customers, that he is removed to the well known corner
house at the Old-slip, where Mr. Gerardus Duyckinck
kept his universal store, formerly known by the sign of
the looking glass, and now by the sign of the blocktin
teapot, where he continues to make, sell and exchange,
wholesale and retail, all sorts of pewter ware, at the
cheapest rate, and where he hopes for the favourable
continuance of his friends and customers. He likewise
gives ready money for old pewter.—*New York Gazette
and The Weekly Mercury*, May 25, 1772.

HENRY WILL.—Notice of John Siemon, Furrier, mentions that he is at Mr. Henry Will's, Pewterer, the Corner

[1] The supplement to No. 479 was mis-dated May 25, 1752.

of the Old Slip.—*The New-York Gazette and The Weekly Mercury,* November 9, 1772.

HENRY WILL, Pewterer, Acquaints, the public, that he is removed to Albany, where he intends to carry on the Pewterer's business in all its branches. As he has hitherto been favoured with the custom of many of his friends in and about Albany, so he hopes to merit their continuance;—an assortment of Pewter ware will be constantly kept by him; old pewter will be exchanged for new, or cash given for it.—*The New-York Journal or The General Advertiser,* April 11, 1776.

JOHN WILL.—To be Sold, by Johanes Will, Pewterer, living in Smith's-Fly, opposite Mr. Robert Livingston. A Parcel of the best New-York distill'd Rum, by the Hogshead, Barrel, or smaller in Quantity, not less than five Gallons; as also a variety of Glass Ware, manufactured at the Glass House in New-Windsor.

N.B. Said Johanes Will, gives ready money for good Wood Ashes, and broken Window and Bottle-Glass, as also old Pewter. Any Person wanting any Particulars of Glass Ware made, may apply to the said Will, and they shall be served with all possible Expedition.—*The New-York Gazette or The Weekly Post-Boy,* September 27, 1756.

JOHN WILL.—This is to give Notice, That John Will, Pewterer, from Germany, living in Smith's Fly, opposite to Mr. Robert Livingston, makes and sells all sorts of Pewter Ware, in the neatest and best Manner, and has also to sell, best Albany peas by the Bushel or Quart, Oat Meal by the Hundred Weight or Quart, best London Mustard Seed by the Bushel, half Bushel, peck or Quart, Buckweed by the Bushel, a small Parcel of Flax Seed; and sundry other Goods at a reasonable Rate for ready Cash.—*The New-York Gazette or The Weekly Post-Boy,* February 4, 1760.

PETER YOUNG.—For the Benefit of the Public in general, I Peter Young, of the city of New York, Pewterer, living at Mr. Fisher's, Barber, in Spring Garden, commonly called Chatham street, was afflicted with an imposthume or sore in my breast with such a violent cough, that I could not rest day or night, spitting and vomitting matter constantly for three months, that I thought I was in a consumption; I applied to several, and tried various kinds of Psysick, until I applied to the French Doctor Blouin, who advised me to make use of his Anti-Venereal Pills, so well known by the name of Keyser's Pills. I followed his advice, and by the use of those pills alone, in a short time I recovered my former health. Witness my hand, PETER YOUNG.—*The Constitutional Gazette,* December 13, 1775.

MISCELLANEOUS PEWTER

PEWTER DISHES.—Among other items exposed to sale by way of Publick Vendue are: one Brass Kittle, four pewter Dishes, eight Pewter Plates, one Iron Chafing Dish, one Brass snuffer, five Chairs and two Tables, one Looking-Glass, one Spinning Wheel, one Chest, four Pewter Basons one Feather Bed and Furniture. . . . — *The New-York Weekly Journal,* February 26, 1739.

PEWTER BUTTONS.—Runaway from Johannes Bratt, a servant. . . . "He had on when he went away an old dark couler'd Coat, with Pewter Buttons, Leather Breeches, and a white shirt; . . . —*New-York Weekly Journal,* June 28, 1742.

PEWTER.—Just imported from Liverpool, and to be sold on board the Snow Nancy, William Beekman Master, Several White Servants; also sundry sorts of Earthen Ware in Casks and Crates, Cheshire Cheese, Loaf Sugar, Cutlery Ware, Pewter, Grindstones, Coals, and sundry other Goods too tedious to mention: by Abraham Van Horne, Daniel & Isaac Gomez or said Master.—*New-*

York Gazette Revived in the Weekly Post-Boy, June 25, 1751.

PEWTER WARE.—Among other items for sale by Abraham Wilson, peruke maker, are: pewter plates, Dishes, basons and spoons, knives, and forks. . . . —*The New-York Gazette*, November 3, 1760.

PEWTER BUTTONS.—Runaway from Abigail Lord an Irish servant man . . . "Had on when he went away, a light colour'd cloth jacket with home made pewter buttons. . . . —The *New-York Gazette and The Weekly Mercury*, July 2, 1770.

LONDON PEWTER.—Cheaper than can be imported. Puffing, and a pompous Parade of cheap selling, is of late become so fashionable among us, that an Advertisement in common Form, no longer attracts the Attention of the Public, it therefore seems necessary to offer something more than the general Declaration of, as cheap as can be imported, or of because purchased at Vendue for less than a Cent, and therefore the Prices are annexed to the following Articles, which are sold by John Thurman, jun. at his Store in Wall-street, which must convince the Public that he not only sells Goods for less than a Cent, or as cheap as can be imported, but even cheaper than can be imported.

As by this kind of dealing the Poor will be enabled to cloath themselves, as it were, from the Hands of the Manufacturers; and it is evident no Profit can possibly arise to the Seller, it is hoped that kind Providence, or the Public will put all such generous Traders in some way of living with the Expence. Best London Pewter Dishes, at 1 shilling 5 per Pound. . . . —*The New-York Gazette and The Weekly Mercury*, November 4, 1771.

PEWTER QUART POT.—Stopped a Pewter Quart Pot, mark'd in the Inside I W, and at the Bottom of the

Outside A D. Whoever owns the same, may know the person who defrauded them of it, by applying to the Printer.—*The New-York Journal or General Advertiser,* July 29, 1773.

FURNITURE

CABINETMAKERS

GILBERT ASH.—For the Benefit of a Poor Widow. On Thursday the 18th Instant, will be open'd, at the City Hall, in the City of New-York, a New Organ, made by Gilbert Ash, where will be performed, A Concert of Vocal and Instrumental Musick. . . . Tickets, at Five Shillings each, to be had at Mr. Cobham's in Hanover-Square, at the Gentleman's Coffee-House, at the King's Arms, at the Province Arms, at the Bible & Crown in Queen-street, and at Mr. Ash's joining Mr. Willet's in Wall-street; who continues the Business of Organ Building, by whom Gentlemen and Ladies, may be furnished with noble Instrument, in a convenient Time after it is be-spoke.—*The New-York Mercury*, March 15, 1756.

GILBERT ASH.—At the Upper End of Wall-Street, near the City Hall, Carries on the Manufactory of hard Soap-boiling, and has now by him a Parcel of very good Soap to dispose of, both brown and white; and also a Parcel of Babary Wax mould Candles. The Shop-Joiner or Cabinet Business is carried on at the same Place, where may be had, all sorts of Work made in that Branch, Tables, Chairs, Desks, &c.—*The New-York Mercury*, October 22, 1759.

GILBERT ASH, in Wall-Street, near the City-Hall, has by him A Parcel of ready made Chairs, Mahogany and Black Walnut, Mahogany Tea Tables, and dining Tables, which he will sell, reasonably; Also a Parcel of hard Soap and Candles, which he will sell cheap.—*The New-York Gazette or the Weekly Post-Boy*, April 14, 1763.

THOMAS ASH, Windsor Chair Maker, At the Corner below St. Paul's Church in the Broad-Way, Makes and sells all kinds of Windsor chairs, high and low backs, garden and settees ditto. As several hundred pounds have been sent out of this province for this article, he hopes the public will encourage the business, as they can be had as cheap and good, if not superior to any imported; he has now by him, and intends keeping always a large quantity, so that merchants, masters of vessels, and others may be supplied upon the shortest notice. N.B. Shop goods will be taken in pay.—*Rivington's New-York Gazetteer*, February 17, 1774.

JOHN BRINNER, Cabinet and Chair-Maker, from London; At the Sign of the Chair, opposite Flatten Barrack-Hill, in the Broad-Way, New York: Where every Article in the Cabinet, Chair-making, Carving and Gilding Business, is executed on the most reasonable Terms, with the utmost neatness and Punctuality. He carves all sorts of Architectural, Gothic and Chinese Chimney Pieces, Glass and Picture Frames, Slab Frames, Gerondoles, Chandaliers, and all kinds of Mouldings and Frontispieces, &c. &c. Desk and Book-Cases, Library Book-Cases, Writing and Reading Tables, Commode and Bureau Dressing Tables, Study Tables, China Shelves and Cases, Commode and Plain Chest of Drawers, Gothic and Chinese Chairs; all Sorts of plain or ornamental Chairs, Sofa Beds, Sofa Settees, Couch and easy Chair Frames, all kinds of Field Bedsteads, &c. &c.

N.B. He has brought over from London six Artificers, well skill'd in the above Branches.—*The New-York Mercury*, May 31, 1762.

THOMAS BURLING.—Whereas the Co-partnership of John and Thomas Burling, expires the first of April next; all those who have any demands on them are desired to call for the same; and all those who are indebted to them are hereby requested to make immediate payment; The more so as one of them is going to live in the Country.—

The New-York Gazette and the Weekly Mercury, February 17, 1772.

THOMAS BURLING, Cabinet and Chair-maker, in Chapple-street, New York, Has opened a yard of all kinds of stuff suitable for country Joiners, which he proposes to sell on reasonable terms.—*The New-York Gazette and the Weekly Mercury,* January 11, 1773.

THOMAS BURLING, Cabinet & Chair-Maker, At the Sign of the Chair, in Beekman-Street, commonly called Chapel-Street, New-York, Executes with neatness and dispatch the different articles in his branch, and will gratefully acknowledge all favours of his friends, and the public in general.

He has now made for sale sundry pieces of furniture, of the best mahogany, which he proposes to sell at the lowest rate good work sells at. Said Burling sells mahogany, ready sawed, fit for carpenters in stair case building and all other kind of stuff suitable for carrying on the joiners business, all which he proposes to sell on the most reasonable terms.[1]—*Rivington's New-York Gazetteer,* September 2, 1774.

HENRY CARMER.—Abraham Willson, Has removed his Furr Store from Little-Dock-street, to the upper end of Wynkoop-street, next to Henry Carmer's, cabinet-maker, . . . —*The New-York Gazette and the Weekly Mercury,* May 9, 1774.

JOHN CLARK,[2] Shagreen and Mahogany Case-Maker, Now lies in the house lately occupied by Mr. Cowperthwait, next door to Mrs. Breese's near the Old Slip Market, and carries on his business as usual. He returns his hearty thanks to the publick in general, for their assistance at the late fire, in which he was a great sufferer.

---

[1] A similar advertisement appeared in 1775.
[2] First advertised in *The New-York Journal or General Advertiser,* July 30, 1767.

—*The New-York Gazette and the Weekly Mercury*, May 2, 1774.

JOHN CROSS.—Run away from his Bail, on Saturday the 4th June, Instant, a Man named John Cross, by Trade a Cabinet maker: He is about 5 Feet 8 Inches high, of a pale Complexion, has black Hair, a long Nose, given much to Liquor, and is very quarelsome. Whoever takes up and secures said Fellow in New-York Gaol, shall have Ten Pounds Reward, and all reasonable Charges paid by Thomas Brookman. N. B. All Masters of Vessels are forbid to take him away.—*The New-York Gazette*, June 13, 1763.

ANTHONY DEMELT.—To be Sold by Helena Mc. Pheadris, A House and Lot of Ground, next Door to Adolph Brass's on Golden Hill: It contains 25 Feet, Front and Rear, and 125 Feet in Length, is now occupied by Anthony Demelt, Chair-Maker.—*The New-York Mercury*, January 23, 1758.

ROBERT DIXSON.—If Robert Dixson, Cabinet-maker, and Joiner, be in this Place, and will apply to John Utte, Breeches-maker living near the Fly Market, or to John Graham, at the Duke of York's Head, at Whitehall Slip, may hear of George Dixon his Brother.—*The New-York Gazette*, November 21, 1763.

ADAM GALER, Windsor Chair-Maker, (lately from Philadelphia,) in Little Queen Street, next door to the Corner of Great George Street, opposite Hull's tavern, Makes and sells all kinds of Windsor Chairs, Any gentlemen or masters of vessels may be supplied with a neat assortment upon reasonable terms.—*Rivington's New-York Gazetteer*, August 25, 1774.

ANDREW GAUTEIR.—To be Sold, by Andrew Gauteir, in Princes-Street, Opposite Mr. David Provoost's in Broad Street; A large and neat Assortment of Windsor

Chairs, made in the best and neatest Manner, and well painted, Viz. High back'd, low back'd and Sackback'd Chairs and Settees, or double seated, fit for Piazza or Gardens. Children's dining and low Chairs, &c.

N.B. As the above Gauteir intends constantly to keep a large Number of all Sorts of the above Chairs by him for Sale, all Persons wanting such, may depend on being supplied with any Quantity, Wholesale or Retail, at reasonable Rates.—*The New-York Gazette or the Weekly Post-Boy,* April 18, 1765.

THOMAS GRIGG, senior, joiner is lately moved to the Cart & Horse, where he continues to make house-chairs, couches, closestool chairs, seats for houses, and easy chairs, likewise all sorts of joiners and cabinet work, done in the best manner: He has to Lett, the stables belonging to the Cart & Horse, very reasonable, to any gentleman or others that may want them.—*The New-York Mercury,* May 27, 1754.

THOMAS GRIGGS,[3] junior, at his house near the Gentleman's Coffee-House, makes house-chairs, easy-chairs, settees, couches, and closestool chairs, in the neatest manner, having a sufficiency of hands, and stuff, for that purpose. Whoever inclines to favour him with their custom, may depend on having their work done with the greatest care and dispatch.—*The New-York Mercury,* April 15, 1754.

THOMAS GRIGG.—This is to acquaint the Public, that Thomas Grigg, Joiner and Cabinet-Maker, Has removed to the house where James Duane, Esq; lived, opposite the Fly-market, where he carries on his business in all its branches; he also has two pleasant rooms to lett, with or without a cellar, fit for a merchant, who may board in the said house, and may have the rooms furnished. It would have an excellent stand for a notary-public.—

[3] Father and son may have spelled their names differently.

The New-York Gazette and Weekly Mercury, May 30, 1768.

CHARLES GULLIFER.—If Charles Gullifer, formerly of West Pennard, in Somerset, in England, by Trade a Cabinet Maker, who came from England about 10 years ago, and followed the Profession of a Schoolmaster, since his Arrival, (as Mr. Williams has been inform'd) is living; and will apply to Mr. Williams, he will hear of something to his Advantage.—*The New-York Gazette and Weekly Mercury*, June 6, 1768.

JONATHAN HAMPTON.—To be Sold, by Jonathan Hampton, in Chapel-Street, New York, Opposite Captain Andrew Law's, A large and neat Assortment of Windsor Chairs, made in the best and neatest Manner, & well painted, Viz. High Back'd, low back'd and Sack-back'd Chairs and Settees or double seated fit for Piazza or Gardens, Children's dining and low chairs, &c.
N.B. As the above Hampton intends constantly to keep a large Number of all Sorts of the above Chairs by him for Sale, all Persons wanting such, may depend on being supplied with any Quantity, wholesale or Retail at reasonable Rates.—*The New-York Journal or the General Advertiser*, May 19, 1768.

JOHN HOFFMAN.—All persons indebted to the estate of John Hoffman, late of this city, Cabinet-maker, deceased, are hereby desired immediately to settle and pay their accounts . . . —*The New-York Journal or the General Advertiser*, September 9, 1773.

HORNER.—To be Sold, At Public Vendue, on the 4th of March, if not sold before at private Sale, The house in beaver-street, opposite Mr. Bayley's Stove-Grate Warehouse, now occupied by Mr. Horner, Cabinet-Maker, . . . —*Rivington's New-York Gazetteer*, January 27, 1774.

HUBBELL & PATTERSON.—The partnership of Hubbell
and Patterson, Cabinet and Chair-Makers, was dissolved
the 20th of June last, the above business is now carried
on by Isaac Hubbel, at his shop in Little-Dock-Street,
near the Coffee-House, where he will always endeavour
to merit the favours of the public.—*Rivington's New-
York Gazetteer,* September 15, 1774.

THOMAS JONES.—Deserted from the Majesty's Army
. . . Thomas Jones, cabinet maker; . . . Born in the
County of Tipperary, Ireland . . . —*The New-York
Gazette and the Weekly Mercury,* September 30, 1771
(*Supplement*).

JOHN KELSO, Windsor Chair-Maker, from Philadelphia, at Mr. Hyer's, in Broad-street, next door to the
General's, Makes and sells all kinds of windsor chairs,
chairs for sulkies, &c. on the most reasonable terms; and
as he served a regular apprenticeship in one of the first
shops in that way in Philadelphia, he is persuaded he can
supply those who may be kind enough to favour him
with their custom, with as well-finish'd, strong, and neat
work as ever appeared in this city; and as the laying-out
as much of our money as possible at home, serves to keep
the balance of trade in our favour, he therefore hopes for
the encouragement of the respectable inhabitants of this
city, as well as those trading to the same, whose favours
by every way in his power to merit them, shall be gratefully acknowledged, by their Most Obedient Humble
Servant, JOHN KELSO.—*The New-York Gazette and the
Weekly Mercury,* August 8, 1774.

WILLIAM NORTON.—To be sold at Mr. Skaats, near the
Meal Market, very good Leather Chairs, by William
Norton.—*The New-York Weekly Journal,* September 29,
1740.

JOHN PARSONS, joiner, has lately set up his business
between the New and Fly-Markets, near his late master

Joshua Delaplains, makes all sorts of cabinet work, sitting and easy chairs, closestool chairs, and all other kinds of household furniture in that way. Those who incline to favor him with their custom, may depend on having their work done in the neatest manner.—*The New-York Mercury*, April 22, 1754.

SAMUEL PRINCE.—John Sheiuble, Organ Builder may be spoke with at Mr. Samuel Prince's Cabinet maker, at the Sign of the Chest of Drawers, in New York . . . — *The New-York Gazette and the Weekly Mercury*, March 30, 1772.

SAMUEL PRINCE.—A partnership has lately commenced between Robert Robinson and Michael Price, who have for sale at their store next door to Mr. Samuel Prince, shop-joiner, in Horse and Cart-street; a general assortment of dry goods . . . —*The New-York Gazette and the Weekly Mercury*, November 1, 1773.

SAMUEL PRINCE, Cabinetmaker, At the Sign of the Chest of Drawers, in William-Street, near the North Church, in New York: Makes and sells all sorts of cabinet work in the neatest manner, and on the lowest terms. Orders for the West Indies, and elsewhere, compleated, on the shortest notice.[4]

He has on hand, for sale, A parcel of the most elegant furniture, made of mahogany, of the very best quality, such as chest of drawers, chest upon chest, cloath presses, desks, desks and book cases of different sorts, chairs of many different and new pattens, beuro tables, dining tables, card tables, breakfast tables, tea tables, And many other sorts of Cabinet work, very cheap.—*The New-York Gazette and the Weekly Mercury*, February 6, 1775.

DANIEL SHAW.—Whereas a Letter directed to Daniel Shaw, Cabinet-Maker, in this City of New York, was on Thursday last delivered by the Letter Carrier thro' mis-

[4] Samuel Prince's advertisements still appeared in 1776.

take to a Person unknown: and as the Letter is supposed to be of some Consequence, it will be taken extremely kind of the Person who has it, if they will send it to the Printer hereof, in Broad Street—it can be of no Service to anyone but the Owner.—*The New-York Gazette,* Feburary 2, 1761.

CHARLES SHIPMAN, Ivory and Hardwood Turner, lately from England: Takes this Method to acquaint all ladies, gentlemen, &c. that having served a regular apprenticeship to a very considerable Turning Manufactory in Birmingham; he purposes carrying on that business here,[5] in all the various undermentioned articles; Therefore all those who please to favour him with their employ, may depend on being served with the strictest assiduity, and on the most reasonable terms. Mahogany waiters and bottle stands, billiard balls, bell handles, cups and balls, dice boxes, pack thread boxes, pepper boxes, soap boxes, washball boxes, patch boxes, raisin boxes, glove sticks, drum sticks and walking stick heads, paste rollers, round rulers and sugar hammers, tobacco sieves, sand dishes, ivory totums, tooth-pick-cases and eggs, nutmeg graters, pounce boxes and ivory thimbles, ivory netting, and knotting needles; tobacco stoppers, and cases for smelling boxes, counting-house seal handles, and steel seals cut with cyphers, ivory counters engraved with alphabets and figures, (very popular for children) back gammons and chess men; Cruet frames repair'd and German flutes tip'd in the neatest manner, oval picture frames, and sundry other articles too tedious to mention. —*The New-York Journal or the General Advertiser,* August 6, 1767.

WILLIAM TILOU.—On Wednesday, at Noon, a Fire broke out in the Shop of William Tilou, a Turner and Chair maker in Maiden-Lane, which immediately burnt to the ground, destroying all his Tools and Stock in Trade, to the entire Ruin of an honest, sober, industrious

[5] Charles Shipman's advertisements still appeared in 1768.

Man, with a distressed Family. The unhappy person is reduced to a State of unspeakable Distress; and as he is an Object deserving the Charity of all the humane Citizens, a Subscription has been opened for his Relief. Any Contribution sent to the Printer, will be most thankfully received, and immediately applied to enable him to commence Business again.—News item in *The New-York Gazette and the Weekly Mercury*, March 27, 1775.

PETER TILYOU.—Whereas a Report hath been industriously propagated, That Peter Tilyou, Senior, of the City of New-York, Chair-maker, has been very ill-used by his Son Vincent, and Ann his Wife; and that the said Vincent and his Wife, dragged the said, Father through the Entry by the Hair of his Head; and that they have from Time to Time gave him great Provocation: Wherefore, in order to Undeceive The Public, the said Vincent Tilyou, and Ann his Wife, being duly sworn on the Holy Evangelist of Almighty God, do depose and say, That the same is all false, scandalous and malicious Report, purely calculated, to injure the characters, of the Deponents, they having always avoided, as much as possible, giving their said Father any Provocation. And Further these deponents say not

Sworn this 15th day of   Vincent Tilyou
March 1770 before me,   Ann   Tilyou
Andrew Gautier Aldm.[6]

The New-York Gazette and the Weekly Mercury, March 26, 1770.

JOHN TREMAIN,[7] having declined the Stage, proposes to follow his Business of a cabinet-maker: and at the House of Mr. Norwood, near Long-Bridge, all Gentlemen and others may be supplied, at the Cheapest Rates, and in the neatest Manner, with all sorts of Cabinet-Work,

[6] The same Andrew Gautier before mentioned as a cabinet maker.
[7] A benefit was given for Mr. Tremain in January, 1752. The performance consisted of the *Tragical History of King Richard the Third*, and the Farce of *Lethe.—The New-York Gazette Revived in the Weekly Post-Boy*, January 20, 1752.

such as Chest-of-Drawers, Desks, Book-Cases, Clock-Cases, Dining and Tea-Tables, plain or scollopt; tea-Chests, Tea-Boards, Dressing-Boxes, Bedsteads &c. Those who incline to find their own Stuff, may have it work'd up with Dispatch, Honesty, and Faithfulness.— *The New-York Gazette Revived in the Weekly Post-Boy,* August 26, 1751.

ROBERT WALLACE, Joyner, Living in Beaver Street, at the Corner of New-Street, makes all Sorts of Cabinets, Scrutores, Desks and Book Cases, Drawers, Tables either square, round oval or quadrile, and Chairs of any Fashion. Any Gentlemen or Ladies who will please to favour him with their Custom, may depend on having their Work done after the best Manner, and at the most reasonable Rates.—*The New-York Gazette or the Weekly Post-Boy,* May 28, 1753.

WILLET & PEARSEE, Cabinet and Chair-makers, at the Sign of the Clothes-Press, nearly opposite the New Oswego market, at the Upper-End of Maiden-Lane. Continues to make in the very best manner Cabinet and Chair-Work of every kind. As they are determined by being punctual in performing, and in finishing their work with the greatest neatness and care, to aim at giving general satisfaction. They humbly embrace this way of offering their service, and will with gratitude acknowledge the kindness of all such as please to favour them with their commands.

They have on hand at present made of the best Mahogany, and in the neatest Manner,

A very handsome Desk and Book-Case,

A chest upon Chest,

A Lady's Dressing-Chest and Book-Case,

Three Desks, Three Sets of Chairs,

A Pair of Card-Tables, and several Tea-Tables, Stands, Breakfast and China Tables, Bureaus &c. &c.

N. B. Two Apprentices are wanting at the above place.— *Rivington's New York Gazetteer,* April 22, 1773.

MARINUS WILLETT, Has remov'd his Vendue Store to the house lately occupied by Waldron and Cornel, next door to Abraham Lotts, Esq; treasurer, and purposes to do all in his power to give satisfaction to whoever may be kind enough to employ him in that way; which he hopes, with the excellency of the situation, will be a sufficient inducement to those who have goods to dispose of by public auction, or on commissions at private sale.

Every article in the Cabinet and Chair way, May be had on the shortest notice, and executed in the best manner, by Willett and Pearsey, at the said vendue store, or at the sign of the clothes press near the Oswego-Market, at the upper end of Maiden-Lane, who will take dry goods in pay.

N.B. There is on hand at either of the above places an assortment of choice Mahogany furniture.—*The New York Gazette and the Weekly Mercury*, May 9, 1774.

MARINUS WILLETT.—Christian Stamler, Taylor and Habit Maker, from London, is removed from opposite the Coffee-House, Hunter's Quay, to the house that Mr. Marinus Willett lives in, in Queen Street near the Fly market. . . . —*The New-York Gazette and the Weekly Mercury*, May 8, 1775.

FURNITURE

FURNITURE OF GOVERNOR MONTGOMERY.—To Morrow being the twelfth day of this instant, at two o'clock in the afternoon, at the Fort, will be exposed to Sale by public Vendue the following Goods, belonging to the Estate of his late deceased Excellency Governor Montgomery, Viz.

A fine new yellow Camblet Bed, lined with Silk & laced which came from London with Capt Downing, with the Bedding, one fine Field Bedstead and Curtains, some blew Cloth lately come from London, for Liveries; and some white Drap Cloth, with proper Triming. Some broad gold Lace. A very fine Medicine Chest with great variety of valuable Medicines. A parcel of Sweet Meat & Jelly Glasses. A Case with 12 knives and twelve forks with Silver Handles guilded. Some good Barbados Rum. A considerable Quantity of Cytorn Water, a Flack with fine jesseme Oyl. A fine jack with Chain and Pullies &c. A large fixt Copper Boyling Pot. A large Iron Fire-place, Iron Bar and Doors for a Copper, A large lined Fire Skreen and Several other things All to be seen at the Fort . . . —*The New-York Gazette,* October 4-11, 1731.

SACKING-BOTTOM BEDSTEAD.—To be sold on Wednesday the 16th of January next, . . . a Suit of red Chaney Curtains, a Sac-king-bottom Bedstead, 3 Feather Beds and Bolsters, 1 Black Walnut Table 1 large Bell-metal Morter . . . —*The New-York Weekly Journal,* December 31, 1733.

HOUSEHOLD FURNISHINGS.—On Wednesday the 16th Instant will be Sold by Auction . . .

A Pair of large Gilt fram'd Sconces	A Parcell of Chairs
A Bean and Waits	A Parcell of black fram'd Pictures
A Tea Table and China	Pewter and Brass
A corner Cubbard	A Chocolate stone and Rowler
A Pair of brass andIrons	A Parcell of old Cordage
A Pair of Iron do	And Kitchen Utensills
A Bed and Bedsted	

The New-York Weekly Journal, April 4, 1740.

FURNITURE OF ANTHONY BYVANCK.—Accounts settled for the estate of Anthony Byvanck . . . all those who have a mind to Buy a Choice Clock, Black Walnut-Cubbord, and other Furniture belonging to the aforesaid Estate, may apply to said Bancker, who is impowered to dispose of the same.—*The New-York Weekly Journal,* April 4, 1743.

HOUSE FURNITURE.—To be sold at Public Vendue . . . House Furniture, as Feather-Beds, Bolsters, Pillows Quilts, Blankets, Curtains and Bedsteads, green Damask seated, red leather and Cane Chairs, Looking-Glasses, dressing and other Tables, a Mahogany Desk and chest of Drawers, Carpets, China, Glasses, a clock, Kitchen Furniture, some Boxes of Candles and a Pair of Gloves.— *The New-York Weekly Post-Boy,* June 16, 1746.

STOVES.—This Evening will be presented, A Comedy called, A Bold Stroke for a Wife. The House being new floor'd, is made warm and comfortable; besides which, Gentlemen and Ladies may cause their Stoves to be brought.—*The New-York Gazette Revived in the Weekly Post-Boy,* November 19, 1750.

CORNISH BEDSTEAD.—To be Sold New Cornish Bedstead, together with the Bed, Bolster, and two Pillars, a Suit of fine Calico Curtains, and all the Furniture belonging to the same; Any Person that inclines to purchase the Bed and Furniture, may apply to the Printer hereof. N.B. It is all New.—*The New-York Evening Post,* April 8, 1751.

MESSACIPIA TABLE.—To be Sold at publick Vendue on the 25th Day of March next, beginning at ten of the Clock in the Morning, at the House and Inn late of Jonathan Ogden, of the City of New-York, deceas'd, . . . The said House and Lot of Land, with Stables. . . . Also divers sorts of Furniture, household Goods, Utensils, one Cow, and a Table called a Messacipia-Table . . . —*The New-York Gazette and the Weekly Post-Boy,* February 26, 1753.

MAHOGANY CHEST OF DRAWERS.—To be Shot for, on Tuesday the 22d. of January next, a good Mahogany Chest of Drawers, with Eagle's Claw Feet, a Shell on each knee, and fluted Corners, with good Brass Work and Locks: Those that intend to try their Fortune for the same, may apply to Mr. George Peters, next door to Mr. Peter Marschalk's, in Broad-Street, at the Corner of Flatten-Barragh, where they may see the above:

There will be Twenty Chances, at 14 Shillings each Chance.—*The New-York Gazette or the Weekly Post-Boy,* December 31, 1753.

✓STOVES.—New-Invented Pennsylvania Stoves, both round and Square, to be sold by, Peter Clopper, opposite the Fly-Market. They are remarkable for making a Room Warm and comfortable with very little Wood.—*The New-York Mercury,* November 9, 1761.

HOUSE FURNITURE.—To be Sold this Day at Public Vendue . . . All the house Furniture; consisting of Feather Beds, Tables, Chairs, Pots, Pans and Kitchen Furniture; Silver Spoons and Silver Punch Bowls, some Liquors and sundry other things too numerous to mention.—*The New-York Gazette or the Weekly Post-Boy,* November 12, 1761.

WINDSOR CHAIRS.—To be Sold, by Thomas & James Franklin, At their Store facing Fly Market; Best Jamaica Spirits, West-India and New-England Rum . . . a Parcel of low and high back Windsor Chairs . . . —*The New-York Gazette,* January 4, 1762.

HANGINGS.—Roper Dawson, has to sell among other things . . . a great variety of Paper Hangings and in Figures, Bass Relievo for Ceilings, &c. Marble Chimney Pieces; gilt Leather for Hangings; Looking Glasses of neatest Patterns . . . —*The New-York Gazette or the Weekly Post-Boy,* June 3, 1762.

SETTEE.—On Wednesday last . . . the Steeple of Trinity-Church in this City was struck with the Lightning, . . . Mr. Callow's House in Wall-Street, was struck much about the same Time, but sustained little or no damage. It came down the Chimney, and run along the Brass Nails that was in a Settee near the Hearth, blackening the Heads of all of them; it then entered the Settee, shivered it to Pieces, and took its Course thro' the Hearth

into the Cellar.—News item in *The New-York Gazette,*
July 12, 1762.

CHEST UPON CHEST.—To be sold household goods
belonging to a gentleman leaving the province. . . . A
book case, chest upon chest, mahogany tables, chairs
&c. &c. looking-glasses, pictures, china . . . —*The New-
York Mercury,* November 29, 1762.

HOUSEHOLD FURNITURE.—To be Sold, by private Sale
by John Martin, in Hanover Square. An exceeding neat
Mahogany Clothes Press, Desk and Book-Case, in a new
Taste, and executed in the neatest Manner a four posted
Mahogany Bedstead, fluted Pillars, with Cotton check
Furniture, fring'd and Tossels. A neat mahogany Field
Bedstead, fluted Posts, with very fine printed Callico
Furniture. A round Mahogany Pillar, and Claw Table.
A Sett of fine Tea Table China. . . . —*The New-York
Gazette or the Weekly Post-Boy,* January 27, 1763.

MAHOGANY DESK.—John Brinner, Cabinet and Chair
maker . . . carves all kinds of bedsteads, with carved or
plain cornishes . . . N. B. A neat mahogany desk and
book case, in the Chinese taste to be sold.—*The New-
York Mercury,* January 3, 1763.

WALL PAPER.—James Walker . . . has to sell very
cheap, the following goods, imported in the last vessels.
Great variety of paper hangings, viz. Flock, or velvet,
and mock chinese, . . . —*The New-York Gazette or the
Weekly Post-Boy,* May 5, 1763.

MAHOGANY FURNITURE.—To be Sold, at Vendue, Sundry pieces of neat mahogany furniture, lately imported
from London by, and was the property of the deceased
Mr. James Morison (one of the unfortunate Gentlemen,
who lately perished in crosing this bay) viz. A mahogany
book case and drawers, in the neatest taste, finely ornamented; a mahogany bed stead, a mahogany desk; gen-

teel mirrors; mahogany chairs; tables; a curious sett of pictures; &c. &c.   Also, a parcel of curious books.—*The New-York Gazette*, November 21, 1763.

FURNITURE OF JOSEPH HAYNES.—To be sold at publick Vendue, on Monday the 17th inst. the household and kitchen furniture, of the late Mr. Joseph Haynes, Consisting of a variety of chas'd and plain plate, mahogany dining, dressing, card, and tea tables, chairs and desks, pier, sconce, and dressing glasses, feather beds, bedsteads, chest of drawers, table cloths, napkins, sheets and pillow cases, with a variety of china tureen dishes; plates and bowls, cups and saucers, &c. . . . —*The New-York Mercury*, March 10, 1766.

SIDE TABLES.—A Few Crates of Stone Ware, with some choice Marble Slabs, for Side-Tables, to be sold cheap by Captain William Stewart, next Door to the Honourable Joseph Reade's, Esq; in King-Street.—*The New-York Mercury*, December 28, 1767.

A BILLIARD TABLE compleat, to be sold.   Enquire of James Wessels, living in Fare-Street.—*The New-York Gazette and the Weekly Mercury*, February 18, 1771.

WINDSOR CHAIR.—A neat Windsor Chair to be sold. Enquire of J. Allen, near the Fly, Also An extraordinary good Saddle and Chair Horse.—*The New-York Gazette and the Weekly Mercury*, April 15, 1771.

PINE CHEST.—Whereas the house of the subscriber was, on the night of the 18th inst. robbed of a pine chest painted prussian blue . . . —*The New-York Gazette and the Weekly Mercury*, January 13, 1772.

FURNITURE OF RICHARD VASSAL.—To be sold at public Vendue, on Tuesday the 7th July next, The sale to begin precisely at 10 o'clock in the afternoon, All the elegant and valuable household furniture of Richard Vassal, Esq;

(who has lately embarked with his family for Jamaica), at his late dwelling-house in Wall-street, belonging to, and formerly occupied by Mr. William Kelly, consisting of handsome pier, and sconce glasses, pictures, china, mahogany four post bedsteads, bureaus, desks, tables, chairs, feather beds, Axminster and Scotch carpets, and a variety of kitchen furniture, the whole little, if any the worse for wear, being lately purchased new from the makers and importers.—*The New-York Gazette and the Weekly Mercury*, June 29, 1772.

MAHOGANY FURNITURE.—At publick Vendue, will positively be sold, to the highest Bidder, at Thomas Nixon's, at the Fly Market, on Tuesday the 4th day of May, a Large quantity of new and second hand Mahogany Furniture, amongst which are two desks with book-cases, two chests of drawers, four desks, four bureau tables, four dining do.. four card tables, four tea do. four setts of chairs, two arm'd do. and a variety of other articles.—*The New-York Gazette and the Weekly Mercury*, April 12, 1773.

CARPETS.—To be sold at public vendue, on the Coffee-House Bridge, on Thursday next, the 26 inst. at XII o'clock: One very large Persian carpet; six Scotch carpets, of different sizes, and three pieces of Scotch carpeting.—*Rivington's New-York Gazetteer*, May 19, 1774.

CARPETS, Of the Royal Manufactory at Challiott, which exceed every other kind of carpets for beauty, strength, and duration of colours, Likewise choice of Turky carpets, to be seen at Christopher Miller's.—*Rivington's New-York Gazetteer*, September 15, 1774.

CARVERS AND GILDERS

NICHOLAS BERNARD, Carver, at Mr. Poree's, Surgeon and Operator for the Teeth, near the Exchange, Broad-street; Has for sale, a very neat Assortment of Looking

Glasses, in the most elegant and newest Fashion, with carved, and carved and gilt Frames, do. Pediments and plain Mahogany and Walnut; also Dressing Glasses, Girondoles, chimney Pieces, Figures of Plaster of Paris, Brackets, &c. Paper Machine for ceilings, the King's Coat of Arms, neatly carved, fit for Church or public Building. N.B. The above Articles will be sold very cheap.—*The New-York Journal or the General Advertiser*, June 1, 1769.

STEPHEN DWIGHT, late an apprentice to Henry Hardcastle, carver, has set up his business, between the Ferry Stairs and Burlington Slip, where he carves all sorts of ship and house work: also tables, chairs, picture and looking glass frames, and all kinds of work for cabinet makers, in the best manner and all reasonable terms.—*The New-York Mercury*, July 21, 1755.

STEPHEN DWIGHT, Takes this Opportunity to acquaint the Public, that he Intends to move the first of May, into the House of Mr. Johnston, Carpenter, and the Shop opposite, where Mr. Osborne, Cabinet Maker, now lives, near the Moravian Meeting, where he intends to follow Carving in general as usual, and also Portrait and History Painting. N.B. He also will teach drawing in Crayon, black and white chalk, Indian Ink, and black Lead Pencil, in the quickest and best Manner.—*The New York Gazette*, April 12, 1762.

DWIGHT & DAVIS.—To be sold a three story brick house . . . apply to subscriber Stephen Dwight. N.B. Said Dwight and Davis continue to carry on the business of carving and gilding as usual, where any ladies or gentlemen may be supplied with girandoles, looking-glasses, and picture frames, &c.—*Rivington's New-York Gazetteer*, March 10, 1774.

HENRY HARDCASTLE.—Run away from Henry Hardcastle, of the city of New York, carver, an apprentice lad . . . —*The New-York Mercury*, June 30, 1755.

JOHN GIBBONS.—Twenty Dollars Reward, Deserted from His Majesty's 29th regiment, 22nd of July last . . . John Gibbons, carver and gilder, aged 27 years, 5 feet 11½ inches high, ruddy complexion, brown hair, light grey eyes, thin visage, and much carbuncled, straight and light made.—*The New-York Gazette and the Weekly Mercury,* September 30, 1771 (*Supplement*)

MINSHALL,[8] Carver and Gilder, from London, lives in Dock-Street, Near opposite Bolton and Sigell's Tavern, Takes this Method of informing Ladies and Gentlemen, where they may have Carved Frames for Glasses, Picture Frames, Tables, Chairs, Girandoles, Chimney Pieces, Brackets, Candle Stands, Clock and Watch Cases, Bed and Window Cornicing: He makes Paper Ornaments for Ceilings and Stair Cases, in the present Mode.—*The New-York Journal or the General Advertiser,* December 7, 1769.

JAMES STRACHAN, Carver and Gilder, from London, in the Broadway near the Old English Church, in New York; Makes and sells all Sorts of Picture and Glass Frames, Tables, Gerendoles, Brackets; and Candle Stands, carved and gilt, in Oil or burnish'd Gold. Likewise all Sorts of House-Carvings, in Wood or Stone, at the lowest Prices.—*The New-York Gazette or the Weekly Post-Boy,* October 24, 1765.

JAMES STRACHAN & DAVID DAVIDSON.—James Strachan, at the Cabinet-Warehouse, upper End of Wall-street, New-York, Begs leave to return his most hearty thanks to the ladies and gentlemen of this city, &c. for their favours during his co-partnership with Mr. D. Davidson, deceased, and hopes for their continuance. As he intends to carry on the business in its various branches, his Customers may depend on every order being fulfil'd with integrity and all possible dispatch, with the best work

---

[8] Name also spelled Minshull. In later advertisements (1771, 1772) Minshall mentions that he teaches drawing.

and materials, having imported by the ship Beulah, Capt.
Henderson, an assortment of brass furniture, &c. of different kinds, and newest patterns; also looking glasses
of different sizes, in carv'd and gilt frames, likewise glass
without frames, so that his employers may chuse frames
of any pattern or price, either in oyl or burnish'd gold.
All sorts of picture frames, gerandoles, brackets, table
frames, &c. House carving of every kind, gilding and all
sorts of cabinet work, perform'd in the neatest manner
and lowest prices. N.B.—He has also imported some elegant plaister busts.—*The New-York Gazette and the
Weekly Mercury,* October 3, 1768.

JAMES STRACHAN.—All persons who have any demands
on the estate of James Strachan, late of this city, Carver
and Cabinet-maker, deceased, are desired to bring in
their accounts, in order for a settlement; and all those
indebted to said estate, are requested to make speedy
payment, to Jonathan Blake, Thomas Barrow, or James
Barrow, who are empower'd to settle and receive the
same, by Catharine Strachan, Administratrix.

N.B. The business of the late James Strachan, will be
carried on in the same shop, as usual; and his widow
hopes for the continuance of the favours of her late husband's friends, and the public in general, which will be
thankfully acknowledged.—*The New-York Journal or
the General Advertiser,* February 9, 1769.

LOOKING GLASS MAKERS

GERARDUS DUYCKINCK.—Lookin-glasses new Silvered,
and the Frames plaine Japan'd or Flowered, also all Sorts
of Picktures, made and Sold, all manner of painting Work
done. Likewise Lookinglasses, and all sorts of painting
Coullers and Oyl sold at reasonable Rates, by Gerardus
Duyckinck at the Sign of the two Cupids, near the Old
Slip Market. N.B. Where you may have ready Money
for old Lookinglasses.—*The New-York Weekly Journal,*
January 6, 1735.

GERARDUS DUYCKINCK, Living near the old Slip Market in New-York, continues to carry on the Business of his late Father deceas'd, Viz. Limning, Painting, Varnishing, Japanning, Gilding, Glasing, and Silvering of Looking-Glasses, all done in the best Manner.

He also will teach any young Gentleman the art of Drawing, with Painting on Glass; and sells all sorts of Window-Glasses, white lead, oil and Painter's Colours.—*The New York Weekly Post-Boy,* August 18, 1746.

GERARDUS DUYCKINCK.—To Be Sold by Gerardus Duyckinck, on the Dock, between the Old Slip, and Coentjes Market. A very fine Assortment of Glass Pictures, Paintings on Glass, prospects, History, Sea Skips and Land Skips & large Assortment of Entry and Stair Case Pieces ready framed, With the Maps of the World: And in four Parts. London all on Rollers, Prints of Sundry Sorts, Do. ready Coloured for Jappanning;

Also a very good Assortment of Limners Colours, Japanners Do. with Gold Leaf, jappanners Gold Dust, Silver Lead and Silver Dust, Painted Colours, Glass of all Sizes, Linsead Oyl, and Sundry other Ship Chandlers Ware.

The said Gerardus Duyckinck, follow the Above Art of Painting, Gilding, Japanning &c. as usual at a Reasonable Rate.—*The New-York Weekly Journal,* March 19, 1750.

JAMES FODDY Looking Glass-Maker, late from London Hath brought a Parcel of very fine Pier Glasses, Sconces with fine Brass Arms; Dressing-Glasses also of sundry sorts, in Glass-Frames, Glass and Gold Frames, Gold Frames Japann'd, Wallnut and Olive Wood Frames.

He is likewise in a readiness to new Quick-Silver and take the stains out of Old Looking-Glasses, which will render them as good as ever.

He also undertakes to square Diamond Cut and Polish Old Looking-Glasses, and converts them to the best Use.

All which he performs at reasonable Rates, at the

House of Mr. Verplank in the City of New-York.—*The New-York Gazette,* October 6-13, 1729.

JAMES FODDY, citizen and Glass-seller of London, who arrived here the latter End of last June and brought with him a Parcel of very fine Looking-Glasses of all Sorts, and likewise appeared several Times in this Paper, to acquaint the Publick, that he undertook to alter and amend Old Looking-Glasses but he not meeting suitable Encouragement, is shortly determined for the West-Indies: All Persons therefore who are inclin'd to have their Glasses repair'd or buy new, may apply to the James Foddy at Mr. Verplank's in New-York.—*The New-York Gazette,* April 21-27, 1730.

JAMES FODDY.—To prevent the Publick from being further imposed upon James Foddy (after two years retirement) is again return'd to the old Bowling-Green, where he Undertakes to remedy and put in order Looking-Glasses that have been injur'd or damaged by ignorant Pretenders to silvering likewise to square, Diamond Cut, Polish, and Silver old Looking-Glasses, and convert them to the best Use, which will be perform'd at Reasonable Rates and the Utmost Expedition. per JAMES FODDY.—*The New-York Weekly Journal,* May 9, 1737.

ANTHONY LAMB.—Foliating, or Quick-Silvering all sorts of Looking-Glasses and Sconces, neatly done with care and expedition, by Anthony Lamb, mathematical instrument maker, living on Hunters' Key; where may be had Godfry's new invented quadrant, for taking the lattitude or other altitudes at sea, hydrometers for trying the exact strength of spirits, large surveying instruments in a more curious manner than usual; which may be used in any weather without exception, small ditto which may be fixed on the head of a walking stick, and lengthened to a commodious height, guaging instruments as now in use, according to an act of assembly with all other mathematical instruments for sea or land, by wholesale or retail, at reasonable rates.—*The New-York Mercury*, June 11, 1753.

JOHN MILLER.—All Persons indebted to the Estate of George Montgomerie, deceased, are hereby desired to pay the same to John Miller, Gardner, at the old Bowling Green . . . —N.B. You may be furnished with the best kind of Garden Seeds, of several Sorts, by the above John Miller. Also, Lookinn-Glasses, that have been abus'd or spoil'd by ignorant Pretenders, to Silvering may be rectified and put in Order.—*The New-York Weekly Journal*, February 17, 1735.

MINSHULL'S LOOKING GLASS STORE, Removed from Smith street to Hanover-square (opposite Mr. Goelet's the sign of the Golden Key,) has for sale, an elegant assortment of Looking Glasses, in oval or square ornamental frames ditto mahogany. The greatest variety of girandoles ever imported to this city. Brackets for busts or lustres and ornaments for chimney pieces, as tablets, frieze's &c. Birds and baskets of flowers, for the top of book cases or glass frames, gilt bordering for rooms by the yard. Engravings by Strange, Wollet, Vivare's & other eminent masters. A pleasing variety of mezzotintos well chosen and beautifully coloured. Also, an elegant assortment of frames, without Glass. Any Lady or Gentleman that have Glass in old Fashioned frames, may have them cut to ovals or put in any pattern that pleases them best. The above frames may be finished white, or green and white, purple, or any colour that suits the furniture of the room, or gilt in oil or burnished gold equal to the best imported.

I flatter myself, from the assurance of my correspondent in London, that when the difference is settled between England and the Colonies, of having my store constantly supplied with the above articles, as will give a general satisfaction to those who please to favour me with their command.

N.B. An apprentice is wanted to the Carving and

Gilding; none need apply but those who have a lad of a sober and promising genius, and are willing to give a Premium. Money for broken Looking Glass are taken in Exchange.—*The New-York Journal or the General Advertiser*, March 16, 1775.

LOOKING GLASSES

LOOKING GLASSES.—To be Sold by Publick Vendue at the Old Slip-Market on Tuesday November 6th, five fine large looking-Glasses.—*The New-York Gazette*, October 15-22, 1733.

LOOKING GLASS.—Among other things sold by the printer . . . Large Looking-Glass, six Foot long and two Foot and half broad.—*The New-York Gazette or the Weekly Post-Boy*, April 12, 1756.

IMPORTED LOOKING GLASSES.—Just imported from London by Sidney Breese . . . Looking Glasses, framed in the Newest Taste, from 8s to £30 a piece . . . —*The New-York Mercury*, June 1, 1761.

LOOKING GLASSES, SCONCE GLASSES, DRESSING GLASSES, UNDRESSING GLASSES . . . imported by Sidney Breese from London.—*The New-York Mercury*, May 23, 1763.

A LOOKING-GLASS GRINDER, and Polisher, is wanted for South-Carolina. If there be such an One at Hand, he may apply to the Printer hereof.—*The New-York Gazette*, January 5-12, 1767.

LOOKING GLASSES.—Sold at Rhinelander's Store . . . Looking-Glasses of all sizes, from 2 l. to 14 l. each . . . —*Rivington's New-York Gazetteer*, January 13, 1774.

LOOKING GLASSES.—A Very elegant assortment of both oval and square, of various sizes, and Scotch carpets and carpeting, to be sold very low, by John Stites.—*Riving-ton's New-York Gazetteer*, May 12, 1774.

UPHOLSTERERS

RICHARD BIRD, Upholsterer, lately arrived from London, Takes this Method to acquaint those Gentlemen and Ladies who will Please to Honour him with their Commands, that he will execute his Business in the Most approved Manner now in Vogue: He is to be heard of (at present) in Cortland Street, opposite the late Alderman Cortland's. N.B. Paper hung on the most reasonable terms.—*The New-York Mercury*, June 15, 1761.

JOHN BROWER, Upholsterer, At the Crown and Cushion, in Broad-Street; Makes all kinds of Beds, Mattrasses, Festeen Window Curtains, stuffs and covers Sophas, Couches, Easy Chairs, French Chairs, back Stools, &c. Paper hangings put up in City or Country in the best Manner: said Brown [*sic*] makes Tents, Camp Equipage, and all Branches in that Business, performed in the best Manner, and at reasonable Rates. It shall be my chief Care and Study, to use my best Endeavours to bring every Thing in the least Compass of Expence possible, to those who shall be pleased to employ me.—*The New-York Mercury*, May 20, 1765.

STEPHEN CALLOW, Upholsterer, from London, Now living at the lower End of Stone-Street, in New-York; Performs all Sorts of Upholsterers Work, Beds, Chairs, Seattees, &c. and likewise hangs Rooms with Paper or Stuff in the newest Fashion. N.B. He also hangs Bells in the best Manner.—*The New-York Gazette Revived in the Weekly Post-Boy*, November 6, 1749.

STEPHEN CALLOW.—All Persons having any Demands on Stephen Callow, of this City are desired to bring in their Accounts and they shall receive Payment; & all those indebted to the said Callow, are desired to dis-

charge the same, by the first of March next, to prevent
trouble, as he intends to leave the City in March.—*The
New-York Gazette or the Weekly Post-Boy*, February
16, 1764.

STEPHEN CALLOW, Upholsterer, Is returned to this
City, and lives at his own House in Wall-Street, being the
Place he usually lived in; where he intends to carry on
his Business in all its various Branches and will be much
obliged to Gentlemen, Ladies, and others, who please to
favour him with their Commands, which he will execute
in the newest and genteelest Taste.—*The New-York
Gazette and the Weekly Mercury*, June 6, 1768 (*Supplement*).

CHRISTOPHER THOMAS CLARKE, In Broad-Street, Corner of Flattin-Burgh Hill, Intending to follow the Cabinet and Upholsterers Business, will sell at publick Sale
all his remaining Store of Dry Goods and Jewellery; the
Sale to begin this Morning and continue till all are sold.
Goods selling daily at Moore and Lynsens's Vendue;
also a valuable Negro Wench, who is a good Cook, and
well recommended, to be sold at private Sale.—*The New-
York Mercury*, August 18, 1766.

JOSEPH COX, Upholsterer, from London, now living in
the house lately possessed by Charles Johnston, next
door to Dr. William Brownjohn, in Hanover Square;
Makes beds, Window Curtains, chairs, &c. and every
other articles in the upholstery way, in the neatest and
most genteel manner, and on the most reasonable terms;
and will be much obliged to all gentlemen, Ladies and
others, for their custom, whose work shall be finished
with care and dispatch.—*The New-York Mercury*, July
19, 1756.

JOSEPH COX.—Just imported in the Minerva, Capt.
Tillet, from London, and to be sold very cheap, by Joseph
Cox, Upholsterer, at the Royal-Bed and Star, in Wall-

street, A Neat Assortment of very handsome Paper
Hangings, and a great Variety of Furniture Checks of
the newest-fashioned Colours, Worsted Damasks, Mor-
reens, Harrateens, and Chineas, Lines and Tossels,
Cotton Counterpaines, green Musqueto Neeting, superfine India Chintz Counterpaines, with every other Article
in the Upholstery Way, and all kinds of Work in that
Branch, done as usual, at the lowest Rates.—*The New-
York Gazette and the Weekly Mercury,* February 22,
1768.

JOSEPH Cox, Upholsterer, Cabinet and Chair Maker
from London, at the Royal Bed and Star, in Wall-street,
New York, Makes all sorts of canopy festoon, field, and
tent bedsteads and furniture; also every sort of drapery,
window curtains; likewise sopha, settees, couches, bur-
gairs, French elbow, easy and corner chairs; back stools,
mewses, ribband back, gothic and rail back chair; ladies
and gentlemens desk and book cases, cabinets, chest of
drawers, commode dressing and toilet tables; writing,
reading, side board, card, and night ditto, cloth presses,
and chest China shelves, ecoinures, fire screens, voiders,
brackets for lustres and busts: with every other article
in the cabinet and upholstery branches: All finished in
the newest Taste, and greatest dispatch.

Likewise just opened, a great variety of lines and
tassels for bed and window curtains, of different colours;
lines, and a few very handsome balance tassels for hall
lanthorns; two sets of black silk tassels for palls, with
a large assortment of bed laces, amongst which is some
white cotton bed lace of a new manufactory; and white
fringers for ditto.

N.B. All sorts of hangings put up in the best manner,
camp equipage compleated, and matrasses of all sorts
and prices.—*Rivington's New-York Gazetteer,* October
7, 1773 (*Supplement*).

JOHN DAVIS, Takes this method to inform his friends
and the public in general, that he has opened a Shop

in the house formerly occupied by James and Arthur Jarvis, in Queen-street, between Beekman and Burling slips, where he proposes to carry on the Upholstery Business in its various branches; viz. tents, camp bedsteads, drums and colours, &c. &c. where all those who are pleased to favour him with their commands, shall meet with general satisfaction.—*The New-York Gazette and the Weekly Mercury*, December 9, 1776.

ELIZABETH EVANS, Takes this method to acquaint her friends and the public, that she is returned to this city, where she has been employed for several years, and given general satisfaction, in making up in the neatest manner and newest taste, all sorts of Upholstery work, such as festoon bed and window curtains, field or camp beds, Ketty fishers, wrought quilts, chair, sopha and settee cases; also ladies boned waiscoats and stays; all which she will execute with care and punctuality. Any commands for her, sent to Benjamin Getfield's, Breechesmaker, No. 198, in Queen-Street, opposite Burling's Slip, will be immediately attended to.—*The New-York Gazette and the Weekly Mercury*, August 26, 1776.

THEODOSIUS FOWLER, Upholsterer, Opposite the old English Church, Great George Street, Makes all sorts of Canopy, festoon, field bed, and window drapery curtains, also stuffed sofas, settees, couches, French, elbow, easy, corner and backstool chairs, with every other article in the upholstery branch, finished in the genteelest and newest taste with the greatest of dispatch. Also just imported, a great variety of lines and tassels for beds and window curtains of various colours, with an assortment of bed lace of different kinds.

N.B. All sorts of paper hangings put in the best and cheapest manner, and all sorts of mattrasses of sundry prices.—*Rivington's New-York Gazetteer*, June 2, 1774.

JAMES HUTHWAITE, Upholsterer and Chair stuffer from London. Now living at Mr. M'Mullan's in Han-

over Square, New-York; Makes up all Sorts of Beds and
Window Curtains in the neatest Manner: Also Matrasses and Beds for Sea: He likewise undertakes to
destroy the Buggs entirely, without damaging the Furniture; And does all Sorts of Paper Hangings after the
compleatest Manner.—*The New-York Gazette Revived
in the Weekly Post-Boy*, June 19, 1749.

JAMES HUTHWAITE AND STEPHEN CALLOW, Uphol-
sterers from London, living in Bridge-Street, near the
Long-Bridge; Makes all Sorts of Beds, Settees, Chairs
and Couches, after the newest Fashion: Likewise stuffs
Riding Chairs, and hangs Rooms with Paper and Other
Things.—*The New-York Gazette Revived in the Weekly
Post-Boy*, April 9, 1750.

GEORGE RICHEY, Upholsterer and Tent-Maker, from
Great-Britain, at his Shop two Doors from the Merchant's-Coffee-House; Makes all sorts of Beds, Chairs
and easy Chairs, Settees, Couch-Beds, Suppose; likewise
Field and Tent Beds, fitting for Gentlemen of the Army;
with all sorts of Tents and Markees fitting for the Cam-
paign, and all sorts of Matrasses fitting for the Sea or
Land Service.
    N.B. He likewise has a great Variety of Paper Hang-
ings for Rooms of the newest Patterns.   All Gentlemen,
Ladies and others, that please to favour him with their
Custom, may depend on having any of the above Articles
on the most reasonable Rates.—*The New-York Mercury*,
July 30, 1759.

GEORGE RICHEY, Upholsterer and tent-Maker, At the
Sign of the Crown and Thistle at the Upper End of
Bayard-Street.   Takes this Method to inform the Public,
that he makes all Sorts of Upholstery Work, in the
newest and genteelest Fashions, practised in London;
such as Beds, Window-Curtains, Chairs, Easy-Chairs,
Couches, setees, Sofa's, Field and Tent Beds, Camp
Tables and Stools, all Sorts of Tents & Markees, square

and Horsemen's Tents, with Valeces for ditto, also Havarsacks, Kettle Bags, and Camp Colours. Paper hung, and all Sorts of Matrasses, proper for either Land or Sea Service, made and sold as above; likewise Tassels for Furniture and Chariots, as good and cheap, as can be imported from England. Any Ladies or Gentlemen, that pleased to favour him with their Employment, may depend upon being well served, and at the most reasonable Rates.—*The New-York Chronicle*, May 8-15, 1769.

JOHN TAYLOR, Upholsterer and House-Broker from London . . . sells the following . . . Four Post, bureau, table, tent, field and turnup bedsteads, with silk and worsted damask, morine, harateen, china, printed cotton for check furnitures; festoon, venetian, and drapery window curtains, easy chairs, sophas, tent and camp equipages; floor and bed side carpets, feather beds, blankets, quilts and counterpains, sconce, chimney pier and dressing glasses in mahogany, carved and gilt frames, card, dining, tea, dressing and night tables; mahogany and other chairs, fire-irons, brass fenders, shovels, pokers, and tongs, copper tea-kettles sauce pans, and all manner of chamber, parlour and kitchen furniture too tedious to mention . . . Funerals decently performed.—*The New-York Journal or General Advertiser*, March 24, 1768.

JOHN TAYLOR, Late of Cow-Foot-Hill in the City of New-York, Upholsterer, but now of the Glass-House, at Newfoundland, in the Out-Ward of the said City, Returns his most grateful Thanks to those Ladies and Gentlemen who were pleased to encourage him in that Business; but finding it not being possible to answer his Expectations, has declined the same, and removed to the aforementioned Place, commonly called or known by the Name of the Glass-House; . . .—*The New-York Gazette and the Weekly Mercury*, June 13, 1768 (*Supplement*).

JOHN TAYLOR, Late of the Glass-House; Returns his most sincere thanks to the ladies and gentlemen of the city, and the public in general, for all the favour they have been pleased to confer on him, and begs leave to inform them he has remov'd into the house next to Mr. Ennis Graham's in Wall-street: where he intends carrying on the business of a cabinet maker, upholsterer, and auctioneer; such ladies, gentlemen, and merchants, who shall be pleased to honour him with their commands, may depend the greatest attention shall be paid to discharge all trusts reposed in him, in a most accurate and early manner. He also proposes buying and selling by public or private sale, estates, ships, stores, all manner of household furniture, linen, china, plate, jewels, books, and all sorts of wares and merchandise, &c. Also takes in exchange for new work executed by him any of the above articles.

The following information is with great deference offered, and humbly conceiv'd it may tend to some recommendation. The buying and selling all the above recited articles has been his sole study for seventeen years, viz. Eight of them under his father, and nine for himself; and farther is at this juncture a sworn exchange broker and appraisor, of the city of London.—*The New-York Gazette and the Weekly Mercury*, June 4, 1770.

RICHARD WENMAN Upholsterer, near the Broad Way, in Little Queen Street, near the Scot's Meeting-House. Being inform'd by some of his good Friends, that it has been publickly reported, he did not carry on the Upholsterer's Business: Takes this Method to inform the Gentlemen and Ladies of this City, that he Makes Beds and Furniture of all Sorts, Tents of all Sorts, Puts up Paper Linings of Rooms, and Performs all Parts of the Upholsterer's Business in the neatest Manner.

Has to sell, Lines and Tossels, Also a Negro Boy, about 15 or 16 Years old, who has had the small Pox.—*The New-York Gazette or the Weekly Post Boy*, January 6, 1763.

RICHARD WENMAN, Upholster, in Little Queen's-Street, opposite the New-York Arms, has to sell; A

Parcel of live Feathers, very cheap for Cash or short
Credit; likewise has to sell, all Sort of bed Binding, of
different Colours; he has likewise to sell, Tossels and
Line for Window Curtains; he likewise follows the Upholsterer's Business, and will do his Endeavour to satisfy
those that is willing to employ him.—*The New-York
Mercury*, March 17, 1766.

RICHARD WENMAN, is once more obliged to acquaint
the Public, that he still continues carrying on the Upholsterers Business as usual, altho' it has been reported by
some malicious Person or Persons, that he had quitted
his Business entirely; which Report, he hopes will be
more to his Advantage than to his Disadvantage. He has
to dispose of some Lines and Tussels of different Colours,
for Window Curtains. The Person who borrowed the
Key that he used to take down Bedsteads with, is desired
to return it again.—*The New-York Gazette and the
Weekly Mercury*, July 16, 1770.

BLANCH WHITE, Upholsterer from London, Two Doors
above Mr. Parker's Printing-office Beaver Street: Makes
all kinds of Bed Furniture, in the newest Fashion, and
at the most reasonable Rates: also Tents, Marquees,
Bell Tents, Horsemen's Tents, private Tents, Drums,
&c. &c.
N.B. The said Blanch White, has followed the Business
for many Years past in Philadelphia, and must be known
to some Gentlemen of the Military in this City, to which
she is now removed; and will be very careful in execut-
ing any Orders with Punctuality and Dispatch.—*The
New-York Journal or General Advertiser*, September 3,
1767.

BLANCH WHITE, Upholsterer and Undertaker, from
London, on the New-Dock, next Door but one to Alderman Livingston's; Makes all kinds of Upholstry-Work,
in the newest Fashion and on the most reasonable
Terms; likewise all kinds of Field Equipage, Drums, &c.

Funerals furnish'd with all Things necessary and proper Attendance as in England.

Mrs. White Begs leave to acquaint the Ladies and Gentlemen, that she washes all Sorts of Gauze Laces, caps, on the Wires; Silk Stockings, &c. in the neatest Manner, she having a proper Frame, and a Stove for bleaching. Flounces and Trimmings for Ladies Robes, neatly pinck'd; also Shrouds and Sheets.—*The New-York Journal or General Advertiser*, January 7, 1768.

POSITION WANTED.—A young man (an upholsterer) lately from London, would be glad of employment from any master upholsterer or cabinet maker, or from any gentleman either in town or country, to do any kind of that business, particularly stuffing chairs, soffas, making up bed hanging, window curtains of all sorts, Venetian window blinds, putting up paper hangings, &c. all which he will do in the best manner; and, as he is a stranger, and wishes for encouragement he will work on the lowest terms. . . .—*The New-York Gazette and the Weekly Mercury*, August 8, 1774.

CLOCKS AND WATCHES

CLOCK AND WATCH MAKERS

JAMES ABBETS.—This is to give Notice to the Publick, That James Abbets, Watch-Maker, in Albany, intends shortly to remove from said Place: all Persons therefore that have any Watches in his Hands, are desired to make speedy Application for them.—*The New-York Gazette or the Weekly Post-Boy*, March 11, 1760.

BENJAMIN BAGNEL.—Run away from Joshua Delaplaine, of New-York Joyner, an Apprentice . . . Whoever shall take up said Apprentice and bring him to his Master; or secure and give Notice to his Master, or to Benjamin Bagnel Watch-maker in Boston . . . shall have Thirty Shilings as a Reward . . .—*The New-York Gazette*, July 30-August 6, 1733.

BARTHOLOMEW BARWELL.—All Sorts of Clocks, Clean'd and mended in the best Manner, and at the most reasonable Rates, with Expedition, by Bartholomew Barwell, lately from the City of Bath: now living at the House of Rene Hett, in the Smith's Fly, near the Fly-Market, in New-York.—*The New-York Gazette Revived in the Weekly Post-Boy*, August 21, 1749.

BARTHOLOMEW BARWELL.—Whereas it has been falsly reported, That I Bartholomew Barwell, of the City of New-York, Clock-Maker, am entrusted with the Care of the Clock belonging to the New Dutch Church of this City, greatly to my Hurt and Prejudice: This is therefore to acquaint the Publick, that I am not in the least concerned with the Care of it, otherwise than when employed to clean it, as it is now, and for many years past

143

has been, under the Care of Mr. Isaac Vanhook. Said Barwell continues his Business of Clock-Mending and Cleaning, at his House in the Fly and shall be glad to oblige all those who may think proper to employ their Very Humble Servant, BARTHOLOMEW BARWELL.—*The New-York Mercury*, December 25, 1752.

BARTHOLOMEW BARWELL, Living next Door to the Widow Derham's, between the Fly and Meal-Markets, has just imported in the Brig Concord, Capt. Jacobson, from London. Some very neat Clocks; and likewise Childrens Leather Shoes, from three Years to fifteen, by the Groce, Dozen, or single pair.—*The New-York Gazette*, August 11, 1760.

RICHARD BRECKELL.—A mechanical puppet show presented by Richard Breckell . . . who mends and cleans all sorts of clocks, reasonably—*New-York Mercury*, December 29, 1755.

CHARLES OLIVER BRUFF, Goldsmith and jeweller, At the Sign of the Tea-pot, Tankard, and Ear-ring, has removed his Shop from Rotten-Row, opposite to the Fly-Market, and but two Doors from the main Street; . . . he mends ladies fans in the neatest manner, and cleans watches, and puts glass in for one shilling a piece; and sells chains, seals, and keys. . . .—*The New-York Gazette and the Weekly Mercury*, June 19, 1769.

JAMES BRUFF.—At the Sign of the Clock and two Watches, opposite to Mr. Roorback's, at the Fly-Market, is made and repaired at reasonable Rates, Clocks and Watches; will keep in Repair by the year, Clocks plain or musical; also is done at the said Shop, fine gilding with Gold, either Watch Cases, Cocks and Slides, Snuff Boxes, Ladies Equipage, &c. in the best Manner; China is also riveted at the said Shop three different Ways, and ornamented with Birds, Beasts, Fish, Flowers, or Piece of Masonry, by a curious and skilful Workman; great Care shall be taken to dispatch whatsoever is undertaken, and doubt not but to give general Satisfaction, to those Gentlemen and Ladies, who will be pleased to favour me with their Custom, and grateful Thanks from their humble Servant, James Bruff.—*The New-York Mercury,* February 3, 1766.

GEORGE CHESTER, Watch-Maker, from London, begs leave to inform, That he has just opened Shop at the Sign of the Dial, on the New-Dock, and next Door to Mr. Van Dyck, the Hatter's; where he intends to sell and repair all Sorts of Clocks and Watches. Those Gentlemen and Ladies who are pleased to honour him with their Employ, May depend on the greatest Care imaginable, and utmost Dispatch, at the most reasonable Prices now in London. Said Chester has a few second Hand Watches to dispose of reasonable, and a very good Eight-day Clock, which will come cheap.—*The New-York Gazette or the Weekly Post-Boy,* March 14, 1757.

ISAAC DOOLITTLE.—We are well assured, that Mr. Isaac Doolittle, Clock and Watch-Maker of New-Haven, has lately compleated a Mahogany Printing-Press on the most approved Construction, which, by some of the best Judges in the Printing Way is allowed to be the neatest ever made in America, and equal, if not superior to any imported from Great-Britain: This Press, we are told, is for the Use of Mr. William Goddard of Philadelphia, Printer of the Pennsylvania Chronicle.—News item from Newport in *The New-York Gazette and the Weekly Mercury,* August 21, 1769.

JOHN ENT, Clock and Watch-maker, at the Sign of the Dial and Time, opposite the Old-Slip-Market, New-York, makes and mends all sorts of Clocks and Watches, in the neatest Manner, as cheap as in London: Likewise repairs and cleans all sorts of Clocks and Watches, with Care and Dispatch, at reasonable Rates.—*The New-York Gazette or the Weekly Post-Boy,* November 8, 1756.

THOMAS EVANS, Watch-Maker, from London, At his Shop opposite the Meal Market, and but two Doors from Mr. Malcom Campbells, Cleans and Repairs all Sorts of Watches, plain, repeating or horizontal Kind. Ladies and Gentlemen, that please to Favour him with their Custom, may depend upon having it performed with Dispatch, and on reasonable Terms, Said Evans cleans and repairs Clocks of all Kinds, and will undertake to look after them by the year.[1]—*The New-York Gazette,* May 26, 1760.

BASIL FRANCIS, Watch-Maker, At the Dial, between the Dutch Church and the Market in Albany; Being regularly bred to the business in London, and having wrought for some of the most eminent masters of that art in said city, as an approved workman; and as he hath given satisfaction to those that have already favoured him with their custom, flatters himself, he shall meet with encouragement from the public, which he will ever endeavour to merit, by his assiduity to satisfy and oblige those who please to employ him. He repairs watches and clocks with accuracy and dispatch, and insures their performance for one year (accidents and mismanagement excepted) as cheap as is consistent with justice to himself and employer.

The great botch-work that is to be observed in many watches, is a convincing proof that there are many pretenders to the business who by their great ingeniuty have learnt to take (or rather break) a watch to pieces, and by their botch-work, before they can set them ticking, often render many good watches almost beyond the ability of the best workmen to rectify, being better skilled in the destruction than construction of the machine. Such must be acknowledged by all to be very dear to their employers, if they were to pay for being so employed.— *The New-York Gazette and the Weekly Mercury,* May 24, 1773.

[1] Advertisements by Evans still appeared in 1763.

BASIL FRANCIS.—Ten Dollars Reward. Whereas a certain William Hill, in the beginning of Sept. last, did in a fraudulent manner, obtain of the subscriber one pinchbeck watch, with a single case, winds up in the face, the hole where the key goes a little flowered. He is a well made man, about 5 feet 7 inches high, dark complexion, with short curl'd black hair, has an odd kind of speech, somewhat like the high Dutch accent, says he is an Englishman, and a gunsmith, but he has wrought at the silver-smith's business, and commonly wears blue cloaths. Whoever apprehends the said William Hill, so that he may be brought to justice and the watch obtained, shall be entitled to the above reward, or for either watch or man five dollars, paid by Basil Francis, Watch and clockmaker, in Albany, Who makes and repairs watches and clocks with accuracy; those who please to employ him, may depend on a full exertion of his abilities to give general satisfaction.—*The New-York Gazette and the Weekly Mercury*, January 3, 1774.

CHARLES GEDDES, Watch-Maker and Finisher, from London, (late from Boston) Begs leave to acquaint his friends and customers, that he has opened shop in Queen-street, between Burling's and Beekman's-Slip, a little north of the Fly-Market; where he carries on his business as usual. He has for Sale, a variety of Watches, in silver and pinchbeck cases, chains, &c.

N.B. Merchants or Masters of vessels having watch materials to dispose of will meet with a purchaser, by apply to Geddes. Wanted a Journeyman, who understands his business, to whom good encouragement will be given.—*The New-York Gazette and the Weekly Mercury*, August 26, 1776.

GLADMAN & WILLIAMS.—Messrs. Gladman & Williams, Clock and Watchmakers, from the late Mr. G. Graham's, Take this Method to acquaint Gentlemen, Merchants, and others, That they have opened a Shop next to St. Sepulchre's Church, on Snow Hill, London; where all

Orders they may be favoured with in that Branch, from any of his Majesty's Colonies, shall be executed in the most masterly Manner and with the utmost Expedition. —*The New-York Mercury*, November 12, 1764.

THOMAS GORDON, Watch-Maker, from London, opposite the Merchant's Coffee-House, in New-York. Carefully cleans and repairs, in the very best Manner, all Sorts of horizontal, Plain, or repeating Watches and Clocks, at reasonable Rates.—*The New-York Mercury*, February 19, 1758.

THOMAS GORDON, Watchmaker from London Who lately lived near the Merchant's Coffee-House in this City, is now moved into the Shop of Mr. Hastier, in Hanover Square, opposite to Doctor Brownjohn's, and next door to the Corner adjoining Wall-Street; where he repairs in the best Manner (as formerly) Repeating, Horizontal, and other kinds of Watches; musical, chyming, and other Clocks, at the most reasonable Prices.[2]— *The New-York Gazette and the Weekly Mercury*, July 24, 1769.

ISAAC HERON.—All sorts of Watches, Clocks, Jewellery and Plate, repair'd in the best manner and upon reasonable Terms, by Isaac Heron, in Bound-Brook, New Jersey. All Watches repair'd by him, he upholds and warrants their Performance for one Year: those he sells, he warrants for a Term of Years, according to their value, provided their failure proceed not from Accident or mismanagement.—*The New-York Mercury*, July 2, 1764.

ISAAC HERON.—Repeating, Horizontal, and all Sorts of Watches repaired in the best Manner, on the most reasonable Terms, by Isaac Heron, Watch-Maker, at Mr. Stuyvesant's Vendue-House, opposite the Meal Market, New-York. He upholds and warrants their Performance for one Year, Provided they fail not through an Accident,

[2] Advertisements by Gordon still appeared in 1771.

or Mismanagement. Those he sells he warrants for a Term of Years, according to their Value.

Said Heron takes this public Method to return the Gentlemen of New-Jersey his sincere and grateful Thanks, for their kind Encouragement of him, whilst he resided at Boundbrook; and hopes that those he has been so happy to Please, will yet, (when Convenient) continue to Favour him with their Employ; to Merit which, he is determined to exert himself; and if any of the Work he has done in the last Year should fail, he begs it may be sent to him being as earnest to Rectify that he is paid for, as to receive his Money when earn'd. Watches left for him, at Mr. Neilson's Store, or at Mr. Duffs' in New Brunswick, Mr. Hetfield's in Elizabeth-Town, Mr. Banks's in Newark, with Mr. Bryan Laverty at Amboy; at Mr. Mellen's in Millstone, Mr. Duyckinck's at the New Branch, at the Union Store; Mr. Stewart's at Hacket's-Town, and Mr. Kinney's in Morris-Town, may depend on their being carefully repai:r'd, justly charg'd for, and return'd with all possible Dispatch, By the Publick's humble Servant, Isaac Heron.—*The New-York Gazette*, May 5, 1766.

ISAAC HERON.—Repeating and plain, gold, silver and pinchbeck watches; jewellery and plate of the newest taste, to be sold by Isaac Heron, watch-maker, at Mr. Stuyvesant's vendue-house, opposite the upper end of the coffee-house-bridge, New-York. N.B. He takes old gold, silver and lace, in exchange. Those watches he sells and repairs, he warrants as usual.—*The New-York Gazette and the Weekly Mercury*, May 2, 1768.

ISAAC HERON.—A Musical Clock, noble and elegant, which cost in England, £ 80. A Gold Repeating Watch neat and good, cost £ 50. both to be sold at (nearly) Currency for Sterling, by Isaac Heron, Watch Maker, facing the Coffee House Bridge.

A neat and extraordinary good chamber Repeating Clock, a few Silver and Pinchbeck Watches, Seals, chains, keys, and Trinkets; Earings of Paste and Marquisette, Enamell and ditto, and Mother O'pearl and ditto, some Wax and Jett ditto, Locket Buttons by the Card or pair, Etwees, Enamel'd Snuff Boxes, plated Buckles, etc. etc. All which he will sell at a very low rate. He humbly entreats those who are indebted to him to pay as soon as convenient, lest his Creditors should begin to think it inconvenient to trust him longer. Those who have Watches in his Care above six Months, are requested to call for them.—*The New-York Gazette and the Weekly Mercury,* July 23, 1770.

ISAAC HERON.—At the Sign of the Arch'd Dial, by the upper End of the Coffee-House Bridge; Isaac Heron Watch-Maker, Has an Assortment of Watches, and the best, second, third, fourth, fifth, bad, and worse Sorts; some very neat, some very ugly, and others—so, so; most of them in plain, and a few in engrav'd, gold, silver, gilt, and shagreen'd, double and single Cases; some he warrants for a long Time, some for a shorter Time, and others for no Time, at all. . . .—*The New-York Gazette and the Weekly Mercury,* April 15, 1771.

ISAAC HERON, Watch-Maker, at the corner by the Coffee-House, sign an arched Dial; has for sale, a Few very fashionable warranted watches, in gold, silver, gilt and green cases, which he will sell as low as they retailed in London. Also, Ladies elegant steel watch-chains; mens do. seals, trinkets, glasses, springs, strings, and keys by the dozen; enamelled-dials; elegant do. for the Craft, Ancient, and Modern. Elegant broach-jewels for their honest breasts; sword knots, sundries, &c. with Sprigs, which more beauteous makes the fair; and lockets, various, for the hair.

These watches he repairs, he does as well and charges as low for, as his neighbours, i.e. as near the London prices as possible. To say more, would neither be prudent nor honest. As usual, he warrants their performance—not for ever, but one year, and if they be not very

bad, for ten; after the first, at 4s. per ann. for each,
cleaning; accidents and mismanagement of them excepted; but,

Should the all-sustaining hand him drop,
His movements all springs, wheels hands must stop!
Then, like the tale of "a bear and fiddle,"
This bargain—"breaks off in the middle."

He is extremely grateful to his friends, and the in-
dulgent public for their smiles and favours, and really
means to merit a continuance of them. . . .—*The New-
York Journal or General Advertiser*, December 24, 1772.

ISAAC HERON.—The Inhabitants are desired to be
careful of their Doors, Windows, &c. as there are a set of
House breakers now in Town. Some of them broke off
one of the Shutters, and a Pane of Isaac Heron's Shop
Window, on Sunday the 27th ult. so early as 9 o'Clock
in the Night. The Noise alarmed the Family, and the
Villains made off.

Isaac Heron presents his Compliments to those Gentry,
and congratulates them on their getting so clean off, on
a Night so very dirty and wet, If they choose to return,
during the cold Season, he will take care to provide them
a warm Reception. And will endeavour to prevail upon
them to leave behind e're they go, some Proof of their
Identity; such as an amputated Limb, or, even a Snuff
box full of Brains. The latter may be of Use to our very
vigilant City Watch, though, it is thought they sleep
pretty sound with the few they have got.—News item in
The New-York Journal or the General Advertiser, January 7, 1773.

ISAAC HERON.—Choice and Cheap, or Union of the
Good and Beautiful, exemplified in an assemblage of
warranted Watches, Isaac Heron, near the Coffee-House,
has received by the Rosamond, Also, a few for jockies,
of that quality which a Frenchman would style patraques,
to which a Dutchman would give the epithet Schlegt;
a Scotchman that of littleguid-warth; and Irishman,

neenshagamagh; an Englishman, poor-thing, runner, bauble, d—d bad, &c. Such to be sure he warrants—not, Patent Keys, trinkets, &c.—*The New-York Gazette and the Weekly Mercury,* April 18, 1774.

ISAAC HERON.— . . . He earnestly, yet humbly entreats those indebted to him, that they will be as speedy as possible in discharging the same (however small the sum) and assist him, in his laudable exertions to crawl from under the debt he owes. Besides, he begs they will deign to consider he has a large family, and that market-money really becomes exceeding scarce.—*Rivington's New-York Gazetteer,* November 16, 1775.

ISAAC HERON.—A Capp'd Silver Watch, H. Thomas, maker, No 5000, stolen. Isaac Heron will amply reward any person who shall produce it, or the thief. Said Heron wants journeymen and materials, such as sizeable springs, glasses, &c. Indeed, his case is pretty similar to that of their High and Mightinesses, the Congress, L—d d—them! (He hopes those three simple consonants won't offend them) who, before the extinction of their northern army, wanted, only men, money and cannon, to make a compleat conquest of All Canada. Coffee-House-Bridge; New-York.—*The New-York Gazette and the Weekly Mercury,* October 21, 1776.

HURTIN & BURGI, Watch makers and Silver-smiths, at Bound Brook, Repairs repeating horizontal, and all sorts of watches and clocks, in the best manner and at the Cheapest rates; Any gentlemen or ladies who are pleased to favour them with their custom, may depend on having their command executed with the greatest care and punctuality. They will exert themselves in the compliance with all reasonable commands that may be given both in the performance of the work and any other way which may have a tendency to merit the custom, favour, and good will of the publick &c. per the publick's humble servants, W. HURTIN and F. BURGI.—*The New-York Mercury,* May 19, 1766.

WILLIAM HURTIN.—Left some parts of a clock, which the owner may have again, by applying to William Hurtin, Watch maker on Golden Hill, proving their property and paying charges.—*The Constitutional Gazette,* May 29, 1776.

SAMUEL JEFFERYS.—Ran away . . . an indented English servant man, named Jonathan Pinkard, by trade a Watch maker from Samuel Jefferys, Watch maker, in Philadelphia.—*The New-York Journal or the General Advertiser,* April 8, 1773.

WILLIAM KUMBEL, Clock and Watch-Maker, at the sign of the Dial, near the Coenties Market, Begs leave to inform the public, that he carries on said business in all its branches; likewise the gold and silver smiths business. Any gentlemen or ladies who favours him with their work, may depend on its being done in the neatest manner, and at the most reasonable rate, with the quickest dispatch.—*The New-York Gazette and the Weekly Mercury,* July 24, 1775.

WHITE MATLACK.—In the advertisement of George Leedell, book binder, mention is made that he has removed to Peck's-slip, next door to Mr. White Matlack's, watch-maker,—*The New-York Gazette and the Weekly Mercury,* May 3, 1773.

WHITE MATLACK.—Lost. Among other things at the dreadful fire last Monday, a plain silver Watch, maker's name White Matlack, in New-York, no 12 or 123. Any person that has found it, and will please to bring it to the subscriber, will greatly oblige an unhappy and distressed sufferer. GEORGE FISHER.—*The New-York Journal or General Advertiser,* May 18, 1775.

WHITE MATLACK.—Lost between Beekman's Slip and the incampment of the first brigade. A Silver Watch, with a china face, steel chain, the swivel has been newly brazed in, and goes stiff, has been lately cleaned by White Matlack of this city, and has one of his papers in the case. Whoever has picked up said Watch, and will return it to the subscriber, in Col. Read's regiment, shall receive a handsome reward. GEORGE WHIPPLE.—*The Constitutional Gazette,* May 11, 1776.

AARON MILLER, Clock-Maker, in Elizabeth Town, East New-Jersey; Makes and sells all Sorts of Clocks, after the best Manner, with expedition: He likewise makes Compasses and Chains for Surveyors; as also Church Bells of any size, he having a Foundry for that Purpose, and has cast several which have been approved to be good; and will supply any Persons on a Timely Notice, with any of the above Articles, at very reasonable Rates. —*The New York Gazette Revived in the Weekly Post-Boy,* January 4, 1748.

PHILIP MILLER.—Whereas on Monday night the 15 inst. the shop of Philip Miller, of this City, watchmaker, was robbed [3] of the folowing articles, viz. 8 pair of solid shoe buckles, 6 pair of open work, ditto, 18 sorted hat buckles, 3 pair of carved knee buckles, 6 silver seals, 4 pair of clasps; 1 pair of little paste buckles, 9 stone broaches, 15 pair of stone buttons, 2 tea spoons, 2 milk pots, one plain, the other chased, 3 punch ladles, 2 china snuff boxes, 1 coral, 2 pair of gold sleeve buttons, 6 heart, and 14 plain gold rings, 10 garnet, ditto, 4 white stone, ditto, 3 double heart and hand gold ditto, 2 garnet and white stone, ditto, 2 common, ditto, 5 men's ditto, and 1 rich stone ear-ring. Whoever apprehends the theif that stole the above mentioned goods, shall have Ten Pounds reward Paid by Philip Miller.—*The New-York Gazette,* August 29, 1763.

[3] The shop of Philip Miller was robbed a second time. See *The New-York Chronicle,* September 14-21, 1769.

JOHN NIXON, Musical, Repeating and Plain Clock and Watch-Maker, Periodical Titivator, the only regular Watch-Maker, (Not of the London Company though) Opposite Hull's Tavern in the Broad-Way, New-York. Begs leave to inform the public, that he has set up his business, and intends to work as well and reasonably as any in the City; he also cleans and repairs clocks and watches by the year, and warrants them. Such gentlemen and ladies that choose to send their work to him, may depend upon being well served By their humble Servant, John Nixon.—*Rivington's New-York Gazetteer,* August 19, 1773.

JOSEPH AND THOMAS PEARSALL, Watch-Makers, have removed from the Place where they formerly lived, to the House nearly opposite, (where Haddock and Browne lately lived) between Beekman and Burling's Slip; where they still continue their Business as usual.—*The New-York Journal or the General Advertiser,* May 17, 1770.

JOSEPH AND THOMAS PEARSALL.—The Copartnership of Joseph and Thomas Pearsall, watch Makers, being dissolved the first of May last, All Persons having any Demands, against said Copartnership, are desired to bring in their Accounts; and all those that are indebted to the aforesaid Copartnership are likewise desired to make speedy Payment.

Joseph Pearsall, has removed to the House lately occupied by Robert and John Murray, Merchants, between Burling's and Beekman's-Slip; where he carries on the business in the Watch and Clock Way as usual; and has imported in the last Vessels from London, Very neat Eight Day Clocks, in Mahogany and Japan Cases: Likewise a Parcel of very good Silver and Metal Watches, by the Dozens, or smaller quantity, which he will dispose of on the lowest Terms.—*The New-York Journal or the General Advertiser,* June 17, 1773.

JOSEPH PEARSALL, Watchmaker, Has removed from between Burling's and Beekman's slip, to the house lately occupied by Cornelius Clopper, merchant, opposite Hugh Gaine's, three doors below James Rivington's. Has imported in the Dunmore, Lawrence, and the Sampson, Coupar, very neat eight day clocks in mahogany cases, moon'd and plain; elegant spring do. black ebony cases, gold watches, capt and jewelled plain do. in shagreen cases, French do.

Likewise a very neat assortment of silver watches, day of the month, capt and plain do. which he will sell on the most reasonable terms, wholesale and retail. N.B. Mens and womens steel watch chains by the dozen.[4]— *Rivington's New-York Gazetteer*, May 26, 1774.

THOMAS PEARSALL.—Left for Sale with Mr. Thomas Pearsal, [*sic*] at his Shop, between Beekman and Burling's Slip, in Queen Street, A very good Gold repeating Watch, which can be recommended by the Watch-Maker who examined it, as a Piece of extraordinary good workmanship, and will be disposed of at a very low Price. —*The New-York Journal or the General Advertiser*, September 9, 1773.

THOMAS PEARSALL, Watch-Maker, Between Beekman and Burling-Slip, Has For Sale, very neat Clocks in Mahogany Cases; moon'd and plain jappan'd and spring ditto; likewise a very good Assortment of new Watches, Day of the Month, capt and plain do. which he will sell at the most reasonable Rates, for Cash or short Credit.— *Rivington's New-York Gazetteer*, February 3, 1774.

WILLIAM PEARSON, Jun. Clock and Watch-Maker, near the Coffee-House, in New-York, Begs leave to acquaint the Gentlemen and Ladies, that he makes, mends, and repairs all sorts of Clocks and Watches, after the best and cheapest Rates, and on the shortest Notice. Said Pearson, has for Sale, some very good neat silver

---

[4] In 1775, J. Pearsall's advertisements still appeared.

and Pinchbeck Watches, which he will warrant for any
reasonable Time. Likewise, a very neat Assortment of
Chain and Seals. N.B. Gentlemen in the Country, that
has Clocks out of Order, by sending a Line, will have
their Orders punctually obeyed, on the shortest Notice.
—*The New-York Gazette and the Weekly Mercury,*
August 29, 1768.

WILLIAM PEARSON, Clock and Watch-Maker, near the
Merchant's Coffee-House, Begs leave to inform the
public, that he makes, mends, and repairs, all sorts of
clocks and watches, after the best and cheapest rates,
likewise has to sell, some very neat silver and pinchbeck
watches, which he will warrant for any reasonable time;
a very neat musical clock, a neat assortment of chains,
seals, &c. All Gentlemen or Ladies, that choose to favour
him with their commands, either in town or county, may
depend on having them executed after the best manner,
and on the shortest notice. By their humble servant.
N.B. He cleans clocks by the year.—*The New-York
Journal or the General Advertiser,* February 23, 1769.

WILLIAM PEARSON.—Clocks. All Kinds of Clocks
made, cleaned, and repaired, by William Pearson, Clock
and Watch-Maker, at the Dial in Hanover-Square: Who
likewise repairs watches at a moderate price, and will
warrant their performance a twelve-month. He likewise
teaches vocal and instrumental music; strings, quills, and
tunes harpsicords, spinnets, claricords, and hand or
barrel-organs, all at a reasonable rate. . . . N.B. He
begs the favour of his former customers (if any there be
that move next May) to give timely notice, and he will
remove their clocks gratis.[5]—*Rivington's New-York
Gazetteer,* April 14, 1774.

THOMAS AND MERVIN PERRY.—Just imported in the
Ship Hope, Capt Benjamin Davies, from London, and
to be sold cheap by Thomas and Mervin Perry, Watch

[5] Similar advertisements continued to appear in 1775.

Makers in the Fly; A Neat Assortment of Gold Watches, plain, silver, and Days of the Months; Gold, Silver and Metal Watch Seals; Silk Watch-strings neat watch Papers, and Materials in the Watch-Branch, necessary for the Business, Wholesale or retail. N.B. Said Mervin Perry, begs Leave to acquaint his Friends, That he likewise mends and repairs all Sorts of watches in the neatest Manner, and at the most reasonable Rates; as he has been over to London for Improvement, and has had Instructions from the most eminent Masters.—*The New-York Gazette or the Weekly Post-Boy,* October 15, 1767.

MERVIN PERRY, Watch-Maker, at the Sign of the Dial, Takes this Opportunity of informing the Publick, and his Friends in Particular, That he still continues carrying on the Business in the same Shop lately occupied by his Father Thomas Perry, between Mr. Noel's and Mr. Cooley's; Those Gentlemen who chuse to honour him with their Commands, may depend on having them executed with utmost Care, Attention, and Expedition. He has to dispose of some neat plain, Gold, Silver, Days of the Month, and Metal Watches; likewise Silver and Steel Chains, Silver Seals, Silk String, neat Watch Papers, with a variety of other Articles for Watch-Makers, too tedious to mention which he will sell at the lowest Rates.—*The New-York Gazette and the Weekly Mercury,* November 14, 1768.

MERVIN PERRY.— . . . All Clocks and Watches that he sells, With his own Name, he will keep in good Repair, the first three Years, Gratis; and will warrant to import and sell Watches and Clocks from the Price of four Guineas to a Hundred, cheaper than any private Gentleman can import them for their own Use. Any Gentlemen that wants to be supplied, are desired to send their Orders to said Shop, and they will be complied with as speedy as possible. . . .—*The New-York Gazette and the Weekly Mercury,* October 21, 1776.

THOMAS PERRY. Watch and Clock-maker from London, Now living next Door to Mr. Depuyster, in Dock Street, near the Long-Bridge, in New-York; Makes, mends and cleans all Sorts of Clocks and Watches in the best Manner, with Expedition; and furnishes any Person with Chains, Seals, Chrystals, Keys, or any other Matters relating to that Business, at the most reasonable Rates. —*The New-York Gazette Revived in the Weekly Post-Boy*, June 19, 1749.

THOMAS PERRY.— . . . He will import, if bespoke, good warranted clocks at £ 14 they paying freight and insurance, and clocks without cases for £ 10.—*The New-York Mercury*, May 3, 1756.

THOMAS PERRY.—All persons who are indebted to the estate of Thomas Perry, late of the city of New York, watch-maker, deceased, are hereby requested to made speedy payment thereof, to the subscriber, who is the Widow and executrix to the last will and testament of the deceased. RUTH PERRY.—*Rivington's New-York Gazetteer*, February 24, 1774.

EBENEZER SMITH PLATT.—Watches of all Sorts, Viz. Plain, horizontal, repeating, and striking, sold and repaired in the cheapest and best manner: Likewise, clocks, musical and plain, equal in quality, and cheaper than can be imported from Europe, made and sold by Ebenezer Smith Platt, between Beekman's and Burling's Slip, in the lower street, New-York. The advertiser wants an apprentice about 14 years old, with a good character.—*Rivington's New-York Gazetteer*, May 26, 1774.

——PROCTOR.—Beatman drops sold at the shop of Mr. Proctor watchmaker, living in the Square, next door to Mr. John Waters Merchant.—*The New-York Weekly Journal*, April 1, 1734.

CARDEN PROCTOR.—Watches and Clocks, Carefully and Expeditiously, Made and Mended, by Carden Procter [*sic*] living in Smith-Street, in the House where Henry De Foreest, Printer, lived in, removed from, opposite to Mr. James Daurcey's.—*The New-York Weekly Journal,* July 6, 1747.

CARDEN PROCTOR, Watch movement maker, and finisher, in Hanover-Square, between the fire-engine house, and the sign of the Unicorn & Mortar, sells and repairs, plain, repeating or horizontal watches: also clocks: He likewise gilds plain or chased cases, lady's chains, snuff boxes, buckles, sword hilts, &c. in the best and cheapest manner; where may be had, his opinion in an impartial manner, of watches to be sold or bought, with intent to put a stop to the many impositions this government labours under, for want of skill in that way.[6] —*The New-York Mercury,* August 18, 1755.

STEPHEN SANDS, Clock and Watch-maker, desires to inform the public in general, and his friends in particular, that he has opened shop at the house wherein Mr. Corn-well Sands now lives, in Peck's Slip, nearly opposite the market, where he proposes carrying on his business; those who please to favour him with their custom may depend upon having their work done with the utmost care and dispatch: Who has also to dispose of Watch Chains and Seals, and almost every article in his way. —*The New-York Gazette and the Weekly Mercury,* February 3, 1772.

STEPHEN SANDS.—Wanted, As an apprentice to the Watch-Making business, A Sober ingenious Lad, of a good character, about 15 years of age. Such a one may hear of a place by enquiring of Stephen Sands, clock and watch-maker, nearly fronting Peck's Slip, New-York.

Stephen Sands has, to dispose of, a very neat assort-ment of mens steel watch chains; likewise Cornelian, Intaglio and common seals; gilt trinkets; joint and com-mon sheet watch keys, and silk strings: also neat fancy

---

[6] C. Proctor's advertisements still appeared in 1768.

and paste knee and stock buckles, &c.—*Rivington's New-York Gazetteer*, June 30, 1774.

MATTHEW SHEPHERD, Clock and Watch Maker from London. Has opened a shop in Rotten Row, late Mr. Lorain's, where he undertakes to rectify all sorts of plain repeating and horizontal watches; likewise, clocks on the most reasonable terms. He has by him a neat assortment of watches, and clocks in mahogany and wallnut tree cases, as also table spring pieces.

N.B. He particularly solicits the favour, if any persons having watches, which stop frequently, or perform meanly, to make tryals, which to convince the publick of his certainty in rectifing, he will undertake upon the terms of no cure no pay.—*The New-York Gazette*, January 21, 1760.

JOHN SIMNET.—Watches Repair'd in a perfect and durable manner, with expedition, at an easy expence, and kept in good order, for 2s 6 Sterling per year, by J. Simnett [*sic*] original maker from London, on the New-Dock, near Murray's Wharf, New-York.—*New-York Journal or General Advertiser*, August 23, 1770.

JOHN SIMNET.—Watches. This Advertiser will continue, (far as it may be put in his power) to prevent you being imposed on by appearance, inability, or covetousness, will labour to save his employers expence, and gain repute to himself, and the real makers in England, desires not to charge twice for mending the same watch, —having dwelt in this city near four years,—if any watch he has practiced on, requires alteration, it shall be done without further charge, whilst the materials it is composed of, can endure.

Price of cleaning, two shillings currency, glasses fitted for one shilling each. The price of joining a broken main spring, or chain, two shillings, if a new one is requisite, eight shillings. All other repairs in proportion, at half what is usually charged, by John Simnet, watch-Finisher, of London, At the new Dial, the low shop beside the Coffee House Bridge, New-York.—Periodical Titivaters instructed by the year or quarter.—*The New-York Gazette or the Weekly Post-Boy*, December 23, 1771.

JOHN SIMNET.—Watches, Neat and Plain; Gold, Silver, Shagreen, and Metal. Some engraved and enamelled, with devices new and elegant; also the first in this country of the small new fashioned watches, the circumference of a British shilling.

Old work repaired and cleaned as usual, in the best and cheapest manner, by John Simnet, removed to the main-street (called the Fly) a low shop, next to the corner of Beekman's-Slip, New-York. The sign of a dial, against the wall.—*Rivington's New-York Gazetteer*, May 12, 1774.

JOHN SIMNET.—Watches. John Simnet, (one of the first in London, who brought this curious and useful manufacture to perfection) continues to repair and clean old watches much cheaper and better than is usual; and sells excellent new watches in gold, silver, metal &c. which will require no expence cleaning or repairing, except abus'd. Best glasses is 1 s.

Remov'd next to the white house, the lower corner of the Coffee-House bridge, New-York. The sign of the dial over the window.—*The New-York Gazette and the Weekly Mercury*, May 22, 1775.

THOMAS SMART, Clock and watch File Maker, at the Sign of the File and Hammer, in Division-street, near St. Paul's Church, Makes and sells all sorts of clock and watch files and tools of several sorts. He has now for sale a good assortment of large files and draw-plates, such as round, half round, four-square, and oval.—*The New-York Gazette and the Weekly Mercury*, October 4, 1773.

CHRISTIAN SYBERBERG, Watch-Maker, now living at the Dial, in the house of Mrs. Mary Kippen, near the Old-

Slip Market: Repairs all sorts of clocks and watches, with the utmost expedition: He has lately imported from London, a parcel of very neat silver and pinchbeck watches, which he'll sell very reasonable for ready money, and will warrant to be good. N.B. He has a choice assortment of silver, pinchbeck seals, steel and pinchbeck chains, keys, leather and silk strings, &c. and gives good attendance to all his customers.—*The New-York Mercury,* August 2, 1756.

CHRISTIAN SYBERBERG.—Whereas about six of the clock, in the night of Friday the 24th of this instant December, a villain run his hand through the shop window of Christian Syberberg; of this city, watch-maker, and took therefrom two watches, and escaped; one of which is pinchbeck, with a green shagreen case, the other a large old-fashioned silver one with a pendulum. All persons are desired to be catious in purchasing the above watches, if offered to sale; and whoever will discover the thief or thieves, so as they may be brought to justice, shall have Forty Shillings reward, paid by Christian Syberberg.—*The New-York Mercury,* December 27, 1756.

WILLIAM THOMPSON, Clock and Watch-Maker, Lately arrived from Britain, Begs leave to acquaint the public, that he has taken a commodious shop in Fair-street, opposite to the North Church, where he intends carrying on his business, in making and repairing all kinds of Clocks and Watches. Those ladies and gentlemen who please to favour him with their work, may depend on having it done in the best manner, and most reasonable terms. He likewise makes those curious and useful instruments called Way Wiser.—*The Constitutional Gazette,* October 14, 1775.

JOHN VOGT, Watch-maker, Now living in the House of Patrick Carryl, in Hanover Square, Makes, Cleans and repairs all kinds of Watches. Gentlemen that please to favour him with their Work, may depend on having it done to their Satisfaction, and on the lowest Terms, by their Very humble Servant, JOHN VOGT.—*The New-York Mercury*, September 11, 1758.

ANTHONY WARD.—Several Bags of good new Hops to be Sold very reasonable for Money or Country Produce. Enquire of Anthony Ward, Watch-Maker in New-York, and know further.—*The New-York Gazette*, February 18-25, 1729.

JOHN WOOD.—Watch Main-Springs Made in Philadelphia, are sold by the manufacturer, Matthias Eyre. Spring-Maker, from London, at his house in Third-street, below South-street, and by John Wood, Watch-maker, in Front-street, and corner of Chestnut-street.

Where watch-makers and others may be supplied with any quantity of springs much cheaper than can be afforded when imported from England, from which circumstance, and the good quality of the Springs, the maker hopes for the encouragement of the watch-makers in this and the neighbouring provinces, whose orders will be gratefully received and faithfully executed. N.B. By the dozen thirty shillings, single spring, three shillings.— *The New-York Gazette and the Weekly Mercury*, February 27, 1775.

JOHN WRIGHT.—Very good Cheshire-Cheese to be Sold by John Wright Watch-maker, at his House in Duke-street, for 8d. per pound by the Single Cheese, and for less if they take a large Quantity.—*The New-York Gazette*, January 2-16, 1739.

JOHN WRIGHT, Watch-Maker, being absolutely determined to leave this City in a Fortnight, or three Weeks at farthest, desires all Persons that have any Demands upon him, to bring in their Accounts, and receive Satisfaction: And all those that are indebted to him, are requested to pay off the same forthwith, and thereby prevent Trouble.—*The New-York Gazette or the Weekly Post-Boy,* October 1, 1753.

JOHN WRIGHT.—In a real estate notice mention is made of John Wright, late of the City of New-York, Watch-maker deceased.—*The New-York Journal or General Advertiser,* September 23, 1768.

JAMES YEOMAN & JOHN COLLINS, from London, Beg leave to acquaint the Ladies and Gentlemen of this City, that they have taken a Shop in Hanover-Square (lately occupied by Mr. Hammersley, and next Door but one to Mr. Charles M'Evers's,) for the carrying on the Watch and Clock Business, where all kinds of Clocks and Watches, will be clean'd and repair'd in a very careful and expeditious Manner. Likewise Gentlemen may have their Guns new stock'd or repair'd, as neat as in England.
N.B. We have imported nothing new at present, nor do not intend to any Thing of the kind, until the Importation becomes general.—*The New-York Gazette and the Weekly Mercury,* September 18, 1769.

JAMES YEOMAN, Watch and Clock-Maker, from London; Begs leave to acquaint his Friends, and other Ladies and Gentlemen of this City, that he has removed from his late Dwelling on Hunter's-Quay, to the House of Mr. Mervin Perry, opposite the Merchant's Coffee-House, where every Branch relative to the above Business will be carefully and accurately performed. N.B. The said James Yeoman, will let Part of the House where he now lives; it is very convenient for a small Family, having a good Yard and Cistern for Water.—*The New-York Journal or the General Advertiser,* October 31, 1771.

JAMES YEOMAN.—Watches, Horizontal, Repeating, or plain; Clocks Astronomical, Musical or Plain, with Weights, or Springs, repaired as cheap as by any Person in this City, by James Yeoman, (at the Sign of the White Dial, nearly opposite the Merchant's Coffee-House) who received his Instructions in the Business from the ingenious Mr. Neale, (whose great knowledge in Mechanics was well known) he can with propriety declare himself a real Manufacturer, having had the Government of a large Manufactory from its Infancy to its Maturity, one Hundred Miles from London.

The above is not the Result of Vanity or Parade, for, should it be doubted, proper Testimonials shall be produced, to prove the Assertion: As it is the sole wish of the said James Yeoman, to obtain Favours only proportioned to the knowledge he has, and the Satisfaction he affords in his Business, on those Foundations he submits his Reputation, as an Artificer, to the Judgment of the Impartial.—*The New-York Journal or the General Advertiser*, March 12, 1772.

JAMES YEOMAN.—Death notice: a native of England; His father is the first of Mathematicians and a Fellow of the Royal Society, himself was an ingeneous Watchmaker. His song and story ever set the table in a roar, and the chearfulness excited by his comic powers, justly entitles his memory to this faithful record of his very pleasant and truly courteous disposition.—*Rivington's New-York Gazetteer*, May 20, 1773.

CLOCKS AND WATCHES

WATCH TO BE MENDED.—Some years past there was a Watch sent from this Place to London, to be Mended. These are to give Notice, That if the Owner of said Watch will apply to the Printer hereof, tell the Marks and pay the Charges, he may have his Watch again.—*The New-York Gazette*, May 17-24, 1736.

THE PRINCIPLES OF MR. HARRISON'S TIME-KEEPER. In this Time-keeper there is the greatest Care taken to avoid Friction as much as can be, by the Wheels moving on small Pivots, and in Ruby-Holes, and high Numbers in the Wheels and Pinions.

The Part which measures Time goes but the eighth part of a Minute without winding up; so that part is very simple, as this winding up is performed at the Wheel next to the Balance Wheel; by which Means there is always an equal Force acting at the Wheel, and all the rest of the Work has no more to do in measuring Time, than the Person that winds time up once a Day.

There is a Spring in the Inside of the Fusee, which I call a Secondary Main Spring; This Spring is always kept stretched to a certain Tension by the Main-spring, and during the Time of winding up The Time-Keeper, at which Time the Main-Spring is not suffered to act, this Secondary Spring Supplies its place . . .[7]—*The New York Journal or General Advertiser,* June 11, 1767.

MUSICAL CLOCK.—John Sebastian Stephany, Chymist, Has for Sale for Cash, a new and ingenious Clock Work, just imported from Germany, and made there by one of the most ingenious and celebrated Clock-makers in Germany: It plays nine different selected musical Tunes, and every one as exact as can be done on the best musical Instrument; and changes its Musick every Hour. It is done will 11 Clocks and 23 Hammers. It has an ingenious striking work for every Hour, and quarter of an Hour; it repeats 8 Days, Hours and Minutes, and shows the Months, and the Days of the Month.—*The New York Gazette and the Weekly Mercury,* June 6, 1768 (*Supplement*).

PUNISHMENT FOR WATCH STEALING.—Richard Ely stole a silver watch out of the shop of Mr. Smith, Brazier . . . was exalted on a Wooden Horse in a Triumphal Carr and in that ignominious manner Rid round the City, with Labels on his Breast . . . after which he was conducted to the public Whipping Post, where he received the proper Chastisement.—News item in *The New-York Chronicle,* September 14-21, 1769.

[7] The article continues at length giving a detailed account of the mechanism of the time keeper.

A MUSICAL CLOCK, plays 6 tunes, Viz. The rakes of Mallow, 2 minuets, symptoms of love, the miller's wedding and the miller of Mansfield: upon 10 bells, two hammers to each, besides the clock bell; plays every third hour a tune thrice over, and every part of the tune repeated; and when, or as often as you please besides. It tells the moon's age, by a beautiful moon, adorn'd with stars in the arch of the face; and the day of the month, as common clocks do. It stands in an elegant mahogany case, about 9 feet high, which cost ten guineas in Liverpool.

This very ornamental useful and entertaining piece of furniture, which should bring £ 120 currency is to be sold for £ 70.—*The New-York Gazette and the Weekly Mercury*, April 29, 1771.

MUSICAL CLOCK.— . . . At public auction, To be viewed at the Coffee house. It plays six tunes four times in 12 hours, and at will: and is by far the most valuable and elegant time piece ever imported to America.—*The New-York Gazette and Weekly Mercury*, July 5, 1773.

BUILDINGS AND BUILDERS

HOUSES AND OTHER BUILDINGS

KITCHEN.—The Lotts and Houses next to the Custom House in New-York, wherein are 9 Fire Places, with a large Yard, a Stable, a Cestern, a Well, and a Pump, in the Kitchin, a Large Crane to the Chimney, with Stones, Dressers, and several other Things, that may be left for the use of a Tenant. . . .—*The New-York Weekly Journal*, August 2, 1725.

WEATHER VANE.— . . . On the house of John Breese, Leather Dresser . . . is erected a Staff on which is a Blue Vane, with white Figures viz. 1741: which Vane is easily seen from the Ferry, from over the Fresh Water, from the North and East River, and very plain from the Commons.—*The New-York Weekly Journal*, August 10, 1741.

FIRE PLACES.—Just published, and to be Sold by the Printer hereof, An Account of the New-invented Pensilvanian Fire Places: Wherein their Construction and manner of Operation is particularly explained; their Advantages above every other Method of warming Rooms demonstrated; and all Objections that have been raised against the Use of them, answered and obviated. With Directions for putting them up, and for using them to the best Advantage. And a Copper-plate, in which the several Parts of the Machine are exactly laid down, from a Scale of equal Parts, (Price 1s.). The above mentioned Fire-places are also to be sold at the Printer's hereof; where one of them just set up may be seen.— *The New-York Weekly Post-Boy*, December 3, 1744.

TRINITY CHURCH.—Friday morning last about 4 o'clock, a violent Fire broke out in the new Free-School-House, kept by Mr. Joseph Hildreth, Clerk of Trinity-Church in this City; which got to such a Height before it was discovered, as to render it impossible to save it from being entirely destroyed; and tho' it stood at a considerable Distance from the Church, yet the Flames ascended so high, and carried with them such Abundance of live Coals, as to put the Church in imminent Danger, particularly the Steeple; which was set on Fire five several Times, almost at the Top, what little Wind there was setting directly on it; notwithstanding which, by the good Providence of God, and the Diligence and Activity of a few Persons within, who broke Holes through, it was happily extinguished, and preserved: There was scarce any Thing saved out of the House, from the Fury of the Fire; and we are assured, besides a great deal of Furniture and other Things, the Records of the Church are entirely consumed. The whole loss sustain'd, is supposed to be near Two Thousand Pounds Value.—News item in *The New-York Gazette Revived in the Weekly Post-Boy*, February 26, 1750.

DWELLING HOUSE.—To be Sold, A very good Dwelling-House in the County of Bergen, of Forty Eight Foot long and Twenty Four Foot broad, with a large Cellar Kitchen, a Dairy and Store-Cellar all joined together, the said Dwelling-House has two large Rooms and an Entry, with a large Flush Garret & Bolting House standing near the same & an old Store House Stable & Negroes Kitchen adjoining to each other, and a well Built Smoak House, with a Fowl House thereunto adjoining, with a very good Garden to the same, . . .—*The New-York Weekly Journal*, January 27, 1746.

FIRE PLACES.—Just arrived, A fresh Parcel of the New Fire-Places, Made by Robert Grace, in Pennsylvania, And Sold by the Printer hereof in New-York. A Pamphlet wrote by the Inventor, which describes the Use and

Advantage of these Fire-Places, is given with them gratis.—*The New-York Weekly Post-Boy,* September 8, 1746.

St. George's Chapel.— . . . Notice is hereby Also Given, That a Committee of the Vestry of Trinity Church, will meet every Friday at 2 o'Clock in the Afternoon, at the House of William Cook, near the City Hall, to treat with such Workmen, Carpenters and Masons, as will undertake, the building and finishing the Galleries and Pews, and other inside Work of St. George's Chappel.—*The New-York Gazette Revived in the Weekly Post-Boy,* January 14, 1751.

Presbyterian Church.—Monday last we had here a pretty hard Gale of Wind at N. E. which broke or bent down the Iron Work, Ball and Cock, on the Spire of the Presbyterian Church in this City: This had been often apprehended, tho' it has stood several harder Gales since it was put up; but 'tis believed, the Gale we had a few Weeks ago crack'd it, and so this last compleated it.— News item in *The New-York Gazette Revived in the Weekly Post-Boy,* February 18, 1751.

Stone Wall.—Last Week as some Workmen were digging down the Bank of the North River, just back of the English Church, in order to build a Still House, a Stone Wall was discovered between four and five Feet thick, near eight Feet under Ground, and is suppos'd to have been the Breast-Work of a Battery, tho' we can't learn that the oldest Men living amongst us, know any Thing of such a Battery being there, which affords some Matter of Speculation to the Curious here.—News item in *The New-York Gazette Revived in the Weekly Post-Boy,* May 6, 1751.

Lighthouse.—To Be Let. Bedloe's Island, alias Love Island, together with the Dwelling-House and Light-House, being finely situated for a Tavern, where all kind

of Garden Stuff, Poultry, &c. may be easily raised for
the Shipping, outward bound, and from whence any
Quantity of pickled Oysters may be transported; it
abounds with English Rabbits.—*The New-York Gazette
and the Weekly Post-Boy*, July 2, 1753.

SNUFF MILLS.—To be Sold, or Lett, The Snuff Mills
that formerly belonged to Mr. Francis Goelet, at New-
Rochell, with 12 molds for snuff, a tobacco engine, with
knives and sives, and all the other working utensils thereunto belonging. For further particulars, enquire of Mr.
Anthony Lispenard, at New-Rochell.—*The New-York
Mercury*, October 14, 1754.

LEAN-TO.—To be Sold. A House with one Room, and
Leanto, a good dry Cellar, and a good Store House 30
by 21 Feet, two Story High, and a Cellar under it, . . .—
The New-York Gazette or the Weekly Post-Boy, March
10, 1755.

BRICK AND STONE HOUSE.—To be Sold by Charles
Arding, The Corner House, and 5 Lots of Ground near
the Revd. Mr. Barclay, and Alderman Van Courtlandt,
fronting to Nassau Street, 128 Feet some odd Inches; and
runing along Fare Street 115 Feet or thereabouts; the
House is new built, with Brick and Stone, 3 large Rooms
on a Floor, a Cellar Kitchen, a good Cellar, and Large
Garrets, seven Fire Places, and the House is two Story
high, there may be 3 Lodgeing Rooms made in the Garrets, being half Stories. Sash Window is in all the House,
a long Entery through the Middle of the House, with a
handsome stare case well ballister'd with curled Maple.
The House is built in the Form of a Square, with a large
Store House on the back Part of said Lots, 42 Feet Long;
the whole is in good Fence, with a long Grass Plat, and
a fine Cistern, with several Fruit Trees already planted,
which will make a very commodious Garden, and very
pleasantly situated for any Gentleman, Merchant or any
other person, having a fine Prospect over the Commons,

and up the North River; . . .—*The New-York Gazette and the Weekly Post-Boy*, April 7, 1755.

RENT.—At the Merchants Coffee-House, will be sold, at publick Vendue . . . a Dwelling House and Lot of Ground, now in the Tenure of Mr. Abraham Abrahams, the lower End of Stone-Street; it is built of Brick, with Sash Windows in front, two Stories high, with several conveniences, it rents for Forty Pounds and the Taxes, per annum. Conditions will be made known at the place of sale.—*The New-York Mercury*, February 9, 1761.

PAPERED ROOMS.—To be Sold . . . A New Well-built House and Lot of Ground, in Little Queen-Street. . . . The House is 34 Feet 6 Inches front; has seven Fireplaces; the Rooms all ceil'd and some of them neatly paper'd; three Feet Gang way; the yard pav'd; and Garden inclos'd with a good pail'd Fence; cistern in the same. . . .—*The New-York Mercury*, January 11, 1762.

NEW DUTCH CHURCH.—On Wednesday last, near 6 o'clock in the Afternoon, the New Dutch Church in this City, was struck and set on Fire by Lightning, which happily was soon extinguished. It is remarkable that in the Course of a few Years, the same Accident has happened to this Church 3 or 4 times.—News item in *The New-York Mercury*, June 20, 1763.

YELLOW BRICK FRONT.—To be Sold, at private Sale, a Very Commodious new Dwelling-House and Lot of Ground, situated in Cherry-Street, and now in the Tenure of William Cobb, The House is three large Stories high, a yellow Brick Front, having eleven Rooms, Seven Fire Places, with a large Cellar Kitchen, and Store Cellar, and a fine Tea-Water Pump in the yard. . . .—*The New-York Gazette or the Weekly Post-Boy*, February 23, 1764.

NEW YORK LIGHTHOUSE.—On Monday Evening last, the New York Light-House, erected at Sandy Hook was

lighted for the first Time. The House is of an Octagon
Figure, having eight equal Sides; the Diameter at the
Base 29 Feet; and at the Top of the Wall 15 Feet. The
Lanthorn is seven Feet high; the Circumference 33 Feet.
The whole Construction of the Lanthorn is Iron; the
Top covered with Copper. There are 48 Oil Blazes. The
Building from the Surface is Nine Stories high; the
whole from Bottom to Top 103 Feet. This Structure was
undertaken by Mr. Isaac Conro, of this City; and was
carried on with all the Expedition that the Difficulty of
passing to and fro on the Occasion could possibly admit
of: It is judg'd to be a masterly Piece of Workmanship.—
News item in *The New-York Gazette or the Weekly
Post-Boy*, June 21, 1764.

CHRIST CHURCH.—Extract of a letter from Great Barrington, in Connecticut [sic]. About three Weeks ago
was laid the Corner Stone, and since is erected the Frame
of an Episcopal Church by the Name of Christ Church
in Great Barrington, 50 Feet by 40, about 26 Feet high
besides the Roof and Underpining, with a handsome
Chancel on the East End, and a Steeple 115 Feet high,
on the West Side. The whole Building (but more especially the Steeple, Chancel and Roof) is excellent Workmanship. Mr. Kilbourn of Litchfield, was the Master
Workman in the Frame; Mr. Easton of Pittsfield, Master Joiner. . . .—News item in *The New-York Gazette
or the Weekly Post-Boy*, July 12, 1764.

LIGHTS OF GLASS.—Whereas the Subscriber proposes
moving to New-York on the first of May, 1766, he would
at private Sale any Time before that Date, sell the
following. . . . Another Farm, about 6 Miles from New-
Windsor, on the aforesaid Road, containing 150 Acres
of Land, whereon is a good House 30 Feet by 32, Two
Stories high, well painted and glazed, having between
2 and 300 Lights of Glass in it; . . .—*The New-York
Gazette or the Weekly Post-Boy*, April 25, 1765.

BED CLOSET.—To be Let, A Very convenient First
Floor, consisting of Four Rooms, with Fire-places, and a
Bed Closet, situated on the New Dock, near the Coffee-
House; it may be entered immediately.   Inquire of
Samuel Dobie, living on the New Dock.—*The New-York
Gazette or the Weekly Post-Boy*, September 26, 1765
(*Supplement*).

A PROPOSAL FOR HEATING HOUSE OF PUBLIC WORSHIP.
—A Proposal to the Publick.   As there is at present a
View for one or more Buildings going on for publick
Worship, and as the Weather is so severe in the Winter
Season, I wonder it has never been put in practice at the
Beginning of such publick Buildings, (when it makes so
little difference in the Expence) in making hollow Wells,
or Flews with a Furnace, or Stoke-Hole at each Side of
(Church or Meeting) at Entrance, when the Congrega-
tion by a small Subscription, or otherwise, at the severe
Time of the Winter, might keep the Building to any
degree of Heat, which would be found very agreeable to
Persons of all Ranks, and with a small Quantity of Fuel,
either Wood or Coals, properly apply'd; (the Trouble or
Expence being a meer Trifle, by known Experience.). . . .
—*The New-York Mercury*, March 10, 1766.

TRINITY CHURCH STEEPLE.—A motion we are told is on
the Point of being made for a compleat Set of 10 Bells
to adorn Trinity Church Steeple, partly to be carried in
Execution by Way of Subscription, and any Deficiency
will no Doubt be made good by the Church.   A noble
Motion indeed, and if carried into Execution with any
Spirit, will give an Ornament to the City few others can
boast of; and 'tis surprizing a Thing of the Kind has been
so long neglected, unless, indeed they were frightned out
of it by the loss of the first Set sent for, which Barbados
now glories in; and which was taken by the Enemy,
retaken, and sent in there.   Philadelphia vaunts in theirs
of a Ring of Eight, in a Steeple not so substantial, and it
was chearfully carried through after the first Motion.

It is doubted but the Generality of the People of all Denominations will approve of it here.—News item in *The New-York Gazette,* July 21, 1766.

LIGHTNING ROD.—Mr. Holt; Sir, Having lately seen in one of the public Paper (but forgot which) an Account of the Light-House being struck by Lightning, I was induced to inquire after the particular Circumstances of that Affair; especially, as I knew it to have had a Metal-line Conductor, and that if it really was so, there would not be wanting those, who, for the Prejudice of Education, and their Non-Knowledge of the Efficacy of conducting Wires, would be ready to infer, and propagate the Inutility of them, for the Preservation of Edifices, &c. You will oblige the Public, and one of your constant Readers, by assuring them, that the Light-House at Sandy-Hook, has not been struck, so as to exhibit any Appearance, or Signs thereof whatsoever, and that the Veracity of the Informant is indisputable, as well as his Knowledge of the Premises, which he derives from his Proximity thereto. I am. &c.—*The New-York Gazette and the Weekly Post-Boy,* July 31, 1766.

TAVERN.—To be sold, at public Vendue, on the 25th Day of January next, at Noon, at the Merchant's coffee-House; The noted tavern, having the Sign of the free-mason's arms, on the west side of the Broad-way, fronting the great square; the house has twelve fire-places, two large dancing rooms, and eight other good rooms, with every conveniency for the reception of company, It was formerly kept by Samuel Francis, and since by the subscriber, and has rented at eighty pounds per annum, besides taxes. Any person inclining to purchase at private sale, may in the meantime inquire of John Jones.—*The New-York Journal or the General Advertiser,* December 17, 1767.

BRICK AND TILE HOUSE.—To be Sold, or Lett, All that Dwelling-House situated in Stone-Street . . . the Dwelling-House is large and commodious, two Stories High, built of Holland Brick, and covered with Tiles, as is also the Kitchen behind said House; there is an excellent Pump and Cistern in the Yard, and a spacious Gang-Way to it, the Lott is 45 Feet in Stone-Street, 75 Feet in Petticoat Lane, and above 200 Feet deep, running from street to street . . .—*The New-York Gazette,* March 16-23, 1767.

WAINSCOTTING.—To be sold at Publick Vendue, . . . One house and lot of ground in possession of Mrs. Eary: The house consists of one large cellar, a cellar Kitchen fitted with dressers, drawers, shelves, and ovens, two pantries, and a closet; on the first floor, two large parlours with marble chimney pieces and hearths, and Wainscotted dado high. On the first story, two large genteel rooms, with marble chimney pieces and hearths; one neat bedchamber and dressing-room. On the second story, two rooms, with fire-places, and closets, and three bed-chambers; a large garret on the whole; In the yard is a wash-house and cistern; The passage from the street and the stair-case is light and large, and wainscotted dado high . . .—*The New-York Gazette and the Weekly Mercury,* August 29, 1768.

LONG ROOM.—At Mr. Cox's Long-Room, near the Liberty pole, to-morrow Evening the 19th inst. will be exhibited, the celebrated Lecture on Heads, with singing by the young man who has already been so justly admired. Tickets 5s. each.—*The New York Gazette and the Weekly Mercury,* January 18, 1773.

BATH HOUSE.—Perth-Amboy, March, 1772. Lately Erected And as soon as the Season will permit, will be opened A New and Convenient Bath In which is a Room properly constructed to undress and dress in, with a Stair-Case leading into the Bathing Room, where Persons of either Sex may bath in Salt-Water, in the greatest Privacy; and for those that chuse to swim off into

deeper Water, a Door is so placed in the Bath, that they
can conveniently go out and return. . . .—*The New-
York Gazette and the Weekly Mercury,* March 9, 1772.

VAUX HALL.—To be Sold at public Vendue, . . . The
large, commodious and well fitted House and Gardens, in
the Out-Ward of this City, wherein Col. James formerly
lived, and is known by the name of Vaux-Hall. The
situation is extream healthy, and pleasant, commanding
an extensive prospect up and down the North-River:
The House has four large rooms on a floor, twelve fire-
places, most excellent cellars, and adjoining the house is
built a compleat room, 56 feet long and 26 wide, very
neatly finished under which is a large convenient kitchen
and other offices, with a coach-house and stables, a well
of the very finest water, pumps, cistern, pigeon-house,
&c.

The gardens are large, and laid out in a neat, genteel
manner. The upper garden is planted with the very
best fruit trees of different sorts; flowers and flowering
shrubs all in great perfection: the lower garden is plenti-
fully stocked with vegetables of every kind, sundry fruit
trees, and every other necessary for the family use,
great quantities of which might be sent to market. . . .
Until the Premises are sold, there will be the usual genteel accomodation, Tea, Coffee, Hot Rolls, &c. &c. and
the elegant Wax-Work Figures to be seen at all hours of
the day.—*The New-York Gazette and the Weekly Mercury,* May 17, 1773.

LARGE COMMODIOUS ROOM.—Edward Barden, Intends
on Saturday the 14th inst. opening the noted tavern the
corner house in the fields, . . . where he intends keeping
a good house as usual, (which is very well known in
general) and will provide tea and coffee mornings and
afternoons; dinners, suppers and entertainments provided at the shortest notice. He has a large commodious
room fit for balls, concerts, or assemblys. . . .—*The*

New-York Gazette and the Weekly Mercury, May 9, 1774.

WINDMILL.—To Be Let, And enter'd on immediately, The Windmill, house and garden, situated in the Bowery-lane, containing six lots of ground, being a thriving neighbourhood and very advantageous for a corn or meal store. For further particulars enquire of the printer.— *The New-York Gazette and the Weekly Mercury*, September 18, 1775.

WINDMILL.—To The Public, William Davidson has opened the noted Wind-Mill, near the one Mile Stone in the Bowery-Lane, and will give constant Attendance; and will grind Wheat, Corn, Oats, Ginger, &c. at the lowest Price.—*The New-York Gazette and the Weekly Mercury*, August 5, 1776.

BUILDERS, ARCHITECTS, AND SURVEYORS

DOBIE AND CLOW, Builders, in Division-Street, Take this Method of informing the Publick, that they undertake to build in Stone or Brick, Plaster and Stocco Work of all kinds, after the London Taste. Any Gentlemen who please to employ them may depend upon having their Work so done, as to bear the nicest Scrutiny. If required, they will also give Plans and Elevations, with Estimates of the Whole in Squares, Rods and Yards, together with the Quantity of Materials Buildings of any Dimension will take, in such a Manner as any Gentleman may know his certain Cost before he begins to build.— *The New-York Mercury*, March 11, 1765.

DANIEL DOOD of Newark in New-Jersey Surveyor, designs to remove to another Place and therefore gives publick Notice in his own Stile of Poetry, Viz.

Let this give Notice to my Friends,
    That I am about to move,
To try to better my Condition
    As it doth me behove
And if that any want that I
    Should Land for them survey,
Let them apply themselves to me
    Before I go away:
But with this Caution well observe
    They don't infringe the Claim
Of them, that Seven hold for One,
    And think it is no Shame;
Who say I help to steal Man's Land,
    And blame me very sore
Which Blame of right belongs to them
    That stole it long before.

But I'm unwilling to offend
    Those Fools as well as Wise,
These Fools I say all those are Fools
    Whose Interest blinds their Eyes.
If any are displeased herewith
    or with that Path I've Trod,
The Auther will maintain the same,
    Whose Name is Daniel Dod.
        —*The New-York Gazette,* December
30, 1729-January 6, 1730.

THEOPHILUS HARDENBROOK.—This is to give Notice,
that Theophilus Hardenbrook, Surveyor, Designs all
Sorts of Building, well suited to both Town and Country,
Pavillions, Summer-Rooms, Seats for Gardens, all sorts
of Rooms after the Taste of the Arabian, Chinese, Persian, Gothic, Muscovite, Paladian, Roman Vitruvian, and
Egyptian; also Water-houses for Parks, Keepers Lodges,
burying Places, Niches, Eye Traps to represent a Building terminating a Walk, or to hide some disagreeable
Object, Rotundas, Colonades, Arcads, Studies in Parks or
Gardens, Green Houses for the Preservation of Herbs,

with winding Funnels through the Wall, so as to keep them warm, Farm-Houses, Town Houses, Market Houses, Churches, Altar Pieces: He also connects all sorts of Truss-Roofs, and prevents their separating, by a new Method; and also all sorts of Domes, Spires, Cupolos, both Pile and hanging Bridges. Note, He designs and executes beautiful Chimney Pieces, as any here yet executed. Said Hardenbrook has now open'd a School near the New-English-Church, where he teaches Architecture from 6 o'Clock in the Evening till Eight.—*The New-York Mercury,* October 2, 1758.

WILLOUGHBY LOFTUS.—The Subscriber takes this Method to inform the Public, that he has by a Number of Years Practice, acquired the Art of forming Designs for Buildings; any Gentlemen (either in Town or County) that pleases to favour me with their Employ, may depend on having their Buildings performed in the newest and neatest Manner now practised in or about London; I having work'd with the best Workmen on the best Buildings, therefore an well acquainted with the best Method of performing the Workmanship: I will take all Manner of Buildings, either by the Lump, or Day; my Character and Abilities, may be well known by several Gentlemen in this City. Those Gentlemen who choose to favour me with their Commands, by leaving a Line or sending for me, opposite to Mr. Garret Noel, Bookseller, they shall be waited on immediately, By their Humble Servant, Willoughby Loftus. N.B. He likewise measures Carpenters, Painter, Masons, and Paviers Work.—*The New-York Gazette and the Weekly Mercury,* July 4, 1768.

FRANCIS MARSCHALK.—To be Leased for a Term of Years. The Lots at the Rear of the College Ground. . . . For Particulars Enquire of Francis Marschalk, City Surveyor.—*The New-York Gazette,* February 9-16, 1767.

THOMAS SHAW AND NATHANIEL SEDGFIELD, lately arriv'd from England, takes this method of acquainting the public, that they are capable of building most sorts of mills, as grist-mills, paper, and oil-mills, Engines for rasping and cutting wood for dying with, Engines for raising water from mines, either by wind, water, or Horses, saw-mills for cutting wood, &c. Any person inclined to employ said Shaw and Sedgfield, by applying to the Printer, may be informed where to meet with them.

N.B. A plan will be drawn, if required, of any of the above works, by the publick's most humble Servants, Thomas Shaw and Nathaniel Sedgfield.—*The New-York Gazette and the Weekly Mercury,* August 15, 1768.

LUMBER

A BOARD YARD, Kept by Thomas Shreeve, House-Carpenter and Joiner, from Burlington, West-New-Jersey, living opposite to William Waltons, Esq; in Queen-Street, and has to dispose of, Pitch-Pine Duck Plank for Vessels, and sheathing Boards for ditto; Pitch-Pine and Cedar Boards of Inch, three Quarter, and half Inch; also Joices of Cedar and Pitch-Pine, of sundry Sizes; likewise Shingles of 3 Feet, and those of 18 Inches in Length; as also Cornish and Indian Gutters, and sundry other Sorts of Boards.

N.B. The Boards are on a Lot of Ground belonging to the Estate of the late Major Van Horne, next to the new Building of the said William Walton, Esq; from whence they may be taken by Water without the Help of a Cart.—*The New-York Gazette or the Weekly Post-Boy,* June 3, 1754.

SAWYER.—Edmund Banton, Sawyer, from Liverpool, having lately set up his Business at the House of Mr. Rosevelt, near the North-River, in this City, takes this Opportunity to acquaint all Cabinet-Makers, Joiners, and Carpenters, that will favour him with any Thing in his Way, that they may depend on having their Work done in the best Manner, with all due Care and Expedition; having every conveniency for carrying on that

Business, and a good House for Keeping Timber from the
Weather. Due Attendance will be given by him at his
Saw-Pitt at the Place above mentioned.

N.B. If he meets with any Encouragement from the
several Tradesmen above mentioned, he purposes to stay
in this Place, otherwise he must be obliged to remove for
better Employ.—*The New-York Gazette or the Weekly
Post-Boy*, June 3, 1754.

LUMBER YARD.—John Blanck, Living at Ellis's-Slip, at
the North-River, Has now by him, at his Lumber-Yard,
(which was formerly kept by Alderman Roosevelt,) a
choice parcel of shingles, gutter pieces and Cornishes,
and all other sorts of timber for building, which he sells
on the most reasonable terms.—*The New York Gazette
and the Weekly Mercury*, June 6, 1768.

BOARD AND TIMBER YARD.—George Bell, Still continues
to keep his Board and Timber Yard, near Ellis's Dock,
at the North-River, where he now has for Sale, Shingles,
and every other Article in the Timber Way, having supplied himself with a large Assortment, and intends to
keep a sufficient Quantity always ready provided for his
Customers; and any Gentleman that please to favour
him with their Commands, may always depend upon
being well served, and at the lowest Prices. Also sells
Rum and brown Sugar by the Barrel, or less Quantity,
with Loaf Sugar, Salt and Indian Corn.—*The New-York
Gazette and the Weekly Mercury*, July 18, 1768.

TIMBER.—To be Sold by Stanton & Ten Brook,[1] on
Dey's Dock; at a small Profit, All kinds of Timber,
Albany Boards, yellow Pine, red and white Cedar for
Gutters, Mahogany of all Sorts for Joiners Work, Albany
Pipe Staves, all Sorts of Shop Work by a Man who is
to give good attendance to the Yard. Stanton and Ten

[1] The partnership of Stanton & Ten Brook was later dissolved by
mutual consent.—*The New-York Gazette and the Weekly Mercury*,
October 15, 1770.

Brook.—*The New-York Gazette and the Weekly Mercury*, April 30, 1770.

LUMBER INSPECTED.—Whereas a Law of the Corporation of the City of New York, has lately passed, to ascertain the Size, Dimensions, and Quality of Staves, Heading, Hoops, Boards, Timber, Shingles and Plank, which shall be brought to this City of New-York, for Sale, from and after the first Day of September, which will be in the Year 1770; Notice is hereby given, that we are appointed Measures and Inspectors of Timber, Plank, Boards, &c. and all Persons are desired to take Notice, that they are requir'd by the said Law, not to deliver to the Purchaser, any Plank, Timber, Boards or Shingles, before they are examined and measured. Isaac Chardavoyne, Francis Many, John Blank, Theop. Hardenbrook.—*The New-York Journal or the General Advertiser*, September 13, 1770.

NORTH AMERICAN LUMBER, Lumber of all kinds for European, West-India, and American Markets, to be sold by Abiel Wood, and Co. at Pownalboro, Sheepscut-River. For Particulars, Prices and Terms of Payment, apply to Robert Gould and Thomas Brown, in Back-Street, Boston, who are ready to treat for several Cargoes of any Kind of Dimensions; and will engage that the greatest Dispatch shall be given.—*The New-York Gazette and the Weekly Mercury*, April 8, 1771.

MAHOGANY.—A Cargo of 60,000 feet choice large bay mahogany, to be sold in lots from 5 to 10,000 in each lot; laying on the wharf between Burling's-slip and the Ferry Stairs; at public vendue, on Wednesday next, between 11 and 12 o'clock.—*The New-York Gazette and the Weekly Mercury*, September 28, 1772.

LUMBER YARD.—To be Sold, At George Stanton's Lumber Yard, at Dye's Dock, near the North-River, All kinds of Albany board and and planck, oak and Jersey

pine, timber of all sorts, the best three feet or long
shingles, lath, &c. by Philip Hone, who gives constant
attendance, and will undertake all kinds of shop-work.—
The New-York Gazette and the Weekly Mercury, July
5, 1773.

BOARD AND TIMBER YARD.—Marsh and Trembly, Inform their Friends and the Public in general, That they
have for Sale at their Board and Timber Yard, (That
formerly kept by George Bell, at the North River) A
Large Quantity of Lumber, among which is all kinds of
Albany and Jersey Plank, with Timber and Boards of all
Sorts and Dimensions commonly used in this city; cieling
Laths, &c. Gentlemen or others will be supplied with
any of the above Articles at the shortest Notice. They
have also a Quantity of Shingles to dispose of. N.B.
Daniel Marsh has for Sale, as usual, Bricks, Lime &c.—
The New-York Gazette and the Weekly Mercury, Sep-
tember 5, 1774.

LUMBER YARD.—To Be Sold, by Hardenbrook and
Dominick, At their Lumber-Yard, in Water-Street, a
little above Dover-Street: Timber, boards and plank of
all sorts and sizes for building, red cedar logs, mahogany,
red and Spanish Cedar boards and plank, mahogany and
Spanish Cedar for stair cases. Likewise at their Lumber-
Yard, in the Out-Ward, near the Ship-Yards, they have
long and short shingles, hand sawed long oak and pine
plank, from one and an half inch to four inches, for ship
building, &c. round and square gutter pieces, square oak
and pine logs, round and square logs for dock building.
Also on the shortest notice can supply any person with
large quantities of lumber for shipping.—*The New-York
Gazette and the Weekly Mercury*, March 6, 1775.

MASONS AND THEIR MATERIALS

STONE LIME.—All Persons who shall have occasion for
good Stone-Lime next Spring or Summer, may be sup-

plyed with what Quantity they have occasion for by
Lewis Gomez in the City of New-York, at a reasonable
Price.—*The New-York Gazette,* September 29-October
6, 1729.

PURPLE STONES.—To be Sold, Wrought or Unwrought,
Curious fine flat purple Stones brought from Hide Park,
for Tomb-Stones, Head-stones, Hearth-stones, Step-
stones, Paving stones, &c. Whoever has occasion for
any of the aforesaid Stones, may apply to John Norris, at
the house of Mr. Edward Hicks, Merchant in New York.
—*The New-York Gazette,* March 24-31, 1735.

QUARRY STONES.—To be Sold, by James Banks, Tavern
Keeper, at Newark. All Manner of the best Sorts of
Quarry-Stones, as Tomb Stones, Platforms, Step-Stones
of any Length, Paving Stones, Curbs for Wells, Rollers
for Gardens, Building Stones, Hearth Stone, and Duck
Puddles; any of which may be had, either rough, hewn
or saw'd, at reasonable Rates.—*The New-York Weekly
Post-Boy,* June 16, 1746.

STREET PAVER.—George Hicks, Street-paver, from
London, Advertises himself, as ready to serve any Gentlemen in that Way, either by the Day or by the Yard, at
the most reasonable Rates. He may be spoke with at the
house of Nicholas Killman, a little below Cortland's
Sugar House, at the North River.—*The New-York
Gazette,* June 23, 1760.

TILES.—To be sold, by Robert Crommelin, living near
the St. George's Chapel: a Parcel of Laths and glaz'd
Tiles, for covering Houses.—*The New-York Gazette,*
September 22, 1760.

BRICKLAYER.—Richard Weston, Bricklayer, from Lon-
don, takes this Method to inform all Gentlemen and
Ladies, and others that he has lately arrived at New-
York, and intends to follow his Business in all its various

Branches; as also causes Suction to Chimnies, to cure
that obnoxious Suffocation that Families so frequently
labour under; Likewise makes Backs, or Water Cisterns
of Brick or Stone, plaister'd with durable Cement; as
also stucco Frontis Pieces, and Arcadias, neatly performed
in their true Orders, and the whole Entablature neatly
performed in Brick Work. Those Gentlemen and Ladies
that think proper to favour me with their Employ, may
be waited on by directing only to my House, in King
George Street, next Door to Mr. William Peck. Mean
Time, I am Gent. and Ladies your most humble and
Obedient Servant. Richard Weston.—*The New-York
Gazette or the Weekly Post-Boy,* August 5, 1762.

LIME.—For White Washing, Exceeding fine unslack'd
stone Lime, which by experience is found to stick best
to the walls, and endure longest white; also, unslack'd
Lime by the hogshead for plastering, or for building;
which will be warranted better than any Rhode Island
Lime; and common slack'd Lime, to be had on the most
reasonable terms, by Ralph Thurman, at the North-
River, near Alderman Roosevelt's.—*The New-York Mercury,* February 25, 1765.

PLAIN TYLES TO COVER BUILDINGS, made by Daniel
Hendrickson, at Middletown Point, the same Sort as are
made Use of in London, and most Parts of England, and
are the soundest and most lasting Covering made use of
(except the best light Sort of Slate) and are greatly
perferable to the Boston Slate, being lighter and cheaper.
No Weather can penetrate, if properly laid, and are the
safest of any covering against Fire, being not subject to
fly by any Heat. To be Sold by J. Edward Pryor, near
the Commissary Lake's, at the North-River, New-York,
or the above Maker. Where also may be had in the
Spring, choice Rubbing Bricks for cutting Arches, or any
Mouldings for Cornises, will also stand Fire for Ovens
or Furnaces.

Best Providence Lime, to be sold by said Pryor, Also

the noted North River Lime, branded J. M. W. for Whitewashing (lately advertised by Ralph Thurman.) And
all kinds of Materials for Buildings provided on the least
Notice, the lowest Rates, with Instructions what Scant-
lings are proper, or other Materials necessary, and their
Quantities in any kind of House Building.

N.B. Said Pryor makes Plans and Estimates, directs
or measures all Artificers Work, belonging to building in
Wood, Brick, or Stone. . . .—*The New-York Mercury,*
December 2, 1765.

BRICKLAYER AND MASON.—The subscriber (with his
wife) lately from Kilkenny in Ireland, and just arrived
with Capt. Gifford from Bristol, by trade a bricklayer
and mason, being indebted for his passage, to Capt.
Gifford, £ 26 current money of New-York, is willing to
enter into contract with any person who will pay the
said money, . . Patrick Blanchville.—*The New-York
Journal or the General Advertiser,* June 2, 1768.

BRICKLAYER.—William Sawyer, Bricklayer and Plaister, late from London, informs the public, That he will
execute his work upon as reasonable terms, and in as
neat a manner as any man in this city. Likewise can
set any kind of fire work in brick; such as coppers, stills,
stoves, dyers kettles, whalebone boilers, tripe pans, tallow chandlers pans, soap boilers pans, smoke jacks, bakers
oven, Dutch ovens, hatters kettles, muffin plates, &c.
Gentlemen wanting any of the above work done, by sending a line to Mr. Robert Merrey, or Mr. Scandrett, near
the Fly-market shall be waited on by their humble
servant, William Sawyer.—*The New-York Gazette and
the Weekly Mercury,* July 3, 1769.

FIRE BRICK, Isaac Conro, Near the Oswego-Market,
Has for sale, best Yellow Stock Brick, which, on repeated
trials at the air-furnaces in New-York and Newark have
proved superior for standing an intense heat, to any
bricks in America; and are equal, if not superior, to the

best Windsor fire bricks: For the truth of this, please to enquire of Messrs Peter T. Curtenius, merchant, and William Lyle, founder, owners of the air-furnace, in New York, and Moses Ogden, manager of the air-furnace, at Newark. Those bricks make the best bottoms for bakers ovens, they are also the most lasting for flues in sugar and pot-ash works; in short, they exceed the Philadelphia soap stone, for standing fire, which has been proved in the steel-furnace in Connecticut; the above mentioned bricks make also beautiful fronts for buildings, nearly resembling in colour the Portland stone.

At the same place may be had, Fire Clay and Sand, of which the morter is made for building of any kind of work for standing fire: Of this sand and clay, crucibles have been made, which are as good as any that are imported. If any gentlemen in the West-Indies, should have occasion for it, for the use of their sugar works, it will be packt up in handy cask fit for exportation. Said Conro has also for sale, marble chimney pieces of the newest fashion, chimney tyle, iron backs, bottoms and side plates; brass wire wove fit for pantries and daries to keep out flies, stone lime. He also cures smooking chimnies: No cure, no pay, for this work.—*The New-York Gazette and the Weekly Mercury,* October 29, 1770.

MARBLE.—Several sets of very curious Italian, Derbyshire, and Kilkenny Marble for Fire-Places, Polished in the best Manner, just imported from England, and to sold by Walter Franklin, and Co.—*The New-York Gazette and the Weekly Mercury,* July 22, 1771.

BRICKS.—To be sold, 15,000 Stock Brick, fit for Furnaces and Forges. The Quality of these Bricks, which were manufactured by Isaac Conro, deceased, is so well known in regard to their Quality for standing the most intense Heat, that it will be needless to say any thing more about them, than that they are well burnt and to be sold by the Subscriber, who will send them to New-York, agreeable to Directions, or deliver them at the Kill, at Amboy. STEPHEN SKINNER.—*The New-York Gazette and the Weekly Mercury*, September 16, 1771.

LAW FOR MAKING BRICKS.—We are desired to publish the following extract of a law of this colony, relative to the making of Bricks, passed the 19th June, in the year 1703; the regulation thereby directed, it is said, not being duly attended to.

That no person or persons, shall make or suffer to made, in any place or places within this colony, any bricks, or kiln of bricks, but such as shall be well and thoroughly burnt, and of the size and dimension following. That is to say, every brick to be and contain nine inches in length, four inches and one quarter of an inch in breadth, and two inches and one half inch in the thickness thereof, . . .—*The New-York Gazette and the Weekly Mercury*, April 6, 1772.

FRENCH BURR MILL-STONES, Made of the first quality, lately imported from France, by the subscriber at his mill-stone-manufactory, at the lower end of Little Queen-Street, at the North-River;

Who will engage to compleat them in a masterly manner, either for merchant or other mills; He has been many years in the business of mill-stone making, And likewise the millers business in general; And as he has been at a very great expense in procuring the Burrs, plaister of Paris, and materials, and being the first person in promoting so useful a manufactory in this Province, hopes for the encouragement from the generality of the merchants, millers, &c. &c. as the Burr-Stones from repeated tryals have been found to exceed any other ever yet found out for grinding wheat, &c. And the public may be asured no pains or expence shall be spared to render them far superior to any ever imported into America, as none but prime stones shall be made use of for that purpose. And as the above stones are of the greatest utility to the colonies in general, he humbly hopes for that encouragement which the merit of his work may justly deserve; which favours shall be gratefully acknowledged by The Public's obedient, humble servant, JAMES WEBB. N.B. Any gentleman may choose out the stones before made up, if he pleases.—*The New-York Gazette and the Weekly Mercury*, June 13, 1774.

TILES.—Weeks and Vallentine, Pan-tile-Makers, at Middletown; Make and sell pan-tiles of the best quality, at eleven Pounds per thousand for glaz'd and nine Pounds for unglaz'd. Gentlemen may be supplied with any quantity by applying to Mr. John Besnit, Bricklayer, opposite Mr. John Wiley's Distillery, New-York. N.B. They will warrant them to stand any weather.—*Rivington's New-York Gazetteer*, July 28, 1774.

MASON.—William Hunt, Mason, from England, Residing at Mrs. Wessels's, in Bridge-street, New-York. Takes this method of informing the respectable public, that he would be very desirous of serving them in any sort of mason work, such as setting of kettles, boilers, stills, stoves, cylinders, ovens, glass and iron furnaces, &c. He will effectually prevent smoaky chimneys or desire no pay. Those persons that please to employ him, are requested to send a line, post paid, and they will be immediately answer'd, or attendance given, by their humble servant. WM. HUNT.—*The New-York Gazette and the Weekly Mercury*, July 10, 1775.

HOUSE CARPENTERS

A CARPENTER'S DAY MADE EASY.—Mr. Zenger: I am a Carpenter by Trade and can read English, therefore I some Times borrow your paper. My fellow Trades Men say, that you are to print every Thing that is good and bad in the Country, and to reward all Men according to their Deserts. I hear that some Body has put a Clapper into the Fort Bell, and that it is to ring at Morning, Noon and Night, as in the old Times. I am heartily glad of it. It will produce a great Reformation. We shall breakfast,

dine, and sup, according to Rule and Compass, and know
how to square our Work as in the Days of our Fore-
fathers. I assure you, Mr. Zenger, that is a good deed,
and ought not to be slighted: Therefore I and the Rest
of the Day Labourers in Town, intend very speedily to
pay our Thanks to that worthy Artist, in a very Handsome Address of which pray take Notice in your Papers.
I am Bob Chizel.—*The New-York Weekly Journal,*
January 7, 1733.

House Carpenter.—To Be Sold, By Peter Hendrick's
House carpenter, near the new dutch Church, several
sorts of Cordials which cures the Hestirk Fitts; Children
of Worms; pangs in the stomach, chollick, and several
other Ailments.—*The New-York Evening Post,* December 19, 1748.

Wage.—For the Encouragement of Ship-Carpenters,
able Seamen, and Labourers, in the Country, and the
neighbouring Provinces, to repair to the City of New-
York, The Merchants of this City have agreed to give to
Ship-Carpenters, Eight shillings per Day, able Seamen,
Five shillings; and Labourers Four shillings; with the
usual Allowance of Provisions; and no other or greater
Wages whatsoever. And all Persons liking the above
Proposals, may be certain of constant Employment.—
The New-York Gazette or the Weekly Post-Boy, Sep-
tember 18, 1758.

Carpenter.—Blake, Carpenter and Joiner, in John-
Street near the Golden-Hill, Takes this Method of informing the Publick, that he undertakes Carpenter's &
Joiner's Work by Measure, or makes Estimates before he
begins to work; so that any Gentleman that pleases to
employ him, may depend on having their Work done
in the best Manner, and knowing their certain Cost.—
The New-York Mercury, April 8, 1765.

House Carpenter.—This is to acquaint all Gentlemen
that have any Buildings to undertake, or carry on that

I John Glover, House-Carpenter from Edinburgh, will endeavour, if applied to, to accomplish the same in the most elegant, substantial and newest Fashion, that is at present in Great-Britain, as I am universally acquainted with the same, and I shall endeavour to use all Gentlemen that will employ me, with the utmost Veracity: I shall say no more, but I hope my Work and Performances will bear me witness of the Truth of the above asserted; I am to be found at the House of John Torry's, near the Scotch Meeting-House. John Glover.—*The New-York Gazette or the Weekly Post-Boy*, February 22, 1768.

HOUSE CARPENTERS.—The partnership of Joseph Peirson and Willoughby Loftus, House Carpenters, being now dissolved; the Business of House-carpenter and Ship-Joiner, is still carried on by Joseph Pierson on the New Dock, who hopes for the continuance of his Friends Custom, which will be gratefully acknowledged by their most obedient Servant. JOSEPH PEIRSON.—*The New-York Gazette and the Weekly Post-Boy*, February 26, 1770.

SOCIETY OF HOUSE CARPENTERS.—To the Public, The Society of House Carpenters, in this City, having fixed on the House of Mr. David Philips, at which to hold their stated Meetings, and transact the Business of the Society, beg Leave to take this Method to acquaint the Public therewith, and to desire the favour of such Gentlemen who shall have Occasion to employ them, either in drawing Plans, Elevations, and Estimates, or to execute any Carpenters Work, that they would be pleased to apply to said Philip's, where they will meet with the Workmen, who will faithfully, and on reasonable Terms, perform the different Kinds of Work which they shall undertake; and will with Gratitude acknowledge any Favours received from their Employers.—*The New-York Gazette and the Weekly Mercury*, November 18, 1771.

METAL WORKERS AND IRON WORKS

BRAZIERS

JAMES BYERS, Brass-Founder, in Bayard Street, next to Mr. Levy's, Makes all sorts of Brass Work, Viz. Andirons, Tongs and Shovels, Fenders, Candlesticks, Buckles: Casts all sorts of Brases for Mills, Brass Chambers for Pumps, &c. &c. Also Makes Wire Cages for Parrots; hangs Bells, Rivets China &c. &c. with Care and Dispatch.[1]—*The New-York Gazette*, December 13, 1762.

JOHN GENTER.—To be sold very cheap for ready Money by John Genter, Brasier, in Duke Street, who intends selling off his Shop, consisting of A Large Sortment of Brass and Copper Kettles, with Three large Soap Kettles, hard Metal, and Pewter of all Sorts, Shovels and Tongs, Hand Irons, Grid-Irons, and most kinds of Founder's, Brasier's and Hard Ware.—*The New-York Gazette Revived in the Weekly Post-Boy*, March 12, 1750.

JOHN HALDEN, Brasier from London, near the Old-Slip-Market in New-York; Makes and sells all sorts of copper and Brass Kettles, Tea-kettles, Coffee Potts, pye pans, Warming-pans, and all other Sorts of Copper and Brass Ware: He likewise mends and tins any sort of Copper and Brass, after the best Manner; at reasonable Rates; and gives Ready Money for Old Copper, Brass, Pewter or Lead.—*The New-York Weekly Post-Boy*, November 19, 1744.

JOHN HALDEN, Brasier from London, near the Old-Slip Market in New-York, Makes and sells all sorts of Copper

---

[1] Byers still advertised in 1771, in *The New-York Gazette and the Weekly Mercury*, February 11, 1771.

and Brass Kettles, Tea-Kitchens, Tea-Kettles, Coffee
Pots, Pye-Pans, Warming-Pans, Chafing-dishes, Candle-
sticks, and all other sorts of Copper and Brass Ware;
Also sells hard-metal Plates and Dishes, Tankards quart
and pint Mugs, Cullenders, Tea-Pots, Salts, Cranes,
Punch-Ladles, Tea Spoons; all sorts of London Pewter,
black japan'd Mugs, Brass Cocks, knives and Forks, Shoe-
buckles, Brass Wire and Hand-irons. Makes and mends
Coppers and Stills; he likewise tins and mends any sort
of Copper or Brass after the best Manner at reasonable
Rates; and gives ready Money for old Copper, Brass,
Pewter or Lead.[2]—*The New-York Weekly Post-Boy,*
February 24, 1746.

THOMAS PUGH, Brass and Bell-Founder, from Birmingham, at his Shop in Maiden-Lane, New-York. Makes
and casts all sorts of Work in the Brass founding Way;
also makes and sells all Sorts of soft and hard white
Metal; likewise Pinchbeck, and Bath Metal, in all its
kinds; He will make House Bells, Clock Bells, or Chim-
ing Bells, for any that shall please to employ him, at
the most reasonable Rates.—*The New-York Gazette or
the Weekly Post-Boy,* May 2, 1768.

WILLIAM SCANDRETT, Brass-Founder, living about the
Center of the Fly-Market, opposite the Widow Tucker's,
Makes and sells all Sorts of Brass and Iron Hand-Irons,
and various other Articles in the Foundery Way; Like-
wise has imported in the Edward, Capt. Davis, and other
Vessels from London, An Assortment of Hard-Ware,
such as Brass Candlesticks, Shovels and Tongs, Chimney
Hooks, Brass Cloke Pins, Brass Cocks, ditto Crane Cocks,
best Wool Cards, London Pewter Plates, Dishes, Basons,
Tankards and Spoons: Likewise Barbers Trimings,
Hones, Razors, Straps, Curling Irons, Scissars, Wig Cauls,
Ribbon, Silk, &c. As Also Ivory and Horn Combs, with
and without Cases; Shoe-Buckles and Sleeve-Buttons, of

[2] Creditors of John Halden met to demand settlement. See *The
New-York Gazette Revived in the Weekly Post-Boy,* May 27, 1751.

sundry kinds, Files, Borax, Shoe and Knee Chapes, Spelter and Spelter Sorters, Silversmiths binding Wire, Brass ditto, Pumis-stone, Rotten ditto, Argil, Sandever and Sand Paper, blue Melting Pots, Crucibles of all Sizes, which he will sell at the most reasonable Rates; likewise has to sell a Parcel of Men's Shoes, which he will sell very cheap; best White-Chapel Needles, four, and four and a half Pound Caulking Pins.—*The New-York Gazette*, April 16, 1764.

JOHN SMITH, Brasier and Copper-Smith, at the Sign of the Brass-Kettle, Tea Kettle, and Coffee-Pot, between the Dwelling-House of Capt. Isaac Sears and Beekman's Slip; begs Leave to acquaint the Public in general, and his Friends in Particular, that he has just open'd Shop at the above-mention'd Place, and proposes to carry on his Business in all its Branches. Those Persons who (willing to encourage a young Beginner) may favour him with their Commands, may depend on having them executed with Punctuality and Dispatch, at a reasonable Rate. N.B. He keeps a neat Assortment of ready made Articles for Sale.[3]—*The New-York Gazette and the Weekly Mercury*, January 16, 1769.

JOHN SMITH.—On Saturday last, Richard Ely (pursuant to his sentence, for fraudulently Attempting to Cheat and Defraud Numbers of the Respectable Inhabitants of this City, and also for attempting to Steal a Silver Watch, out of the Shop of Mr. Smith, Brazier on the Dock) was exalted on a Wooden Horse in a Triumphal Carr, and in that ignominious manner Rid round the City, with Labels on his Breast. . . .—News item in *The New York Chronicle*, September 14-21, 1769.

RICHARD SKELLORN, Brass-Founder, in Beaver-Street, near the King's Statue, New-York, late from London:

---

[3] Death notice of John Smith, brass founder and copper smith, from Island of St. Croix, appeared in *The New-York Gazette and the Weekly Mercury*, August 8, 1774.

Makes the following articles from the newest patterns now in vogue in London. All sorts of fine and common candlesticks, brass and irons, fret fenders, coach and cabinet work, all sorts of brass weights, mortars, and mill work; bells cast, Likewise Clock, watch, and gun work in general.

N.B. The best allowance made in exchange for old metal. An Apprentice of credible parents will be acceptable for the above trade.—*Rivington's New-York Gazetteer,* May 18, 1775.

JOHN TAYLOR.—. . . Campbell and Gault have their shop in Maiden Lane between the house of Mr. Jacob Allen's Gun-smith, and Mr. John Taylor, Brass-founder. . . .—*The New-York Journal or the General Advertiser,* February 25, 1773.

MOSES TAYLOR, removed from the Fly-market to the Old Slip market, makes and sells Brass and Copper Kettles, and most other kinds of Braisier's Goods. He gives ready money for old Brass and Copper.—*The New-York Gazette,* August 12, 1751.

JACOB WILKINS, Near the Old-Slip Market, at the Sign of the Brass Andiron and Candlestick, in New-York, Has for sale a neat and pretty assortment of brass andirons of the newest fashion, and a larger assortment of iron andirons with brass heads, (different sizes) from sixteen to fifty shillings per pair; also a few dozen of shovels and tongs, suitable to the above; a few brass fenders, also brass shovels and tongs, brass and pinchbeck knee buckles; makes all kinds of brass work, mill brass and pump chambers, also branding irons of metal that will not rust, also brass fenders, melting pots No. 15, No. 12. . . .—*The New-York Gazette and the Weekly Mercury,* August 26, 1771. Also *N. Y. Mercury,* May 20, 1765.

THOMAS YATES, Brass Founder, and Copper-Plate Printer, from Birmingham, living in Fincher's Alley, near

the Bowling Green, New-York; Makes all Sorts of Hand
Irons, Buckles, Buttons, &c. Likewise makes all sorts
of small Steel and Iron Tools for Cabinet-Makers, Carv-
ers, Silver Smiths, and Engravers, such as Chizzels,
Gouges, Drills, Scorpers, Gravers, Punchers, &c. &c. Also,
House Bells hung in the neatest and best Manner. N.B.
He makes, mends and repairs all Sorts of Locks. *The
New-York Gazette*, November 19, 1759.

CUTLERS

EDWARD ANDREWS Cutler, who served an Apprenticeship to the famous Mr. Henry Jones of Sweething's Alley
by the Royal Exchange London, arrived in this Place
last Week in the Irene, Capt. Garrison, and has taken a
Shop in the House, late in the Possession of Mrs. Easom,
next Door to Mrs. Groesbeck's near the Merchants
Coffee-House; where Gentlemen, Ladies, and others, may
depend on having all kinds of Cutlery-Work done by
him, in the newest and neatest Fashions now in Vogue
at London, and at reasonable Rates. He has brought
over with him a small but choice Assortment of Goods in
his Way, such as Table-knives, Butchers-knives, and Pen-
knives, Razors, Lancets, and Scissers; Buttons, Buckles,
Cork-screws, Seals, and noted Constantinople Razors-
Cases and Strops, &c. &c.—*The New-York Gazette and
the Weekly Post-Boy, Supplement*, dated May 18, 1752.

JOHN ARIS at the Cross Guns in Market Field Street,
near the N. E. Bastion of the Fort, Makes, Mends, and
Grinds all Sorts of Cutlery Ware and Surgeon's Instru-
ments. You may also have all sorts of White Smith's
Work done by him, all at a very reasonable Rate.—*The
New-York Weekly Journal*, January 11, 1742.

BAILEY & YOULE, Cutlers from Sheffield at Their Shop
Near the Merchants Coffee-House, Makes all sorts of
surgeons instruments, trusses, steel collars for children,
irons for lame legs, and silversmiths tools; likewise grinds

all sorts of knives, razors, shears, and scissars, to look as neat as when new; also fixes new blades into any kind of hafts; cut gentlemen and ladies names, with numbers for numbering linen, and books, wherewith they give either red or black ink which will not wash out, and may be used by any person without trouble or inconveniency.

They likewise have for Sale, Silk stockings, silver hafted knives and forks, ivory and ebony ditto, red wood, plain and silver ferrel'd ditto, stag, buck and bone ditto, carving knives and forks, pen-knives of all sorts, pocket, garden ditto, razors of all sorts, bones and razor straps, fine cast steel scissars, common ditto of all sorts, taylors shears and thimbles, tortoiseshell combs, and common butchers knives, saws, steels and cleavers, shoemakers knives of all sorts, cock gaffs, netting and knitting needles, sword canes with cocks, plain ditto, silver seals and steel blocks, silver plated ditto, double and single plane irons, carving gouges and chissels of all sorts, watch chrystals, and silver buckels of the newest fashions. N.B. They give the greatest price for old gold and silver lace, and old gold and silver.—*The New-York Gazette and the Weekly Mercury,* March 4, 1771.

THOMAS BROWN.—William Gale, who formerly lived in Duke-Street, next to Mr. Bayard, has imported Clothier's Shears, Cards &c. he is to be spoke with at the House of Thomas Brown, Cutler in Hanover-Square, in New-York.—*The New-York Weekly Journal,* November 30, 1741.

THOMAS BROWN, is removed to the Sign of the Cross-Daggers in Smiths-Fly, near the Fly-Market, and sells all Sorts of Ironmongery and Cutlery Ware, by Wholesale or retail; as Locks, Hinges, Gimblets, Bolts, Latches, Pullies and Sash Line, dripping and frying Pans, Carpenter's Hammers, Chizzels, compasses and Rules, Drawing Knives, Stone and Brick Trowels, London Glue, Wooll-Combs & Cards, Brass Handles & Escutcheons, and all other Materials for Cabinet-Makers, Broad axes,

Hand-saws & Iron Squares, and all sorts of Coopers Tools, all sorts of knives, Scissars, Lancets, Razors, Coat & Breast Buttons, Thimbles, Pins and Needles; all sorts of Shoemakers Tools, Smith's Anvils & Vises, German & English Steel, all sorts of London soft & hard Metal Pewter & all Sorts of sadlery Ware. He likewise grinds Razors, scissars & Lancets, as usual.—*The New-York Weekly Post-Boy,* May 19, 1746.

JOHN FLANNER, Cutler, from London, now living near the Fly-Market in New-York; Makes and sells all sorts of Cutlery Ware, and Grinds scissars, Razors, Pen Knives, or any other sort of Instruments, after the best Manner, with Expedition.—*The New-York Gazette Revived in the Weekly Post-Boy,* September 21, 1747.

WILLIAM JASPER, cutler, Just arrived from England, is now settled in New York, near the Fly, Queen-Street, near the Burling's and Beekman's Slip, next Door to Mr. Murray's, takes this Method to acquaint the publick, That he makes all kinds of Surgeons instruments, and grinds and cleans them; makes Razors, Pen knives, scissars, and all kinds of Edge Tools, which he also grinds; and makes Cutlery in general; makes Buckles of the best Block-Tin, wrought and plain Men's Gold and Silver Ware; Pinking-Irons of all Sorts; Sadlers Tools; Fret-Saws; Hatters knives; likewise draws Teeth with great Ease and Safety, being accustomed to it for many Years. He likewise has brought over a Quantity of Copper and Tin Hard-Ware. All Persons that please to favour him with their Custom, may depend upon being served in the best and cheapest Manner.—*The New-York Gazette,* August 29, 1763.

LUCAS & SHEPARD, White-smiths and Cutlers, from Birmingham and Sheffield, At their shop at the Fly-market, near the Ferry-Stairs, make all sorts of surgeons instruments, all sorts of jointed irons for lame legs, steel trusses, and steel collars for children, all sorts of double jointed plyers, steel pads with sets of bits; silver-smiths, braziers, and tinners tools; turning lathes for any trade, tobacco engines, stove grates, iron bed steads, winding up and smoak jacks coach smith's work, new locks, and any sort of keys made to old ones, coopers vices, all sorts of gimblets, plane irons double and single center pins, cork screws, all sorts of carving tools and white smith's work. Likewise makes all sorts of knives and forks, pocket and pen knives, shoemakers knives, tobacco knives, razors, lancets, fleams, butcher's steels, knives and cleavers. Also grind all sorts of knives, razors, scissars, shears, fleams and lancets, and all parts of sword cutling; put new blades into any sort of hafts. We having wrought with Mr. Bailey for three years past, hope gentlemen and ladies will favour us with their custom, as they may depend upon being well used, and that the above articles are made here.—*The New-York Gazette and the Weekly Mercury*, May 20, 1771.

LUCAS & SHEPHERD.—As the Co-partnership of Lucas and Shepherd, expired the first of May last, Sebastian Lucas, Whitesmith and Cutler, from Birmingham, Takes this opportunity to acquaint the public in general, and those in particular whose friendship he has already experienced, that he still carries on the busines, at his shop . . .—*The New-York Gazette and the Weekly Mercury*, September 13, 1773.

RICHARD SAUSE, Cutler, Has removed from the Corner of the Slote, in Smith-street, next door to Messrs Thompson's and Selby's Saddlers, near the coffee house, where he continues to carry on the cutlery business, in various branches, Viz—New works of various sorts, surgeons instruments of all sorts, ground, glazed, polished and set-swords, pistols, guns, &c. cleaned and polished, silver-smith's, brasier's and tinmen's tools of all sorts ground and polished; taylors, glovers, and all other shears; Choping knives, saddlers, shoe-makers and butcher knives; fleams, razors, scissars, pen knives, (and any

other things to tedious to mention) ground and finished
in a neat manner.

N.B. Said Sause, returns thanks to the Publick for
their favours, and hopes by his care and assiduity for a
continuance of the same.—*The New-York Gazette*, April
6-13, 1767.

JOHN SCULTHORPE. — Whereas John Sculthorpe,
Peruke-maker, near the Fly Market, has, for several
Years past, carried on the above said Branch, and Cutlery
grinding, and intends now to decline one of them, as he
cannot attend them with such Dispatch he would chuse.
He therefore informs any Persons of either of the said
Business, that they may enter into a good accustomed
Shop, by applying to him, who will agree for the same
on reasonable Terms.

N.B. As due Attendance cannot be given to both, he
hopes to serve his Customers, in the continued one of
Peruke-making, in a more regular and expeditious Manner. To be entered into on May Next.—*The New-York
Gazette*, January 28, 1760.

NICHOLAS VANDYCK, Cutler, Living on the Dock near
the Ferry-Stairs in New-York. Grinds Razors, Scissars,
Pen-knives, Lancets and all sorts of Instruments, after
the best Manner with Expedition: He also grinds
Fuller's Sheers, approved to be well done by Mr. Gale:
Likewise makes or mends Bellowses for Goldsmith or
Blacksmiths, after the newest Model. He makes and
sells Brass Buckles, wholesale or retail, as also Brass
Boxes for Mill Brushes, with sundry other Things in the
Brass Foundry Way, all expeditiously, and at reasonable
Rates.—*The New-York Gazette Revived in the Weekly
Post-Boy*, October 5, 1747.

JOHN WALLACE, who lately lived by the Old Slip Market, is Removed to the Sign of the Cross-Swords, next
Door to Mrs. Byfield, near the Fly-Market, who makes,
mends and grinds all sorts of Knives, Razors, Scizers, and

Pen-knives. Surgeons may be supplyed with very good Lancets and other Surgeons instruments. Gentlemen may be furnish'd with all sorts of Kitchin Furniture that belongs to a Smiths Trade. Barbers may have their Razors ground for four Pence a Piece. He puts up and mends all sorts of Jacks, Makes Multiplying Wheels for Jacks. He mends Locks and makes Keys, and Stillards also. He also sells all sorts of Cuttlery-Ware. And all at Reasonable Rates.—*The New-York Gazette,* June 12-20, 1737.

WHITESMITHS

JOHN ABEEL.—Anchors, From two hundred to seven hundred two quarters made of the very best bar iron, by the best anchor-smith in America equal if not superior in Quality to any made in Europe, to be sold by John Abeel, near the Coenties-Market, who can supply any Gentleman on a short notice with Anchors from 1000 to 1500 Weight.—*The New-York Gazette and the Weekly Mercury,* July 18, 1768 (*Supplement*).

ROBERT ANDREWS, Air-Jack-Maker from England, living on the Hill commonly called Pot-Baker's Hill, next door to Mr. Roorbach's. Makes and mends all sorts of Jacks: Also makes scale-Beams, or hangs Bells in Gentlemen's Houses; and all sorts of White-Smith's work after the best Manner. The Air-Jacks are of great Service to Chimnies that don't draw the smoke well; several has been already prov'd in this City. Any Gentlemen or Ladies that will be pleased to favour him with their Custom, may depend upon being faithfully serv'd, by their Humble Servant, ROBERT ANDREWS.—*The New-York Gazette and the Weekly Post-Boy,* May 7, 1753.

ROBERT ANDREWS, White-Smith and Jack-Maker, in Wall-street, near Mr. Christopher Bancker's, Makes and sells, Iron Pales for Ashes, at 24 s. Tests for Stoves, at 2 s. Also Iron Scale Beams, and all other Sorts of

Smith's Work, at a reasonable Rate.—*The New-York Mercury*, November 6, 1758.

ELIAS BONNELL & ROBERT FARRIS, in Wall-street, in the shop that Mr. Robert Andrews lately kept, next Door to Mr. Banker's, Makes, and sells smoak Jacks, in the best manner, with Care and Expedition; As also all sorts of White Work, together with ship and shop stoves; Ash-Pails; Stove Tests; horse shoeing, and Farriery; with all sorts of House Work; and Edge Tools done in the best manner, by ELIAS BONNEL, and ROBERT FARRIS. —*The New-York Gazette*, June 23, 1760.

JOHN BURCH, Tin-Plate Worker and Japanner, from London, Has removed from the Fly, to the house in Hanover-Square lately occupied by Mr. Lloyd Daubney, and opposite Mr. Gaine's printing-office, where he carries on both branches in the most extensive manner. He has by him a large collection of tin ware of all kinds, both plain and japan'd, which he will sell as cheap as they can be bought in London. Those who buy to sell again will have a large allowance made them. As several parts of his business are entirely new in this country, he hopes for such encouragement as will induce him to continue them.

N.B. Many block-tin articles for kitchen use, warranted to stand the fire, and not have any pernicious quality, as many other metals have.—*The New-York Gazette and the Weekly Mercury*, May 3, 1773.

JOHN BALTHUS DASH, Tinman, from Germany; At his house near the Oswego Market, makes the best of French Horns, Philadelphia Buttons and Shoe Buckles, and will sell them very reasonably by wholesale or retail.—*The New-York Mercury*, March 18, 1765.

JOHN DIES, of this City, Iron-Monger, intends, next May, to decline that Business: . . . N.B. Isaac Goelet and Peter Curtenius, in Partnership, intends to carry on the same Sort of Business, in the same House, at the Golden-Key, in Hanover-Square.—*The New-York Gazette or the Weekly Post-Boy*, February 4, 1754.

NICHOLAS GODDARD.—Run Away . . . from William Puntiner . . . an English servant man, named Nicholas Goddard, by trade a tinman. . . .—*The New-York Gazette*, January 14, 1760.

JOHN GRAHAM, Tinman, Informs his friends and customers, that he is removed from the house where Mr. Baltus Dash formerly lived to the next Door but one where Mr. Whiteman used to live, in the Broad-Way, near the lower end of the Oswego market, where he makes and mends all kinds of tin work as usual; he also does all kinds of copper-smith's and braziers work, and makes brass buckles, tins copper and brass in the best manner. All those that will favour him with their custom, will be served at the most reasonable rates, By their humble Servant, JOHN GRAHAM.—*The New-York Gazette and the Weekly Mercury*, April 23, 1770.

SAMUEL KEMPTON.—This is to acquaint the Publick, That Samuel Kempton, his Shop on Hunter's-Quay, near the Coffee-House: Makes and sells all Sorts of Tin-Ware, fit for Shipping, or the Army: Any Gentlemen that please to favour him with their Custom, may depend upon being Expeditiously and Reasonably served, by their humble Servant, SAMUEL KEMPTON.—*The New-York Gazette or the Weekly Post-Boy*, October 30, 1758.

WILLIAM RICHARDSON, Lock Smith and Bell Hanger from the City of London. Makes all sorts of Iron-Work, scrole-works, Leafage or Foldage, all sorts of Doctors Instruments Capital or Pocket, Spring Trusses, Bag Trusses or Spring Bandages for Ruptures, all sorts of Jacks made and fixed Horisantical or Vertical, likewise makes secret Padlocks for secret Places, or Spanish ditto. Any Person may be supplyed at the cheapest Rate, at his

House in the Broad-Way, New-York.—*The New-York Weekly Journal*, May 22, 1749.

RIGGS & HADDEN.—Wanted, A Person that understands the nailing business in its different branches, or has been employed in that manufactory. Such a person bringing proper recommendations, will meet with good encouragement, by applying to Joseph Riggs, Esq; or Joseph Hadden, in Newark, New-Jersey, who are entring largely into that business.—*The New-York Gazette and the Weekly Mercury*, April 11, 1768 (*Supplement*).

SEAGER & SMITH.—Whereas John Seager and Samuel Smith, Nail-Makers, of this City declared off Partnership the 10th Instant; and John Seager only, now carries on the Business as usual, on Mr. Brazier's Wharf, near the Ship-Yards, where all his old Customers may be supplied as formerly; assuring them and all others, they shall be served to the utmost Satisfaction of their humble Servant, JOHN SEAGER.

N.B. It is desired that none of the Debtors to the Partnership will pay any Money to the said Samuel Smith.—*The New-York Gazette*, January 12-19, 1767.

TIN-MEN wanted. Very good encouragement will be given to fifteen or twenty persons, who understand the working of flat-iron into kettles, if they apply to Samuel Ogden, at Boonetown, in Morris County, New Jersey; who hath rod and sheet iron of all sizes to dispose of. Apply to Josiah Shippey, at Mr. Isaac Roosevelt's, New-York.—*The New-York Gazette and the Weekly Mercury*, August 12, 1776.

TIN PLATE WORKER will have constant Employ & good Wages by applying to Smith at the Corner of Burling's Slip, in Queen's Street.—*The New-York Gazette and the Weekly Mercury*, December 9, 1776.

HENRY USTICK.—Nails, Made and sold by Henry Ustick, At his Nailery in Smith-Street, on Pot-baker's-

Hill, near Judge Horsmanden's, Four-penny, 10, 12, 20, 24, and 30 d. Nails; sheathing, drawing, Jack and sugar cask nails; and spikes of all sorts, coppers rivets, &c. by the cask or lesser quantity. Orders for any sort of nails complied with on the shortest notice. . . .—*The New-York Gazette and the Weekly Mercury,* February 17, 1772.

JOURNEYMEN NAIL-MAKERS, Are wanted immediately. —Such, properly qualified, will meet with good Encouragement, by applying to William Ustick, at the Sign of the Lock and Key, between Burling's and Beekman's slip, in New-York.—*The New-York Gazette and the Weekly Mercury,* September 12, 1768.

IRON WORKS

AMERICAN COMPANY'S IRON WORKS, Notice is hereby given, to all those indebted to the American Company, by bond, note, book debt, or otherwise, at Ringwood, Long pond, and Charlotteburg works, or elsewhere, that Robert Erskine, the present manager, the company's agent in New York, or such person or persons as he or they shall appoint, are alone authorized to receive debts due to the company, and to give proper discharges for the same. Whoever therefore shall pay any debt or balance to any other person, will undoubtedly, be again sued for the same by ROBERT ERSKINE.[4]—*The New-York Journal or the Grand Advertiser,* April 1, 1773.

ANDOVER PIG-METAL, To be sold by the subcriber, at Elizabeth-Town. Gentlemen in New-York may be supplied with any quantity, on giving the shortest notice to John Blanchard.—*The New-York Gazette and the Weekly Mercury,* January 18, 1773.

[4] The American Company Iron Works of New-Jersey authorized Reade and Yates as well as Robert Erskine to be agents.—*The New-York Gazette and the Weekly Mercury,* September 28, 1772.

CHARLOTTEBURG FURNACE.—Ore Carters for Charlotteburg Furnace. Notice is hereby given to those who
usually carted ore from Hibernia mine to the above
furnace, or others, that those who choose to commence
carting on or before the 10th of October next, and who
shall deliver a quantity not less than three tons a week,
till it amounts to 30 tons, shall be paid as formerly, 10 s.
6d. New-York Money per ton; and for their further
encouragement, they shall have the same price in sleighing time. Those who begin carting after the 10th of
October, will receive 10 s. per ton, and if the quantity
carted amounts to 20 tons, they shall receive 9s. per ton
in sleighing time.

N.B. None except those who cart at the above rates,
shall have the privilege to sleigh at the foregoing prices;
all others who only sleigh, are desired to remember that
no more than 8s. per ton will be given in sleighing time.
If through unavoidable misfortune, the carters shall fall
short of their stipulated quantity, they may depend on
all reasonable indulgence from the manager. ROBERT
ERSKINE.—*The New-York Journal or the General
Advertiser,* September 17, 1772.

ETNA FURNACE.—At Etna Furnace, in the County of
Burlington, New-Jersey: Founders who can execute the
moulding and casting of flasked and unflasked or open
Iron ware, both hollow and flat, with neatness and Expedition: Any Person who can make Brass or mixed Metal
Moulds for castings, and any Workman who well understands the making of such Moulds as are made of Wood
and of Flasks, and can produce good Characters, may
meet with extraordinary Encouragement. It is expected
that the Mould should be finished with great Skill and
Accuracy, and may be made at the Workman's place of
Abode, if in this or the neighbouring Provinces . . .
Good Colliers, Keepers and Stocktakers are wanted at
two Furnaces and two Forges there lately erected. . . .—
The New-York Gazette or the Weekly Post-Boy, January
25, 1768.

FORGE.—Two thirds of a good Forge or Ironworks, with Hammers Anvils, Bellows, running Gear, &c. in good Order, and a new Grist-Mill, having one pair of Stones, and a Boulting-Mill, commodiously situated on Black-Creek, one half Mile from Borden-Town, . . . N.B. The Purchaser may buy the other third Part of the said Works upon reasonable Terms of William Yard, and the payment may be on the same conditions as above. He also may buy a parcel of Coal Wood already set in Pits to make Coal, so that he may soon begin to go to work.— *The New-York Weekly Post-Boy*, July 18, 1748.

FORGE.—To be Sold, or Let, for a Term, The Moiety, or one Half of a Forge for making Bar Iron, &c. with Carriages, Privileges of Land and Water, Houses, Coals Sheds, with the Appurtenances, situated at a place called Murders Creek, on the West Side of Hudson River, at the North Side of the High Lands, where the same Creek empties into the Hudson's River. Any Person inclining to purchase the same may apply to John Alsop, in Hanover Square in the City of New-York, and agree upon reasonable Terms, and receive a good Title. JOHN ALSOP.—*The New-York Gazette*, May 28, 1759.

FORGE AND HAMMER MEN.—Thirteen of the best Hammer-men and Forge-men in the Iron Manufactory have been engaged to come from Sheffield to America, for which a handsome premium is given them; and great wages for two years certain, and six shillings a week to each of their wives and families as stay behind for that time. They have also given one hundred guineas for each of the best Saw-makers, and the same money for their wives that stay. (If provisions are kept up at the rate they at, the Americans will soon have hands enough to carry on the manufactories, without giving premiums, —News item from London, July 13, in *The New-York Journal or General Advertiser*, October 8, 1767.

FOREST OF DEAN FURNACE.—To be Sold, A Lease, of which seven years are unexpired, from the 26th Septem-

ber next, of Forest of Dean Furnace, together with all
the appurtenances and stock necessary to the well conducting thereof, situated in the Highlands of New-York.
. . .—*The New-York Gazette and the Weekly Mercury,*
April 9, 1770.

FURNACE.—To be sold, a new well-built furnace, good
iron mines near the same, two forges, one with 3, and the
other with 2 fires; a saw mill, several dwelling-houses
and coal-houses, and several tracts of land adjoining;
. . . The furnace and forges are situated on a good
stream, 28 miles from Acquackanung landing, and 36
from Newark. Whoever inclines to purchase the same,
may apply to Nicholas Gouverneur, in New-York, or to
David Ogden, sen. Samuel Gouverneur, and David
Ogden, jun. at Newark, who will agree for the same.—
The New-York Mercury, March 5, 1764.

FURNACE.—The Blast Furnace, with the coal houses
and other appurtenances at Bloomingdale, near Pomp-
ton, late the property of John and Uzal Ogden, Esquires,
will be sold at public vendue at the Coffee-House in the
city of New-York. . . .—*The New-York Gazette and
the Weekly Mercury,* June 22, 1772.

WILLIAM HAWXHURST.—William Hawxhurst, has
lately erected a finery and great Hammer, for refining
Sterling Pig Iron into Bar and takes this Method to
acquaint his old Customers, and others that they may
by applying to him in New-York, be supplyed with flat
and square Bar Iron, Cart, Waggon, Chair, and Sleigh
Tire-Mill Spindles; Wrines Cranks, and Iron Axletrees,
Cast Mill Rounds, and Gudgeons. He continues to make
Anchors as usual.—*The New-York Gazette or the
Weekly Post-Boy,* October 2, 1766.

HIBERNIA PIG IRON (which is found to make as good
Bar Iron as any in America) Plates for Chimney-Backs,
Cart and Waggon-Boxes, West-India Bars, for Sugar

Works, &c. to be sold by Gerard Bancker.—*The New-York Journal or the General Advertiser*, June 11, 1767.

HIBERNIA FURNACE, Morris-County, New-Jersey, The late Hibernia Company at this place is dissolved, and the works are now carried on for account of the Right Honourable the Earl of Sterling, the present sole proprietor thereof. A number of wood-cutters are now wanted at these works, also some good miners. A plentiful supply of all kinds of necessaries for the workmen, is now laid in, and will constantly be kept up. Three shillings per cord will be allowed for wood-cutting: Whoever inclines to work at this place, may depend on meeting with civil treatment, honest dealing, and punctual pay, from Joseph Hoff, Manager.—*Rivington's New-York Gazetteer*, February 3, 1774.

HIBERNIA FURNACE.—Wanted immediately, At the Hibernia Furnace, in Morris-County, New-Jersey, belonging to Messrs. Robert and John Murray, of New-York, a Number of Wood Cutters. Two Shillings and Nine-Pence per Cord will be given, and the Balance paid as soon as the Quantity agreed for is completed, by the subscriber living at the Works. Joseph Hoff.—*The New-York Gazette and the Weekly Mercury*, January 1776.

IRON MANUFACTURE.—An Easie Way to get Money and be Rich, Just Published, A Scheme by striking Twenty Thousand Pounds Paper Money) to encourage the raising of Hemp, and the Manufacturing of Iron in the Province of New-York, with some Observations, shewing the Necessity and Advantages thereof. Sold by the Printer hereof, Price 6d.—*The New-York Gazette*, March 15-22, 1737.

LEAD MINE.—As we have but little material Intelligence to present our Readers with this Week; we hope it will not be disagreeable, to inform them, that we have been credibly assured that a valuable lead Mine was lately discovered in Dutchess County, in this Province; and that some of the Ore having been tried, yielded in the Proportion of three Quarters of a Pound of fine Lead, to a Pound of Ore: 'Tis said, it lies in great Quantities near the surface of the Earth, and that the Owners of the Land are resolved to set about the improving it with all possible Diligence; so we hope it may turn out to their, as well as the Country's Advantage.—News item in *The New-York Gazette Revived in the Weekly Post-Boy*, March 26, 1750.

LIVINGSTON'S FORGE.—To be Sold by Robert Livingston, junr. A Parcel of choice Pigg Iron, at Eight Pound per Tun. Ready Money, or Rum, Sugar, Molasses at Market Price. N.B. It's Manufactur'd, at Ancram in Manner of Livingston.—*The New-York Weekly Journal*, April 2, 1744.

LIVINGSTON'S FORGE.—Wanted, at Robert Livingston's Junr. new Forge in Mannor Livingston, which will be ready in three Weeks Time; Three good Refiners, to make bar-iron, with each a good hand to work with them: Stock will never be wanting. Good encouragement will be given for refining and drawing bar-iron, with good accomodations. For further particulars, enquire of Peter R. Livingston, Merchant in New-York or Robert Livingston Junr. at his seat in said Mannor.—*The New-York Mercury*, October 27, 1760.

MOUNT HOLLY.—To be sold by the Subscriber, the Iron-works known by the Name of Mount Holly Iron-Works, Viz. One Forge or Finery, with three Fire Places, and three Pair of Bellows, and all the Utensils thereunto belonging: Also one other Forge or Chafery, with one Fire Place, and one Pair of Bellows, with all the Utensils belonging to it, built for the Conveniency of the hammer Man, where he meets with no Interruption from the Finers, both built upon the main Branch of Ranchocus Creek; Water Carriage from the Forges to Philadelphia;

. . . Any Person inclinable to purchase, and will come
and view the Premises, may be informed of the Price,
and the Incumberances upon it, by Peter Bard.—*The
New-York Mercury,* November 7, 1763.

MOUNT HOPE, pig and bar iron, of as good a quality as
any made in America, to be sold by Mr. Nicholas Hoffman, in New-York, Mr. John Blanchard, at Elizabeth
Town, or by Messrs. Faish and Wrisberg, the proprietors,
at Mount Hope, in New-Jersey, where particular drafts
of iron will be drawn on the shortest notice, and executed in the neatest and best manner.—*The New-York
Gazette and the Weekly Mercury,* July 5, 1773.

NEW FOREST PIG IRON.—The best of New Forrest Pig
Iron, by the Ton, . . . To be sold, by John Abeel.—*The
New-York Mercury,* December 17, 1764.

NEW-YORK AIR FURNACE.—Gilbert Forbes, At the Sign
of the Broad-Ax . . . sells Ironmongery, Cutlary, Sadlery, and Brass Furniture of all Sorts, Pots and Kettles,
cast at the New-York Air Furnace, which are very thin
and light, not inferior to the Holland, for Use or standing
the Fire.   Also, Iron Sauce Pans, Cart, Waggon, and
Chair Boxes, Pot-Ash Kettles and Coolers, Chimney-
backs and Plates of any Size; and many other Things
in that Way.—*The New-York Gazette,* January 12-19,
1767.

NEW-YORK AIR FURNACE.—To the Public, The New-
York Air Furnace Company, Have lately erected an Air
Furnace near the City, which after a considerable Expence, they have now got in proper Order, for Casting
in the neatest Manner, the under mentioned Goods,
which are equal to any imported from England, Scotland,
Ireland, or even Holland, either for Shape, Lightness,
boiling white, or standing Fire: They therefore hope
the Publick will encourage the Works, by giving the
Preference to what is American Make, especially when

the Price is full as low as any can be afforded for, that are imported from Europe. viz. Pots, Kettles, skillets, pot-ash kettles, and bottoms for calcining pot-ash, which they will warrant for three months, chimney backs, layers and jamb-plates, agreeable to any pattern that shall be sent, forge and fullers plates, hatters basons, forge hammers and anvils, sugar house boilers, stoves, pipes and grates, round and square stoves for work shops or house-use, ships cabooses, perpetual ovens, pye-pans, . . . —*The New-York Gazette,* August 17-24, 1767.

NEW-YORK AIR FURNACE.—Peter T. Curtenius, At the Sign of the Golden Anvil and Hammer, . . . has also for Sale the following Goods, made at the New-York Air Furnace, viz. Best Pot-Ash Kettles and Coolers, Hearths, Bars and Doors for Pot-Ash Works, Forge Hammers and Anvils, Chimney Backs, Bottoms and Jamb Plates, Ship's Cabooses, Cart, Waggon, and Chair Boxes, Pots and Kettles, Pye-pans, Sugar-Boilers, Rollers and Gudgeons, Large Screws and Nuts for Spermactic Works, Fullers Screws and Plates; besides many other articles in the cast Iron Way: And if Persons want any new Article done in that Way, they may have it cast to any Pattern they shall leave at the Furnace, or at my House.—*The New-York Gazette or the Weekly Post-Boy,* February 4, 1771.

NEW-YORK AIR FURNACE.—Between 12 and 1 o'Clock last Friday Morning, a Fire broke out at the Air Furnace belonging to Messrs Sharp and Curtenius, in the West Ward of this City; Its Situation being pretty remote from the Town, and a Wooden Building, the same was almost consumed before the Inhabitants could be collected, notwithstanding which every Measure was pursued for the Preservation of the Materials belonging to the Furnace; though the loss 'tis said will amount to, at least 400£.—News item in *The New-York Journal or the General Advertiser,* November 26, 1772.

New-York Air Furnace.—To the Public, Sharpe, Curtenius, and Lyle, Have rebuilt (at a considerable Expense) The New-York Air Furnace, In a much completer Manner than before it was burnt down; and as they provided themselves with a sufficient Stock of Pig-Metal, &c. they propose to carry on the Foundery Business in all its Branches with great Diligence, and flatter themselves that the Friends of America will encourage them, by preferring Goods manufactured in their own Country, especially when they are as good, and sold as cheap as they can be imported from Europe. . . .—*The New-York Gazette or the Weekly Post-Boy,* April 12, 1773.

Noble & Townsend's Forge.—A forge with Six Fires, to be built near Sterling, for Mess'rs Noble and Townsend, who will give Great Encouragement to any person that will erect and compleat the same. Anyone that inclines to undertake it, must give in their proposals before the 25th of January, as immediately after that, it is intended to set about cutting and drawing the timber. As the roughness of the country makes it necessary to collect the timber while the snow is on the ground, the person that applies ought to be strong handed. For further particulars apply to William Hawxhurst in New-York.

N. B. Good encouragement will be given to those who understand making steel from Pig metal, in the German method, as the above Forge is designed to be employed in that business.—*The New-York Journal or the General Advertiser,* December 28, 1775.

North Carolina Forge.—Any persons that are well acquainted with the method of casting cannon, mortars, shells and shot, and also the common sorts of hollow ware, such as pots, kettles, &c. and are willing to go to North-Carolina, may have extraordinary encouragement, by applying to the Delegates of that state, in Philadelphia. The Expences of their removal will be defrayed, by that state, and it is not doubted but such persons as may undertake to go will find it very easy to procure good land for themselves and families, as there are many thousand acres of vacant land convenient to the works. —*The New-York Gazette and the Weekly Mercury,* September 28, 1776.

SAMUEL OGDEN'S IRON WORKS.—Samuel Ogden, Manufactures in the best manner, at his works in Booneton; bar iron for rudders, grist-mills; share moulds, large and small, square and flat iron of all sizes; and also cart, and waggon and chair tire: Which he will deliver at New York on the most reasonable terms, drawn agreeable to any given directions, immediately after application made there fore, to him at said works, or to Mr. Nicholas Hoffman merchant, in New-York.—*The New-York Gazette and the Weekly Mercury,* December 21, 1772.

PRINCIPIO IRON WORKS.—Run away the 15th of this instant August, 1728, from Stephen Onion, & Company, of Principio Iron-Works in Cæcil County in the Province of Maryland, two Servant Men. . . .—*The New-York Gazette,* August 19-26, 1728.

RINGWOOD IRON WORKS.—Wanted, at Ringwood Iron-Works, in the Jersies, Sober Men, that understand driving a Horse Team, any such, of good character, will meet with Employment, in that way, by applying as above.—*The New-York Gazette and the Weekly Mercury,* September 12, 1768.

SALISBURY FURNACE.—To be Sold, At Salisbury Furnace, in Connecticut, For Cash, or Produce in Hand: A Pair of Hessian, or Wooden Furnace Bellows, . . . N.B. The Furnace at Salisbury, is now re-building, and will require larger Bellows than the above, which is the sole Reason of their being offered to Sale.—*The New-York Gazette or the Weekly Post-Boy,* July 2, 1770.

SALISBURY FURNACE.—To be Sold, and possession given in February next, or sooner, if required. The Furnace Situated in the town of Salisbury, and province of Connecticut in New-England, having been lately rebuilt on the most approved plan, . . . Also to be Sold a Compleat double Forge With four fires and two hammers (now at work) together with all necessary utensils; situated in Colebrook, in Connecticut, near the road from Hartford to the furnace; built in 1771. . . .—*The New-York Gazette and the Weekly Mercury,* November 29, 1773.

STEEL.—American Steel, Manufactured by John Zane, at Trentown, esteem'd quite equal, if not better in quality than what is imported from England, may be had of Bowne and Rickman, at their store in the house of Peter Clopper, facing the Fly-market, on reasonable terms, in half faggots, or blister'd, by Ct. wt.

N.B. If on tryal any bar proves faulty, it will be received back, and the money return'd. They have an assortment of Dry Goods as usual.—*The New-York Gazette and the Weekly Mercury,* June 8, 1772.

STERLING IRON WORKS.—Good Encouragement given by Hawxhurst and Noble, at Sterling Iron Works, for Wood-cutters, Colliers, Refiners of Pig and Drawers of Bar Iron. Also a Person well recommended for driving a four Horse Stage, between the said Works and the Landing. N.B. Pig and Bar Iron, and sundry English Goods to be Sold by William Hawxhurst in New-York.—*The New-York Mercury,* October 29, 1759.

STERLING IRON WORKS.—Whereas the Copartnership, between Hawxhurst and Noble, in the Sterling Iron Works, expired on the 19th Day of October last; all Persons who have any Demands on the said Copartnership, are desired to bring in their Accounts to said Hawxhurst, at New-York, to receive Satisfaction. The Works are still carried on by said Hawxhurst, and the best Encouragement given for a Founder, Smith, Anchor Smiths, Miners, Carpenters, Colliers, Wood Cutters, Carters, and common Labourers: They will be paid ready Cash for their Labour, and be supplied with Provisions there upon the best Terms. . . .—*The New-York Mercury*, September 28, 1761.

STERLING IRON WORKS.—W. Hawxhurst, Still carries on the Sterling iron works, and gives the best encouragement for founders, miners, mine burners, pounders, and furnace fillers, bank's-men, and stock takers, finers of pigg, and drawers of bar; smiths, and anchor smiths, carpenters, colliers, woodcutters, and common labourers; They will be paid ready cash for their labour, and will be supplied with provisions there, upon the best terms. . . .—*The New-York Gazette and the Weekly Post-Boy, Supplement* for November 3, 1763, dated November 4, 1763.

THE STERLING ANCHORY Which was burnt down in May, 1767, is rebuilt, and carried on by Noble and Townsend; all Gentlemen, Merchants, and others, that will be kind enough to apply to William Hawxhurst, in New-York, may be supplied with Anchors warranted for a Year, made out of refin'd Iron wrought from the Sterling Pigs. . . .—*The New-York Gazette and the Weekly Mercury*, April 17, 1769.

TANTON FORGE.—A New Forge or Bloomery, called Tanton, is now finished on a Stream never failing nor subject to Back-Water or hasty Freshes, about sixteen Miles from Burlington, and the same Distance from Philadelphia, in a Country remarkably healthy, and has a good Stock of Coal housed.

Good sober Workmen are wanted to carry her on, and extraordinary Encouragement will be given to One who will have a more general Oversight, and shall come well recommended, with or without a Family.

Good Master Colliers to Coal by the Load, bringing

Recommendations with them, will be encouraged at Tanton and Atsion Forges, which are near to each other, and where the Business of Coaling has every Convenience possible. Wood Cutters are also wanted. For further Particulars, enquire of Charles Read, Esq; at Burlington.—*The New-York Gazette and the Weekly Post-Boy*, December 25, 1766.

UNION IRON WORKS.—To be sold, two tracts of land, one of 750 acres, part in the county of Hunterdon, and part in the county of Morris, divided by a run called Spruce-Run (which run turns the Union-Iron-Works) is about 8 miles from said works, about the same distance from Johnson's furnace, and about 12 miles from Robinson's works. . . .—*The New-York Mercury*, August 22, 1757.

VESUVIUS FURNACE, at Newark, in New-Jersey; A Single Man, well recommended, who understand moulding and casting of Iron Hollow Ware, in all its branches, may hear of good Encouragement, by applying to Mr. James Abeel, Merchant, in New-York, or to Moses Ogden, at said Furnace.—*The New-York Gazette and the Weekly Mercury*, March 28, 1768.

VESUVIUS FURNACE.—To Be Sold, By James Abeel, Near the Albany-Pier; Hollow-Ware of all kinds, made at Vesuvius Furnace, at New-Jersey, and allowed by the best Judges to be far preferable to any made in America. Likewise Old West-India and N. York Rum, and best Muscovado Sugar by the Hogshead.—*The New-York Gazette and the Weekly Mercury*, July 4, 1768.

VESUVIUS FURNACE.—Wanted immediately, At Vesuvius Air-Furnace, at Newark, East New-Jersey, two Persons who understand molding or Hollow Ware in Sand; such will meet with good Encouragement, by applying to Edward Laight and James Abeel, in New-York, or to Moses Ogden, at the said Furnace.—*The*

New-York Gazette and the Weekly Mercury, March 12,
1770.

VESUVIUS FURNACE.—At Laight & Ogden's Air-
Furnace, Are made Iron Castings of every Kind, equal
in Quality to any imported from Europe. They now
have for Sale at the Store of Edward and Wm. Laight,
Pot-Ash kettles, coolers, cauldrons of forty gallons; iron
pots and kettles from 28 to 1 gallon, lighter than Holland
or English: iron stoves of various sizes; plates for chimney backs and jambs; iron sash weights, by the use of
which instead of lead, every purchaser saves two-pence
per lb. ox-cart and waggon boxes; iron tea kettles and
pye pans; griddles, swivel guns, &c. &c.

Any, or every of the above enumerated articles are
made at the shortest notice, agreeable to any pattern or
dimensions, to be left at Mr. Moses Ogden's, at the
furnace in Newark, or at the aforesaid store of Edw. and
Wm. Laight, near Burling's-Slip, New-York, where may
be had as usual on the lowest terms a universal Assortment of Ironmongery and Cutlery, Also Indigo, Oil &
Blubber, &c.—*Rivington's New-York Gazette,* November
18, 1773.

METAL WORK

IRONMONGERY.—Choice Bohea Tea, also Sheathing
Duck Nails, and Spikes, and all Sorts of best London
Nails, Long Scythes, Sicles, Dutch Scythes, Spades, Shod,
Shovels, Iron Hoops, best London Steel long and short
Handle Frying Pans, Anvils, and Vices, also Anchors and
small Swivell Guns.   And several other sorts of Iron
Ware to be Sold by JACOB FRANKS.—*The New-York
Weekly Journal,* April 23, 1739.

BRASS KNOCKERS.—Whereas some low-liv'd People
have, on Saturday the 3d Instant, at Night, broken off
and stolen the Brass Knockers of several Doors of Gentlemen's Houses, in this City: which vile and infamous
Practice hath, for some Years past, been frequently

repeated, not only to the Loss of the particular Persons suffering by such mean Practices, but also to the frequent Disturbance and Alarm of the Neighbourhood, wherein the said Villany has from time to time been perpetrated. This is therefore to give Notice, That if any Person or Persons shall discover the said Criminal or Criminals, to the Printer hereof, within Ten Days after this Date, and support his or their Accusation or Information, by Proof sufficient to convict the said Criminal or Criminals, in a Court of Justice; he or they so discovering shall be intituled to the Sum of Sixty Pounds, current Money of this Province, from the Persons whose Names are herewith given to the said Printer, subscribed to a Paper, whereby they bind themselves to pay the said Reward to such Informer or Informers; which Paper the said Printer will be ready to show the Person or persons so informing as aforesaid.—*The New-York Gazette Revived in the Weekly Post-Boy,* March 12, 1750.

BELL.—To be Sold by John Dyer of the City of New-York, a very good Bell, of a very good Size and Sound, fit for any Country Church or Court-house, &c. being about 120 lb. Weight, and will be sold very Reasonable. Any Person inclined to purchase the said Bell may apply to the above said John Dyer, and agree on reasonable Terms, or to the Printer hereof.—*The New-York Gazette,* May 14-21, 1733.

COPPER.—A very good Copper that hold 120 Gallons, being very strong and fit for any Use, to be Sold by John Dyer of the City, very Reasonable.—*The New-York Gazette,* September 10-17, 1733.

METAL WARE.—Lately imported, and to be sold very cheap, by Lodowick Bamper, at his House, in Beekman Street: A choice Assortment of Copper Tea Kettles, and Pye-Pans, Brass Candlesticks and Chafing-Dishes. . . .

—The New-York Gazette Revived in the Weekly Post-Boy, May 27, 1751.

CHIMNEY BACK.—Lately Stole out of a House rebuilding in Bever-Street a small Iron Chimney-back, with the Figures of a Parrot in a Ring on it: Also a pretty large Iron Hearth-Plate, plain: If any Person can give Intelligence of them, so that the Thief may have Justice done him, or the Plate got again, they shall have twenty shillings Reward, paid by the Printer hereof.—*The New-York Gazette Revived in the Weekly Post-Boy,* July 1, 1751.

ASH PAILS.—A Parcel of choice Iron Ash-Pails, proper for taking up hot Ashes from Hearths, to let them cool in; and are very useful as a Preservative against Fire; to be sold by Gerardus Beekman, opposite to the Fly Market.—*The New-York Gazette Revived in the Weekly Post-Boy,* January 27, 1752.

IRON WARE.—Just imported, and to be sold very cheap for Ready Money, By Rip Van Dam, at his Store near the New-Dutch Church; A very good Assortment of Iron Ware, viz. Skillets, from one Pint to six Quarts, small French Lancaster Kettles, Iron Pots and Kettles by the Ton, Iron and Lead Weights from 1 Quarter to 56 lb. Iron Chimney Backs, Sash Weights, Cellar Window Bars, large and small Morters, Cart and Waggon Wheel Boxes, Iron Cyder Mills, and a Parcel of Iron Boilers of 50 Gallons to be set in Brick; also an Assortment of Cutlery, Snuff Boxes, Chalk Corks by the Gross, and single-refin'd Loaf Sugar, &c.—*The New-York Mercury,* August 31, 1752.

TOOLS.—Just imported in the last Vessels from England, and to be sold cheap by Joseph Hallet, . . . Long, midling, and short scythes, ivory, buck and horn handle knives and forks, cutteau, jack and pruning knives; large midling and small sicles; mill cross cut and hand saws, ship carpenter's axes, adzes and mauls, blacksmith's vizes, sledges and hammers, screw plates of several sizes, long and short handle frying pans, locks and hinges of all sorts, dripping pans, pie pans and tea-kettles, very neat branched and brass candlesticks, a large assortment of files and rasps, house carpenter's broad axes, adzes and chisels, brass kettles bail'd and unbail'd, a good assortment of pewter, watches, glasses, keys, springs, seals and chains.

N.B. Said Hallet sells refin'd and common iron pots, cart, waggon and chair boxes.—*The New-York Mercury,* June 8, 1761.

BAR IRON.—To Be Sold, by Ludlow and Hoffman, in Bayard-Street, Refin'd Bar-Iron, Wholesale and Retail, stamped with the Letters D O noted for its being of the best Quality, and well drawn; where all Smiths and others, that have Occasion for particular Drafts of Iron, may apply, and depend on having them drawn in the best and most expeditious Manner, and most reasonable Terms. Good Beef, Pork, and a Parcel of oats, with an Assortment of Dry Goods.—*The New-York Gazette,* April 4, 1763.

HARDWARE.—Peter Goelet, At the Sign of the Golden-Key, in Hanover-Square, sells Wholesale and Retail, the following Articles (Part of which is just imported per the William and Mary, from Bristol). All sorts of Ship and House-Carpenters Tools, Goldsmiths, Gunsmiths, Blacksmiths, Shoemakers, and Turners ditto, Brass & Iron Door Locks, Padlocks; Chest, Cupboard, Draw, Desks, Book-case, and Stock ditto: Hinges of all Sorts and Sizes; Brass Furniture for Desks and other Cabinet Work: a Variety of Cloak Pins; Glass Supports, all Sorts of Nails, Tacks and Brads, Pocket Pistols, neat Fowling Pieces, Gun-barrels and Locks, Chimney Hooks, Tongs and Shovels, Andirons, Garden Shears, Chafing-dishes, Scythes, and Sickles, Brass Cocks, Tea-Kettles, Crusibles and blue Melting Pots, Steel Plate Mill-Saws, Cross-cut

Whip, and Frame ditto, Trace-Chain, Brass and Iron Knockers, . . .—*The New-York Gazette,* May 16, 1763 (*Supplement*).

HARDWARE.—Peter T. Curtenius, At the Sign of the Golden-Anvil and Hammer, opposite the Oswego-Market, has just imported for Sale in the Grace from Bristol, and in the other Vessels from Europe, Nails of all sizes, manufactured by the best makers in England; neat brass headed shovels and tongs, chamber and kitchen bellows, with all kinds of household furniture in the ironmongery way, locks and hinges of all sorts, together with all the necessaries for building; carpenters, joiners blacksmiths, and shoemakers tools of all sorts, besides a great variety of other articles, the whole making out a compleat assortment of ironmongery, cutlery, and brazery ware.—*The New-York Mercury,* November 7, 1763.

IRON WARE.—It is computed the demands from New England for iron ware have this year sunk upwards of ten thousand pounds; as the people of that province now fabricate the more common articles among themselves. —News item from London, October 19, 1764, in *The New-York Gazette or the Weekly Post-Boy,* January 3, 1765 (*Supplement*).

METAL WARE.—Henry Brevoort, At the sign of the Frying-Pan, in Queen's-street . . . will sell on the lowest terms, wholesale and retail; A Neat and general assortment of ironmongery viz. iron pots kettles skillets, dogs, and cart boxes, brass kettles, Dutch and English tea kettles, copper, brass, and iron chafing dishes, chamber and common bellows, brass and iron candlesticks, brass and steel snuffers and stands, Dutch and English chimney backs, sheet iron, hearth tiles, . . .—*The New-York Journal or the General Advertiser,* December 10, 1767.

AN IRON CHEST, As good and safe, as almost any in the Province, with two Keys; to be sold cheap, the

Owner having little Occasion for the same at present: It is three Feet long, 19 Inches deep, and 18 in Breadth. For further Information apply to H. Gaine.—*The New-York Gazette and the Weekly Mercury,* October 10, 1768 (*Supplement*).

IRONMONGERY.—John Morton, At his Store in Queen-Street, near the Fly-Market, Has for Sale, Forge Hammers of a superior quality, car and waggon boxes cast in flasks, backs for chimnies, cast iron dogs and stoves of different kinds; where forge-masters and ironmongers may be supplied with any quantity of those articles (warranted) on the most reasonable terms. . . .—*The New-York Gazette and the Weekly Mercury,* January 15, 1770.

MILL WORK.—To Be Sold, a Variety of Mill-Work, such as Cog Wheels, large and small, with and without Axle-trees; a different Assortment of Running-Geers for ditto, completely finished, with Iron Works, as Gudgeons, Bolts with Screws, Boxes and Hoops, &c. &c. may be made answerable for any kind of Mill Work, will be sold very reasonable: Inquire of the Printers.—*The New-York Gazette and the Weekly Post-Boy,* February 1, 1773.

IRONMONGERY AND CUTLERY.—Nicholas Carmer, Has for sale at his store at the sign of the cross hand-saws, at the lower end of Maiden-lane, and near the Fly-market; A Large and compleat assortment of iron-mongery and cutlery ware, which he will sell both wholesale and retail, on the most reasonable terms, viz. Mill, cross-cut, hand tenant and sash-saws; carpenters tools of all sorts, shoemakers do. blacksmith do. spades and shovels, tongs and shovels, and files of all sorts, locks and hinges of all sorts, brick and plaistering trowels, frying pans and grid-irons, copper and iron tea-kettles, chafing-dishes both square and round, brass cocks of all sorts, best White-chapel darning and common needles,

large and small scale beams and steel-yards, paper and
brass ink-stands, brass and iron candlesticks of all sorts,
with very large single and double branch sconces, iron,
gilt and brass knockers, best ivory, buck and common
handle knives and forks, best pen knives and carving do.
common and best temple spectacles, fine do. with spare
glasses, brass and iron wire, best holland quills, . . .—
The New-York Gazette and the Weekly Mercury, February 21, 1774.

ANDIRONS.—Jacob Wilkins, At the sign of the Gold
Andiron and Candlestick, . . . Has for Sale, A Large
quantity of brass and iron andirons, of the newest patterns, and of different sorts of sizes, and a few dozen of
tongs and shovels, and fenders to suit the andirons.
Also plated shoe, knee, and stock buckles, and very neat
japanned waiters. The subscriber makes mill brasses,
and pump chambers; also branding irons, and sundry
sorts of brass work, &c. . . .—*The New-York Journal or
the General Advertiser*, August 11, 1774.

IRON UNTENSILS.—. . . Said [George] Ball has likewise imported a large assortment of the useful and wholesome iron utensils, so much recommended by physicians
for their safety, and so generally and justly prefered to
copper, by all the house keepers in England, for two of
the best reasons in the world, viz. That they are entirely
free from that dangerous, poisonous property, from
whence so many fatal accidents have been known to
arise amongst those who use copper vessels, and because
they never want tinning as copper vessels do.
Tea kettles from three quarts to six, Four gallon pots
with covers, to five quarts, Pie pans, two gallon oval pots,
Stew pans and covers, of several different sizes, Fish
kettles of six different sizes, with strainers, Sauce pans,
from six quarts to one pint. For cabin use on board of
shipping, they are far preferable to copper, as no danger
(however careless the cook, or long the voyage) can possibly happen from using them, as too often has through

those causes, from the use of copper. They are all wrought according to the most approved patterns now used in London, and will be sold very low.—*The New-York Journal or the General Advertiser,* August 3, 1775.

CANDLESTICKS.—Fifes and Sword knots to be had at the Printers's: Also Handsome Brass Candlesticks at 22s. 18s. 6d and 16s. a pair.—*Rivington's New-York Gazetteer,* September 28, 1775.

REFINED BAR IRON, Directly from the Works, Sold by Robert Erskine, Near Whitehall Ferry Stairs, New-York. N.B. Orders, for Iron drawn to any Size, from three Quarters to three Inches square, and from one and an Half to five Inches flat, executed with Punctuality and Dispatch. Mill Irons, Rudder Irons, &c. drawn to Patterns.—*The New-York Gazette and the Weekly Mercury,* August 26, 1776.

STONE CUTTERS

CHARLES BROMFIELD. — Liverpool, 1770. Charles Bromfield, Begs leave to acquaint his Friends and the Public, That he is establish'd in the Marble Trade, on a very extensive Plan, having a Large and curious Assortment of all the different Kind that is produced in Italy, and the valuable Sorts of other Countries: Any Gentlemen who are pleased to apply to him, at his Yard in Williamson's Square, for any kind of manufactured Goods, may depend on having their Orders executed with the greatest Punctuality, in the neatest and cheapest Manner, having ready made a Variety of Chimney Pieces, Statues, Busts, Urns, Vases, Tables, Water Closet Cisterns, Mortars, &c. &c. He makes Monuments, Fonts and Tombs.

N.B. He also will supply the Inland Manufacturers with Marble in the Block, on as good Terms as from any other Part of this Kingdom.—*The New-York Gazette and the Weekly Mercury,* February 5, 1770.

THOMAS BROWN, and Com. from London, Beg leave to inform the Publick, that they have open'd a Marble Quarry, in this Government, little inferior to the Italian, out of which will be made Chimney Pieces, Marble Tables, Monuments, Tombs, Head Stones for Graves, &c. in the compleatest Manner, and on the most reasonable Terms: As we shall make it our constant Endeavour to oblige all such as shall favour us with their Custom, we flatter ourselves no one will be backward to incourage a Business, which in Time may prove a Benefit to this Country. Likewise the useful and necessary Arts of Drawing, and Architecture will be taught, in the most methodical Manner, in Water-Street, on the upper Side of Peck-Slip.—*The New-York Gazette or the Weekly Post-Boy,* August 30, 1764.

THOMAS BROWN.—Italian, English, and Irish Marble for Chimney Pieces, &c. &c. To be sold as cheap as can be imported, By Thomas Brown, Marble Cutter, in Chapel-Street. Also Grave Stones and Jersey Stone Chimney Pieces, executed in the neatest Manner.—*The New-York Gazette and the Weekly Mercury,* July 26, 1773.

ANTHONY DODANE.—To the Public, That Anthony Dodane, Marble Cutter, has Chimney Pieces both of Marble and Red Stone, that will serve for Jams and Hearth Pieces of all Kind. He also furnishes Slabs, and mends those that are broken, (provided they are not in too many Pieces) at a reasonable Price. He may be spoke with at his Shop, behind the Old English Church, on the Dock. Those who please to favour him with their Commands, shall have them punctually observed, by their humble Servant, Anthony Dodane.—*The New-York Gazette and the Weekly Mercury,* July 4, 1768.

ANTHONY DODANE.—. . . Begs Leave to inform the Public, that he makes all Sorts of Chimney-Pieces in the most Elegant Manner, both of White and Vein'd, (Italian and American) Marble and Red Stone, he also cut Tomb and Head-stones. . . .—*The New-York Chronicle,* September 14-21, 1769.

ANTHONY ENGELBERT.—Ran away the 30th of last Month, from Anthony Engelbert, of this city, Stone-Cutter, a High-Dutch Servant Man, . . .—*The New-York Gazette,* June 4-13, 1739.

WILLIAM GRANT, from Boston, makes all sorts of Tomb-Stones, Head Stones, and other Kind of Stone, Cutter's Work; He may be spoken with at the House of Mr. John Welsh, Sexton of Trinity Church, in New-York.—*The New-York Weekly Journal,* October 6, 1740.

WILLIAM GRANT AND SAMUEL HUNTERDON.—This is to give Notice to all Persons Whatsoever, That William Grant Stone-cutter, and Samuel Hunterdon, Quarrier of Newark lately arrived from England, carves and cuts all Manner of Stones in the neatest and most curious Fashions ever done in America. The said Grant is to be spoke with at Mr. Welsh's Sexton to Trinity Church, in New-York.—*The New-York Weekly Post-Boy,* September 30, 1745.

ROBERT HARTLEY, Stone-cutter from Kingston upon Hull, at Hunter's-Quay, near the merchant's coffee-house, New-York; Acquaints the public that he executes stone work in general; and in the neatest and best manner, finishes all sorts of marble monuments, tombs, grave stones, head-stones, &c. makes and finishes in the newest and most genteel fashion, marble chimney pieces, and Bath stove grates. Also has brought with him for sale, a good assortment of Bath stoves of the newest patterns, marble slabs, marble for chimney pieces, neat marble mortars, and stone slabs for hearths and chimney pieces. Also sells and fixes new invented perpetual ovens, which are constructed upon such a plan as has not yet been known in this city, having a contrivance for heating smoothing irons, without any obstruction to the ovens baking.

Any gentlemen who will favour him their orders, may depend upon the greatest dispatch in business, and of being served upon the most moderate terms.—*The New-York Gazette and the Weekly Mercury,* September 30, 1771.

GEORGE HASS, Stone Cutter, and Mason, Lately arrived in this City, Begs Leave to inform the Publick, that he has learn'd both the said Branches of Business in the best Manner; therefore, if any Gentlemen would please to favour him with Employment, in either of said Branches, they may depend on his rendering them entire Satisfaction. Inquire for him of Mr. Lodowick Bamper, near the New English Church, . . .—*The New-York Gazette or the Weekly Post-Boy,* January 19, 1764.

LINDSAY AND SHARP, At the foot of Ellis's-Slip, takes this Method of informing the Public, that they carry on the Business of Stone-Cutting in its different Branches; they also undertake building of Stone-Cisterns, and will demand no pay unless they hold tight. Gentlemen favouring them with their Work, may firmly depend on having it done in such a Manner as will give them the utmost Satisfaction, and upon the most reasonable Terms.—*The New-York Mercury,* August 18, 1766.

JOHN NORRIS.—On Tuesday last John Norris, a Stone-Cutter of this City and his Partner were, in eminent Danger of being smother'd under Ground; for as they were at Work in a Shaft to lay a Drain, about 15 foot below Surface of the Earth one of the Stanchions which Supported the Earth, on the Sides gave Way, . . .— News item in *The New-York Weekly Journal,* November 21, 1737.

UZAL WARD.—Newark Quarry Stone. Whereas many persons in New-York, who have had occasion for Newark quarry stone, have met with difficulty and disappointment in being supplied, not knowing where or to whom properly to apply. The public have therefore this notice, that I the subscriber, who have in my hands all the quarries lately belonging to Samuel Medlis, deceased, and keep a number of workmen constantly employed therein, will endeavour speedily and punctually to supply all demands for such stone; and that, for the greater conveniency of such persons who may want to be supplied, there are two boats constantly plying between New-York and Newark, . . . UZAL WARD.—*The New-York Gazette and the Weekly Mercury,* April 8, 1771.

JAMES WILSON.[1]—Run away on Wednesday last, the 24th Inst. from James Wilson, of this City, Stone-cutter, a Servant Boy. . . . *The New-York Gazette and the Weekly Post Boy,* April 29, 1754.

[1] "On Tuesday last, after diligent Search, grounded on a violent suspicion, a large Sum of Money was found in the House of one James Wilson, an Inhabitant of this City, Stone-Cutter; which on the Confession of the said Willson before Alderman Livingston, appear'd to be the Cash stolen . . . . . he was accordingly tryed, convicted, and condemned; . . . . and is to be hanged on Friday." . . . .—News item in *The New-York Gazette or the Weekly Post-Boy,* January 22, 1759.

PAPER MANUFACTURERS, PRINTERS, AND BOOKBINDERS

PAPER MANUFACTURERS

HUGH GAINE.—Ready Money for Clean Linen Rags, May be had from H. Gaine. And for the further Encouragement of such poor Persons as are willing to employ themselves in procuring Rags, the following Premiums will be given.

To the Person that delivers the greatest Quantity of good clean dry Linen Rags to H. Gaine, in the Year 1765, not less than 1000 lb. Ten Dollars, besides being paid the full Value of the Rags.

To the Person that delivers the second greatest Quantity of Rags, of the same kind, not less than 800 lb. in the Year 1765 Eight Dollars.

To the Person that delivers the third great Quantity of Rags, of the same Kind likewise, in the Year 1765, Five Dollars.

A Book will be kept to enter the Names of all such Persons, as bring Rags and the Quantity the deliver; and the Premiums will be paid in the first Day of the Year 1766, by H. Gaine.—*The New-York Mercury,* December 17, 1764.

HUGH GAINE.—The printer of this paper, in conjunction with two of his friends, having lately erected a Paper-Mill at Hempstead Harbour, on Long-Island, at a very great expence, the existence of which entirely depends on a supply of Rags, which at present are very much wanted; He therefore most humbly intreats the assistance of the good people of this province, and city in particular, to assist him in this undertaking, which, if attended with success, will be a saving of some hun-

dreds per annum to the colony, which has been constantly sent out of it for Paper of all sorts, the manufacturing of which has but very lately originated here; but
should the publick countenance the same it is more than
probable that branch will be brought to considerable
perfection in this place. The highest price will therefore be given for sorts of Linen Rags, by the Public's
Humble Servant, HUGH GAINE.—*The New-York Gazette
and the Weekly Mercury*, October 11, 1773.

HUGH GAINE.—Linen Rags. The salutary Effects re-
sulting from the Paper Manufactory lately erected in
this Province, is very sensibly felt by the Inhabitants
thereof, who consume many Thousand Reams of Paper
annually, that for 40 years past were imported from a
neighbouring Colony, to the very great Detriment of
this, as the Cash transmitted from hence on that Account
never returned again, the Ballance of Trade being so very
great against us. And as no Manufactory can be carried
on to any Purpose without a Sufficiency of rough Materials to work on, and as Rags is the Principal used in the
Paper Branch, it may be necessary to inform the Publick,
that the Paper-Mill at Hempstead-Harbour, on Long-
Island, is now in great Want of a Quantity of that Com-
modity, . . . Hugh Gaine. N.B. Three Pence Per Pound
will be given for the Best Rags, and in Proportion for
those of an Inferior Sort.—*The New-York Gazette and
the Weekly Mercury*, January 23, 1775.

JOHN KEATING.—Ready Money for clean Rags, May
be had of John Keating, between Burling's-Slip and the
Fly-Market, in Queen-Street. All those that really have
the welfare of their country at Heart, are desired to consider seriously, the Importance of a Paper Manufactory
in this Government, and how much Good they may do
it by so small a Matter, as saving only the Linen Rags,
especially the fine ones, that would be otherwise useless.
This saving is recommended not so much for the Value
of the Money that any one may immediately receive for

the Rags, which can be a trifle at first, as for the Benefit
the Public will receive, if the Manufactory is properly
encouraged, so as to supply us without importing paper
from Abroad. . . .—*The New-York Journal or the General Advertiser*, February 18, 1768.

JOHN KEATING.—The New-York Paper Manufactory.
John Keating, Takes this Method to inform the Public,
that he manufactures, and has for sale, Sheathing, packing, and several Sorts of printing Paper. Clean Linen
Rags, are taken in (for which ready Money will be given)
by said Keating, at his Store, between the Fly and Burling's-slip; and by Alexander and James Robertson, at
their Printing-Office. A very curious Address to the
Patriotic Ladies of New-York, upon the utility of preserving old Linen Rags, will make its appearance in the
next Chronicle.—*The New-York Chronicle*, August 17-
24, 1769.

JOHN KEATING.—Sixty Pounds per Year, with Meat,
Drink, Washing and Lodging, will be given by John
Keating, to a Man who understands the Paper-making
Business well, in all its Branches, and good Encouragement for Journeymen Paper-makers; likewise ready
Money for good clean Linen Rags.—*The New-York
Gazette and the Weekly Mercury*, October 7, 1771.

JOHN KEATING, at his Paper Manufactories, At and
near New-York, makes All sorts of Paper and paste
board; viz.

> Brown, whited brown
> Blue, and grey
> Purple sugar loaf,   }Paper
> Cartridge and press
> Waste or wrapping, different sizes

Printing and writing paper of various sorts and sizes
Paste board of all qualities and sizes. Which are to sold
at the lowest prices, at his store in Queen-street, near
Burling's slip, where he gives the best prices for Linen

Rags, according to their quality and fineness. . . .—*The New-York Journal or the General Advertiser*, May 21, 1772.

JOHN KEATING.—The First Paper Manufactory Established in this City of New-York, by John Keating, is now removed to Peck's-Kill, and is in great want of a large quantity of fine and coarse Linen Rags, . . .—*The New-York Gazette and the Weekly Mercury*, July 11, 1774.

SAMUEL LOUDON.—Parchment Manufactured in the Country, Sold by Samuel Loudon. As Latin and Greek School Books are much wanted, and as it is probable there are many families in this city, who have some of them useless, they would do the Public a benefit by sending them to Samuel Loudon, who will give ready Cash or new Books for them. Greek Lexicons, Greek Grammars, Virgils, and Cicero's Orations are most wanted.—*The New-York Packet and the American Advertiser*, May 16, 1776.

SAMUEL LOUDON.—Three Pence per Pound Given by Samuel Loudon, for the best sort of clean, white linen Rags, and so in proportion for that of an inferior sort.— *The New-York Packet and the American Advertiser*, May 9, 1776.

PAPER MILL.—This is to give Notice, that there is come to the Place, last Month from England, a Person that knows the Preparation and making of all sorts of Paper, and it appearing to him that that Branch of Business will answer to good Profit in this Place; any Gentleman that has a good and constant Stream of fresh Water, and will erect a Paper-Mill thereon; that the Proposer will go half with him; the Gentleman to receive all the Profits, only subsistence Money, 'til the Proposer's Half of the Building shall be discharged, also an Allowance for the Water. He may be heard of at Mr.

Anneyley's, Gun-Smith, in New-York.—*The New-York Mercury,* March 7, 1760.

PAPER HANGING MANUFACTORY.—A new Manufactory for Paper Hangings is set up at New-York, which is an article in great demand from the Spanish West-Indies.— News item from London, April 10, *The New-York Gazette or the Weekly Post-Boy,* June 6, 1765 (*Supplement*).

A PAPER MILL, To be Sold: . . . It is situated at Spotswood, in New-Jersey, about 10 miles from Amboy ferry, in very good order, 50 feet in length, and 30 in width. . . . Whoever may be inclin'd to purchase said mill, are inform'd that the proprietor Frederick Roemer, will engage to instruct one or two persons in the business. For farther particulars, apply in New-York to John Klein, baker, or on the premises, to Frederick Roemer. —*The New-York Gazette and the Weekly Mercury,* May 18, 1772.

JOHN SCULLY, Next Door to Alderman Roosevelt, at the Fresh-Water Manufactures all kind of Paper Hangings, of the newest Patterns, (to which Business he served a regular Apprenticeship,) and hangs the same in the neatest Manner with Borderings suitable to the Paper, which he also Manufactures himself.

N.B. The said Scully, hangs English Paper at Eighteen Pence per Piece, and will wait on any Gentleman, Lady or other, who may be pleased to favour him with their Commands, on the shortest Notice.—*The New-York Gazette,* November 23-30, 1767.

WILLIAM SHAFER.—Ready Money for all Sorts of clean Linen Rags, paid by William Shafer, Paper-maker, living at the Fresh-Water Pump, who likewise has for sale All Sorts of Paper, and will dispose of it cheaper than any imported from Europe. A Person that understands the Paper-making Business, and brings a good Recommenda-

tion, may have employ, by William Shafer, Paper-Maker.
—*The New-York Journal or the General Advertiser,*
November 21, 1771.

SIMSON's.—Manufactured, and to be Sold at Simson's
in Stone-Street, New-York, by Wholesale, cheap for
Cash, Wrapping Paper, fit for Shopkeepers, Tobacconists,
Chocolate-Makers, Tallow-Chandlers, Hatters, &c. Blue
Paper for Sugar-Bakers, Printers Paper &c. Where
Orders for every Kind of Common Paper, Pasteboard,
&c. may be comply'd with on proper Encouragement.
Rags are taken in and paid for, by Frederick Ramer, at
the Mill, in Spotswood, and by Michael Housewort, next
Door to Weyman's Printing Office.—*The New-York
Gazette,* September 24, 1764.

ROBERT WOOD.—Parchment, which by those who have
tried it, is esteemed superior to most imported from
England, Made and sold at reasonable rates, by Robert
Wood, in Fifth Street, a little below Walnut Street, in
Philadelphia.
  Sold also by Joseph Crukshank, Printer, in Market
Street, between Second & Third Streets, and by Isaac
Collins, Printer, in in Burlington, Hugh Gaine and John
Holt, Printers, in New York, and by Joseph Dunkley,
Painter and Glazier, opposite the Methodist Meeting
House.
  The Demand for this Parchment being much increased
of late, has encouraged said Wood to extend his Works
so that he now expects to be able to supply his Cus-
tomers in a manner more satisfactory than heretofore,
without Fear of a Disappointment.—*The New-York
Journal or the General Advertiser,* November 17, 1774.

PRINTERS OF NEW YORK NEWSPAPERS

JOHN ANDERSON, Takes this Method to inform the
Public in general, and his Friends in Particular, that he
has removed his Printing-Office from Battoe-Street, to

the lower Corner of Beekman's Slip, where he continues carrying on the Printing Business in all its Branches, with Neatness, Accuracy, and Dispatch, at the very lowest Prices; and hopes for a Continuance of the Favours of his former Friends and Customers, whose Kindness he will endeavour to merit, by his Assiduity to serve them with Punctuality and exactness.

Advertisements, Hand Bills, &c. (of a moderate Length) are printed at an Hour's Notice. Also, may be had at said Office, Bibles, Testaments, Spelling-Books and Primers, Blank Bonds, Powers of Attorney, Bills of Sale, Bills of Lading, Penal Bills, and all other kinds of Blanks used in this Province.

Said Anderson has likewise for Sale, Spiritous Liquors, Dry Goods, and Earthen Ware, with many other Articles as usual.—*The New-York Gazette and the Weekly Post-Boy,* October 12, 1772.

JOHN ANDERSON & SAMUEL PARKER.—To the respectable Publick, Samuel F. Parker, and John Anderson, Of this City, Printers, Have entered into Partnership together, for the carrying on that Business in all its Branches; and propose in August next, to publish the New-York Gazette or the Weekly Post-Boy, which was published for many Years by said Parker's Father, and esteemed to be a Paper of as good Credit and Utility as any extant since the first Commencement thereof; . . . Printing in all its Branches will be carefully executed and further Particulars thereof published in due Time. —*The New-York Journal or the General Advertiser,* April 8, 1773

WILLIAM BRADFORD.—Last Saturday Evening departed this Life, Mr. William Bradford, Printer, of this City, in the 94th Year of his Age: As the Printer of this Paper liv'd upwards of eight Years Apprentice to him, he may be presumed to know something of him: He came into America upwards of 70 Years ago, and landed at the Place where Philadelphia now stands, before that City was laid out, or a House built there: He was Printer to this Government upwards of 50 Years; and was a Man of great Sobriety and Industry; . . .—News item in *The New-York Gazette Revived in the Weekly Post-Boy*, May 25, 1752

SAMUEL LOUDON'S CIRCULATING LIBRARY [1] Will be opened the first day of January 1774; subscriptions for reading, are taken in at his house, at 20 shillings per annum, half to be paid at subscribing. Occasional readers to pay by the week, or volume; the prices for which, with rules for reading, will be particularly affixed to the catalogue, which is now printing, and will be ready to deliver to the subscribers, and other readers, next month.

The design is set on foot at the desire of several very respectable inhabitants, and shall be conducted with all possible fidelity and diligence, in providing books, both instructive and entertaining, and written by authors of the most established reputation. It is hoped that all who approve of the undertaking, will do their utmost to encourage it, and without delay, as every body may see that it's existence and perfection, depends on the encouragement it meets with, by enabling the undertakers to provide, and keep in order, a sufficient number of valuable books.—*Rivington's New-York Gazetteer*, December 30, 1773.

JAMES RIVINGTON.—Last Thursday was hung up by some of the lower class of inhabitants, at New-Brunswick, an effigy, representing the person of Mr. Rivington, the printer at New-York, merely for acting consistent with his profession as a free printer.—News item in *Rivington's New-York Gazetteer*, April 20, 1775.[2]

[1] In the *New-York Gazette*, September 24, 1764, notice is given that "Noel's Circulating Library, Is now opened for the second year," . . . .
[2] In the same issue of the newspaper, Rivington inserted an illustration of himself hanging in effigy with a note to the public. . . . . "He has considered his press in the light of a public office, to which every man has a right to have recourse. But the moment he ventured to publish sentiments which were opposed to the dangerous views and designs of certain demagogues, he found himself held up as an enemy to his country," . . . . . .

JAMES RIVINGTON.—Thursday Morning about 12 o'Clock, a Party of Light Horse from Connecticut, amounting to about 100, entered this City, and in the utmost regularity proceeded to the House of Mr. James Rivington, Printer, and after surrounding the same, with bayonets fixed, a number alighted and placed three centinels at each door; when a few of the party entered the house, and demanded his types, which were accordingly surrendered, and put up in bags, then they destroyed the whole apparatus of the press. The business being thus finished without the least noise or opposition, the surrounding spectators consisting of about fifteen hundred inhabitants signified their approbation by three huzzas, and immediately the party went out of town with their booty, without offering the least insult to any of the inhabitants.—News item in *The Constitutional Gazette,* November 25, 1775.

JOHN PETER ZENGER.—The Printer [John Peter Zenger] now having got his Liberty again, designs God Willing to Finish and Publish the Charter of the City of New-York, Next Week.—*The New-York Weekly Journal,* August 11, 1735.

JOHN PETER ZENGER.—There is now in Press, and will be Published with all imaginable Speed, A brief Narative of the Case and Tryal of John Peter Zenger, Printer of the New-York Weekly Journal. Containing a brief Account of the Proceedings against him, and of this Tryal, for Printing his Journals, No 13 & 23 both before and during his 9 Months Imprisonment on that Pretence.—*The New-York Weekly Journal,* September 23, 1735.

JOHN PETER ZENGER.—There is now Published Remarks upon Mr. Hamilton's Arguments in the Tryal of J. P. Zenger, for Lybelling against the Government. To be Sold by the Printer hereof.—*The New-York Gazette,* October 17-23, 1737.

JOHN ZENGER.—Mr. John Zenger, Printer in this City, being lately deceased, and having no Person qualified to carry on his Business: This is to give Notice, that the Printing Press and Materials lately occupied by him, will be exposed to Sale at publick Vendue, on Tuesday the 30th of this Instant July, at the Dwelling House of the Deceased: The Press is esteemed a good One; and much of the large Letter in good Order.—*The New-York Gazette Revived in the Weekly Post-Boy*, July 1, 1751.

OTHER PRINTERS

ROBERT BELL.—This Day is published, And now selling by Robert Bell, Printer, and Bookseller, next door to St. Paul's Church Third-Street, Philadelphia. Also in New-York by William Green, Bookseller and Book-binder. Complete in three volumes, with neat bindings, . . . Political Disquisitions; . . . By J. Burgh, Gent. . . .—*The Constitutional Gazette*, November 22, 1775.

BENJAMIN FRANKLIN.—Whereas on Saturday Night last, the House of Benjamin Franklin, of the City of Philadelphia, Printer was broke open, . . .—*The New-York Gazette Revived in the Weekly Post-Boy*, November 5, 1750.

HODGE & SHOBER.—. . . Printing, in all its different Branches, performed by said Hodge and Shober, in the neatest Manner, with Accuracy, Dispatch, and at the most reasonable Prices. As they are young Beginners, they earnestly request the Favour and Encouragement of the Public, which they will endeavour to merit, by their Assiduity to satisfy and oblige those who are pleased to employ them.—*The New-York Gazette and the Weekly Mercury*, January 25, 1773.

MILLS, HICKS AND HOWE, Printers and stationers, Have just opened their Printing-Office and Shop in Queen-street, near the Fly-market, and Have for Sale,

Stationary of all Kinds Particularly a very fine Assortment of Writing Paper, viz. Atlas, Imperial, Royal, Super Royal, Medium, Demy, Thick and thin Post, Foolscap, gilt and plain, . . . N. B. The above assortment was ordered by the Stationers to the Hon. Board of Commissioners for their own use, previous to their leaving America, and is therefore very suitable for public offices, as well as gentlemen of the navy and army in general, being of the best quality.—*The New-York Gazette or the Weekly Mercury,* August 26, 1776.

BOOKBINDERS

T. ANDERTON.—Lately arrived from England . . . T. Anderton, Book-Binder, Letter Case, and Pocket Book-Maker; Makes and sells wholesale and retail, all sorts of letter cases, desk cases, travelling cases and travelling boxes either with or without shaving equipages; Ladies travelling writing desks, fishing cases, solo cases. . . .

The said T. Anderton, performs book-binding in its full perfection, in all sorts of plain and rich bindings; marbles and gilds the edge of books, gilds and letters libraries, or parcels of books, and rules paper or bill books, day books, journals and leidgers, &c. (as exact to any pattern) but with greater ellegancy that if taken from copper plate, and binds in parchment, or vellum, either with or without Russia bands. Gentlemen and Ladies who please to try his abilities may always depend on being well used on the very lowest terms. New pocket books, made to old instruments.

At the same place may be had, when ready, a curious black writing ink improved from a prescription which the late right hon. Henry Pelham, esq; gave 36 guineas for; what is ramarkable in this ink is, time will not afface nor any spirit destroy it from the face of paper, or parchment, but it always remains of a fine jett black: It flows finely from the pen, and never grows thick by the keeping. . . .—*The New-York Mercury,* December 24, 1764.

BOOKBINDER.—A Journeyman Book Binder, May hear of Encouragement, according to his abilities, by applying to the Printer hereof.—*The Constitutional Gazette*, June 22, 1776.

PHILIP BROOKS, Book Binder from Dublin, Carries on that business in all its branches, at his shop in Dock street, between the Coffee house and Old-slip bridge. New or old books lettered, gilt and rebound in the neatest manner; merchants and others supplied with blank books, either ruled or plain, on the shortest notice; pocket books, memorandum books, &c. He will study to give general satisfaction to his customers, and flatters himself the public will favour him with some encouragement. . . .—*The New-York Gazette and the Weekly Mercury*, September 25, 1775.

SAMUEL BROWN.—Charles Morse moves to the house . . . being the second House above Mr. Samuel Brown's, Printer and Book Binder, . . .—*The New-York Gazette or the Weekly Post-Boy*, June 20, 1765.

HENRY DE FOREEST.—Books neatly Bound, Gilded and Lettered, Account-Books Rul'd & Bound, in Vellum, Parchment, Calf, or Basil, by Henry De Foreest, enquire for him at the House of John Peter Zenger, or at his House opposite to the Sign of the Black-Horse.—*The New-York Weekly Journal*, May 19, 1735.

SAMUEL EVANS, Book-Binder from London; Begs leave to inform the Gentlemen of this City, that he still carries on his Business, at his House, next Door to Mr. Doughty's Taylor, in Beaver-Street, where all Gentlemen and others may depend on having their Work done in the neatest and best Manner, either in Morocco, Calf, or Sheep-Skin, by their very humble Servant, SAMUEL EVANS.—*The New-York Gazette or the Weekly Post-Boy*, June 11, 1761.

GEORGE FISHER.—Virginia, Williamsburg, August 2, 1765. Broke goal, last Saturday night a servant man, named George Fisher, by trade a book-binder. . . .—*The New-York Gazette or the Weekly Post-Boy,* September 19, 1765.

WILLIAM GREEN.—Just published and to be sold by William Green, Bookbinder, . . . An Earnest Address to such of the people called Quakers, . . .—*The New-York Journal or the General Advertiser,* March 16, 1775.

JOHN HINSHAW.—The Book of the Chronicles of His Royal Highness, William Duke of Cumberland . . . likewise to be had at Mr. John Hinshaw's, Book-Binder near the Old-slip Market.—*The New-York Weekly Journal,* July 28, 1746.

WILLIAM HOUGH, Book-binder, at the House of Mr. William Milliner, at the Corner of Beaver-Street; Binds all sorts of Books, either printed or for Merchants and Shop-keepers Use, after the neatest and best Manner now in vogue in London: He likewise rules Musick to the greatest Perfection; and being but a Beginner, hopes to give entire Satisfaction to all Gentlemen and others, either in Town or Country, who shall please to favor him with their Custom.—*The New-York Gazette Revived in the Weekly Post-Boy,* October 2, 1752.

JOSEPH JOHNSON of the City of New-York Bookbinder, is now set up Book-binding for himself as formerly, and lives in Duke-street (commonly called Bayards-street) near the Old-Slip Market, where all Persons in Town or Country, may have their Books carefully and neatly new Bound with Plain or Gilt, reasonable.—*The New-York Gazette,* September 23-30, 1734.

JOHN JONES.—Book-Binding, in all its parts, performed by John Jones, in Elizabeth-Town, living near to Mrs. Cheetwood's mill.—*The New-York Mercury*, September 5, 1757.

GEORGE LEEDELL, Book-Binder, late of London, Begs leave to return his thanks to his friends and customers, and the publick in general, for their past favours, and hopes for the future continuance of them, which he will endeavour to deserve. He has removed to Peck's-slip, next door to Mr. White Matlack's, watch-maker, where he proposes to continue to carry on his business in all its different branches, as neat as can be done in London. Merchants and others, may be supplied at a very short notice, with all kinds of books (such as ledgers, journals, and waste books) as cheap as they can be imported. Where may be also had his much admired Black and Red Ink, and Hudson's Bay Quills, so long wanted in this country; spelling books and primers, books marbled on the edges, as in London; and paper gilt and blackt.— *The New-York Gazette and the Weekly Mercury*, May 3, 1773.

ROBERT M'ALPINE, Binds, Gilds, and Letters, all Sorts of Books, to Perfection; He may be spoke with at the dwelling House in Hanover Square, next Door to Dr. Nicolls, N.B. He also sells sundry Sorts of Books.—*The New-York Weekly Journal*, November 30, 1741.

NUTTER AND EVANS, Book-Binders, acquaint their Friends and the Public in general. That they have opened a Shop on Rotton-Row, in the House of Mr. John Jones, where they may have all manner of Book-binding done in the neatest and most elegant taste (either in gilt or plain Covers) and on the shortest notice. Ruling (in whatever Form required) performed to Satisfaction; and all other the business of Book-Bindering done on reasonable Terms, and with great Accuracy. And earnestly sollicits for the Public's Favour, particularly those who are willing to encourage new Beginners, assuring them, that they will make it their unwearied

Study to serve them to the utmost of their Abilities, whenever they shall please to favour them with their Commands. They have for Sale, Chapman's Books, Primmers, Almanacks, Paper, Quills, &c. and the best of both Red and Black Inks, made and sold by themselves. Likewise Phials of almost any Size, may be had at the said Shop.—*The New-York Chronicle,* September 28-October 5, 1769.

VALENTINE NUTTER.—Just published, and to sold by Valentine Nutter, Book Binder, opposite the Coffee-House. Josephus's Works, 4 Vols. octavo, neatly bound and lettered, much superior to any that have yet made their appearance, at the moderate price of 36 s. per set. He has likewise for sale, day books, all of his own manu-facture. As he continues to carry on the book binding business in all its branches, he hopes for the continuance of his former customers, and the public in general, being determined to do his work as cheap and good as can be done in this city. Old books from the country will be done neatly, and returned immediately. . . .—*The New-York Journal or the General Advertiser,* October 19, 1775.

PRINTER.—Blanck Book for Merchants, such as Day Books, Ledgres or Journal, made and sold by the Printer [3] hereof, and old Books New Bound.—*The New-York Gazette,* September 24, 1744.

JAMES WATT, Book-binder, Is removed into Broad-Street, next Door to William Alexander's where Book-binding, in general is neatly and expeditiously performed. —*The New-York Mercury,* May 8, 1758.

JAMES WATT.—Best black and red Ink, made and sold by James Watt, Book Binder, on Rotten-Row. The Red is made of the Best Brasiletto, Gum-Arabick, &c. and

[3] Some time between the years 1742 and 1743, William Bradford took H. De Foreest, his former apprentice, into partnership. The printers of *The New-York Gazette* at this time were thus Bradford & De For-eest.

the Black of the best Aleppo Nut Galls, Gum Arabick, &c. estem'd by Experience, much better than any made of the best Ink Powder; Vials to be had from 1s 6 to 6d. Those that find Bottles at 3s. per Quart; and smaller Quantities in Proportion.   N. B. The above Watt binds all Manner of old and new Books and sells all sorts of Blanks, Blank Books and other Stationary &c. &c.—*The New-York Gazette or the Weekly Post-Boy,* September 12, 1765.

STEWART WILSON, Bookbinder and Bookseller, opposite the Main Guard, in Albany; Has to dispose of, a great Variety of Books, upon every Subject, and more especially those suited to the Taste of America. Said Wilson binds all Kinds of Books in the newest and neatest Manner.   Any Gentlemen in the Army or elsewhere, that please to favour him with their Orders for Books or Stationary of any kind, may depend on being punctually served.—*The New-York Mercury,* October 22, 1759 (*Supplement*).

FABRICS AND NEEDLEWORK

FLAX CULTURE

MACHINES FOR CLEANING FLAX SEED.—Machines for cleaning Flax Seed. James Parsons, In Queen Street, next Door to Wm. Walton, Esq, near Peck's Slip, Has to Sell, Brass Wire Machines, for cleaning flax Seed in the best Manner for shipping; likewise Cockie Skreens, very useful for Millers, and all Persons concern'd in Cleaning Grain.—*The New-York Gazette or the Weekly Post-Boy,* June 30, 1763.

FLAX.—A Large quantity of good well drest spinning Flax, is wanted for the Factory in New-York: All Persons who have such to dispose of, at reasonable rate, by applying to Obadiah Wells, in Mullbery-Street, near the Fresh Water, may have ready Money for it. N.B. None but, the best sort will have the preference. Also the spinners in New-York, are hereby notified, that due Attendance will be given, every Tuesday, Thursday, and Saturday, in the Afternoon, to give out Flax and receive in Yarn; by said Wells, and to prevent Trouble, no Person who has not been an Inhabitant in this City ever since May last, will be admitted as a Spinner in the Factory. Also the said Wells, still continues receiving and selling in the Market, all sorts of Country Manufactories, such as Linens and Woollen Cloth, Stockings &c. &c. at five per cent for Sales and Remittances.—*The New-York Gazette or the Weekly Post-Boy,* May 8, 1766 (*Supplement*).

FLAX DRESSING.—This is to acquaint the Publick, That George Robinson from England, carries on the Flax-Dressing, at his House next Door to the Sign of the Orange-Tree, near Golden-Hill, after the English Manner, and sells it either ruff, heckled, or hetcheled. Also dresses Flax for any Person that chuses to send it ruff, at the most Reasonable Rates (according to the Fineness ordered) by the Pound, and all possible Care will be taken to give content to all Persons that may be pleased to encourage this new Branch of Business.—*The New-York Gazette and the Weekly Mercury*, April 17, 1769 (*Supplement*).

METHOD OF PREPARING FLAX.—The Method used in French Flanders, Of raising and preparing Fine Flax, For making the finest Hollands, Lawns, Cambricks and Laces, (Lately discovered in Great Britain, and much encouraged there) Being the most profitable article of agriculture that ever was produced in any country, both as it is a certain and inexhaustable source of wealth to the farmer, and of national advantage . . .

The whole process of raising and managing this flax is inserted in Freeman's New-York Almanack for the year 1770.—*The New-York Journal or the General Advertiser*, December 14, 1769.

FLAX INSPECTION.—An Act for the Inspection of Flax in the City of New-York Passed the 24th Day of March 1772. Whereas the cleaning of Flax in this Colony to prepare it for Spinning and Rope Making, has become an Object of some Importance, and as Abuses are committed in the Sale of Flax, altogether unfit for the said Purposes, to the great Damages of the Purchasers; for the Prevention therefore of the said Evil for the future . . .[1]—*The New-York Gazette and the Weekly Mercury*, April 6, 1772.

FLAX SWINGLERS.—Wanted immediately, seven or eight good flax swinglers, who understand that business well; they may have employment for some time, and shall be paid ready money for their work, Enquire of

[1] The entire text of the Act follows.

Comfort Sands, or Obadiah Wells. Said Sands has by him a choice parcel of inspected flax for sale.—*The New-York Gazette and the Weekly Mercury,* May 4, 1772.

FLAX HECKLED.—The public is hereby inform'd, that all persons who chuse to send their flax to heckle, to George Robinson, in the Fly-Market, can have it done reasonable, and at any fineness as in England, with the utmost integrity. He has always an Assortment for sale. —*The New-York Gazette and the Weekly Mercury,* September 7, 1772.

FLAX DRESSING.—George Williamson, Lately from Ireland, but last from Philadelphia, Hereby informs the public, that he has at a great expence furnished himself with all necessary utensils and conveniencies for dressing of Flax, according to the most approved method used in the linen manufactories in Europe; and has for sale at his shop in Fly-street, at the Corner of Queen-street, a great Variety of Dressed and Shoe Flax.

And as this kind of manufactory is become not only the grand interest of this province, but of importance to almost every Particular family in it, he hopes his endeavours (which so evidently tend to the public utility) will meet with general encouragement by all who are disposed to introduce a manufacture so necessary as is that of linen; all of whom may depend on being supplied with flax of the best quality, and dressed to as great perfection as any in the old countries.

Also tow of every quality, and undressed flax, may be bought at the lowest prices, at the same place.—*The New-York Gazette and the Weekly Mercury,* January 25, 1773.

FLAX DRESSING.—Allan Grant, Flax-Dresser, from Edinburgh, Informs the publick, that he has set up his business in Partition-street, formerly called Division-street, near St. Paul's Church; where he hatchels flax in the best manner, and sells the same together with tow;

and as he has brought with him a compleat set of tools to answer all sorts of flax, he humbly hopes for encouragement from all well wishers to this province. He also proposes to hatchel flax in the best manner for all persons who pleases to favour him with their custom.

N.B. Any person who has a parcel of well scutched and wholesome flax, may apply to said Grant for sale.—*The New-York Gazette and the Weekly Mercury*, August 8, 1774.

SILK CULTURE

THE CULTURE OF SILK or, an Essay [2] on its Rational Practice and Improvement. . . . By the Rev. Samuel Pullein, M A. . . .—*The New-York Gazette or the Weekly Post-Boy*, January 8, 1767.

SILK WORMS IN SOUTH CAROLINA.—We have the pleasure to acquaint the public, that the succesful introduction of the Silk Manufacture in this province bears a promising aspect, as we hear there are great quantities of Silk-Worms raised in almost every family in Purrysburg parish, and some by the French of Hillsborough, and the English and Germans near Long Canes, and that several gentlemen and ladies, near Charleston, will make the private amusement of raising Silk Worms, tend to the public benefit, by shewing how easy the knowledge thereof may be acquired, . . . Mr. John Lewis Gilbert, a native of France, who is employed by the gentlemen concerned on behalf of the public, in the encouragement of this manufacture, to wind, and teach the windings of silk, has now a considerable number of silk-worms, in the old school-house, . . .

Workmen are now employed in building an oven for curing the cocoons, erecting four machines, and all other necessaries for winding silk, with all expedition, in rooms adjoining Mr. Gilbert's, in order that the filature may be set to work as soon as the cocoons are fit, which may

---

[2] Installments of the essay appeared in the issues of the *New-York Gazette or the Weekly Post-Boy* for the first half of the year 1767.

be in about three weeks.—News item from Charleston,
S. C., May 8, in *The New-York Gazette or the Weekly
Post-Boy*, May 28, 1767.

SILK.—Extract from letter from Leicester, June 14,
1771. The silk of your manufacture I exhibited to the
best judges in London, and they unanimously pro-
nounced it equal to any, except, China. There wants
no improvement in it—there wants only quantity. I am
now manufacturing it into stockings.—News item from
Philadelphia, September 19, in *The New-York Gazette
and the Weekly Mercury*, September 23, 1771.

SILK WORMS.—It is said that a considerable number
of French refugees, well skilled in the management of
silk worms, and making of wines, have within these few
days, engaged themselves on very advantageous terms
to go to New-York, and South-Carolina, where the culti-
vation of these two lucrative branches is carrying on with
great spirit.—News item from London, July 15, in *The
New-York Journal*, September 23, 1773.

SILK MANUFACTURE.—James Wallace, At the Sign of
the Hood, In Water-street, opposite to Mr. Van Zandt's,
near the Coffee-House, New-York, Begs leave to inform
the Ladies and Gentry, that he makes and sells, black
and white silk patent lace for ladies aprons, handkerchiefs &c. White thread do. for ladies and gentlemens
ruffles; hoods, aprons, and tippets, and several other
things in that way; silk and thread gloves and mitts, the
silk of which is American produce: He therefore hopes
to be honoured with the commands of those who wish to
encourage their own manufacture. Stockings made in
the best manner, for those that bring their own stuff.
N.B. Silk stockings drest in the neatest manner, as in
London and Dublin, thereby preserving their gloss and
colour to the last; stitches taken up in the best method,
at the most reasonable rates.—*The New-York Journal
or the General Advertiser*, July 6, 1775.

IMPLEMENTS

CARDS.—Any one may be furnished with good large Wool Cards at 32s. per Doz. Fine Cotton Cards at 34s. per Doz. likewise scribling and small Cards at very reasonable Rates by William House, the Maker, in William Street opposite to Mr. Witts's at the King's Head in New-York. Any Person bringing old Boards may have new Cards put on them, and be allowed.—*The New-York Weekly Journal,* July 31, 1738.

FOOT LINEN WHEELS.—Good Foot Linnen Wheels made by William Stoddard, at Oysterbay and to be sold by Henry Chadeayne, in Beekman's-Street, near the New-English-Church, in New-York.—*The New-York Gazette Revived in the Weekly Post-Boy,* March 11, 1751.

NEEDLES.—John Ernst Juncken Needle-maker, living in Second-street, near the Dutch Vendue House, in Philadelphia: Hereby gives Notice to the Public, that he makes and hath to sell, at a reasonable Rate the following Commodities, Víz. Test Hooks, washed over with Pewter, small Hooks and Eyes, fit for Regimentals, Worms for Gunns, Brass and Iron Chains, and Brushes for Musquets, Chains for squirrels, Cages for Parrots, and other Birds &c.—*The New-York Gazette or the Weekly Post-Boy,* January 1, 1759.

SPINNING WHEELS.—Wanted (by the Society for promoting Arts, &c.) 50 Spinning Wheels, Any Persons having it in their Power to furnish that Number immediately, are requested to apply to Messrs. Obadiah Wells, James Armstrong, and John Lamb, who will agree with them for the same.—*The New-York Mercury,* February 25, 1765.

NEEDLES, Both White Chaple and common, and all kinds of Fish Hooks, made by William Sheward, in Pennsylvania, and sold on his Account by Watson and Murray, in New-York: They are equal if not superior in Quality to any imported from Europe; and always free from Rust, which by the frequent Damps in Vessels, European made are always liable to. As that laudable Disposition of encouraging Our American Manufactories, so much abounds in this Province, the Makers flatters himself of the Merchants here, favouring him with their Orders, by applying as above.—*The New-York Mercury*, September 2, 1765.

CARDS.—Scribling cards, stock cards, cotton and woollen do. sold by Mr. Mathew Paterson, in Horse and Cart Street; by Mr. Richard Minifie, shop-keeper, at the Fly-Market; by Mr. John Carns, Cooper and Shop-keeper, near Peck's Slip, and by the maker at Capt. Waller's in Broad Street, near the Bowling Green.

These cards are made of good calf-skin, and will stand re-setting, if kept dry; whereas the woollen cards imported are sheep-skin; the scriblers, &c. wore out, and the cotton old scriblers cut down and set again; therefore the maker hopes he will gain the approbation of all those who are friends to the prosperity of America.—*The New-York Gazette and the Weekly Mercury*, December 18, 1769.

REED MAKING.—The subscriber willing to assist in promoting manufactures in America, (especially at this critical and alarming juncture) has lately set up the business of Reed-Making, where all weavers and others, both in town and country, may be supplied with reeds of all kinds, as neat and good as any imported. Those persons who will be pleased to oblige him with their custom may depend upon being served with great exactness, and at the shortest notice, by applying at the subscribers house, in Wood-bridge, East New-Jersey, and their favours will be gratefully acknowledged by their humble servant, Nathaniel Pike.—*Rivington's New-York Gazetteer*, July 7, 1774.

TAMBOUR NEEDLES.—Tambour Silks, Needles, and
Cases, Just imported per the ship Lady Gage, a compleat
assortment of Tambour Shades on Silk and Shaneil, with
the best London made Tambour needles, and cases, to
be had of William Long, in Great George-Street.—
Rivington's New-York Gazetteer, July 7, 1774.

PINS.—Richard Lightfoot, from Dublin, at his Pin
Manufactory at the Crown and Cushion, in Water-Street,
near the Coffee-House in New York. Takes this method
to inform the Ladies, and the Public in general, that he
makes and sells all sorts of pins equal to any made in
London or Dublin, and superior to any manufactured
elsewhere; he likewise draws harpsichord, spinnet, forti-
piano, dolsemor, and all other kinds of music wire; silver
profile for gentlemens buttons and tambour works; brass
and iron knitting needles, black and white hair pins,
chains, brushes and pickers for soldiers firelocks, pins for
linen printers and paper stampers; laying and sewing
wire for paper makers, card makers wire, skeleton and
pound wire for ladies caps, hackle teeth, and several
other things in that way, and as he is the first that ever
attempted any of said branches on this continent, he
therefore hopes for the countenance of those who wish
to encourage their own manufactures.—*The New-York
Gazette and the Weekly Mercury*, July 10, 1775.

FLAX WHEELS.—Wright and M'Allister, Flax Wheel
Makers, at the Spinning-Wheel, nearly opposite St.
Paul's Church, Broad-Way, Offer their service to the
encouragers of American Manufactories, who may be
supplied on the shortest notice, with Wheels of different
kinds, at reasonable prices: And, as their attention will
be chiefly engaged in this branch of the turning business,
they hope to merit the encouragement of the public, and
answer any commissions they may be favoured with
from the country.—*The New-York Packet and the
American Advertiser*, June 13, 1776.

KNITTING NEEDLES.—Joseph Plowman, Pin-Maker in Water-Street, near the Coffee-House. Begs leave to inform the public, That he still continues carrying on that manufactury, and has now for sale the following goods: Pins, brass and iron knitting-needles, iron wire, binding and card ditto, hooks and eyes, fishing hooks, brass rings for buttons, priming brushes and wires for soldiers, files and knives &c. &c. He likewise makes moulds for paper makers with sewing wire.—*The Constitutional Gazette,* June 22, 1776.

SPINNING AND WEAVING

WEAVING ENCOURAGED.—We hear from Maryland, that Subscriptions have been lately made among the Gentlemen there, for encouraging the Manufacture of Linen: The Mayor and Common Council of Annapolis, have promised to pay as a Reward the Sum of 5 £ to the Person that brings the finest Piece of Linen, of the Growth and Manufacture of Maryland, to next September Fair; for the 2d. Piece in Fineness 3 £. and for the 3d, 40 s. the Linen to continue to be the Property of the Maker. Like Rewards are offered in Baltimore County, and 'tis thought the Example will be followed in all Counties in Maryland.—*The New-York Gazette,* May 3-10, 1731.

STOCKING WEAVING.—John George Cook, Stocking Weaver, Gives Notice, That every Body may be supply'd with all Sorts of Stockings, such as Worstead three threads, and Full'd Stockings, & Fine Cotton, and Linnen Stockings, living at the House of John Peter Zenger, Printer in Stone Street.—*The New-York Weekly Journal,* January 28, 1744.

STOCKING WEAVING.—This is to give Notice, that John George Cook, Stocking Weaver, has now three different Looms for either Country Yarn, Silk, Cotton, Worsted or Linnen. . . .—*The New-York Weekly Journal,* July 14, 1746.

SPINNERS EMPLOYED.—St. Andrew's Society. Whereas
the St. Andrew's Society, at New-York in the Province
of New-York, are willing and desirous to employ, such
poor scots Women, as are capable of working, and for
want of employ, become the Objects of the Society's
Charity. These are therefore to desire and advertise, all
those who are able to spin, either Flax, Wool or Cotton,
(but particularly Cotton Wick) that they shall be furnished with proper Materials to employ them, and
sufficient Wages allowed them, by Messrs David Shaw,
and David Milligan, Merchants in New-York, who are
appointed by the said Society, as a Committee for that
Purpose. DAVID MILLIGAN, Secry.—*The New-York
Gazette or the Weekly Post-Boy,* February 18, 1762.

LINEN MANUFACTORY IN BOSTON.—At the Linen
Manufactory, in Boston, there has been made within the
three last Months Four hundred Yards of Bengals,
Lillepusias, and Broglios, which were bought off by some
of the principal Ladies in this Town for their own and
their Children's Winter Wear: And as the Ladies have
set the Example, I hope the Gentlemen will follow this
laudable Custom, as they may be supply'd in the Spring
with several Sorts of Summer Wear.

Bridgewater Flax to be sold by 6s O. T. per Pound.
JOHN BROWN.—News item from Boston, January 24, in
The New-York Mercury, February 11, 1765.

JOURNEYMEN WEAVERS.—Five or Six good Journeymen
Weavers, may have immediate Employment, by apply-
ing to John Woods, at the Factory, near Fresh Water, in
New-York.—*The New-York Gazette or the Weekly
Post-Boy,* October 17, 1765.

SOCIETY FOR PROMOTING ARTS.—Whereas it has been
found, that the Society for promoting Arts, &c. has
answered great and valuable purposes, particularly in
the Encouragement of raising Flax and manufactoring
Linnen. And besides what has been done by them for

that laudable Purpose, there was some Time since, put into the Hands of those Gentlemen and Trustees, the Sum of Six Hundred Pounds, to encourage the Linnen Manufactory in this City, which Sum they put into the Hands of Mr. Obadiah Wells, to employ Weavers and Spinners; which Trust, they believe, he has honestly and faithfully performed, by employing above Three Hundred poor and necessitous Persons for 18 Months past in this City, in the above Business. As the said Trustees have at present, to the Value of £ 600, in Linnens manufactored in this City and County, to dispose of, which while lying on Hand, disables them from farther prosecuting the benevolent Purposes; they intend therefore to send them about the City, to be sold and distributed, hoping that the good and charitable Inhabitants will purchase them; by this Means, the Linnen Manufactory may again be carried on, the publick Interest greatly promoted, many penurious Persons saved from Beggary, and great Expence to the Corporation, by relieving Numbers of distressed Women, now in the Poor-House. And the Publick may be assured, that the said Linnens have been manufactured on as low Terms as possible, and are now ordered to be sold without any Advance, with the Price of the Cost per Yard, marked on each Piece.—*The New-York Gazette or the Weekly Post-Boy,* December 31, 1767.

FAMILY WEAVING.—. . . Related at a Meeting of the Society of Arts in New-York City. . . . As a farther Specimen of the Practicability of manufacturing our own Cloaths in this Country, We can assure the Public of the following Persons in Woodbridge in New Jersey, making in their respective Families, within the Year past, both Woollen and Linnen of their own raising, the Quantities of following Viz. Mr. Isaac Freeman, 599 Yards, Mr. James Smith, 567 Yards and Mr. Nathaniel Heard, 414 Yards.—News item in *The New-York Gazette or the Weekly Post-Boy,* January 18, 1768.

FAMILY WEAVING IN NEWPORT, R. I.—Within Eighteen Months past 487 Yards of cloth and thirty six Pair of Stockings, have been spun and knit in the family of Mr. James Nixon of this Town.

Another Family in Town, within four Years past, hath manufactured 980 yards of Woollen and Linen Cloth, viz. in 1764, 340 Yards; in 1765 and 1766, 500 Yards; and in 1767, 140 Yards; besides two Coverlids and two Bedticks, and all the Stocking Yarn for the Family, Not a Skein was put out of the House to be spun, but the whole performed in the Family.

We are credibly informed, that many Families in this Colony, within this Years past, have each manufactured upwards of seven hundred Yards of Cloth, of different kinds.

These Instances of Industry are mentioned with a View to demonstrate how easily it will be for those Colonies, in a short Time, to be independent of any other Country, for Cloathing; and at the same Time to excite others to imitate Examples so highly beneficial to themselves and the community.—News item from Newport, R. I., January 18, in *The New-York Gazette and the Weekly Mercury*, February 1, 1768.

JOURNEYMEN WEAVERS.—We are told, that in the course of this week, upwards of 100 Journeyman weavers have engaged to go to New-York and Boston, where they are promised constant employment. (Doubtful).— News item from London, November 1, 1767, in *The New-York Gazette or the Weekly Post-Boy*, February 1, 1768.

KNITTING.[3]—I can with Pleasure inform you, that Industry is so prevalent in this Metropolis, that within six Months a Lady of Distinction, tho' infirm, and of a very delicate Constitution, has knit thirty-six Pairs of Stockings, besides having the Care of a large Family.

[3] An extract from a letter sent from a Gentleman at Amboy to a friend in New York.

Tea is much laid aside here by the first Families, and it is confidently asserted that another Lady being pregnant actually longed for Labrador Tea.—News item in *The New-York Gazette or the Weekly Post-Boy*, February 29, 1768.

WEAVER.—John Woods, Weaver, the Factory, at Fresh-Water, and right back of Mr. Obadiah Well's Takes this Method of informing the publick, that he intends to dye Cotton and Linen Yarn, the best blues, as cheap as in Europe, he likewise, will supply any Person with the best Checks and linens, and on the most reasonable Price. N.B. Any Person wanting any Work done by applying as above, may have it done in the best Manner, and on the shortest Notice.—*The New-York Gazette and the Weekly Mercury*, April 18, 1768.

WOOLEN MANUFACTORY.—Kelly & Culver, Beg Leave to inform their Friends, and the Public, That they have effectually established the New-York wollen manufactory, in Chapel-street, where is to be sold, wollen cloths of different kinds and prices, by wholesale and retail, executed in the best manner. A fulling mill, and all its apparatus, being compleatly finished, is ready to take in all country and other goods, where due care will be observed, to finish such in the neatest and most expeditious manner.

Kelly and Culver, express their highest sense of obligation, to the particular gentlemen who have so generously extended their encouragement from the infancy of this manufacture to its present perfection.—*The New York Gazette and the Weekly Mercury*, February 6, 1769.

WOOL MANUFACTURE.—A Scheme, by James Popham, of Newark, in New-Castle County, for Manufacturing Two Hundred Stone of Wool, at Sixteen Pounds to each Stone, together with the Expences of Labour, Utensils, Houses, &c. which will employ the Number of Hands as mentioned underneath.

Expence of Utensils.

1 Pair Wool-combs, ... £ 3 0 0
1 Pair Stock-cards, ...   0 12 0
6 Pair Hand Ditto, ...   1 1 0
Warping Mill, ...   2 0 0
Twisting Mill for Worsted, ...   5 0 0
4 Looms and Tackle, ...   12 0 0
Furnace for dying, ...   20 0 0
Fulling Mill, ... 100 0 0
Houses for carrying on the Work 100 0 0

£243 13 0

Expences of Wool, Dying Stuffs, & Workmens Wages

200 Stone of Wool, at 24s. per Stone, ... £240 0 0
Dying Stuffs of all Sort, ...·....   30 0 0
1 Comber may earn per Annum, ...   40 0 0
4 Weavers ditto, ... 160 0 0
15 Spinners, ... 220 0 0
3 Winders of Worsted and Yarn, ...   35 0 0
2 Boys, ...   30 0 0
1 Manager, ... 100 0 0

£855 0 0

The Produce of one Year may be about 6000 Yards of
different Sorts, such as Camblets, Callimancoes, Cambletees, plain, striped, and figured Stuffs, Druggets, Sag-
gathies, German Serges, Everlastings, Plushes, &c. The
aforesaid Number of Yards may be computed on an
Average worth Four Shillings per Yard, which will
amount to £1200 0 0
Expences of Wool, &c. 855 0 0
_____
Leaves an annual Profit of £ 345 0 0
. . .—News item in *The New-*
York Gazette or the Weekly Mercury, January 29, 1770.

WEAVING.—Such a spirit of Industry prevails among
the Inhabitants of the Town of Lancaster, in Pennsylvania, that upwards of 27,739 Yards of Linens, stuff, &c.
have been manufactured in that Town since the first of
May 1769.—News item in *The New-York Journal or the*
General Advertiser, June 28, 1770.

SPINNING.—We hear from New-Fairfield, in Connecticut, that the wife of Samuel Hungerford, of that Place, (who is 43 years of Age, and has now living 12 of her own children, and 5 Grand-children) on the 21st. Day of September last, spun by Day-light in about 12 Hours, on a common Spinning-Wheel, 126 Skeins of good fine Worsted Yarn, tho' under the Disadvantage of having a sucking Child to take care of. This can be attested by two young women who carefully reel'd the Yarn. The laudable Ambition of both Sexes, and all Degree of People in the British Colonies (notwithstanding the Discouragement of some few among them) still increases, to encourage Industry, Frugality and Manufactories among ourselves, that we may not long depend on the Necessaries of Life, upon those who would ungratefully take Advantage of our Necessities to deprive us of our natural Rights and Liberties.—News item in *The New-York Gazette and the Weekly Mercury*, October 29, 1770.

TREATISE ON WEAVING.—Proposals for printing by Subscription, A Treatise on Weaving. Consisting of near 300 different Draughts, with full and plain Directions of the Preparations of the Yarn, Warping, and Weaving of Barrogan, Tammy, Durant, Paragon, Duroys, Sergedenim, Grogram, . . . By David Valentine of Suffolk County, Long-Island. . . .—*The New-York Gazette or the Weekly Post-Boy*, January 6, 1772.

WEAVER.—William Elliot, Weaver, Just arrived from Newcastle, Would be glad to serve any gentleman in that business; he has a very competent knowledge of the different branches of manufacturing linen, woollen and sail cloth to No. 1. For particulars enquire on board the ship Molly, Capt. Cowan, at Murray's Wharf.—*Rivington's New-York Gazetteer*, May 26, 1774.

FABRICS

LINENS.—At Mr. Gouvernier's Storehouse on the Dock, near to Mr. John Reads there are all sorts of

Course Kearseys and Course Linnens and several sorts of Merchandize, to be Sold by Allen Patchat, at very Reasonable Rates.—*The New-York Gazette,* December 30, 1729-January 6, 1730.

CALICOES.—John Brown at Mrs. Beurks over against the Market-house by Burgers Path sells all sorts of Linnens broad & narrow, striped & Flowered Muslings Callicoes, Alamodes, Diapers, Searsuckers, Linnen Checks, Fustians, Cambricks, Hankerchiefs and Ribbands &c. at reasonable Rates and takes in Pay, flour, Bisket, Beef, pork & Gammons.—*The New-York Gazette,* May 19-26, 1729.

EUROPEAN AND EAST INDIA GOODS.—On the Monday the 17th of April, next at ten in the Morning there will be exposed to Sale at publick Vendue, on Credit, at the Store-house of David Clarkson over against the Fort, Sundry sorts of European and East India Goods, being the Remainders of several Cargoes, viz. Fine Spanish Cloths, Shaloons, Camblets, Camblet Stuffs, Callimincoes, Durants, English Damasks, Ditto India, China Tafities, plain, striped and flowered Persians, Cherry-derries, Gingrams, Grograms, Sattins, Cheerconnies, Sooseys, Atchabannies, Threads, Mohair, Buttons, Callicoes, Chints, Muslins, Garlicks, Hollands Linnen, Cambricks, Diapers, Books for Accounts, Indian Gunns, and Brush Ware, with several Parcels of Haberdashery, Cutlery, Iron Ware and other Goods.—*The New-York Gazette,* March 27-April 3, 1732.

FABRICS.—Just Imported from England, and to be Sold by whole sale at a Store in Duke-street, over against the House of Mr. Samuel Bayard, a large Sortment of Goods, viz. Broad Cloths, Druggets, Duroys, Shalloons broad and narrow plain and striped Tammys, ditto Callimancoes, silk and worsted Camblets Mourning Crapes, worsted and cotton Stockings ditto Caps, New-fashion Buttons and Mohair, Linnen of divers sorts,

Muslins, Handkerchiefs of many sorts, Bed-ticks, Fustians colour'd & white, fine and coarse, Hats Ribbons plain and flowered, Fans and Girdles, sewing and stiching Silk, Cutlery Ware of all sorts, Nails Sadlers Ironmongery, Lace for Caps, Silver Lace for Hats and shoes, Brass and Copper Ware, with Abundance of other Things too tedious here to incert.—*The New-York Gazette*, May 8-15, 1732.

KERSEY.—At the House of John Bell, Carpenter, over against Capt. Garret Van Horne, there is to be Sold, Broad Cloths, Kersey's, Kersey Plains, Frize, Green Colloured Duffills, Druggets, Shalloons, Mimikin Blew Bases, Frize, and Plains, and some Ready made Cloaths, &c. By Wholesale and Retail at Reasonable Rates. Also, looking Glasses, and Eight Day Clocks with Japan Cases. N.B. And he will Truck for Beef, Pork, Bread, Flouer, and Gammons.—*The New-York Gazette*, Dec. 9-17, 1734.

IRISH LINEN.—To be sold, near the House of Mr. Lynch on the New Dock, sundry Sorts of Irish Linnen from 2s. to 7s. on the most reasonable Terms, for ready Money.—*The New-York Weekly Journal*, December 15, 1735.

FABRICS. Just Imported, And to be Sold at a New Store in Hanover-Square near the Old Slip Market, Several sorts of Goods entirely fresh, Viz. Kerseys, Broad Cloths of most Prices, Cloth Serges, Druggets, Plushes, striped Cottens, Mourning Crapes, Plain & Flower'd Yard-wide Stuffs; Flower'd Damasks & Ruffels; Plain and Striped Callaminco's, and superfine Black Callaminco, Fine Worsted and Silk Camblets; best London & Bristol Shalloons; Mens Caps, Stockings, Persians, Taffetys, Silk Damasks, Sattins, Gressets; Silk Paplins, Shaggareen, black Mantua, Paduasoys, Lutestring & Velvet; Checks of several sorts, Striped Hollands, Bed-Ticks, Fustians and Dimety; Dutch Holland of several

Prices; Cambricks, Chints, Callico's, Flower'd Linnens,
. . .—*The New-York Gazette*, May 31-June 7, 1736.

FULLING MILL.—The Grist Mill, Fulling Mill, with all
the Utensils belonging to each of them which lately belonged to Obadiah Williams. Absconded; are to be sold
at publick Vendue on the 10th Day of March next, The
Mills are in good order, the Grist Mill having good new
Boulting cloaths, and the fulling mill has two dying
furnaces two Pair of Shears, a Press House, a Press Plate,
Screw, and other necessary Tools, . . .—*The New-York
Weekly Journal*, February 6, 1738.

EUROPEAN AND EAST INDIA GOODS.—Sold at the Store
house of David Clarkson . . . several sorts of European
and East India goods . . . Cloths, Kersey's Druggets,
Mohair, Buttons, Indian Damask, stript plain and Bird-
Eye Taffeties, Strip't and plain Muslins, Callicoes,
Chints, Romalls, Brawles; Guinea stuffs, Thread Laces,
fine Cambricks, spotted Lawns, fine Laces and other
Millanary's Hatts, Indian Guns and flower'd Brimston.
—*The New-York Gazette*, September 18-25, 1738.

FABRICS.—To be Sold by Shefield Howard, At his
House, opposite the Rev. Mr. Vesey's, for Ready Money;
Cambricks, Muslins, Ginghams, Chelloes, Callicoes,
Camblets, Cambletees, Ruffels, Callimancoes, Taffaties,
Barcelona Handkerchiefs, Cotton Romalls, Scotch Hand-
kerchiefs, Byjutaponts, Bed-Ticks, Double and Single
Allopeens, Crapes, Duroys, Scarlet & Green Knaps,
Cotton Caps, colour'd Threads, Mohair and Mettal But-
tons, Felt Hats, Ozenbrigs . . .—*The New-York Weekly
Post-Boy*, May 12, 1746.

LACE.—Naphtaly Hart Meyers, Being removed opposite the Golden Key, in Hanover Square, continues to
sell for ready Money or short Credit, the following
Goods, Mechlin and Brussels Lace, Dresden Work, 12 yd.
16 yd. and 18 yd. Calicoes, English Chints, Persian white

Padusoy, Ducape, white Satten, pink Persia, Silk
Romals, spotted Bandanoes, Muslins, clear ditto, Lawn
Handkerchiefs, flowered Minionet, 7-8, 3-4 Linnens,
Russia ditto, Scotch Ozenbrigs, Ravens Duck, Broad
Cloths and Shalloons, Barragons, corded Druggets, Saga-
thies, brown Fustians and Dimettes, Bombazeens,
Women crape Hatbands, ditto Love for Hoods, Wool
Cards, . . .—*The New-York Gazette and the Weekly
Post-Boy*, May 5, 1755.

MANUFACTURER.—This Day is opened at Hammers-
ley's in Hanover Square New-York, By the Manufacturer
Thomas Fogg, from Wigan in Lancashire, The Check
Warehouse. Where are sold a very great Variety of
Checks, Strip'd Cottons and other Manufactured Goods,
as made at Manchester and Wagan, for Ready Cash or
short Credit. He is really the Manufacturer, and all
Merchants and others may be assured of being dealt with
him on the most reasonable Terms.—*The New-York
Gazette or the Weekly Post-Boy*, June 16, 1763.

SHOP LIFTER.—Monday last a Woman lifted a couple
of Pieces of Callico off of Mr. Milligan's Shop Window;
but a Negro happily seeing it, immediately gave intelligence thereof; Whereupon Pursuit was made, the
Woman overtaken, and the Callico found upon her:
She was carried before an Alderman, who committed her
to Jail; and 'tis said she is to have her Trial To-day.—
News item in *The New-York Gazette or the Weekly
Post-Boy*, February 19, 1767.

LINEN.—Extract of a Letter from a Gentleman in London, to one of the Members of the Society for Arts in
this City, dated July 22, 1767. . . . The People of New-
York, seem to me, to be too infatuated with a foreign
Trade, ever to make any great Progress in Manufactures;
and unless you sell your Linnen, at least as cheap as they
can have it from Silesia, Austria, Bohemia, and Russia,
thro' England, Holland or Hamburg, I fear you will not

establish an extensive Manufactury:—You live in as plentiful a Country as any, and your People might work as cheap: I don't mean in the City of New-York; Cities are not calculated for Manufactures, since its always dearer living in them than in the Country.—News item in *The New-York Gazette or the Weekly Post-Boy,* October 15, 1767.

LINEN.—Extract of a letter from a Gentleman in London, to one of the Society Manufactures in New-York August 26, 1767.

I received a Piece of Linnen from the Society:—it being brown, I desired my Linnen Draper to get it bleach'd; he told me, that during 45 Years that he has been a Draper, he had never seen such an excellent Piece of Linnen; that as he had got a Fortune out of North America, it gave him Pleasure to hear it was Manufactured there, but as a Linnen Draper he was sorry for it. It has been 6 weeks on the Grass, and the Bleacher says it must be in his Hands 6 more, before it will be well whiten'd; for that he never saw a Piece equal to it, and desired to know of what Fabrick it was. Such are the Praises of your Manufacture; I hope soon to see the Day, that we shall import great Quantities of Linnen from New-York, into this kingdom as well as from Ireland and Scotland, and that Germany shall be excluded. —News item in *The New-York Gazette or the Weekly Post-Boy,* November 5, 1767.

SHALLOONS AND SERGES.—By a Gentleman arrived in town from Perth Amboy, in America, we are informed, that a manufactory of Shaloons and serges, very good in quality, has lately been set on foot there; and at Staten-Island they make blankets, ticking, &c. sufficient to supply the Country round. (I don't remember that there is one weaver in the capital part of Perth-Amboy, neither have the whole corporation sheep for a manufactory.)— News item from London, December 29, 1767, in *The*

New-York Gazette or the Weekly Post-Boy, March 21, 1768.

BROADCLOTH.—They write from Perth Amboy, in America, that many hundred yards of broad Cloth, lately manufactured there, had been sold at public vendue for 12 s. sterling per yard, esteemed little inferior to the best English drab.—News item from London, March 12, in *The New-York Gazette and the Weekly Mercury,* May 9, 1768.

BROADCLOTH from the New-York Manufactory, to be sold, by Hercules Mulligan, Taylor: in Chapel Street.— *The New-York Journal or the General Advertiser,* September 22, 1768.

FULLING MILL.—To Gentlemen, Farmers, &c. A Manufacturer, just arrived from England, has taken the Fulling-Mill of Mr. Polhemus, the South of Jamaica, on Long-Island, where all Sorts of Woollen Cloths, Serges, Linceys, &c. are completely dressed, and coloured in the English Manner; where all possible Care will be taken. Cloths, &c. is taken in at Mr. Richard Minifie's Shopkeeper, at the Fly-Market, at Mr. Samuel Casey's Silk Dyer, in Maiden-Lane; and at Mr. John Anderson's at the Ferry.—*The New-York Gazette and the Weekly Mercury,* December 4, 1769.

LACES.—Henry Wilmot, in Hanover Square, near the Old-Slip market, Has a quantity of Exceeding Good rice which he will sell very cheap for Cash, also a parcel of blond and thread laces, gold laces, Vellums, and gold Mecklenburgh bindings, plain and figured modes, variety of figured sarsenets. . . .—*The New-York Gazette and the Weekly Mercury,* January 1, 1770.

SWANSKIN BLANKETS.—A Parcel of Swanskin Blankets, 9-4, and 10-4 wide, of the first Quality, to be sold at P. M'Davett's Store, near the Fly-Market. Also yellow and red Flannels, embossed Serges; Mens and Womens worsted Hose, with a few Pieces of superfine Cloths.—*The New-York Journal or the General Advertiser,* December 20, 1770.

WOOLEN CLOTHS.—Stone and Price, Manufactures, Have imported in the Beaver, Captain Kemble, a large Assortment of Woolen Cloths, consisting of Broad-Cloths, German Serges, Bath Beaver, Naps, &c. &c. To be sold on the lowest Terms, for Cash for short Credit, at the Store of Mr. Ennis's opposite the Lutheran Church, Broad-Way.—*The New-York Journal or the General Advertiser,* December 27, 1770.

IRISH LINENS, from 18 d. to 8 s. per Yard, Callicoes, Cottons and Chintzes, Tabborets, Moreens, &c. &c. to be sold upon very reasonable Terms, for Cash, three or six months Credit, by John Woodward, At his Store, near the Fly Market, who has also for Sale a Quanty of best New-York Rum.—*The New-York Journal,* December 23, 1773.

VENDERS OF FABRICS

ABEEL & NEIL's Vendue House.—sells Irish linens— *The New-York Gazette and the Weekly Mercury,* January 9, 1769.

CHARLES ARDING.—Imports European materials.—*The New-York Gazette Revived in the Weekly Post-Boy,* April 16, 1750.

CHRISTOPHER BANCKER.—Keeps store of materials.— *The New-York Gazette and the Weekly Mercury,* April 5, 1773.

RICHARD BANCKER.—Imports materials from London at his Linen Drapery Store.—*The New-York Gazette or the Weekly Post-Boy,* January 2, 1766.

SIDNEY BREESE.—Imports materials from London.—
The New-York Mercury, June 1, 1761.

SAMUEL BROOME & Co.—Imports materials from London and Bristol.—*The New-York Gazette and the Weekly Post-Boy*, January 21, 1771.

SAMUEL BROWNE.—Imports materials from London.—*The New-York Gazette Revived in the Weekly Post-Boy*, June 3, 1751.

CAMPBELL & GAULT.—Sells materials at their store.—*The New-York Gazette and the Weekly Mercury*, March 1, 1773.

WILLIAM COBHAM.—Sells materials at the Sign of the Hand.—*The New-York Mercury*, February 13, 1758.

JOHN DALGLISH.—Sells materials at the Sign of the Royal-Bed.—*The New-York Mercury*, February 6, 1758.

BENJAMIN DAVIES.—Imports materials from London.—*The New-York Gazette and the Weekly Mercury*, April 29, 1771.

MARY DERHAM, Milliner, Imports materials from London.—*The New-York Gazette*, September 10, 1759.

PHILIP DOUGHTY, Taylor at the Blue Ball imports materials from London.—*The New-York Gazette*, September 10, 1759.

THOMAS DUNCAN.—Sells materials at his store in Wall Street.—*The New-York Gazette Revived in the Weekly Post-Boy*, October 20, 1746.

ABRAHAM DURYEE.—Imports materials from Europe.—*The New-York Gazette or the Weekly Post-Boy*, March 6, 1769.

JOHN ERNEST.—Imports materials from London.—*The New-York Gazette and the Weekly Mercury*, October 10, 1768.

SUSANNAH FAIRCLOTH.—Imports materials from London.—*The New-York Gazette and the Weekly Mercury*, February 10, 1772 (*Supplement*).

JOHN FELL.—Imports materials from London.—*The New-York Gazette Revived in the Weekly Post-Boy*, May 27, 1751.

SAMUEL FOURDET.—Imports materials from England. —*The New-York Gazette*, July 7-14, 1735.

WALTER FRANKLIN & Co. Imports silks from London. —*The New-York Gazette and the Weekly Mercury*, February 3, 1772.

PETER GORDON.—Sells materials at public vendue.— *The New-York Mercury*, April 1, 1765.

ENNIS GRAHAM.—Imports materials from London and Bristol.—*The New-York Gazette*, June 13, 1763.

THOMAS GUMERSALL.—Imports woollen goods from the manufacturer from Leeds, in Yorkshire.—*The New-York Journal or the General Advertiser*, February 6, 1772.

HALLETT & HAZARD.—Imports materials.—*The New-York Gazette and the Weekly Mercury*, April 29, 1771.

NATHANIEL & SAMUEL HAZARD.—Imports materials from England.—*The New-York Gazette Revived in the Weekly Post-Boy*, November 2, 1747.

JOHN HUNT.—Imports materials from London.—*The New-York Gazette and the Weekly Mercury*, October 19, 1772.

ROBERT HYSLOP.—Imports materials.—*The New-York Gazette and the Weekly Mercury*, July 5, 1773.

JOHN LAWRENCE, JUN.—Imports materials from London.—*The New-York Gazette Revived in the Weekly Post-Boy*, June 20, 1748.

ROBERT G. LIVINGSTON, JUN.—Imports materials.—*The New-York Gazette and the Weekly Mercury*, January 7, 1771.

JOHN R. MARTIN.—Imports materials from Bristol. —*The New-York Gazette Revived in the Weekly Post-Boy*, August 29, 1748.

PATRICK M'DAVITT.—Vendue store sells assortment of Irish Linens.—*The New-York Gazette and the Weekly Mercury*, December 25, 1769.

WILLIAM NEILSON.—Imports materials from Liverpool and London.—*The New-York Mercury*, August 17, 1767 (*Supplement*).

JOHN MERRETT.—Imports materials from Europe.— *The New-York Weekly Journal*, November 10, 1740.

ELEAZER MILLER, JUN.—Imports materials from London.—*The New-York Gazette and the Weekly Mercury*, October 10, 1768.

JOHN MILLIGAN.—Imports materials.—*The New-York Gazette*, September 10, 1759.

MOORE & LYNSEN.—Materials sold at auction rooms. —*The New-York Gazette and the Weekly Mercury*, February 13, 1769.

JOHN MORGAN.—Imports materials from England.— *The New-York Weekly Journal*, November 8, 1742.

JOHN MORTON.—Sells the remains of his stock.—*The New-York Gazette and the Weekly Mercury*, October 30, 1769.

MURRAY & PEARSALL.—Imports materials from London.—*The New-York Gazette*, September 10, 1759.

JOHN R. MYER.—Imports materials from London.— *The New-York Gazette Revived in the Weekly Post-Boy*, February 20, 1749.

JOHN READE.—Imports materials.—*The New-York Gazette and the Weekly Mercury*, April 8, 1771.

JOHN SCHUYLER.—Imports materials from London and Bristol.—*The New-York Gazette and the Weekly Mercury*, January 7, 1771.

TEMPLETON & STEWART.—Materials sold at the new auction rooms.—*The New-York Gazette and the Weekly Mercury*, July 17, 1769.

JOHN WADDEL.—Imports materials.—*The New-York Gazette Revived in the Weekly Post-Boy*, October 22, 1750.

CHARLES WATKINS.—Imports materials from London. —*The New-York Evening Post*, November 2, 1747.

THOMAS CHARLES WILLETT.—Sells materials.—*The New-York Journal or the General Advertiser*, October 5, 1769.

THOMAS & JOHN WILLET.—Imports materials from London.—*The New-York Gazette Revived in the Weekly Post-Boy*, September 12, 1748.

WILLIAM WILSON.—Imports materials from London.—
The New-York Gazette, February 7, 1763.

JOHN WOODWARD.—Imports materials.—*The New-York Gazette and the Weekly Mercury,* January 25, 1774.

WILLIAM WRIGHT.—Imports materials from London.
—*The New-York Mercury,* December 17, 1753.

NEEDLEWORK

TEACHES NEEDLEWORK.—Martha Gazley, late from Great Britain, now in the City of New-York, Makes and Teacheth the following Curious works, Viz. Artificial Fruit and Flowers, and Wax-work, Nuns-work, Philligree and Pencil Work upon Muslin, all sorts of Needle-Work, and Raising of Paste, as also to Paint upon Glass, and Transparant for Scones, with other Works. . . .—
The New-York Gazette, December 13-21, 1731.

STOCKINGS.—All sorts of Stockings new grafted and run at the Heels, and footed; also Gloves, mittens and Children's Stockings made out of Stockings; Likewise plain work done by Elizabeth Boyd, at the Corner House opposite to Mr. Vallete's.—*The New-York Gazette Revived in the Weekly Post-Boy,* September 26, 1748.

PLAIN WORK.—Lately arriv'd in this city from Great Britain, Mrs. Mary Gray, who professes teaching all sorts of Plain Work in the Neatest manner, Dresden work in all its varieties; Ladies capuchins, and childrens frocks in the newest fashion. Ladies that have a desire of seeing any of her work, may see it at Capt. Heysham's, in the upper end of Broad-Street, near the City-Hall, where the said Mrs. Gray Teaches. Likewise teaches to work ladies gloves.—*The New-York Mercury,* October 8, 1753.

GOLD LACE.—John Forrest, Taylor, is removed from Smith's Fly, to the Sign of the Gold-Lac'd Waistcoat, at

the corner of the Moravian Church Street, being a few
doors above the Horse and Cart; where gentlemen and
others, may have either plain, gold or silver lace work,
done in a plain, or full laced manner, as compleat, and
as much to their satisfaction as in London.—*The New-
York Mercury,* May 19, 1755.

QUILTING.—Mrs. Carroll proposes teaching young
Ladies plain work, Samplars, French Quilting, knoting
for Bed Quilts or Toilets, Dresden, flowering on Cat Gut,
Shading (with Silk or Worsted on Cambrick, Lawn, or
Holland.—*The New-York Mercury,* May 6, 1765.

NEEDLEWORK.—. . . But my Wife's notion of education differ widely from mine. She is an irreconcileable
enemy to Idleness, and considers every State of life as
Idleness, in which the hands are not employed or some
art acquired, by which she thinks money may be got or
saved.

In pursuance of this principle, she calls up her Daugh-
ters at a certain hour, and appoints them a task of
needle-work to be performed before breakfast. . . .

By this continual exercise of their diligence, she has
obtained a very considerable number of labourious performances. We have twice as many fire-skreens as
chimneys and three flourished quilts for every bed. Half
the rooms are adorned with a kind of futile pictures
which imitate tapestry. But all their work is not set out
to shew; she has boxes filled with knit garters and
braided shoes. She has twenty coverns for side-saddles
embroidered with silver flowers, and has curtains wrought
with gold in various figures, which she resolves some time
or other to hang up. . . .

About a month ago, Tent and Turkey-stitch seemed
at a stand; my Wife knew not what new Work to introduce; I ventured to propose that the Girls should now
learn to read and write, and mentioned the necessity of
a little arthmetick; but, unhappily, my Wife has discovered that linen wears out, and has bought the Girls

three little wheels, that they may spin hukkaback for the servants table. I remonstrated, that with larger wheels they might dispatch in an hour, what must now cost them a day; but she told me, with irresistable authority, that any business is better than Idleness; that when these wheels are set upon a table, with mats under them, they will turn without noise, and keep the Girls upright; that great wheels are not fit for Gentlewomen; and that with these, small as they are, she does not doubt but that the three Girls, if they are kept close, will spin every year as much cloth as would cost five pounds, if one was to buy it.—A letter to the Printer in *The New-York Mercury,* October 16, 1758.

EMBROIDERER.—Levy Simons, Embroiderer from London, informs the Ladies and Gentlemen, That, besides Gold and Silver, he works in Silk and Worsted, Shading; likewise Robins and Facings, Shoes &c. He Cleans Gold and Silver lace, takes Spots out of Silk and Cloths, &c. &c. to be heard of at I. Abrahams, near the Kings Arms. —*The New-York Gazette or the Weekly Post-Boy,* November 6, 1758.

SHADING WITH SILK OR WORSTED.—Mary Bosworth, Lately from London, takes this method to inform the public, that she has opened a school in Cortlandt street, near Mr. John Lary's; wherein she teaches young masters and misses to read, and learn them all sorts of verse; she likewise learns young ladies plain work, samplairs, Dresden flowering on cat gut, shading with silk or worsted, on Cambrick, lawn, or Holland: she draws all sorts of lace in the genteelest manner. Those gentlemen and ladies that will be pleased to favour her with care of their Children, may be assured that she will make them her chief study to deserve their approbation.—*The New-York Mercury,* May 20, 1765.

FLOWERING.—I Take this Method to inform the Publick, that I intend keeping a Sewing-School, on Golden

Hill, next Door to the Sign of the Harp and Crown, on the first day of May next, and will teach young Ladies to flower on Cambrick, Lawn, Gauze, or Muslin, scolloping of Catgut, crowning and flowering of Children's Caps, as also working of Samplers and sewing of plain work. Those Ladies who please to encourage me may depend on their being carefully instructed in the above mentioned, and several Pieces of Needle Work too tedious to mention. By their humble Servant. Isabella Jones.— *The New-York Mercury*, April 27, 1767.

PLAIN WORK.—Mrs. Edwards, Lately from England, Begs Leave to acquaint the Public, that she proposes opening a School and Boarding, for young Ladies, on Monday the 9th of October 1768, opposite Mr. Benjamin Moore's Sail-maker, near Peck's-Slip where will be taught—

Reading, all kinds of plain Work, Samplers, Cat Gut, Dresden Work, imitation of Lace, Sprigging on Muslin and Lawn; likewise all kind of Needle Work most in Fashion in Europe; and she will instruct young Ladies to make up their own Things in the Millenary Way, &c. Ladies and Gentlemen, may depend on the greatest Care being taken for the Improvement of such Children as are under her tuition.

N.B. Young Ladies, either in Town or Country, may be boarded after the genteelest Manner and easiest Terms.—*The New-York Journal or General Advertiser*, October 13, 1768 (*Supplement*).

NEEDLEWORK.—Clementina & Jane Ferguson move their school . . . teach . . . reading, writing, plain needle work, sampler, crowning, Dresden and catgut; shading in silk on holland or cambrick, and in silk or worsted on canvass; as also all sorts of needlework in use for dress or furniture . . .—*The New-York Gazette and the Weekly Mercury*, April 17, 1769.

EMBROIDERER.—Bernard Andrews, Embroiderer, in Broad-Street, at Michael Houseworth's, nearly opposite his Excellency General Gage's; Makes and mends all Sorts of Embroidery Work, in Gold, Silver and Silk, for Ladies and Gentlemen, in the newest and neatest Fashion; likewise Pulpit Cloaths and Tossels. He likewise buys, cleans, and mends, old Gold and Silver Lace. Said Andrews makes and sells all kinds of Paper Work in the neatest Manner, as Hat, Patch, and Bonnet Boxes, at the most reasonable Rates.

If any Ladies should have an inclination to learn Embrodiery, or any of the above-mentioned Work, he will attend them either at his Lodgings, or at their own Houses, as it shall best suit.—*The New-York Gazette and the Weekly Mercury,* April 16, 1770.

WORK ON CANVAS.—Sarah Hay, Takes this method to inform the public, that she purposes to open a Boarding School, the first of May next, in the house where she formerly lived, in Smith-street. She undertakes to teach young Ladies reading English with the greatest correctness and propriety, both prose and verse; plain work, dresden, catgut, and all kinds of Collar'd work, on canvass and camblet; all in the neatest manner and newest taste. She instructs them in the strictest principles of religion and morality, and in the most polite behaviour, and takes the utmost care to instruct them in a perfect knowledge of the subjects they read, (as far as their capacity can take) and provides the principal part of the books proper for their improvement, at her own expence. She also takes day scholars, which will have the same improvement as the boarders. If any that board their children choose they should learn the French language, she will have a master attend at her house.—*The New-York Gazette and the Weekly Mercury,* March 29, 1773.

WORKER IN TAMBOUR AND EMBROIDERY.—Mrs. Cole, from London, worker in Tambour and Embroidery, Has taken apartments at Mr. Matthew Ernest's, opposite the Mr. Andrew Hammersley's, near Coenties Market; where she works in Tambour ladies robes, ruffles, muffs, tippets, work bags, quadrille baskets, gentlemen's waiscoats, knee garters, sword knots, &c. Any Ladies and Gentlemen who favour her with their commands, may depend upon her best endeavours to please, particularly in propriety of shading elegance of design. N.B. She teaches Ladies the Tambour Work expeditiously, and on the most reasonable terms.—*The New-York Gazette and the Weekly Mercury*, September 6, 1773.

TAMBOUR WORK.—William and Sarah Long, from London, Have taken the house lately inhabited by Captain M'Donald in King-Street, and have opened a boarding and day School, for educating Young Ladies in reading, writing, arithmetic, needle work, &c. Also the Tambour compleatly taught, in gold, silver, silk and cotton. The strictest attention is given to morals and behaviour of the young ladies. Grown Ladies may be taught the tambour by lesson, as a room is set apart for that purpose. A Compleat assortment of the very best tambour silk for shading, are provided, with the best needles and cases, and will be sold at the lowest prices.—*The New-York Gazette and the Weekly Mercury*, March 7, 1774.

PRICES QUOTED.—Mrs. Cole, Tambour and Embroiderer, at Mr. Wilks's, near the Exchange, Begs leave to inform the public, that she continues to teach the tambour for a Half Johannes each person. Ladies will be waited on at their own houses, one hour in the day, for Five Pounds currency, each, or Five Shillings a lesson. Those who please to favour her with that honour, may depend on her utmost assiduity to instruct them in the tambour, in muslin, open work, the elegance of shading, to spangle and purl. . . .

N.B. Ladies gown neatly work'd, silk and drawing, for Two Dollars per yard; suits of linen done very cheap, gentlemen's waistcoats done from 24 s. to 40 s. and in gold 3 £ to 5 £ ruffles, sword knots, &c. done on reasonable terms; and shoes work'd for One Dollar. Frames to be sold from 16 s. to 3 £.—*The New-York Gazette and the Weekly Mercury*, April 4, 1774.

CLEANING AND DYEING OF FABRICS

SPOTS REMOVED.—Daniel Wright, now living in Mr. Pecks Slip near the Ship-Yard, in the City of New-York, can clean all sorts of Cloath's or Cloths, likewise Silks, Sattins, Velvet, Stuffs &c. And takes out all Manner of Spots or Stains whatsoever, and brings it to it's former Colour again; any Gentleman or Merchant, or others that have a mind to imploy him in any Thing above mentioned shall be serv'd at reasonable rate by Daniel Wright.—*The New-York Evening Post*, July 7, 1746.

DRY SCOURER.—Thomas Davis, Dry-Scourer from London, now lives at the House of Mr. Benjamin Leigh, School-Master, in Bridge-street, near the Long Bridge, New-York; where he cleans all sorts of Gentlemen and Ladies Cloaths, Gold and Silver Lace, Brocades and imbroidered Work, Points d' Espagne, Cuffs and Robings, Wrought Beds, Hangings and Tapestry, flower'd Velvets and Chints, without hurting their Flowers, at a reasonable Rate.—*The New-York Gazette Revived in the New-York Weekly Post-Boy*, September 17, 1750.

DRY SCOURING AND SILK DYEING.—Samuel & Marmaduke Foster, from Philadelphia, begs leave to acquaint the Publick, that they do carry on the Business of Dry-Scowring and Silk-Dying, at their House In Prince-Street, opposite Mr. Gautier, where they dye all Sorts of Silks and Broad-Cloths, takes Stains and Mildues out of all kinds of Stuffs, Silks, Broad-Cloths, Fustians, and Woollens; they also dye whole Pieces of Ribbons of any Colour, either for Merchants or Shopkeepers; they likewise cleans, and dyes all Sorts of Silk Gowns either plain or water'd, in the neatest Manner; they also clean long

or short Scarlet, or other colour'd Clokes. These Gentlemen and Ladies that please to favour them with their
Work, may depend on having it done in the best Manner
and quickest Dispatch.—*The New-York Gazette or the
Weekly Post-Boy,* August 9, 1756.

SILK DYEING AND SCOURING.—John Hickey, Silk-Dyer
and Scowerer, from Dublin, living in the House and Place
of Mr. James Willson, (much known for the said Business) purposes to scower Men and Women's Garments,
either wet or dry, to dye all Sorts of Colours on Silk,
Cloth, Linnen, Cotton, Leather, &c. All Gentlemen,
Ladies and others, willing to favour him with their Custom, may depend on being well served at the most
reasonable Prices, by the Subscriber, living opposite to
the late Alderman Cortlandt's.—*The New-York Gazette
or the Weekly Post-Boy,* November 22, 1756.

WASHING.—Silk Stockings washed and brought to a
proper Colour, in the nicest and best Manner; at One
Shilling a Pair by Mary Callander, in the Carter's-street,
directly opposite to Colonel De Lancey's, in the Broad-
Way.—*The New-York Gazette or the Weekly Post-Boy,*
May 21, 1759.

SILK AND CLOTH DYEING.—Moore and Collins, Silk
and Cloth-Dyers from London, at Sign of the Two Blue
Balls and Hand, in the Broad-Way, near Oswego Market,
Scours and Dyes all kinds of Silks, Sattins, Cloths,
Camblets, scarlet Cloaks, Stuffs, Brocades, Damasks, &c.
with the utmost Dispatch, and as neat as in London.
—*The New-York Gazette,* April 23, 1764.

SILK DYER AND SCOURER.—Dallas, Silk Dyer and
Scourer, from London, at the Sign of the Dove and Rain-
bow, in Chappel Street, New-York; Cleans and Dyes all
Sorts of Silks, Satins, Velvets, Ducapes, Padusoys, Brocades, Bedhangings, &c. Scarlet and Camblet Cloth
Cloaks and Cardinals, Clean'd or dyed. He will likewise
engage to dye or take Spots out of Broad Cloth, or Silks,

let them be ever so much damaged, that they shall look equal to any new imported. As he hath every necessary Dye-Stuff, and proper Utensils superior to any ever erected in America, and having served a regular Apprenticeship to the Business, he flatters himself he cannot fail of giving general Satisfaction. N.B. Gentlemen's Clothes, either laced or plain, cleaned to the greatest Perfection.—*The New-York Gazette,* June 23, 1766.

SILK DYER AND SCOURER.—Samuel Casey, Silk Dyer and Scowerer, from London, Begs Leave to return Thanks to Ladies and Gentlemen, (those in particular who have favoured him with their Commands since his Commencement of Business in this City) and to the Public in general, for the Encouragement he has received; and informs them that he has set going a blue vat for dying any Sorts of blue, either Woollen, Silk or Linen, at his House in Maiden Lane, nigh the Fly-Market, where he continues to dye all Colours, as usual on the lowest Terms.—*The New-York Gazette and the Weekly Mercury,* August 21, 1769.

SILK DYER AND SCOURER.—Henry Brabazon, Silk-dyer and Dry-scower, from Europe, late from Philadelphia, now residing at the Sign of the Two Dyers, in Mr. Brassier's House on Golden-Hill, near the Harp and Crown: Dyes Saxon greens and Saxon blues; also cotton and wollen or linen, dyes a good blue, and several other colours; and retrieves and re-dyes scarlets damaged at Sea or otherwise: He likewise cleans gentlemen and ladies clothes, scarlet roqueleaus, long and short cloaks, silver orris and brocades, without damaging the ground or flower, in as neat a manner as those done in London. He also dyes and cleans plain and flower'd velvets, and raises the pile again; takes mildews from goods damaged by salt water, or otherwise, and dyes cotton velvet as fine a black, and to as good perfection, as those in Manchester; . . .—*The New-York Gazette and the Weekly Mercury,* July 16, 1770.

DYEING AND CLEANING.—To the Gentlemen and
Ladies of the City of New-York, and the Public in general, Dying, scouring, cleaning and pressing of cloths,
silks and clothes of every kind; as also stoving or white-
ning blankets, swanskins, silk stockings or silks of any
kind; also damaged cloths of any colour, cleaned and
pressed; and made equal to what they were at first by
Thomas Rhodes, in Gold-Street, on Golden-Hill, New-
York, who for many Years, followed the dying business
in Great Britain and Ireland. Scarlet cloaks cleaned or
dyed in the best manner, by said Rhodes.—*The New-
York Journal or General Advertiser*, January 10, 1771.

DYERS.—These are to inform the Public, That the
manufactory lately carried on by Washington and Gant,
at Oyster-bay, on Long-Island, Queen's County, will still
be carried on by Messrs Hunt and Chew, who having
furnished themselves with all manner of utensils and
proper ingredients from England, doth undertake to dye
all manner of wooded blues and greens, Saxon green, fay
and pay greens, and all sorts of ware Colours, and grain'd
Colours, if required; also linen and cotton yarn dyed
blue, so as it will be warranted to stand; and the public
may depend on having their cloth finish'd off in the
neatest manner; also shalloons, tammies, or camblets
water'd or glaz'd in any colour, and at as reasonable a
price as can be afforded; also they will take wool or yarn
to make into cloth.

N.B. Said Washington having been at an immense
expence to procure said workmen, can assure his customers that he hath had the pleasure to prove both said
workmen, as they came from the west of England about
two years ago, and find them men very capable of their
business.—*The New-York Gazette and the Weekly
Mercury*, September 23, 1771.

DYEING AND SCOURING.—Baker and Yearsley, Silk
Dyers and Scowerers from London, Beg leave to inform
the public in general, that they have begun their business

in all its various branches, at the upper end of Maiden-Lane, near Doctor Vanburen's; such as dying, scowering, and dressing all kinds of silk, in the piece or garment, &c. Gentlemen cloaths either wet or dry scowered. They likewise clean and dye scarlet cloaks, coats and jackets, or any kind of scarlet cloth, and make the colour fresh and beautiful. They dye and dress camblets, cambletees, and grograms; clean Turkey and wilton carpets, and make the colour quite fresh. As they have erected every thing convenient for carrying on their business, they hope to give satisfaction to all those that please to favour them with their commands, and may depend on having it perform'd as well as in London.—*The New-York Gazette and the Weekly Mercury,* December 23, 1771.

CALENDER.—To inform the Publick, That there is erected of the best construction, an elegant new Calender, for smoothing all sorts of linen and cotton cloaths; It is carried on in the same manner as in Great-Britain, where they are esteem'd greatly superior to smoothing-irons, both for beauty, advantage, and safety in preserving colours and making them look equally good as when new. . . . Cloaths are taken in at Mrs. Jane Wilson's, the corner of the Fly-market, at the following prices viz. Sheets, 6d. each pair or 5s. per doz. window curtains 6d. per set, women gowns 6d. each, women's sack and petty-coat 6d. womens pettycoats 3d. each . . .—*The New-York Gazette and the Weekly Mercury,* August 3, 1772

WASHING of all kinds for Gentlemen and Ladies, Done in the best Manner, and on the most reasonable Terms, by Mary Campbell, (In Kings-Street, next Door to Mr. M'Ready, Shoemaker). Particularly silk stockings, chintzes &c. which she washes so as to preserve the gloss and colour, and make them look as well as when new—also linen of all kinds, laces &c.—*The New-York Journal or the General Advertiser,* June 17, 1773 (*Supplement*).

TRADES AND OCCUPATIONS

ACTORS.—Last Week arrived here a Company of Comedians from Philadelphia, who we hear, have taken a convenient Room for their Purpose, in one of the Buildings lately belonging to the Hon. Rip Van Dam, Esq., deceased, in Nassau-street; where they intend to perform as long as the Season lasts, provided they meet with suitable Encouragement.—News item in *The New-York Gazette Revived in the Weekly Post-Boy*, February 26, 1750.

ACTOR.—By advice of his Friends, Mr. Kean causes to be presented this evening, for his benefit, (instead of what was advertised in our last) a Comedy called the Busy Body, with the Virgin unmask'd; with singing by Mr. Woodham, particularly the celebrated Ode call'd Britain's Charter.

As this will positively be the last Time of Mr. Kean's appearing on the Stage, he humbly hopes all Gentlemen, Ladies, and others, who are his Well-wishers, will be as kind as to favour him with their Company. Tickets to be had at the Theatre, and at the New Printing Office in Bever-street.—*The New-York Gazette Revived in the Weekly Post-Boy*, April 29, 1751.

ACTOR.—Lewis Hallam, Comedian, intending for Philadelphia, begs the favour of those that has any demands upon him, to bring in their accounts, and receive their money.—*The New-York Mercury*, March 18, 1754.

ACTOR.—Mr. Douglass, Who came here with a Company of Comedians, having apply'd to the Gentlemen in Power for Permission to Play, has (to his great Mortification) met with a positive and absolute Denial: He has in vain represented, that such are his Circumstances, and those of the other Members of the Company, that it is impossible for them to move to another Place; and tho' in the humblest Manner he begg'd the Magistrates would indulge him in acting as many Plays as would barely defray the Expences he and the Company have been at, in coming to this City, and enable them to proceed to another; he has been unfortunate enough to be peremptorily refused it.   As he has given over all Thoughts of acting, he begs Leave to inform the Publick, that in a few Days he will open An Histrionic Academy,[1] of which proper Notice will be given in this Paper.—*The New-York Mercury*, November 6, 1758.

ACTOR.—The Mandolin.   By Mr. Wall, Comedian. Those ladies and gentlemen who may think proper to employ him, by sending to his lodgings at Mr. Thomas Petit's, will be immediately waited on.—*The New-York Gazette and the Weekly Mercury*, April 19, 1773.

ACTORS.—By letters from Charlestown we are informed, that the Government of South-Carolina and Georgia, had prohibited all Trade and Intercourse with the Creek Indians.   The Theatre in that City was closed, after performing fifty-one Plays; and that Mr. Lewis Hallam, and Mr. Woolls, were embarked for England. The Rest of the Company are expected very soon in this City.—News item in *The New-York Gazette and the Weekly Mercury*, June 27, 1774.

ANODYNE NECKLACE.—Imported from London, and to be sold by the Printer hereof; (Price 16 s.) The famous Anodyne Necklace for Children's Teeth recommended in England by Dr. Chamberlen, with a Remedy to open and ease the sore Gums of toothing Children, and bring their Teeth safely out.

[1] In *The New-York Mercury*, December 11, 1758, David Douglass denied a statement which accused him of having opened his Academy to "Act Plays, without the consent of the Magistracy."

Children on the very Brink of the Grave, and thought past all Recovery with their Teeth, Fits, Fevers, Convulsions, Hooping and other violent Coughs, Gripes, Loosenesses &c. all proceeding from their Teeth, who cannot tell what they suffer, nor make known their Pains, any other Way, but by their Cryings, and Moans; have almost miraculously recovered, after having worn the famous Anodyne Necklace but one Night's Time. A Mother, then, would never forgive herself whose Child should die, for Want of so very easy a Remedy, for its Teeth. And What is particularly remarkable of this Necklace, is this, that of those vast Numbers who have had this Necklace for their Children, none have made Complaints, but express how glad they have been, that their Children would have been in their Graves. All Means having been used in vain, till they had this Necklace.—*The New-York Gazette revived in the Weekly Post-Boy,* October 17, 1748.

BAKER.—William Muckelvain, Baker, at the Sign of the Three Bisquets, on Pot-Baker Hill, will continue to heat his Oven at Ten o'Clock, every Day during the warm Weather, for baking Dishes of Meats, Pyes, &c. N.B. He likewise continues baking of Flour into Bread for Family Use, &c.—*The New-York Gazette,* April 18, 1763.

BAKER.—Sarah Sells, Muffin-Maker, in Broad-Street: Takes this Method of informing her Friends, and the Publick in general, that she continues making Muffins and Crumpets hot twice every Day; humbly thanks her Friends for their former Favours, and intreats Continuance of them, which she will make it her constant Endeavour to deserve, and which will be ever gratefully acknowledged.—*The New-York Gazette or the Weekly Post-Boy,* February 29, 1768.

BALANCING EXHIBITION.—The Noted Henry Hymes, Lately from Sadler's-Wells, begs Leave to acquaint the

Public, that he has had the Honour to perform before most of the Nobility and Gentry in Europe and America, and will perform to-morrow Evening, and continue the same every other Evening, Sunday excepted, at the House of Mr. Miller, near the Oswego-Market as follows,

First, he balances a Ladder with four chairs upon his Chin, takes it off with one Hand and rises with it.

Second, He raises an Iron Bar 35 lb. Weight, and swings it on the out-side of his Thum, without the Help of his Fingers.

Third, He balances a Pyramid near six Feet high, with 12 Wine Glasses full of Liquor, on his Chin.

Fourth, He balances a Number of naked Swords on his bare Fore-head.

Fifth, He balances a naked Sword, as a Needle, on the Edge of a Wine-Glass, and makes it spin as swift as the Wind.   With several other curious and surprising Balances, such as Pipes, Tables, Plates, Hoops and Straw &c. &c,

With a curious Magick Lanthorn, which presents several images near six Feet high, &c. &c. with five Images dancing to a Piece of Musick in the Form of Clock-work.

Price for grown persons 2s. and 1s. for Children. Tickets to be had at the House of the Performance, with good Musick to entertain the Company, particularly by Mr. Hymes, on a new invented instrument made by himself.

Gentlemen and Ladies, who will please to favour him with their company, he makes no doubt of gaining their applause.—*The New-York Mercury*, April 13, 1767.

BALANCING EXHIBITION.—By Permission of His Worship Whitehead Hicks, Esq; Mayor of New-York. Benjamin Abram, Who has had the honour of performing before the Kings of Prussia and Denmark, &c. will, on Tuesday the 9th, and Thursday the 11th inst. at the house of Mr. Robert Hull, in the Broadway, at VI o'clock in the evening, Exhibit Balancing.

I. Sets a chair on his forehead, and balances it by musick.

II. Sets a wine glass to his mouth and puts the point of a sword on the edge of the glass, and lets the sword spin round.

III. Claps a plate on the top of the sword and lets it spin round on the edge of the glass.

IV. Takes a tobacco pipe of eight inches long and puts the end of it on the edge of the glass, and the sword in the bowl of the pipe.

V. Balances a peacock's feather and himself with one foot.

VI. Balances the peacock's feather upon his nose, lays down upon his back and gets up again by musick.

VII. Makes the feather jump from one part of his body to another, up and down.

VIII. Balances the feather streight forward.

IX. Balances 6 or 7 pipes one upon another. . . .—
The New-York Gazette and the Weekly Mercury, November 8, 1773.

BLACKSMITH.—George Appleby, Black-smith, who lately lived on the New Dock, near the Major Vanhorne's is removed into the little Street near Mr. Harmanus Rutgers's, where he continues to make Axes after the best Fashion, which he warrants to be good: He likewise makes and sells all Sorts of Edge Tools, at reasonable Rates.—*The New-York Gazette Revived in the Weekly Post-Boy,* March 14, 1748.

BOTTLING BEER.—Benjamin Williams, from Bristol, Begs leave to acquaint his friends, and the public in general, that he is remov'd . . . he intends carrying on the business of bottling beer as usual. Repeated trials have prov'd it will stand the West-Indies. Captains of vessels may be supplied with what quantity they please, on the shortest notice, at ten shillings per dozen; gentlemen in town (for present use) on the same terms, or seven shillings, if they return the bottles.

N.B. Fine cyder of a peculiar quality and flavour, per dozen as above. A good price will be given for empty quart bottles.—*The New-York Gazette and the Weekly Mercury*, May 23, 1774.

BELL HANGER.[2]—Lately come to this City from Philadelphia, John Elliott, who hangs House and Cabin Bells, in the neatest and most convenient Manner, as done at London, with Cranks and Wires, which are not liable to be put out of Order, as those done with Pullies. He Also gives ready Money for broken Looking-Glasses; and may be heard of at John Haydock's, in the Fly, opposite Beekman's Slip. N. B. His Stay in Town will be but short.—*The New-York Gazette or the Weekly Post-Boy*, August 16, 1756.

BOAT BUILDER.—Noah Toveker, shipwright at Saybrook, in Connecticut, will undertake to build vessels of any kind, for privateers, or merchantmen, on reasonable terms, he having all the materials and a sufficient number of hands ready to go to work immediately.—*The New-York Mercury*, November 29, 1756.

BOAT BUILDER.—This is to give Notice, that John Stocker, Ship Wright, has set up a Yard to grave, mend, on new Plank any Vessels for any Ton, Boats, Sloops, or any, to one Hundred and Twenty Tons, and has got Plank, Oakum, Pitch, Turpentine, and all sorts of Necessaries, and can and will give good Attendance to any one that pleases to come to him. The said John Stocker lives on Long-Island, in the Township of Hempstead, on Cow-Neck, at the Mouth of Dogee's Creek, near Stephen Thorn's, about half way or better up Cow-Bay, on the North-East Shore, where there is a good Harbour, good Bottom and smooth Water.—*The New-York Mercury*, June 1, 1761.

[2] This was the first illustrated advertisement of a craftsman to appear in a New York City newspaper.

BOAT BUILDERS.—This Day was launched the Ship Britannia, built by Messrs. Totten and Crosfield, for Captain Thomas Miller; supposed to excel in all Respects, any Ship heretofore built in this Continent.—*The New-York Journal or the General Advertiser*, August 17, 1769.

BOAT BUILDERS.—City of New-York. Peter Arell, of said city, Boat Builder, being duly sworn upon the Holy Evangelists of Almighty God, deposeth and saith, that the boat or barge which Mr. Henry Sheaf was lately building for his Majesty's ship Asia, and destroyed by some person or persons unknown to this deponent, and that he neither advised, aided, or abetted in destroying said boat, and this deponent further saith, that he hath not been in said Henry Sheaf's work-shop for four years last past, and further saith not. Peter Arell. Sworn the 2d day of October, 1775, before me Benjamin Blagge, Alderman.—*The Constitutional Gazette*, October 7, 1775.

BOOKKEEPER.—Any Merchant, or others, that wants a Book-Keeper, or their Accounts started after the best Methods, either in private Trade or Company, may hear of a Person Qualified. Enquire at the Post Office or Coffee-House.—*The New-York Gazette*, July 7-14, 1729.

BRUSH MAKER.—Richard Fitzgerald, Brush-Maker from London, now living at the House of Mr. Taylor, Hatter, near the Old Slip Market, Makes and sells all sorts of Brushes and Mops, such as Painter's, Hatter's, Scowrers, Barber's, & Weaver's Brushes, Stair, House & Hearth Brushes of all kinds, Shoe and Buckles Brushes, Horse Brushes, Hair Brooms and Flesh Brushes; with all sorts of double & singled wired, besides several other sorts too tedious to mention. All Gentlemen and others who will please to favour him with their custom, may depend on meeting with civil Usage. N.B. Said Fitzgerald gives ready Money for any Quantity of Hog's Bristles.—*The New-York Gazette*, July 29, 1751.

BRUSH MAKER.—This is to inform the public that John Facey, Brush-Maker, from Bristol, next Door to the Factory in Chapel-street, Makes and sells all kinds of Brushes, Viz.

Sweeping, scrubbing, scouring, cloth, hat, banisher, dusting, horse, painted hearth, fan, buckle, water, round table, and square curtain brushes

Wheel and stove polishing, hard blacking, barbers, shaving, bonders, short and long white washing, all manner of painting, large clothier's, fuller's, weaver's, coach and harness, buckles and painters tool, and all manner of other brushes

Likewise shoe-makers bristles to be had of the public's very humble servant, John Facey. N.B. Ready money for hogs bristles one shilling a pound, long horse hair, woollen and worsted thrums. It is hoped the Gentlemen both in town and county will encourage the brush manufactory.—*New-York Journal or the General Advertiser,* September 8, 1768.

BUTTON MAKER.—Whereas I Henry Witeman having served my Apprenticeship with Casper Wister, Brass Button-Maker in Philadelphia, have now set up the same Business in New-York, where all Persons that shall please to favour me with their Custom, may depend on having the work done in the best Manner, and at reasonable Rates; at my Shop in Maiden-Lane, between the Fly-Market and the New Dutch Church.—*The New-York Gazette Revived in the Weekly Post-Boy,* September 17, 1750.

BUTTON MAKER.—Henry Whiteman, At the Sign of Buttons and Buckles, near the Oswego Market, as usual, Makes Philadelphia Buttons and Buckles: Wholesale or Retail, as cheap and as good as can be purchased in Philadelphia. As there are a great many of the counterfeit Sort sold in this City, for Philadelphia Buttons, which, upon Trial, has been found to break very soon, and the Purchasers thereof considerably imposed upon;

he gives this Notice to the Publick, that he calls those of his Make, New-York Buttons, which has been well tried amongst all his Customers, and from whom he has heard no Complaint.

The said Whiteman, likewise sells all Sorts of Buckles and Buttons Retail; and a fine Assortment of Tin Ware; black and China Jacks, and some fine Block-Tin Platters, fit for Officers of the Army, Copper Tea Kettles and Sauce pans; with a great many other Goods and reasonable. Also Brass and Steel Buts, Chapes and Tongues, in all sorts of Buckles.—*The New-York Gazette*, October 13, 1760.

CHANDLER.—All sorts of Sope and Candles, made and Sold by John Ditcher, Tallow-Chandler and Sope Boiler, late from London, now living in the House of Mr. Jacobus Roosevelt's, in the Slote; He makes Candles and Soap for those who are pleas'd to find their own Tallow at reasonable Rates: Said Ditcher has his Tools well fix'd after the London Manner.   He would be glad of a Partner with a little Cash.—*The New-York Gazette or the Weekly Post-Boy*, January 28, 1754.

CHANDLER.—Abraham Bendix, Wax-Chandler, lately from London, at the House of Mr. Jonas Phillips, at the East Side of Pecks-slip, gives this public Notice, That he makes and sells the best Sort of Sealing-Wax and Wafers cheaper than they can be imported, of different Sorts and Prices: He likewise makes the best of black and red Lead Pencils, Prussian Blacking-Ball, and Wash-Ball, &c.   Those that will be pleased to favour him with their Custom, may depend on being well served, and with the best Sort, at the lowest Prices.—*The New-York Mercury*, March 4, 1765.

CHANDLERS.—Spermacæti Candle Work.   The Proprietors of the Spermacæti Work, in this City, beg leave to acquaint the Public, that they have erected this (the first of the Kind in the Province) Work at a considerable

Expence, and having brought it to as great Perfection as any on the Continent, they flatter themselves their Candles and Oyl, will have the Preference with the Gentlemen of this City, while the Quality is as good and the Price the same as the best at Market. Those who shall please to favour us with their Orders, may be supply'd, by applying to Isaac Stoutenburgh, Senior, or Junior; William Heyer, in Smith-Street, or James Jarvis, Hatter in French Church-Street.—*The New-York Gazette and the Weekly Mercury*, May 16, 1768.

CHIMNEY SWEEPING.—Mr. Zedtwitz Acquaints his subscribers, and the public in general, that he has provided, agreeable to his printed proposals, hands to carry on the business of Chimney-Sweeping, and by sending to his office in New Dutch-street, near Mr. Leslie's, peruke-maker, his subscribers, and others, shall be duly served at any time; He gives this public notice that his subscribers should not employ any other hands to sweep in the interim, in order that he may perform agreeable to his proposals, and to avoid blunders. Should his people omit any house in its regular time, be indecent, or misbehave to any individual, he will take it extremely kind to acquaint him thereof, that he may give the injured full satisfaction, which is his wish and desire.— *The New-York Gazette and the Weekly Mercury*, May 2, 1774.

CHOCOLATE MAKER.—Made and Sold by Peter Swigard, Chocolate-Maker, in Bayard-street, opposite Mr. John Livingston's Store-House; Choice Chocolate, at the new current Price.—*The New-York Gazette or the Weekly Post-Boy*, September 18, 1758.

CHOCOLATE MAKER.—Peter Low, Living at the Upper End of Maiden-Lane, near the Broad-Way, and opposite to Lairy's-Street. Makes and sells Chocolate, equal in Goodness to any made in this City, at the current Price; and hopes for the Favour and Encouragement of his old

Customers and others. For the greater convenience of my Customers, I constantly keep a Parcel of Chocolate at Mr. Nicholas Low's on the Great Dock, near Coenties Market, where they can be supplied as well as by myself. Gentlemen who chuse to have any Quantity made, shall have it done at a reasonable Rate.—*The New-York Gazette or the Weekly Post-Boy,* October 23, 1769.

CHEMIST.—Richard Speaight, Chymist and Druggist, At the sign of the Elaboratory, between Burling's and Beekman's slip, Begs leave to inform the practitioners in town and country, that he has just imported, . . . a large assortment of Drugs and Medicines. . . . Store keepers and apothecaries in the country may be supplied with the chymical and galenical preparations, as cheap and as good as they can import them from London; as he prepares most of them himself, can warrant the quality of them.

Patent medicines, hair powder, and ivory black, as usual. Likewise sells, wholesale and retail, West-India rum, Jamaica spirits, wine, Muscovado and loaf sugar, pepper, pimento, tea, coffee, and chocolate, with sundry other articles in the Grocery way, too tedious to mention; all of which will be sold as low as any in town.—*Rivington's New-York Gazetteer,* May 12, 1774.

CITY SEALER.—John Ide Myer, City Sealer. Begs Leave to acquaint the Publick, that he has lately removed from Little Dock Street, to the White Hall Slip, where he has erected a very good and commodious Hay Scale, and will give constant Attendance, and the strictest Care taken to do Justice to all who please to favour him with their Employ, as he can depend on the Exactness of his Beam (having spared no Cost to have it as good a one as could be made) doubts not of its giving general Satisfaction; to accomplish which, will be the constant Endeavour of the Publick's, Most obedient humble Servant, John Ide Myer. N.B. All Weights and Measures (as usual) regulated and adjusted in the carefullest Manner.

—*The New-York Gazette or the Weekly Post-Boy,* July 25, 1768.

COMB MAKER.—John Crosby, Comb-Maker, from London: Takes this Method to inform the Gentlemen and Ladies, that he makes all Sorts of Ladies Combs, Tortoiseshell and Horn, and dressing Combs of different Sorts; which may be had at his House in Horse and Cart-Street, near Chappel-Street, or at Mr. Deas's, Wig-Maker and Hair-Dresser, in Broad-Street, opposite to General Gage's. N.B. Any Gentlemen or Ladies, having Turtle-shell by them, may have it made up, on the most reasonable Terms.—*The New-York Gazette or the Weekly Post-Boy,* September 11, 1766.

COMB MAKER.—Lately came from Dublin, a Person who hath had the Honour to serve most of the Nobility in that City, in turning Horn, Ivory, or Tortoiseshell, and makes all Sorts of Combs in the newest and neatest Manner; likewise gives ready Money for Horn, Ivory, or Tortoiseshell; but any Person having either Horn, Ivory or Tortoiseshell, and chuse it to be worked up in any Form relating to his Business, may depend on having their Orders complied and on the lowest Terms, with all convenient Speed, By their humble Servant, Thomas Dunn, Living on Cowfoot-Hill, near the Hay Scales.— *The New-York Gazette and the Weekly Mercury,* July 3, 1769.

CORK CUTTER.—Jervis Robuck, Cork Cutter, from London; Cuts and sells all Sorts of Corks, all Sizes, Wholesale and Retail, at the Foot of Potbakers-Hill, near the new Low Dutch Church: Where may be had, at the lowest Prices, A good Assortment of China raild, Prussia, and Mosaick Soop Tureens; Dishes and Plates: Also Delph, Flint, and Stone Ware. An Assortment of Glass Decanters, Beer and Wine Glasses, Tumblers, &c. suitable for Town or Country Shops. Also, imported in the Snow King William, from London, A neat Assortment of

Looking-Glasses: A Quantity of Iron Pots of different Sizes, Daffy's Elixer, Bateman's Drops, Hooper's Female Pills, a Parcel of Onions, Ginger, Pepper, Allspice, Coffee, white and brown Sugar, &c.—*The New-York Gazette or the Weekly Post-Boy,* February 12, 1759.

COSMETICS.—To be Sold, At Mr. Edwards next door to Mr. Jamison, opposite the Fort Garden, an admirable Beautifying Wash, for Hands, Face and Neck, it makes the Skin soft, smooth and plump, it likewise takes away Redness, Freckles, Sun-Burnings, or Pimples, and cures Postules, Itchings, Ring-Worms, Tetters: Scurf, Morphew and other like Deformities of the Face and Skin, (Intirely free from any Corroding Quality) and brings to an exquisite Beauty, with lip Salve and Tooth Powder, all sold very Cheap.—*The New-York Weekly Journal,* March 29, 1736.

COSMETICS.—The Venetian Paste, So well known to the Ladies for enameling the Hands, Neck and Face, of a lovely white: It renders the most rough Skin smooth and soft, as Velvet, and entirely eradicates Carbuncles and all other Heats in the Face, or Nose and cracking of the Lips at this Season of the Year. Sold only by Hugh Gaine, at 6s. per Pot.—*The New-York Gazette and the Weekly Mercury,* January 24, 1774.

COSMETICS.—Lady Molyneux's Italian Paste. So well known to the Ladies for enamelling the hands, neck, and face, of a lovely white; it renders the most rough skin smooth and soft as velvet. There is not the least grain of paint in it; and Ladies who use it cannot be tanned by the most scorching heat. If it is used to infants in the month, it secures them a delicate skin; nor can the most servere frost crack the skin. Sold by Hugh Gaine. —*The New-York Gazette and the Weekly Mercury,* May 9, 1774.

DANCING, is Taught by the Subscriber, in a genteel and easy Method; at the House in Chaple Street, next

Door to the Play-House, and at Mrs. Demot's on Flatten-Barrack-Hill; He assures all Gentlemen and Ladies that please to Favour him with their Company, that they shall meet with Satisfaction, and that great Care and Due Attendance will be given, by their Humble Servant, John Trotter.—*The New-York Mercury*, June 30, 1766.

DENTIST.—Teeth drawn, and old broken stumps taken out very safely and with much Ease by James Mills, who was Instructed in that Art by the late James Reading deceased, so fam'd for drawing of Teeth, he is to be spoke with at his Shop in the House of the Deceased, near the Old Slip Market.—*The New-York Journal*, January 6, 1735.

DISTILLER.—Joseph Greswold, Disteller from London, Selleth by wholesale or Retail, all sorts of Spirituous Liquors as Rum, Brandy, Geneva, Anniseed Water, Orange Water, Clove Water, Cenamon Water, and sundry other Liquors, at the Sign of the Lyon and Still, in Pearl-Street, New-York.—*The New-York Weekly Journal*, July 6, 1747.

FENCING.—These are to give Notice, To all Gentlemen who desire to learn the right Method and true Art of Defence, and Pursuit of the Small-Sword in its greatest Perfection, and extraordinary quick and speedy, with all the Guards, Parades, Thrusts and Lessons thereunto belonging, fully described, and the best Rule for Playing against Artists or Others with Blunts or Sharps; That they may be taught the same by Me Richard Lyneall, Professor and Master of the said Art, who is to be spoke with at the house of Mrs. Elizabeth Parmyter, in Beaver-Street.

Note, He teaches Gentlemen either Private or Publick, by the Month or by the Whole. Likewise, he has Commodious Lodging for Gentlemen or Ladies.—*The New-York Gazette Revived in the Weekly Post-Boy*, June 22, 1752.

FIRE ENGINE MAKER.—A Fire-Engine that will deliver two Hogsheads of Water in a Minute, in a continual Stream, is to be Sold by Wiliam Lindsay, the Maker thereof. Enquire at Fighting Cocks, next Door to the Exchange-Coffee House, New-York.—*The New-York Gazette,* May 2-9, 1737.

FIRE ENGINES.—Yesterday Capt. Knox arrived here in 15 Weeks from London, but last from Rhode Island: We are assured he has brought over with him two fine Fire-Engines, for the Use of this City, which were sent for by our Corporation; These, with the four already here in Possession of the Corporation, sufficiently prove the Care of our Magistrates for the Preservation of the City as far as lies in their Power.—News item in *The New-York Gazette Revived in the Weekly Post-Boy,* February 5, 1750.

FIRE ENGINE MAKER.—Fire Engines. Whereas it has been the Custom for several Years past, for the Inhabitants of North-America to import Fire Engines from foreign Parts; this is to inform the Publick, that they are made in the City of New-York, as cheap and as good as any imported from England, by Davis Hunt.—*The New-York Mercury,* April 27, 1767.

FIRE ENGINES.—To be Sold, Three small Fire-Engines. N.B. Are very fit for a small Town, or a Gentlemen's County-Seat. Inquire of Jacobus Stoutenburh, Overseer of the Fire-Engines for the City of New-York.—*The New York Journal or the General Advertiser,* June 4, 1767.

FIRE ENGINE.—To be sold by William Shipman, In Beaver-Street, opposite the New-Printing-Office, A Large Fire-Engine, which will with ease command the highest Dwelling-House in this City; she throws her water in a large Body, to a considerable Distance, and will discharge upwards of 200 Gallons in a Minute; is new and in good Order, and works with ease. Has for Sale likewise a few Pair of very elegant polished Steel Snuffers, with open Work Stands, and Ladies and Gentlemens Watch Chains, &c.—*The New-York Gazette and the Weekly Mercury,* July 10, 1769.

FIRE ENGINE MAKER.—Davis Hunt, Engine-maker, at the Fresh-Water, has for Sale, A complete Engine, which he will warrant, and can afford to let the Purchaser have much cheaper than any imported from England. His long Experience in that Branch, and the Number he has made for this City and Country in general, to the Satisfaction of the Buyer, has rendered his Character so far established, that he has no Occasion for a further Recommendation. Any Person, on the shortest Notice, can be supplied by said Hunt. He likewise makes Smiths Bellowses, in the best and cheapest Manner; begs the continuance of his Customers.—*The New-York Gazette and the Weekly Mercury,* February 5, 1770.

FIRE ENGINE.—We can with Pleasure, assure the Public, that the Fire Engine of the Water Works was work'd many Days last week, greatly to the Satisfaction of vast Numbers of People who went to see it. This Engine carries a Pump of 11 inches in diameter, and 6 Feet Stroke, which contains

	29 Galls
Makes 10 Stroke a Minute	290
In one Hour, 174 Hogsheads	17400
In 12 Hours, 2088 ditto	208800
In 24 Hours 4176 ditto	417600

The Well is 30 Feet diameter, and 30 deep, contains 8 Feet depth of Water. The Water is inexhaustable, for the Pump, tho' continually work'd, cannot lower the Water more than two Feet. A Cord and ¼ of wood will work the Engine for 24 Hours.

It is proposed to work the Engine for some Days longer, for the further Inspection of the Public, of which

Notice will be given by hoisting a Flag.—News item in
The New York Gazette and the Weekly Mercury, March
11, 1776.

FISHERY.—We have Advice from Halifax in Nova-
Scotia, that there is such a Number of New-Yorkers got
to that Place, since the first Settlement of it, as will
nearly fill one of the Largest Streets in the Town, and
that they are about to form themselves in one Street,
into a Society or Company, by the Name of the Free
New-York Fishery Company At Nova Scotia; and that
all that shall hereafter come there from New-York, provided they come as one of King David's Soldiers, (see
1 Sam. XXII. Cap 2 Ver.) Shall be permitted to join
them, and draw Shares according to the Stock they bring:
some of these Gentlemen have wrote to their Friends
here, that for their Encouragement to send Merchandize
to them, they will engage that whatever they send, they
will make it all Sterling.—*The New-York Gazette Revived in the Weekly Post-Boy,* September 9, 1751.

GARDENER.—Thomas Vallentine, Bred under the ablest
Master in Ireland, who for some Years after his Apprenticeship conducted the Gardening Business for the Right
Hon. The Earl of Belvedere, a Nobleman remarkable
for elegant Taste, extensive Gardens and Plantations,
the major Part of which were made immediately under
said Gardner's Direction, during his Service with him;
and has been afterwards employed by several of the
Nobility and Gentry, to lay out their Gardens and Improvements. He also surveys Land, makes Copies and
traces Maps, draws Designs for Gardens, Plantations,
Stoves, green Houses, forcing Frames, &c. &c. and will
execute the Plans if required. He is willing to attend
any Gentleman's Gardens within ten or twelve Miles of
this City, a Day or two in the Week, and give such
Directions as are necessary for completing and keeping
the same in proper Order. He has sufficient Certificates
setting forth his Character and Abilities, and can be

further recommended, if required, by a Gentleman near this City. Any Gentleman having Occasion to employ said Vallentine, may hear of him at the Printer's Exchange.—*The New-York Gazette and the Weekly Mercury*, August 8, 1768.

GLUE FACTORY.—To encourage a Manufactory of Glue, in or near the City, (which is much wanted,) Any Person inclining setting up that Business here, (will by inquiring of the Printer) hear of a Person who will take of him Five Thousand Weight, yearly for Three Years, if his Price is approved of; and if his Glue is very good, will be further encouraged.—*The New-York Gazette*, February 17, 1766.

GROCER, CHANDLER AND SOAP BOILER.—John Richardson, Grocer, Chandler, and Sope-Boiler, from England; Takes this Opportunity to inform the Public, that he hath open'd Shop in the House where John Baster, Breeches-maker, lately lived near the Old-Slip-Market, in this City, where Groceries, Candles, and Soap are sold on the lowest Terms, and will be very glad to have the Pleasure of serving Captains and Masters of Vessels with Candles by the Box, &c. And all Favours most gratefully acknowledged, by your most obedient Servant to command, JOHN RICHARDSON.—*The New-York Gazette and the Weekly Mercury*, January 22, 1770.

GUNFLINT CUTTER.—To the Society of Gentlemen for the Encouragement of Arts in the different Provinces of America. John Morris, Gunflint-Cutter to his Majesty's Board of Ordnance, in the Kingdom of Ireland, is willing to come and establish that Branch in any of his Majesty's Colonies or Plantations in America, if properly encouraged for establishing such an useful Branch, whereon depends the Safety and Protection of his Majesty's Royal Person, his Dominions and Subjects in general. It has always been my Study to propogate such useful Arts, as tends to the Public Good, therefore I

earnestly entreat your Consideration on this Branch;
likewise the Art of Mines, Minerals, and Mineral Waters,
and refining Lead and Copper. I am Gentlemen, a
Friend to Liberty and Freedom, JOHN MORRIS. Dublin
20th Jan. 1768.
    N.B. Please to send your proposals directed to me at
William Gun's Esq; in Peter-Street, Dublin.—*The New-
York Journal or the General Advertiser*, May 5, 1768.

GUNSMITH.—To be sold Cheap by Edward Annely,
Gun Smith, at the Fly Market, A Large Assortment of
Guns and Pistols all Tower proof; as also some Birding
Pieces, with Bayonets in their Buts for Gentlemen's Use,
and Guns with Bayonets fit either for Military Use or
Fowling; long Pieces for shooting Geese, Ducks &c.
The right sort of Indian Guns, with Gun Barrels and
Locks of all Sorts; He likewise makes Guns and Pistols
as any Gentleman shall like, and does all Things be-
longing to the Gun-Smith's Trade; and engraves Coats
of Arms on Plate, &c.—*The New-York Gazette Revived
in the Weekly Post-Boy*, August 1, 1748.

GUNSMITH.—Gilbert Forbes, Gun Maker. At the
Sign of the Sportsman in the Broad Way, opposite Hull's
Tavern in New-York. Makes and sells all sorts of guns,
in the neatest and best manner; on the lowest terms;
has for sale, silver and brass mounted pistols, rifle barrel
guns, double swivel and double roller gun locks; common
do. 50 ready made new bayonet guns, on all one size
and pattern.—*The New-York Journal or the General
Advertiser*, March 16, 1775.

HOSTLER.—Waterman, At his repository for horses and
carriages, at the New-York Arms, in the Broad-Way, . . .
N.B. He also wants a good hostler, that will be (if requested) indulged to get drunk twelve times a year.—
The New-York Gazette and the Weekly Mercury, September 23, 1771.

INOCULATION.—Sutton and Latham, Have open'd Apartments for Innoculation, where Patients will be carefully attended, and every Thing necessary provided. Their Price for Innoculation, is Three Pounds Four Shillings, New-York Currency.

As there may be some Persons willing to be innoculated, but who cannot conveniently pay even so small a Sum as Half a Johannes, they are inform'd, that the Price shall be adapted to their Circumstances.

Mr. Latham innoculates from Six Weeks old; and every Month in the Year. For further Particulars, Application to be made to Mr. Latham, at his House in Broad-street. —*The New-York Gazette and the Weekly Mercury,* January 7, 1771.

INSURANCE OFFICE.—The Old Insurance-office Is kept at the Coffee-House, as usual; where all Risques whatsoever, are under wrote, at very moderate Premiums, and due Attendance given from Twelve to One, and from Six to Eight, by Keteltas & Sharp, Clerks of the Office.— *The New-York Mercury,* October 29, 1759.

JACK OF ALL TRADES.—John Julius Sorge. Very much noted among the Nobility in Germany, for divers curious Experiments, lately arrived in this City, hereby gives Notice, that he,

I. Makes all Sorts of Fruits, viz. Pruens, Cherries, Peaches, Grapes, Appricocks, &c. of the same natural Taste and Colour as those that grow, and as perfect, that no Distinction between them and the natural Ones can be perceived.

II. He also makes all the abovementioned Fruit, &c. to the same Perfection, without any Taste.

III. Makes all Sorts of Japan-Work, of divers fine Colours, to that Degree, that none heretofore hath ever exceeded him in that Art.

IV. Makes a Spirit which has the Quality to take out of Clothes and Hats, any Stain or Spot whatsoever, without taking away the Glaze.

V. He prepares a fine Water for Ladies to wash themselves with, in order to preserve their Beauty.

VI. Makes Muscadine Wine, and knows how to cure Wines if spoiled.

VII. Makes a Soap-Liquor, of which take 10 or 12 Drops, and put into a Cup of Water, and you will have sufficient Suds to wash or shave yourself.

VIII. He knows how to wash Gold and Silver Lace, in a very particular Manner.

IX. He makes a Sort of Candles, without any Wax, Tallow, or Fat whatsoever; which Candles are much finer, and gives more Light than any others; they make no Smoke, neither do they want snuffing.

X. He prepares a Spirit which destroys Bugs, and offers any some for Trial.

XI. He knows a special Remedy, to take out the Hair out of Ladies Foreheads and Hands, without any Pain.

XII. He has also knowledge of many other Experiments, too tedious to mention.

N.B. Said Sorge may be spoke with every Afternoon at the House of Mr. Edward Willet, Tavernkeeper, at the Sign of the New-York Arms in the Broad-Way, or at Mr. Koch's, where all Gentlemen and Ladies who will please to favour him with their Custom, may depend upon being duly satisfied.—*The New-York Gazette or the Weekly Post-Boy*, June 16, 1755.

MATHEMATICAL INSTRUMENT MAKER.—All Sorts of Mathematical Instruments, either in Silver or Brass, are made or mended by Charles Walpole, Citzen of London, and most Sorts of other Work done at reasonable Rates at his Shop, at the Corner of Wall-Street, near the Meal Market. N.B. He also gives ready money for Old Copper or Brass.—*The New-York Evening Post*, May 26, 1746.

MATHEMATICAL INSTRUMENT MAKER.—The late invented and most curious Instrument call'd an Octant, for taking the Latitude or other Altitudes at Sea, with all

other Mathematical Instruments for Sea or Land, compleatly made by Anthony Lamb in New-York: where
all Persons may be supply'd with German Flutes, and
sundry other small Works in Wood, Ivory, or Brass, and
Books of Navigation; and a proper Direction given with
every Instrument. Ready Money for curious hard Wood,
Ivory, Tortois-Shell, and old Brass.—*The New-York
Gazette Revived in the Weekly Post-Boy*, January 23,
1749.

MATHEMATICAL INSTRUMENT MAKER.—James Ham,
mathematical instrument-maker, at the house wherein
the Widow Ratsey lately lived, near the Old-Dutch-
Church, in Smith's Street, makes and sells all sorts of
mathematical instruments, in wood, brass or ivory, as,
Theodolite's circumferenter's, sectors parallel rulers, protractors, plain scales and dividers, the late instrument
called an octant, Davis's quadrants, gauging rods, sliding
and gunter's scales, amplitude wood box and hanging
compasses, pocket, do. ship-wright draught bows, bevils,
walking-sticks neatly mounted, surveying chains, japan'd
telescopes, dice & dice boxes, quarto waggoners, Atkin-
son's epitomes, mariner's kalenders and compasses, and
sundry other things, at the most reasonable rates.—*The
New-York Mercury*, May 27, 1754.

MATHEMATICAL INSTRUMENT MAKER.—William Hin-
ton, Mathematical Instrument Maker, at Hadley's Quadrant, facing the East Side of the New Coffee House,
Makes and sells all sorts of Mathematical Instruments,
in Silver, Brass, Ivory, or Wood, viz. Hadley's Quadrants,
Davis's do. Crostaf's Nocturnals, Gunters Scales, Plot-
ting do. Cases of Instruments, Surveyors Chains, Dividers with and without Points, Protractors, paralelled Rulers, Rods for Guaging, Amplitude, hanging and common
Wood Compasses, Pocket do. three Foot Telescopes,
Pocket do. Backgammon Tables, Dice and Dice Boxes;
Billiard Balls and Tacks, Violin Bows and Bridges; with
a Variety of other Articles too tedious to mention: And

as he is a young Beginner, he flatters himself, he shall
meet with Encouragement; and all those who please to
favour him with their Custom, may depend upon having
their Work done in the neatest and best Manner, and at
reasonable Rates.—*The New-York Gazette and the
Weekly Mercury*, May 4, 1772.

MIDWIFE.—Mrs. Ridgely, Midwife from London: Having practised for many Years in that opulent City, with
great Success; but some Affairs relative to the Death of
her Husband, making it indispensibly necessary for her
coming over to this City, she intends during her Stay
to resume that Practice, on a proper Recommendation,
from Gentlemen of the Faculty; and will most carefully
tenderly and punctually attend those Ladies who may
please to favour her with their Commands, on a firm
Dependance of exerting her Ability and utmost Endeavours, not only to merit their Esteem, but to prove
herself on all Occasions, the Publick's very respectful,
and obedient humble Servant. SARAH RIDGELY. . . .—
The New-York Gazette or the Weekly Post-Boy, June 13,
1765

NET MAKING.—This is to give Notice to all Gentlemen,
That John Beals, intends to carry on the Business of Net
Making, at the House of Mr. Samuel Foster, Silk-Dyer,
in Prince-street; such as Horse Nets, to keep the Flies off
them in Summer, Caston-Nets, Shuting Bages, Partridge,
Pigeon, Clue, Tramel, and other Sorts of Nets made and
mended by John Bales, These Gentlemen that please to
favour me with their Work, may depend on having it
done in the best Manner as in London. N.B. Said John
Bales [*sic*] plays on the Violin and Hautboy, for Assem-
blies, at private Balls, or any other Entertainments.—
The New-York Gazette or the Weekly Post-Boy, June
20, 1757.

NUREMBURG PLASTER.—The much famed Genuine
Nuremburg Plaister, is made and prepared in this City,

by G. Gyselbrecht, Surgeon and Practitioner in Physick, and to be sold at his House near Oswego Market, at 2s. and 3d. the largest Box; 1s 2. the second Sort, and 7d. the smallest; with Allowance to Shop-Keepers, who purchase a Quantity to sell again.—*The New-York Gazette Revived in the Weekly Post-Boy*, March 23, 1752.

OIL MEN.—Cressy and Drury, Oilmen, Lately from England, in Prince's Street Have to sell, wholesale or retail, genuine Linseed Oil, manufactured in this City, and refined in the best Manner, fit for finest Painting; also inferior Oils, at different Prices, and Cakes, which is excellent Feed for Cattle, by the Thousand, Hundred, or single Cake. All Gentlemen, Painters, and others, that please to favour us with their custom, may depend on the best Usage, and their Favours gratefully acknowledged, by their Most humble Servants, JAMES CRESSY & EDWARD DRURY. . . .—*The New-York Gazette or the Weekly Mercury*, March 12, 1770.

MACHINES FOR DRESSING WHEAT AND FLOUR.—The Patent Machines (For dressing wheat and flour) of John Milne, and Sons, of Manchester, Are to be sold by Daniel Neil, near Acquakanack, New-Jersey; and by Templeton and Stewart, in New-York. To prevent trouble, the price of the flour machine is thirty three pounds, and the wheat machine twelve pounds, New-York currency. . . . —*The New-York Gazette and the Weekly Mercury*, November 29, 1773.

POST RIDER.—Too all those gentlemen beyond Albany and elsewhere, who receive this paper by the Albany Post-Rider:
Gentlemen,
These may serve to inform you, that I have faithfully served you by day and night, through cold and heat, near four years, and have now almost worn out myself and many good horses, in delivering your paper: some of you have paid me most honourably,

others, perhaps for want of an opportunity have not. These are therefore to inform you, whenever you pay the Printers for their papers, to pay them also for the Rider, who have agreed to receive it for me. Your compliance, gentlemen, will greatly oblige, Your most humble Servant, THE ALBANY POST RIDER.—*Rivington's New-York Gazetteer,* November 17, 1774.

PUBLIC WHIPPER.—The Public Whipper of the City of New-York being lately dead: if any Person inclines to accept the Office with Twenty Pounds a Year, he may apply to the Mayor, and be entered.—*The New-York Gazette Revived in the Weekly Post-Boy,* February 11, 1751.

GOOSE QUILLS.—Mr. Gaine: The following Method of Manufacturing our own Country Goose-Quills has been found to make them equal to any English or Holland Quills imported: And as it may be of Use to the Public, you will be pleased to insert it in your Paper.

First scrape gently the Outside of the Quill, make a Vent or cut off a small End of the Pith; then tye them up in a Bundle, and sink them down into a Kettle of Water, so that the Water may come just above the Pith, and boil them for about three Hours, or 'til they boil clear; then drain out the Water, and Bake them in an Oven at Pleasure.—*The New-York Mercury,* February 11, 1765.

SCHOOL MASTER.—On the 15th of September next at the Custom-House, in this City (where a convenient Room is fitted up) James Lyne designs to Teach in the Evenings (during the Winter) Arithmetick in all its parts, Geometry, Trigonometry, Navigation, Surveying, Guaging, Algebra, and sundry other parts of Mathematical Learning. Whoever inclines to be instructed in any of the said Parts of Mathematical Knowledge, may agree with the said James Lyne at the House of William

Bradford, in the City of New-York.—*The New-York Gazette*, August 31-September 7, 1730.

School Master.—These are To Give Notice, That Persons of both Sexes from Twelve years of Age to Fifty, who never wrote before, are taught to write a good legible Hand in five Weeks at an Hour per Day at home or abroad; and such as write but indifferently may have their Hands considerably improved by Mr. Elphinstone, living in the lowermost of Mr. Haines's New-Buildings in New-Dutch Church Street: where Specimens of Persons writing in the above time may be seen.—*The New-York Gazette or the Weekly Post-Boy*, October 15, 1753.

School Matron.—School for French and English. Maria Gibbon, Who was educated in France, and is lately arrived from London, proposes to open a School, on Monday the 7th of January where young Ladies may be taught to speak and read French and English. She likewise will teach fine and plain Work. More Particulars may be known of Mrs. Gibbon, at Mr. Dudley's, in Maiden-Lane, or she will do herself the Honour of waiting on those Ladies, who shall please to favour her with their Commands.—*The New-York Gazette or the Weekly Post-Boy*, January 14, 1771.

School Master.—To be Public. The Mattisonia Grammar-School in the lower-Freehold, is still continued under the Patronage of Rev. Messrs. William Tennent, Charles M'Knight and William Ayers, and Doct. Nathaniel Scudder, who purpose constantly to provide said school with an able Teacher, and visit as often as may be necessary.

The Gentleman who now presides in the School, and gives singular Satisfaction, is Mr. Moses Allen, late of Nassau-Hall.

He teaches the Latin and Greek Languages with Accuracy, and is particularly attentive to the Reading and Pronunciation of the English Tongue.

The Situation of the School is such, that the Pupils are perhaps as little exposed to Temptation, or any Thing that may corrupt their Morals, as in any Part of America.

N.B. Board, including Washing, Fire-Wood and Candles, is at present no higher than Seven Shillings and Six Pence Proclamation Money, per Week.—*The New-York Journal or the General Advertiser*, January 30, 1772.

SHEARS MAKER.—Cornelius Atherton, (of the Great Nine Partners in Dutchess County.) Begs leave to inform the public, particularly Clothiers, that he has set up the Business of making Clothier's Shears, which he warrants to be equal in Goodness to any imported, and are to be Sold upon as good Terms, which he hopes may be an Inducement for such as want to apply to him. He has made a considerable Improvement in the Construction of these Shears, so that they may be taken a part with a Screw, to be Ground without putting them out of the proper Order, which kind, on account of the additional Workmanship and their great Conveniency, come something higher than the Common. Any Person by applying to him as above, can be supplied on a short Notice.—*The New-York Journal or General Advertiser*, September 13, 1770.

SLEIGHT OF HAND ARTIST.—This is to give Notice to all Gentlemen Ladies and others, that on Monday the 18 of March at the House of Charles Sleigh, in Duke-Street is to be seen the famous German Artist, who is to perform the Wonders of the World by Dexterity of Hand: The Things he performs are too many to be enumerated here. He here with invites all to be Spectators of his Ingeniuty, 1s. 9d. & 6d. is the Price for Admitance. He begins at 7 o'Clock in the Evening. To be continued every night in the Week. Saturday Nights excepted. To be performed by JOSEPH BROOME.—*The New-York Weekly Journal,* March 25, 1734.

SLEIGHT OF HAND ARTIST.—This is to acquaint the Curious, That there is just arrived in this City, a famous Posture-Master, who transforms his Body into various Postures, in a surprising and wonderful Manner, with many Curious Dancings and Tumblings, exceeding any thing of the kind ever seen here. He also Performs the Slight of Hand, with great Dexterity, and Art; and to make the entertainment more agreeable, the Company will be diverted with the Musick of a Dulcemer . . . exhibited by their very humble Servant, RICHARD BRICKELL.—*The New-York Gazette Revived in the Weekly Post-Boy,* April 27, 1752.

SLEIGHT OF HAND ARTIST.—For the Benefit of Mr. Bayly, On Tuesday Evening the 14th of April, Inst. Will be presented, his uncommon Performances by Dexterity of Hand, in a Manner, different from all other Performers of that Art, without the use of Pockets, Bags, or Sleeves. When besides his usual, he will exhibit several Others never attempted before, particularly he will raise an Apple-Tree by Fire, which will bud, blossom, and bear Fruit, in presence of all the Company.

Mr. Punch begs leave to inform the Ladies and Gentlemen, that by him, his Merry Family, and Company of Comedians, will be presented several Drolls, Burlettas, &c. &c. Particularly a New Farce, call'd The enchanted Lady of the Grove. With a curious View of the Sea, in which are seen several Ships Engaging, Fish, Sea Monsters, &c. &c. Swimming: And the Men of War taking the Island of Goree.

End of Part the First, will be a Grotesque Interlude of Dancing, call'd The Drunken Peasant. The Peasant, by Mr. Tea. Clown, by Mr. Bayly. End of Part the Second, a Pantomine, call'd Harlequin and the Miller. The Miller, by Mr. Bayly. Harlequin, by Mr. Tea. End

of Part the Third, a Negro Dance, In Character, by
Mr. Tea.

Ladies and Gentlemen may be assured the strictest
Regularity will be observed as Mr. Bayly has taken Care
to remove every Obstacle that might tend to interrupt
the Company, or, the Performance.

Boxes 4s. Front Seats 3s. Second Seats 2s. The Door
to be open'd at 5, and begin at 7 o'clock. Tickets to be
had only of Mr. Bayly, at the Place of the Performance.
Vivant Rex Et Regina.

To Conclude with a Hornpipe, by Mr. Tea. If
Tuesday Evening proves bad Weather, it will be post-
poned till next Evening The Tuesday following will be
for the Benefit of Mr. Tea.—*The New-York Journal or
the General Advertiser*, April 9, 1767.

SMELTER AND REFINER OF GOLD, SILVER.—Chepman
Ashers, Smelter and Refiner of Gold, Silver, Copper and
Lead, is lately arrived from Germany where he has been
employed as such, in several Smelting and Refining
Works, and particularly those of the Elector of Saxony.

He proposes to smelt, separate, and refine, in this, or
any of the neighbouring Colonies, the above mentioned
Metals, from any Ore delivered to him for that purpose,
and promises to save 50 per Cent. of the Expence usually
paid by the Americans, who sent their Ore to England
to be smelted or refined there. But then the Works must
be erected near a navigable River, and in a Part of the
Country where there is a great Plenty of Wood for making Charcoal. If any Gentlemen inclines to employ the
said Ashers in that Capacity, he doubts not his giving
full Satisfaction respecting his Abilities and Character. He is determined not to contract for a Salary, but
a Share in the Produce of the Works, which if undertaken, will be first of the kind carried on in North-
America, and must prove highly beneficial. For further
Particulars inquire of himself, at Mr. Samuel Israel's in
Little-Dock-Street.—*The New-York Gazette and the
Weekly Mercury*, March 14, 1774.

SNUFF MAKERS.—Maxwell and Williams From Bristol. Where they for many years carried on a large and extensive Trade in the Snuff and Tobacco Manufactories, Have erected in this City, a complete Apparatus for carrying on the said Business in all its Branches.

They have now ready for sale, at their Store, near the lower end of Wall-Street, All sorts of best Scotch and Rappee Snuff, Pigtail, Rag, and fine mild smoking Tobacco. The Public will find upon Trial, the Snuff manufactured by them, to be equal in Quality and Flavour to any imported from Great-Britain; being made of the best Materials, and in a Manner superior to any Thing of the kind yet attempted in the Country: And as an Encouragement to those who are inclined to countenance Manufactories set on Foot in America, purpose selling their Snuff on lower terms than can be imported. . . .— *The New-York Journal or the General Advertiser*, May 13, 1773 (*Supplement*).

SPLINT MAKER.—Lewis Nichols, At Newark, New-Jersey, Makes and Sells, Sharp Splints for Legs and Thighs, universally made use of by Surgeons. Doctor Treat of New-York has been supplied with a number of sets of his make, and he has left a set to be seen at Mr. James Thompson's, at the corner of Beekman's Slip, where a letter left for him will be forwarded, and a number of sets got ready at the shortest notice, and at a moderate price.—*The New-York Journal or the General Advertiser*, May 2, 1776.

SPLIT PEAS MANUFACTURED.—Split Pease, Manufactured in the best manner by John Arthur, near opposite Mr. William Walton's, above Peck's-slip; where any quantity may be had on the shortest notice, put up in bushel and half bushel kegs, or by measure. The said Arthur has likewise received per the last vessels from London, a variety of seasonable goods, amongst which are . . . Henry and Andrew playing cards, . . . barrel and square glass lanthorns, loose and paper pins of all sizes, and a large assortment of Paper Hangings, in which are two elegant India patterns; has also for sale, coffee, loaf, lump and muscovado sugars, rice, chocolate, allspice, &c.—*The New-York Gazette and the Weekly Mercury,* November 22, 1773.

SUGAR REFINING.—Publick Notice is hereby given, That Nicholas Bayard of the City of New-York has erected a Refining House for Refining all sorts of Sugar and Sugar-Candy, and has procured from Europe an experienced Artist in that Mystery. At which Refining House all Persons in the City and Country may be supplyed by Wholesale and Re-tale, with both double and single Refined Loaf-Sugar, as also Powder and Shop-Sugar-Candy, at Reasonable Rates.—*The New-York Gazette,* August 10-17, 1730.

SURGEON.—Elias Wollin of Bohemia, who has served in his Imperial Majesty's Army as Chirurgeon four Years infallibly and instantly Cures the Tooth Ach to Admiration, also Bleeds without any Manner of Pain, Cups in the Like Manner, Wounds, Swellings, and Sores are also cured, wonderfully by him in a Short Time he has made sundry Cures of the Tooth Ach in the Presence of many. He is to be spoke with at the House in Stone Street lately Occupied by Mr. Soloman Myers, opposite to Mr. Lynsen, the Baker.—*The New-York Weekly Journal,* May 25, 1741.

SURGERY.—To be Sold, Heister's Surgery, the whole illustrated with thirty eight Copper-plates, exhibiting all the Operations, Instruments, Bandages, and Improvements, according to the modern and most approved Practice; Sharpe's Surgery, Smellie's Midwifery, Capital Instruments, in Cases, one lin'd with green Velvet, the other with Bays, the best were made by Stanton, all new; likewise a large Medicinal Chest fitted with large and small square Bottles, Wanting but very Trifles to make it compleat for Sea. Enquire of the Printer hereof.—*The New-York Mercury*, July 16, 1759.

TANNERY.—Hugh Hughes Informs the Public that he has a Tan-Yard, and Currying Shop, in Ferry-Street, near Peck's Slip, where the Business is carryed on as usual. And (in a general Way) the following Sorts of Leather may be had, viz.

Harness, Skirting, Bridle, Stirrup, Covering, and Seat-Leather. Also: Soal and upper Leather, Calf Skins, and Sheep Skins, fit for Saddler's or Book Binder's Use, N.B. A good Price is given, by said Hughes, for good Hides, Bark, Oyl and Tallow.—*The New-York Gazette or the Weekly Post-Boy*, October 7, 1762.

TOBACCO PIPES.—A very good dwelling house with a Kitchin and store House a good Stable, a pleasant Garden with an Orchard and about Twenty Acres of Clay ground fit for making Tobacco Pipes, with two Negro slaves, utensils and other conveniencies to carry on that business. It lyes opposite to Froggs Point at White Stone in the Township of Flushing, in Queens County. . . .—*The New-York Gazette*, March 24-March 31, 1735.

TOBACCONIST.—Whereas the Subscriber has followed the Business of a Tobacconist in this City for several Years past, and by his Care and Skill has acquired some Credit with his Tobacco, whose Papers are known by the Mark B. M. And some other Tobacconist envying his Success, or coveting to take away his Bread and Credit, have manufactured and sold their Tobacco, with the Marks M. B. and imposing it on the Publick for the Subscribers: This is therefore to notify to all concerned, that whatever Tobacco is sold by the subscriber, has only the Marks B. M. on the Papers, and any other Mark with a Pretence of its being the Subscriber's, is an Imposture. BLAZE MOORE.—*The New-York Gazette or the Weekly Post-Boy*, January 4, 1768.

TOBACCONIST.—Best Tobacco, manufactured by Stephen Hitchcock, a little below St. George's Chapel; Where the Publick will be supply'd with best Pigtail Tobacco, Cut Tobacco for chewing or smoaking, or the genuine Quality, clear of Sand or Dust, and fine Shag. As he is a new Beginner, he will strive to merit the Approbation of the Publick. N.B. Country Merchants and Seamen, supply'd at the cheapest Rate.—*The New-York Gazette and the Weekly Mercury*, June 17, 1771.

TOBACCONIST.—This is to inform the Publick, That the Tobacconist Business is carried on by the Widow Pell, and the Papers being formerly sign'd by Samuel Pell, are now stamp'd Widow MARY PELL.—*The New-York Gazette and the Weekly Mercury*, July 1, 1771.

TOBACCONIST.—Dennis MacReady Tobacconist. Begs leave to acquaint, friends and customers, and the publick in general, that he has removed his tobacco manufactory from horse and cart street, towards the lower end of Wall-street, at the sign of the bladder of snuff and roll tobacco, where he intends to carry on the business as usual, and has for sale best inspected leaf tobacco by the hhd or barrel fit for shipping &c. superfine pigtail, common do. hogtail and cut tobacco, scotch and rappee snuff. . . .—*Rivington's New-York Gazette*, May 13, 1773.

WATER WORKS.—Mr. Parker, As no doubt you'll advertise the Readers of your weekly Paper of the late Fire in the South Ward of this City; please to add those few Hints, for our future Safety.

It is well known, that the Fires in this Town of late, as that in Duke Street, the School House, and This, happen'd to be situate within Reach of the Rivers; by which Means, the Engines could be supplied without great Difficulty; and thus, to our happy Deliverances, those raging Fires were extinguished.

But suppose a Fire should come to a Head, as either of those did, in the Heart of our City, how should we master it? . . . I propose, that a Drain, or Brick Channel, may be carried up at Low-Water Mark, from under the Long-Bridge, in Broad-Street; [3] . . . Some may object perhaps, that such a Course of Salt Water will spoil the Wells near it, and make the Water brackish; even this I question, as it is confined in a Brick Channel; and if it should, Tea-Water is daily brought at the Doors, and the other will do to wash their Houses.—Letter to the printer in *The New-York Gazette Revived in the Weekly Post-Boy*, November 5, 1750.

WATER WORKS.—Stephen Hitchcock, Living near Peck's-slip, on the dock below Mrs. Walton's, and opposite Capt. Rose, Has erected gutters from the well known pump of water of Mr. Van Horne, formerly occupied by Richard Cornwel. Which water is equal in goodness to any in this city; and which pump has supplied almost all the shipping in the harbour. The gutters extend down to the end of Capt. Rose, and Mr. Laight's new dock, and is so convenient that any vessel may be supplied with water much easier and with less trouble than any other place in the city, as it can be filled in the vessel or boat, as they lie along side of the dock.— *The New-York Gazette and the Weekly Mercury*, September 13, 1773.

WATER WORKS.—Last Thursday sen'night the Corporation of this City met, and agreed to Mr. Christopher Colles's Proposal for supplying this City with fresh Water, by Means of a Steam Engine, Reservoir, and Conduit Pipes; and in order to carry the said useful and laudable Design into immediate execution, they resolved to issue Promissory notes as the Work shall advance.

According to this design, the Water will be conveyed through every Street and Lane in this City, with a perpendicular Conduit Pipe at every Hundred Yards, at which Water may be drawn at any Time of the Day or

[3] A detailed description of the proposed water works follows.

Night, and in case of Fire, each conduit Pipe will be so contrived as to communicate with the extinguishing Fire-Engines, whereby a speedy and plentiful Supply of Water may be had in that calamitous Situation.—News item in *The New-York Gazette and the Weekly Mercury*, August 1, 1774.

WATER WORKS.—New-York Water Works. Notice is hereby given, that a large quantity of pitch pine logs will be wanting for the New-York Water Works; Such persons as are willing to engage to furnish the same, are desired to send their proposals, in writing, before the 20th of October next, to Christopher Colles, contractor for said Works.

These logs must be of good pitch pine, streight and free from large knots, and 20 feet long; one fourth of the number of logs to be 12 inches diameter, exclusive of sap, at the small end; and the remaining three fourths of 9 inches diameter, exclusive of sap, at the small end.—*The New-York Gazette and the Weekly Mercury*, September 5, 1774.

WHALEBONE CUTTING, in all its parts out of the slabs, for stay or hoop-makers, performed by David Philips, at his house near the Widow of Harmanus Rutgers, opposite the Sign of the Three Pidgeons. All persons who may think proper to employ him in the above business, may depend on having their work done, with care and dispatch.—*The New-York Mercury*, February 10, 1755.

WHEELWRIGHT.—James Hallet, Wheel-Wright, on Golden Hill, in New-York, Makes and mends all sorts of Wheels or Carriages for Chaises, Chairs, Kittereens, Waggons or Carts, after the best Manner, with all Expedition, at the most reasonable Rates.—*The New-York Gazette Revived in the Weekly Post-Boy*, February 13, 1749.

WHEELWRIGHT.—Dominicus Andler, Wheelwright, from Germany, Acquaints the public, That he can make most sorts of mills, such as grist, oil, fulling, paper, and saw-mills; also forges and furnaces, to work either by water, wind, or horses; likewise water engines, to take the water out of mines, or other places where water is to be taken out. He has practis'd for many years in Germany, and had the honour to be employed by most of the Princes. For further particulars, enquire of John Entrest, at the North-River, where some of his drafts may be seen. Those Gentlemen who shall be pleased to employ him, may rely on having their work perform'd with the utmost accuracy and dispatch, by their humble Servant, Dominicus Andler.—*The New-York Gazette and the Weekly Mercury,* October 31, 1768.

WHIP MAKER.—John Amory, Whip-Maker, Manufactures and sells all sorts of the best and newest fashioned Horse-Whips, opposite the Old English Church Yard, and next Door to the Shop he formerly carried on that Business in, in Company with John Johnson; and as he is determined to manufacture the best Stuff, and in the newest Taste, he hopes for a Continuance of his Friends and the Public's Encouragement, whose past Favours he most gratefully acknowledges.—*The New-York Gazette and the Weekly Mercury,* October 2, 1775. See also *The New-York Gazette and the Weekly Mercury,* May 25, 1772.

WIND MILL.—At the Wind Mill, near the Bull's Head Tavern, in the Bowery, All kinds of grain, ginger, &c. &c. with every thing that can be manufactured in a grist mill, done in the best manner by George Traile, who will take particular care that strictest justice be done, and all possible dispatch given, to those who may be pleased to favour him with their custom. And at the Snuff Mills, in the Bowery, said Traile manufactures as usual, Scots snuff, rappee of all kinds, and Irish high toasted, equal (baring prejudice) to any imported from Europe, choice pigtail, hogtail and cut tobacco.

For the conveniency of city customers, a small assortment of the above articles will be kept at Capt. Robert Sinclair's-store, on the Hunter's Quay, where orders for quantities will be taken, and executed with punctuality. N.B. It is requested that as much time as possible may be given.—*The New-York Gazette and the Weekly Mercury*, June 1, 1772.

COSTUME

WEARING APPAREL.—Ran away on Sunday the 12th Instant July, from Phillip Livingston, two Irish Servants, . . . They have taken with them brown Frize close-body'd Coats, the Back lin'd with brown Flannel, narrow Sleeves, & Bath-mettle Buttons made after the French Fashion, two ditto Wastcoats, four pair Leather Breeches, four pair Ozenbrigs ditto, five Guinea-Stuff Shirts, and four strong Holland-Linen ditto, five pair Stockings, two Felt Hats, two Silk-romal Handkerchiefs, two Cotton ditto, one Worsted Cap, a Bayonet, and Sundry other Things. . . .—*The New-York Gazette*, July 13-20, 1730.

STAYS.—James Munden, Partner with Thomas Butwell from London, Maketh Gentlewomens Stays and Childrens Coats in the Newest Fashion, and so that Crooked Women and Children will appear strait. By whom Gentlewomen and Ladies in City & Country may be faithfully served by the said JAMES MUNDEN and THOMAS BUTWELL.—*The New-York Gazette*, January 28-February 4, 1735.

BROCADE GOWN.—Lost some Time last Week a Brocade Gown, white Ground, and red and Green Flowers, Wrapt up in a purple Calico Peticoat and half a yard of New Brocade of the same in it. Whoever brings it to the Printer hereof shall have Forty Shillings Reward, and no Questions asked.—*The New-York Journal*, April 11, 1737.

GREAT COAT.—Taken from John Croker at the Fighting Cocks New-York, in the Room of another a light coloured Cloth great Coat with Button Holes in the Inside under a Flap a Capt Cape and the Button Holes in threes down before. Whoever has got the Coat is desired to return it, and take their own, or whoever will inform the said Croker who has the Coat, so as he may have it again, shall have Ten Shillings as a Reward paid by JOHN CROKER.—*The New-York Weekly Journal,* December 3, 1739.

MUFFS.—Peter Ruston living near Mr. Anthony Rutgers, Brewer, Dresses all sorts of Furrs and makes Muffs for Men or Women.—*The New-York Weekly Journal,* November 22, 1742.

WRAPPER.—Lost a Chocalat Colour'd Cambleteen Wraper, small white streeks running crossways, at an uncommon Distance, the Sleeves were not yet sew'd in. Whoever brings it to the Printer hereof, shall be well rewarded and no Questions ask'd.—*The New-York Weekly Journal,* February 4, 1745.

CLOAK.—Last Night was taken out of a House in this City suppos'd by Mistake, a blue Broad-cloth Cloak, with light blue silk Frogs on it with a double Cape, and Silver Hooks & Eyes; . . .—*The New-York Weekly Post-Boy,* December 29, 1746.

GARTER.—Lost on Monday Night last, between the Fort and the Slip-Market, a black Silk Garter, lin'd with red, with a Stone Buckle set in Silver; Whoever finds it, and will bring it to Mrs. Hogg's in Broad-Street, or to the Printer hereof, shall receive half a Pistole Reward. —*The New-York Weekly Post-Boy,* February 22, 1748.

MILLINERY.—Margaret St. Maurice, Lately from London, at Mr. Cook's on Bayard's Dock; Makes and Sells all sorts of Men's and Women's Jockey Caps, Men's

Morning Caps, Masks for Ladies, Bath Bonnets, Bags and Roses for Gentlemen's Wigs, Palareens and Hooks, Silk Hats for Children; after the newest Fashions.— *The New-York Gazette Revived in the Weekly Post-Boy,* May 8, 1749.

WIGS.—Alexander Lindsay and Robert Johnston, peruke-makers. . . . Where Gentlemen may be supplied with all kinds of Perukes, Tets and Fox-Tails, &c. after the most genteel Fashions now used in London; Ladies may also be furnished with Tets and Wigs in perfect Imitation of their own Hair. They also cut and dress Ladies and Gentlemen's Hair, in the London Mode. Orders from the Country shall be punctually complied with, as if given in Town. . . .—*The New-York Gazette Revived in the Weekly Post-Boy,* May 7, 1750.

WIGS.—This is to acquaint the Publick, that there is lately arrived from London, the Wonder of the World, An honest Barber and Peruke-maker, who might have worked for the King, if his Majesty would have employed him; it was not for the Want of Money that he came here, for he had enough of that at Home; nor for the Want of Business that he advertised himself. But to acquaint the Gentlemen and Ladies, That Such a Person is now in Town, living near Rosemary-Lane, where Gentlemen and Ladies may be supplied with the Goods as follow, Viz. Tyes, Full-bottoms, Majors, Spencers, Fox-Tails, Ramalies, Tucks, cuts and bob Perukes; Also Ladies Tatematongues and Towers, after the Manner that is now wore at Court. By their humble and obedient Servant, JOHN STILL.—*The New-York Gazette Revived in the Weekly Post-Boy,* May 21, 1750.

STOCKINGS.—This is to give Notice, That Elizabeth Boyd, is going to remove next Door to the Widow Hog's in Broad Street, near the Long Bridge, and will continue, as usual, to graft Pieces in Knit Jackets and Breeches, not to be discern'd, also to graft and foot Stockings, and Gentlemen's Gloves, Mittens or Muffatees made out of old Stockings, or runs them in the Heels. She likewise makes Children's Stockings out of old ones; at a very reasonable Rate.—*The New-York Gazette Revived in the Weekly Post-Boy*, April 1, 1751.

CLOAK.—Lost last Wednesday, a blue Cloak, with two Capes, one of them Velvet, and under one of the Capes are three red Seals, with a Coat of Arms. . . .—*The New-York Gazette Revived in the Weekly Post-Boy*, April 15, 1751.

GENTLEMEN THIEF ATTIRE.—Runaway thief from the house of Mrs. Mary Bradock . . . wore a Silver-lac'd Hat, a dark cut Pigtail Wigg, a Cloth-colour'd Fustian Coat very short, with Velvet Cuffs and Collars, Breeches of the same with strings, a scarlet Vest, a light colour'd Duffle Great-Coat, a Pair of fine ribb'd worsted Stockings to roll over the knee, no Boots, a Pair of small Silver Buckles in his Shoes. . . .—*The New-York Gazette or the Weekly Post-Boy*, July 30, 1753.

WIGS.—Me givee de Avertisement to every Body of New-York . . . Yes, dammee, me advertisee for makee de Vig, Cuttee and curlee de Hair, dressee and shavee de Beard of the Ghentleman, selle de Pomate, and de Powdre, so sweet for de Hair, and de Vig, for makee de bon Approach to de Madam-moselle: . . . N. B. Me makee all in de Bon Taste, Alamode de Paris; and me no chargee above three Hundred per Cent. more dan all de Workmans in Town.

Me havee de Prises so.

For dressee de Hair,	£0	6	6
For Curlee de Hair,	0	4	0
For Cuttee de Hair,	0	6	6
For makee de Bag,	0	10	6
For makee de Ramille,	de Half de Pistole.		
For makee de Toupee,	de Half of de Pistole.		
For Von Stick de Pomat.	£0	2	6
For Von Bottle de Lavender,	0	4	0

And so in de Proportion.—*The New-York Gazette or the Weekly Post-Boy,* January 5, 1756.

FASHIONS FROM LONDON.—Mary Wallace and Clementia Ferguson, Just arrived from the Kingdom of Ireland, intend to follow the business of mantua-making, and have furnished themselves from London, in patterns of the following kind of wear, for ladies and gentlemen, and have fixed a correspondence so as to have from thence and London, the earliest fashions in miniature: They live at Mr. Peter Clark's within two doors of William Walton's, Esq; in the Fly. Ladies and gentlewomen that will employ them, may depend on being expeditiously and reasonably served, in making the following articles, that is to say, Sacks, negligees, negligee-night-gowns, plain night-gowns, pattanlears, shepherdesses, roman-cloaks, cardinals, capuchins, dauphnesses, shades, lorrains, bonnets and hives.—*The New-York Mercury,* January 3, 1757.

GOLD LACED HAT.—Lost, on Sunday the 6th instant, in the evening, between Blooming-Doll and New-York, a New Gold-Laced Hat. Whoever has found the same, and will bring it to the Printer hereof, shall be handsomely rewarded for his trouble.—*The New-York Mercury,* December 5, 1757.

SHOES.—Knight and Company, at the London Shoe Ware-House, at Whitehall at the House of the late Captain Moore. Where is to be sold by wholesale or retail, on the most reasonable terms, a good assortment of London made men's single channel pumps, neat shoes and pumps, with strong double soal shoes for working men, all sorts and sizes of boys and girls leather shoes, also a compleat assortment of Women's Calimancoes, everlasting and damask shoes made in the newest taste; with women's strong toed clogs for the winter.

N.B. As they intend dealing only in the above articles; the publick may depend on being always supplied, as they will have a fresh assortment by every vessel from England.—*The New-York Gazette,* October 29, 1759.

STAYS.—Clarke, Stay-Maker from London, makes Childrens Stays, Coats, Sullteens, Holhipt Stays, in the newest Fashions: Ladies that chuse to employ him, he is to be found the next Door to Mr. Roberts's in the Broad-Way, opposite the Bowling Green.—*The New-York Mercury,* June 30, 1760.

BREECHES.—John Baster, Leather-Seller and Breeches Maker, from London, at the Sign of the Buck and Breeches, opposite the Old Slip Market, Where he makes all Sorts of Leather Breeches, such as Buck, Doe, Lamb and Black, in the neatest Manner. Such of the Nobility, Gentry, and others, who please to favour him with their Custom, may be supplied with the best in their Kind, By their most humble Servant, JOHN BASTER.—*The New-York Gazette,* October 5, 1761.

FURS.—Alexander Solomons, Skinker [*sic*] and Furrier from London, at his Store, opposite to Henry Holland, Esq; near the long-bridge, has just finished, and has for Sale, a fresh and genteel Assortment of the following Goods, viz. Muffs and Tippets, made of Ermine and Mock-Ermine, Sable and Mock-Sable, Squirrel and Mock-Squirrel, Superfine white Swanskin ditto, Furr

Trimmings for Cloaks of all sorts to suite Muffs and Tippets; all manner of Cloath lined with Furr and Furr caps made after the neatest Manner; Skins dressed. . . .—*The New-York Gazette*, October 26, 1761.

SHOES.—To be Sold, by Alexander Montgomery, At the Fly-Market, next door to Mr. Brovort's, opposite Mrs. Rutgers's; A Parcel of greass'd leather, double and single channel'd pumps, stitch'd heel'd shoes and pumps, of the very best sort, from 14 to 26 s. per pair; women's leather shoes and goloshoes, also a few boots and women's stays, with a general assortment of dry goods of all sorts, which he sells cheap for cash, short credit, or Connecticut lawful money, as he is newly set up there.—*The New-York Mercury*, January 3, 1763.

CLOAK.—Taken by mistake, from the King's arms tavern, last week, a Portugese cloak of brown camblet, lin'd with green baize, with a hood to it, mark'd on the inside W. The Gentleman who has it is desired to return it to the said tavern, which will oblige the owner.—*The New-York Gazette or the Weekly Post-Boy*, December 1, 1763.

STOCKINGS (*Annapolis, Maryland*).—There has lately been made and sold at Mr. Beall's Stocking Manufactory in this City, a large Quantity of Thread Stockings with this Device in Place of the Clock, ∀ Ɯ Ǝ ᴚ I Ɔ ∀ .— News item from Annapolis, Maryland, August 16, in *The New-York Gazette or the Weekly Post-Boy*, August 30, 1764.

DRESS REGULATIONS IN BOSTON, MASSACHUSETTS.—It is with Pleasure we hear some of the principal Merchants in Boston, have come into a Resolution to curtail many Superfluities in Dress; and that upwards of fifty have already signed a certain Agreement for that Purpose. Lace, Ruffles, &c. are to be entirely laid aside: No English cloths to be purchased but at a fixed Price; The

usual Manner of expressing their Regard, and Sorrow
for a deceased Friend, or Relation, by covering them-
selves in Black, is also in the List of Superfluities, and no
Part thereof but the Cape [*sic*] in the Hat is retained;
instead of which, a Piece of Crape is to be tied upon the
Arm, after the Manner of the military Gentlemen.—
News item from Newport, R. I., August 20, in *The New-
York Gazette or the Weekly Post-Boy*, August 30, 1764.

SHOES.—Women's best Calemanco Shoes, Made in
New-York, Equal, if not superior, to any made in England; sold near Coentus's-Market, by James Wells, Who
has also, a great Quantity of Men's and Boys Shoes for
Sale.—*The New-York Mercury*, June 10, 1765.

HATS.—Nesbett Deane, Hatter from Dublin, begs leave
to acquaint the publick, that he has open'd shop in
Broadstreet, near the Royal Exchange, in New-York,
where he manufactures and sells, all kinds of hats, viz.
Finest beaver hats for clergymen, or other gentlemen;
beaveret and castor hats; black or white, plain or furr'd,
riding hats for ladies; and black or white, plain or furr'd,
hats for children. . . .—*The New-York Mercury*, October 21, 1765.

STAYS.—To be Sold by John M'Queen, At the Sign of
the White Stays, in Smith-Street, near the Mayor's; A
neat Assortment of Women and Maid's Stays, in the very
newest Fashion, directly from London. Womens Pack-
thread Jumps. New fashioned Crashets, fit for Ladies
Morning Dress. Misses neat thin bound Stays of
different Sorts and Sizes. Misses and Childrens Pack-
thread Stays from one Month to seven Years old. . . .
—*The New-York Gazette*, February 24, 1766.

ARTIFICIAL HAIR.—. . . It is now the Mode to make
the Lady's Head of twice the natural Size, by the Means
of artificial Pads, Boulsters, or Rolls, over which their
Hair is carefully combed, or frizzled to immitate the

shock Head of a Negro. It would be ridiculous to endeavour to expose the Absurdity of Matters which would
never bear reasoning about; but I have often wondered,
since every Female Body is so disposed to enlarge their
Stock of Hair, whence they procure a Sufficiency of Hair
to cover the Rolls, of all Colours and Shades, which are
exposed to Sale in every Milliner's Shop: And I cannot
say but I was much diverted the other Day, when I was
casually in a Harberdasher's Shop, where these Rolls
were sold, and happened then to engage the Conversa-
tion of the Customers. This Question was started by a
young Girl, Where the Hair came from which covered
these Rolls? Which an old Woman undertook to answer
from her own Knowledge. She said, that in the Hospitals, whatever Patients died, their Hair became the
Perquisite of the Nurses, who carefully sheared them, to
supply this great Demand for Human Hair. That both
the Small Pox, and a Distemper still more disagreeable,
supplied the greatest Part: . . .—Letter to the Printer
in *The New-York Journal or the General Advertiser*,
November 26, 1767.

DRESS REGULATIONS IN NEW LONDON, CONNECTICUT.
—New London town meeting . . . And we further agree,
That we will not, at any Funerals, use, any Gloves (black
excepted) but what are manufactured here, nor procure
any new Garments upon such Occasion, but what shall
be absolutely necessary.—News item from New London
in *The New-York Journal or the General Advertiser*,
February 11, 1768.

SPATTERDASHES.—Aaron Eaton (jointly with his
Father) Spatterdash-maker to his Majesty, lately arrived
from London, Begs Leave to inform the Publick, that
he has opened his Store at Mr. Ettridge's, Sadler, near
the Oswego-Market, where he has to sell, on the most
reasonable Terms, a general Assortment of long and
short Spatterdashes, the latter being much used at
present by the Gentlemen of the Army in England; . . .

—*The New-York Gazette and the Weekly Mercury*, May 23, 1768.

WIGS.—John Cadogan, Peruke maker, and Hair Dresser, Makes bold to acquaint the ladies, gentlemen, and others, that he keeps a shop next to John Cruger, Esqrs, near the Old Slip Market; where he makes all manner of wigs in the newest taste now in vogue; also side locks and crown sheads, ladies crape fronted French curls, newest crape or plain stuffed rolls or towers; the best roll and soft pomatum; royal, chymical, and marble wash balls and perfumed hair powder. . . .—*The New-York Gazette and the Weekly Mercury*, January 1, 1770

UMBRELLA.—Mary Morcomb, Mantua-Maker, from London; Living at Mr. Robert M' Alpine's, Book-Binder, in Beaver-Street; Makes all sorts of negligees, Brunswick dresses, gowns, and every other sort of lady's apparel; And also covers Umbrelloes in the neatest and most fashionable manner, at the lowest prices. . . .—*The New-York Gazette and the Weekly Mercury*, May 7, 1770.

AMERICAN MANUFACTURE.—Last Tuesday, Henry Lloyd, Esq; set out [from Boston] on a Journey to New-York, Philadelphia and the Southern Colonies. And it was observed that that Gentleman's whole Apparel and Horse Furniture were of American Manufacture. His Clothes, Linnen, Shoes, Stockings, Boots, Gloves, Hatt, Wigg, and even Wigg Call, were all manufactured and made up in New-England—An Example truly worthy of Imitation!—News item from Boston, March 26, in *The New-York Gazette and the Weekly Mercury*, April 2, 1770.

FUR HATS.—Nesbitt Deane, Hatter, Having lately returned from Montreal, in Canada, with a good assortment of different furs, for the carrying on his business in the city of New-York, takes this opportunity to acquaint the public, that he has opened shop opposite the Merchant's coffee-house, where he carries on his business as usual, by making the best of beaver hats, both for ladies and gentlemen, and children's ware, both ruff and plain, either black, white, blue, green or red: He also makes good castor ditto, for men or children. . . .—*The New-York Gazette and the Weekly Mercury,* February 11, 1771.

HATS, Manufactured by the Advertiser, to exceed, in Fineness, Cut, Colour and Cock; and by a Method peculiar to himself, to turn rain, and prevent the Sweat of the Head damaging the Crown. Such Gentry and others, who have experienced his Ability, 'tis hoped will recommend. Encouragement to those who buy to sell again. Nesbitt Deane. Aside the Coffee-House Bridge, New-York.—*The New-York Gazette and the Weekly Mercury,* July 1, 1771.

MEN'S APPAREL.—William Thorne, Taylor and Shop Keeper . . . will undertake to make middle sized men's cloths at the undermentioned prices, viz.

	£ s d
A plain suit superfine cloth,	8 10 0
Half trimmed, ditto,	9 0 0
Full drest, ditto,	10 0 0
Coat and waistcoat superfine cloth,	6 15 0
A suit best velvet any colour, lined with satin,	38 0 0
Suit figured Manchester velvet,	15 10 0
Suit ratteen trimmed with feather velvet and gold buttons,	21 0 0
Pair silk velveret breeches,	2 0 0
Single coat superfine cloth,	5 0 0
Plain suit second best cloth,	7 0 0
Coat and waistcoat ditto,	5 5 0
Surtout coat, best Bath beaver,	2 15 0
Plain cloth suit livery,	5 16 0
Ditto, with shag breeches,	7 0 0
Thickset frock and waistcoat,	3 16 0
Liver surtout coat,	3 16 0

Gentlemen who chuse to employ him, may depend on having their cloaths done in the genteelest manner.

Good encouragement to Journeymen Taylors.—*The New-York Journal or the General Advertiser*, March 2, 1775.

STAYS.—John Jones, Stay-Maker, from London, . . . Takes this method to acquaint the ladies and gentry, that he makes all sorts of stays, both turn'd and single; pack thread or bone, whale, waist, or French hips, &c. . . .— *The New-York Gazette and the Weekly Mercury*, January 11, 1773.

WIGS.—Rawdon, Peruke-maker, and operator for Ladies and Gentlemens Hair, Has the pleasure of informing the ladies, that he has acquir'd the true method of making the deservedly celebrated Hollow Toupees or Tates, which are held in such high estimation, that few ladies would choose to be without them. They are so light that they can scare be felt on the head, and may be worn with or without a hat, it being impossible (from their curious construction) for any pressure to injure them; they answer all the purposes of a hair dresser, never requiring any sort of repair from the time of their being made. . . .—*The New-York Gazette and the Weekly Mercury*, August 2, 1773.

UMBRELLA.—A Scarlet Coloured Umbrella, considerably faded, but not half worn, left by a Lady about 4 weeks ago, at some house not recollected. . . . CATH: VAN DYKE.—*The New-York Journal or the General Advertiser*, June 30, 1774.

DRESS OF APPRENTICES AND SERVANTS

BRUSH MAKER.—William Fletcher, a bought Servant, is Run away from his Master. . . . He had on, when he went away, a dark colour'd Kersey Coat with Brass Buttons, and lined with Duroy, has leather Breetches, Short dark Hair, by Trade a Brush maker, pretends to be a Turner, he makes Mops, makes and mends Bellows. —*The New-York Gazette*, April 11-18, 1726.

BLACKSMITH.—Run away . . . a Servant Man named
William Gillam a Black smith by Trade. . . . He was
but indifferently Cloathed when he went away, having
but Part of a Shirt to his Back and a yellow coloured
Jacket with Pewter Buttons; . . . Forty Shillings Reward. . . .—*The New-York Gazette,* December 30, 1729-
January 6, 1730.

MAN SERVANT.—Run away from Richard Bishop, a
Servant Man named John Farrant, about nineteen years
of Age, . . . he had on when he went away a brown
livery Coat and Breeches, the Coat lined and cuffed with
blue, a blue Shoulder knot a black Natural Wig, and a
Pair of red Stockings. Whoever takes up the said Servant and bring him to Mr. Charles Robinson at Capt
Courter's on the Dock shall have Five Pounds Reward.
—*The New-York Gazette,* August 10-17, 1730.

WOMAN SERVANT.—Ran away from Joseph Reade of
the City of New-York, Merchant the 14th of November
1732 a likely Mullatto Servant Woman, named Sarah,
she is about 24 years of Age, and has taken with her a
Callico Suit of Cloaths, a striped Satten Silk Wast-coat,
Two Homespun Wast-coats and Petty-coats; she is a
handy Wench, can do all sorts of House-work, speaks
good English and some Dutch. . . . Five Pounds as a
Reward. . . .—*The New-York Gazette,* November 13-
20, 1732.

BRICK MAKER.—Runaway on Tuesday last from
Nathaniel Hazard of New-York, a lusty lad about 18 or
19 Years of Age, named Robert Hill, a West Country
Man . . . had on when he went away, a Cinnamon
colour'd plain course Kersey Coat, with large flat metal
Buttons, a pair of Tow Trowsers, thick Shoes, an old
Felt Hat, a Brick-maker by Trade, and understands
something of Farmers Work. . . . Forty Shillings as a
Reward. . . .—*The New-York Weekly Journal,* Decem-
ber 31, 1733.

JOINER.—Run away from Thomas Rigby, of the City of New-York, Joyner, an indented Servant Man named John Howey, about 21 years of Age. He is an Irish Man, and a Joyner by Trade, of a middle Stature, . . . he wears a Wigg, had on when he went away a blew Duffels Coat, Ozenbrigs Wast-Coat, and a Pair of Buck-Skin Britches, a Speckl'd Shirt, a new Felt Hat, and a Pair of Yarn Stockings . . . 5 Pounds as a Reward. . . .— *The New-York Weekly Journal*, October 14, 1734.

MAN SERVANT.—Run away from Hugh Waddell, of the City of New-York, Merchant, a Servant Man named Adam Gray, about 19 Years of Age, had on when he went away a blew Coat, edged with Red, and Yellow Metal Buttons, a red Wast-coat with yellow Metal Buttons, Leather Breeches very greasy, gray Stockings, a Pair of small steel Buckles in his Shoes and wears a black Wigg. He also took with him a Steel Gray Cloath Coat trim'd and lin'd with Black, and a Snuff coloured Wast-Coat . . . 30 s. as a Reward. . . .—*The New-York Weekly Journal*, October 14, 1734.

MAN SERVANT.—Ran away from John Lester of Hempstead in Queens-County on Nassau Island, a Servant Man. . . . He had on when he went away, a Red Duffi's Coat, a brown Broad cloth Wastcoat, a light Coloured Durois Coat, and a black Caliminco Wastcoat & Breeches. Twenty Shillings Reward. . . .—*The New-York Gazette*, December 8-15, 1735.

MAN SERVANT.—Ran away from John Wallace of the City of New-York, a Servant Man. . . . He is mark'd on one of his hands with I. B. has a homespun grey Coat, brown Ozenbrigs, or whitish Cloth Breeches, blackish Woolen Stockins, and brass Buckles, has a white Shirt, a Woolen Cap, a Silk Muzlain Handkerchief, and an old Felt Hat. . . . Forty Shillings Reward. . . .—*The New-York Gazette*, September 20-October 4, 1736.

NEGRO MAN.—Ran away from John Wooly in the Township of Hempstead in Queens-County on Nassau Island, in the Province of New York, a Negro Man, about the Age of Twenty Three years; had on when he went away, a course Felt Hat, a grey Home-spun Drugget Coat, about half worn, a Vest of the same, short Toe-Oznabrig Trowzers, grey Yarn Stockins, . . . Forty Shillings as a Reward, . . .—*The New-York Gazette,* July 11-18, 1737.

NEGRO WOMAN.—Ran away from John Bell of the City of New-York, Carpenter, one Negro Woman, named Jenney, . . . had on when she went away, a Birds ey'd Waistcoat and Pettycoat of a darkish colour, and a Callico Waistcoat with a large red flower, and a broad stripe, a Callico Pettycoat with small stripes, and small red flowers. . . . Three Pounds as a Reward. . . .—*The New-York Gazette,* December 12-19, 1737.

MAID SERVANT.—Run away from Capt. Langden of the City of New-York a Servant Maid . . . had on when she went away, a homespun striped wastcoat and Peticoat, blew-stockings and new Shoes, and with her a Calico Wraper, and a striped Calamanco Wrapper, besides other Claaths; . . . Twenty Shillings Reward. . . .—*The New-York Weekly Journal,* January 22, 1739.

ENGLISH SERVANT.—Run away from William Maugridge, of this City, Ship-Joiner, an English Servant, . . . Had on when he went away a Bever Hat, white linnen Cap, mixt Duroy Coat, ozenbrigs Trowsers, worsted Stockings, and new shoes. . . . Forty Shillings Reward. . . .—*The New-York Weekly Journal,* July 6, 1741.

MAN SERVANT.—Run away a Servant Man named Francis Jones . . . had on when he went away a felt Hat, a new worsted Cap, a Surtute Frize Coat, a new Check'd Shirt, a pair of Silk Camblet Breeches, a pair of new homespun thread Stockings, a new pair of Shoes, and sundry Old Cloaths. . . . Twenty Shillings Reward. . . .—*The New-York Weekly Journal*, July 20, 1741.

FIDDLER.—Run away a Negro Man. . . . He had on when he went away a brown Kersey Wast-coat lined with Red Penistone a Black Stock with a Silver Clasp a Pair of Osenbrigs Trowsers and Breeches and Osenbrigs Shirt, a strip'd Wollen Cap, square toed Shoes, and an old Hat, he took with him a red double Breasted Stroud Wast-coat, lined with blue Shallon and trim'd with Black, he is a Fidler. . . . Reward of Three Pounds. . . .—*The New-York Weekly Journal*, September 7, 1741.

IRISH SERVANT.—Run away from his Master . . . an Irish Servant . . . had on when he went away a dark Drab Cloath Coat, red Shaloon Lining and large Brass Buttons; . . .—*The New-York Weekly Journal*, December 21, 1741.

IRISH SERVANT.—Runaway from Samuel Brant . . . An Irish Servant Man . . . had on when he went away, a Felt Hat, a blue drab jacket, an outside Jacket black and white, homespun drugged shorter than the blue one, Buttons covered with the same, lin'd with blewish homespun duroys, a pair of Leather Breeches, blewish Yarn Stockings, and a pair of double Soal'd Shoes, . . . Forty Shillings as a Reward. . . .—*The New-York Weekly Journal*, March 22, 1742.

ENGLISH SERVANT.—Ran away on Wednesday the 25th of January last, from Thomas Stanaland, near Bristol, in Bucks County, and Province of Pensilvania, an English Servant Man . . . had on when he went away, a light-colour'd plain Duroys Coat with Mohair Buttons, one Button at each Pocket, a Pair of Breeches of the same, with three Buttons at each Pocket, and five at each Knee, two Jackets, one striped Linnen and the other

brown Woollen, Woollen Stockings, good Shoes, and a
good Felt Hat. He took with him a Bundle in which was
an old Pair of Leather Breeches, Trousers, Shoes and
Stockings, also some Knives, Razors and old Buckles.
. . . Three Pounds Reward. . . .—*The New-York
Weekly Post-Boy,* February 6, 1744.

MAN SERVANT.—Run away from Rice Williams of the
City of New-York, a Servant Man. . . . Had on when
he went away a dark colour'd Coat, a Linnen Jacket, a
Worsted Cap, two Ozenbrigs Shirts, a Pair of blew Cloath
Breeches, a Pair of new Shoes with Brass Buckles, Yarn
Stockings, . . . Forty Shillings as a Reward. . . .—*The
New-York Gazette,* August 13-20, 1744.

WOMAN SERVANT.—. . . Gone from her Lodgings at
Long-Island Ferry, . . . had on when she went away a
white Quilted Peticoat, a black and white Calicoat &
Wraper and also a Stuff red and white striped Wraper.
. . .—*The New-York Weekly Journal,* October 15, 1744.

ENGLISH MAN SERVANT.—Run away the 16th Inst.
from Peter Cochran, of the City of New-Brunswick, an
English Servant Man. . . . He had on when he went
away, a red Cloath Coat with metal Buttons, slash
Sleeves and striped homespun Lining, a blue Cloath
Jacket, a check Shirt, Leather Breeches, light colour'd
Worsted Stockings, new Shoes, a Felt Hat, and a Linnen
Cap or a Wig: . . . Forty Shillings New-York Currency,
Reward. . . .—*The New-York Weekly Post Boy,* June
3, 1745.

APPRENTICE.—Runaway . . . Irish apprentice Lad.
. . . Had on when he went away, blue Drugget coat
Jacket and Breeches check Trowsers, several check Shirts,
black Worsted Stokings old Shoes with Brass Buckles,
a Felt Hat and a Worsted Cap. . . .—*New-York Weekly
Journal,* June 10, 1745.

NEGRO MAN.—Run away . . . a Negro Man . . . had
on, a darkish Colour'd Woolen Coat, Country Make,
brown Jacket, old Buck-Skin Breeches, and an old
Beaver-Hat . . . forty Shillings Reward. . . .—*The
New-York Evening Post*, February 10, 1746.

NEGRO MAN.—Run away from Barent Van Deventer,
of Flat-Bush, . . . a Negro Man . . . had on When he
Went away a Linning striped, Jacket, a Pair of Home-
spun Breeches, a Blewish Pair of Stockings, and an old
Pair of Shoes, a good Felt Hat . . . 30 Shillings Reward.
. . .—*The New-York Evening Post*, November 24, 1746.

IRISH MAN SERVANT.—Run away . . . an Irish Ser-
vant named Cornelius Sullivan, . . . Had on when he
went away, a Castor Hat almost new, a brown Broad
Cloth Coat, Oznabrigs Shirt, petticoat Trowsers, yarn
Stockings, Calf Skin Shoes with Buckles in them. . . .
N.B. The above Fellow says that he work'd last winter
at the Iron Works, above New-York, and since follow'd
Boating to and from New-York, during which Time he
had deserted his Masters Service, and on the 27th of
August was brought home, and has again deserted.—*The
New-York Gazette Revived in the New-York Weekly
Post-Boy*, September 11, 1749.

MAN SERVANT.—Run-away from Cornelius Vanhorne
of the City of New-York, Merchant on or about the 22
of December last, a Servant Man, . . . Had on when he
went away, a Cloth Jacket faced with Velvet, a dress'd
Sheep-Skin Breeches, a pair of homespun Stockings, a
Leather Jockey Cap, is a pretty talkative Fellow, pretends to be a Coachman, and brought up to attend a
Table. Whoever takes up and secures said Servant, so
that he may be had again, shall have a Pistole Reward
and all reasonable Charges, paid by CORNELIUS VAN-
HORNE.—*The New-York Gazette Revived in the Weekly
Post-Boy*, January 8, 1750.

NEGRO WENCH.—Run away on the fourth of February last, from Robert James Livingston, a tall likely Negro Wench, named Nell, about 36 Years of Age: Had on when she went away, a blue Penniston Petticoat, a short blue and white homespun Gown, with a short blue Duffils Cloak and Straw Bonnet; she is mark'd with nine Spots on each Temple, and nine on her Forehead. Whoever takes up said Wench so that her Master may have her again, shall have Twenty Shillings Reward, and all reasonable Charges, paid by ROBERT JA. LIVINGSTON.—*The New-York Gazette Revived in the Weekly Post-Boy,* March 5, 1750.

IRISH MAID SERVANT.—Run-away the 3d. Inst. from Francis Dudley of this City, carpenter, an Irish Maid Servant. . . . Had on when she went away, a brown and yellow strip'd Stuff Gown, fac'd and rob'd with green Silk, and has been since seen with a blue Gown on, and a blue Petticoat. . . . Twenty Shillings Reward. . . .— *The New-York Gazette Revived in the Weekly Post-Boy,* March 18, 1751.

MAN SERVANT.—Run away yesterday, from Nicholas Bayard, a Bristol Servant Man named James Caselick. . . . Had on when he went away an Ozenbrigs Coat, a green Ratteen Vest, new brown Cloth Breeches, new brown Wig, and a Beaver Hat about half worn; he also took with him a red Ratteen Coat with Brass Buttons one of the Sleeves having a long Cut in it, as also speckled Trowsers; . . . Three Pounds Reward. . . .— *The New-York Gazette Revived in the Weekly Post-Boy,* October 8, 1750.

MAN SERVANT.—Run away . . . man servant. . . . Had on when he went away, a brown jacket, Check Trowers, Shoes and Stockings, an old Castor Hat, and a white Linnen shirt; he has stolen from his said Master, a dark grey Coat, a silk Jacket of orange and purple Colour, with the back Parts of light colour'd Fustian, a scarlet Waistcoat, two grey wigs. . . . Three Pounds Reward. . . .—*The New-York Gazette Revived in the Weekly Post-Boy*, August 19, 1751.

MAID SERVANT.—Ran away last night from Moses Clement, in the Broadway, an Irish Servant Maid. . . . Had on when she went away a light brown Camblet gown, a brown quilted Petticoat, a pair of Stays, white apron and white Handkerchief. . . .—*The New-York Gazette Revived in the Weekly Post-Boy*, January 6, 1752.

MAN SERVANT.—Runaway on Wednesday 22 of January last, from George Burns, Tavern-keeper in New York, near long-Bridge, a Servant Man, of about 23 years of age. Had on when he went away a Bearskin Coat made Frock Fashion, with a scarlet Jacket with green Velvet Lepells, and a strip'd Flannel Jacket under it, a check Shirt, and Buckskin Breeches, white or blue Worsted Stockings, a brown bob Wig, and a large brim'd Beaver Hat, round toe'd Shoes, with square Steel Buckles. Whoever takes up said Servant, so that his master may have him again, shall have Forty Shillings Reward, and all reasonable charges Paid by GEORGE BURNS.—*The New-York Gazette Revived in the Weekly Post-Boy*, February 17, 1752.

CHIMNEY SWEEPER.—Ran away . . . a chimney-Sweeper by trade. Had on when he went away, a new Homespun Kersey Coat, of a mix'd Colour and a jacket of the same kind somewhat worn, Leather Breeches, blue stockings, new shoes ty'd with Leather Strings, Oznabrigs Shirt, with a Linnen Handkerchief round his Neck, and an old Wool Hat, with a Tow String for a Hatband; . . . Forty Shillings Reward. . . .—*The New-York Gazette Revived in the Weekly Post-Boy*, April 20, 1752.

MEN SERVANTS.—Runaway from Elias Degrushe, of this City, Rope-maker, . . . two Servant Men; one named Richard Poole, a West Countryman, . . . had on when he went away short black Hair, a new English Castor-Hat, a half-worn light-colour'd Frize Coat, scorch'd at the Bottom of the left Skirt, a blue Serge Jacket, and a red Cloth one without Sleeves, a Check Shirt, blue Camblet Breeches, brown Yarn Stockings, and new Shoes with broad rimm'd Brass Buckles in them. He may probably pass for a Rope-maker. The other named Thomas Jenkins, . . . had on when he went away, a half-worn Beaver-Hat, worsted Cap, a light-colour'd Cloth Coat, a blue Serge Waistcoat and a Flannel one, Check Shirt, light colour'd Dimity Breeches, Yarn Stockings and new Shoes. . . . Three Pounds Reward for each, . . .—*The New-York Gazette Revived in the Weekly Post-Boy,* May 25, 1752.

INDIAN WENCH AND CHILD.—Runaway on the 4th of December last, from Peter Brouwer, of the City, an Indian wench named Mary, with her Child named Hannah . . . had on when she run away, a purple Calico Wrapper, a homespun short Gown, homespun striped Petticoat, and a green Quilt; Her child had on, a double Stuff Gown the one Side a Bird Eye, and the other blue, a homespun Gown, blue Camblet Petticoat, and a striped Flannel one. . . . Forty Shillings Reward. . . .—*The New-York Gazette and the Weekly Post-Boy,* February 5, 1753.

NEGRO WENCH.[1]—Run away, from the subscriber, in New-York, on Friday the 6th. Instant, a well-set negro wench, named Jane: Had on when she went away, a green waistcoat and blue pettycoat; and is supposed to be harbour'd by some of her own colour in or about this City. Whoever takes up and secures the said wench, so that her master may have her again, shall receive Twenty Shillings reward, and all reasonable charges paid by ANTHONY LAMB.

[1] This is the first time an advertisement accompanied by a picture of a runaway slave or servant appeared in any New York City newspaper.

N.B. Said Wench lately belonged to John Burling, who gave her a note or pass, to look for a master, which she may possibly make use of now, the better to go unmolested.—*The New-York Mercury*, April 30, 1753.

NEGRO SLAVE.—Run away . . . a Negroe Man Slave, . . . Had on when he went away, a course Linnen Jacket and Trowsers, old Shoes and Stockings, he has been formerly out a Privateering with Capt. Tingley, and it is suppos'd he may attempt to get on board some Vessel to go out. . . .—*The New-York Gazette and the Weekly Post-Boy*, July 30, 1753.

COPPERSMITH.—Run away on the 27th of February last, from Richard Kip, of this City, an Apprentice Lad. . . . Had on when he went off, a green Jacket, with a green under One, blue Breeches, grey stockings, large Pewter Buckles, Castor Hat, has a check shirt, is a copper by trade, . . . three Dollars Reward. . . .—*The New-York Gazette or the Weekly Post-Boy*, April 10, 1758.

WOMAN SERVANT.—Run-away from Judah Hays, of this City of New-York, Merchant . . . a German Servant Woman. . . . Had on when she went away, a striped linsey Josey, and a blue Half-thick Pettycoat, She has also taken with her, a striped Bird's-Eye Stuff Gown, one red Calico, do. a red Calico Josey and Pettycoat, and sundry other wearing apparel. . . . Forty Shillings Reward. . . .—*The New-York Mercury*, May 29, 1758.

SHOEMAKER.—Run away . . . an apprentice lad named George M'Clary, about nineteen years of age, by trade a shoemaker, . . . Had on when he went away, a blue cloth coat and breeches, the coat lined with white, two blue waistcoats, one pair of worsted stockings, one pair yarn ditto, both light blue, new shoes with odd buckles, and a half worn castor hat: . . . Thirty Shillings reward. . . .—*The New-York Gazette or the Weekly Post-Boy,* October 30, 1758.

SERVANT MAN.—Three Pounds Reward, Run-away from the Subscriber in Trenton, a Servant Man, named Peter Marsh, about 30 Years of Age. . . . Had on and took with him, an old Felt Hat, a Half worn blue Broadcloth Coat, with short close Cuffs, long Waiste, and short Skirts, blue Cloth Jacket, with brass Buttons and red lining; Ozenburgs Shirt, but probably may have other fine Shirts with him; a Pair of black Knit Breeches; brown ribbed and grey Yarn Stockings, and may also have some black Worsted ones; half worn Shoes, with plain Brass Buckles in them. . . . RALPH NORTON.— *The New-York Gazette or the Weekly Post-Boy,* April 5, 1764.

APPRENTICE BOY.—Run away . . . an Apprentice Boy. . . . Had on when he went away a blue Cloth Coat, a striped Cotton Waistcoat, a brown Pair of Breeches, a narrow brim'd Hat, bound with Tape . . . 40 s. Reward. . . .—*The New-York Gazette or the Weekly Post-Boy,* May 31, 1764.

GUNSMITH.—Fifty Dollars Reward. Run-Away from the subscriber, an English convict servant man, named Benjamin Sagers, a blacksmith and gunsmith by trade, . . . Had on when he went away, a white shirt, blue coat, striped trowsers, spotted stockings, new pumps, and an old beaver hat cut in the fashion, . . . Whoever takes up and secures the said servant in any of his Majesty's gaols, so that his master may have him again, shall have, if twenty miles from home, Forty Shillings, if forty miles, Four Pound, if eighty miles, Eight Pounds, and if one hundred miles, the above reward, and reasonable charges, if brought home, paid by Averay Richardson.—*The New-York Gazette and the Weekly Mercury,* October 16, 1775.

NEGRO MAN.—Run away . . . a Negro man named
Glasgow . . . had on and took with him a light grey
home spun coat, very large and lined with striped linsy,
a dark brown waistcoat, with white metal buttons and
lined with the same cloth of his coat; buckskin breeches,
mended in the seat, a narrow brimmed felt hat; two pair
of grey stockings, one ditto worsted, and a pair of half
worn shoes, with brass buckles . . . eight dollars reward,
. . .—*The New-York Journal or the General Advertiser,*
January 22, 1767.

APPRENTICE.—Five Pounds Reward.   Run-away the
6th instant, July, from Joseph Wicks, of Huntington, on
Long-Island, Copper, an apprentice named David Kelly,
a lusty young man, of about 19 years of age, . . . had
on when he went away, a blue broad cloth waistcoat,
white shirt, whitish strip'd or tow trowsers, a felt hat,
worsted stockings, and old shoes. . . .—*The New-York
Journal or the General Advertiser,* August 6, 1767.

CAULKER.—Run-away from his Master, Caleb Corn-
well, living in Hempstead, . . . a Negro Man named
Shier, about 40 Years of Age . . . is by Trade a Caulker:
Had on when he went away a Castor Hat, homespun
Cloth Colour'd Jacket, Trowsers, blue rib'd Stockings,
and Brass Buckles in his Shoes . . . Twenty Shillings
Reward. . . .—*The New-York Gazette and the Weekly
Mercury,* June 27, 1768.

MAN SERVANT.—Run-away . . . an Irish Servant
Man. . . . Had on when he went away, a white Jacket
with Sleeves, a Pair of Long white Trowsers, Check Shirt,
and a good Hat with a Large Brim . . . Fifty Shillings
Reward. . . .—*The New-York Gazette and the Weekly
Mercury,* June 25, 1770.

NEGRO MAN.—Run away . . . a negro man named
Bristol; . . . Had on, when he went away, a dark brown
cloth coat, with pinchbeck buttons, Jacket of a lighter

colour, with wooden buttons; a beaver hat, about two thirds worn, white shirt, white Jane Breeches, yarn or worsted hose, brown colour; thin shoes with buckles, and is very subject to drink . . . thirty shillings reward. . . . —*The New-York Journal or the General Advertiser,* June 25, 1772.

MEN SERVANTS.—Eight Dollars Reward. Run away . . . John Brown . . . had on when he went away, a dark coloured Bear-Skin Jacket, blue Plush Breeches pieced behind with Buck-Skin, an old Felt Hat, blue Stockings, old ribbed leggings over them, old Shoes that have been soaled, the little Toe of his right Foot stands up. The other named David Smith, . . . had on when he went away, a dark Bear-Skin Jacket, a light coloured under ditto, the hind Part of which is of a darker colour, old Leather Breeches patched before, a half worn Wool Hat, coarse light coloured ribbed Stockings, old Shoes, . . .

Whoever takes up and secures said Servants, so that their Master may have them again, shall receive the above Reward, or five Dollars for Brown, and three for Smith, . . .—*The New-York Journal or the General Advertiser,* April 15, 1773.

NEGRO MAN.—Twenty Shillings Reward, Ran-away . . . a negro man named Tom, had on when he went away, an old beaver hat, a blue homespun coat and jacket, greasy leather breeches, old grey stockings and half worn shoes, speaks Low Dutch and English.

Whoever apprehends him on this side of Kingsbridge, shall have the above reward, and if on the other side Forty Shillings paid by me. DANIEL ENSLEE, Butcher in the Fly Market.—*The Constitutional Gazette,* April 27, 1776.

PAINTING AND GLAZING

PAINTERS AND GLAZIERS

THOMAS & JAMES BARROW, Painters, in Broad-street, near the City-Hall, have for sale, Best London red lead, dry, at 40s. per C. wt. fine Ball Whiting for whitewashing, Lampblack by the Paper or small Barrel, Linseed Oyl, Window Glass and Putty, also Painters and Limners Colours of all sorts, prepared and sold at a reasonable Rate.—*The New-York Gazette and the Weekly Mercury,* September 7, 1772.

JOHN BALDWIN, Begs Leave to acquaint the Public, that he will perform House painting, gilding, glazing, &c. after the most accurate Method now followed in London, Viz. Dead White, and all Sorts of shining Colours, in the most beautiful and exquisite Manner; destroys the knots that defects the painting, likewise purifies and strengthens the Oyl, especially for out-side Work, which is greatly required being the Sun is so penetrating. Those Gentlemen that would be pleas'd to favour him with their Custom, may depend upon having it done efectually, after the cheapest and expeditious Manner, that shall bear the nicest Inspection. By the publick's most obedient humble Servant, JOHN BALDWIN. N.B. Please to enquire for said Baldwin, at Mr. John Edward Pryer's, Master Builder, in Oswego-Street.—*The New-York Mercury,* March 10, 1766.

JOHN DELAMONTAINE.—. . . Request to settle the estate of John Delamontaine, painter and glazier . . . CATHERINE DELAMONTAINE, Executrix.—*The New York Journal and the General Advertiser,* January 7, 1773.

GERARDUS DUYCKINCK, Living near the old Slip Market in New-York, continues to carry on the Business of his late Father deceas'd, Viz. Limning, Painting, Varnishing, Japanning, Gilding, Glasing, and Silvering of Looking-Glasses, all done in the best Manner.

He also will teach any young Gentleman the art of Drawing, with Painting on Glass; and sells all sorts of Window-Glasses, white lead, oil and Painter's Colours.— *The New-York Weekly Post-Boy,* August 18, 1746.

WILLIAM DOWDALL, Ship and house painting, glazing and graining mahogany, gilding on oyl, and distemper, with cleaning of pictures, in the neatest and best manner, by the subscriber, to be found at Capt. Doran's on the dock. WILLIAM DOWDALL.

Whoever chuses to employ the said William Dowdall, may depend on having their work done in such a manner, that if it does not please the employer, no reward will be required.—*The New-York Gazette and the Weekly Mercury,* June 1, 1772.

JOHN EARL.—To be Sold. An assortment of Choice Window-Glass, by the Box, half Box or single Pane, of all Sizes, at reasonable Rates; As also Painting and Glazing Work is done after the best Manner with all Expedition, by John Earl, living at Beekman's Slip.— *The New-York Weekly Post-Boy,* August 7, 1749.

FLAGG & SEARLE, Glaiziers and Painters, in Broadstreet, opposite Mr. William Gilliland's Store; Take this Method to inform the Publick, that they do all Sorts of Glaizing, House, Ship and Coach Painting; likewise Jappaning, Lacquering, &c. after the neatest Manner. Any Gentleman that please to favour them with their Custom (as they are young Beginners) may depend upon their Commands being executed with care and Dispatch. N.B. At the same Place may be had, a few Painter's Colours, Brushes, Tools, &c.—*The New-York Mercury,* July 1, 1765.

SEBASTIAN GUEUBEL.—To the Nobility and Gentry, Sebastian Gueubel, Just arrived in this City, Has for sale, a quantity of beautiful Furniture, elegantly painted and varnished in the Japan Taste; he has some compleat Toilets, He also undertakes to paint and varnish coaches and chairs in the same manner; Hopes the gentlemen and ladies will favour him with their custom, at his lodgings at Mr. Cornelius Sebring's, in Wall-street, where his work may be seen.

N.B. Any Gentlemen and ladies desirous to learn painting and drawing will be carefully taught by their Most humble servant, SEBASTIAN GUEUBEL.—*The New-York Gazette and the Weekly Mercury*, July 1, 1771.

——GUEUBEL, Coach Painter and Gilder, At the upper End of New-Street, near the City-Hall, Paints all Sorts of Flowers, Coats of Arms, etc. in the Neatest Manner.— *The New-York Gazette and the Weekly Mercury*, July 27, 1772.

JOHN HAYDOCK.—Run away the 26th of September last, from John Haydock, of this City, Painter, a German Woman . . . —*The New-York Gazette and the Weekly Post-Boy*, October 1, 1753.

JOHN HUMBLE.—Just imported from London, and to be sold by John Humble, Painter and Glazier, opposite the French Church in New-York. White lead, red lead, Spanish brown, spanish white, venetian red, English oker, spruce yellow, blue smalt, vermillion, prussian blue, india red, verdigrease, umber, white vitriol, gold and silver leaf, brushes, tools, pencils, oyl, and sundry other things relating to the business: As also all sorts of Crown window glass to be sold by the pane or box, at reasonable rates.—*The New-York Gazette Revived in the Weekly Post-Boy*, September 26, 1748.

PETER NORIE.—Sign, Ship, and House Painting, Performed in the neatest manner, and at the most reasonable rates, by Peter Norie, Living in Roosevelt-Street, opposite Mr. Sigard's Blacksmith.—*The Constitutional Gazette,* June 8, 1776.

CHRISTIAN LIVINGSTON.—To be sold . . . A House and Lot of Ground on Cow-foot-Hill, near the New Sugar House, now occupied by Christian Livingston, Painter, being Part of the Estate of Peter Swigard, deceased. . . . —*The New-York Gazette or the Weekly Post-Boy,* October 26, 1772.

JOSEPH NORTHRUP.—This is to give Notice, That Joseph Northrup is removed into the Sloot, behind Mr. Henry Cruger's, in the House Obadiah Wells, formerly liv'd, where he sells all Sorts of Paints made fine by Hundred or small Quantities, Dry or ground in Oyl Glazing Lead, Glass, Painting brushes, &c. and does all Sorts of Painting and Glazing Work at reasonable Rates. N.B. He gives ready money for Hogs Bristles.—*The New-York Evening Post,* June 12, 1748.

JACOBUS TIEDEMAN.—To be Sold . . . two good Dwelling-Houses . . . lately in the Possession of Jacobus Tiedeman, Painter. . . .—*The New-York Gazette Revived in the Weekly Post-Boy,* October 2, 1752.

JOHN WATSON.—In a real estate notice mention is made of a John Watson, painter.—*The New-York Mercury,* January 21, 1765.

OBADIAH WELLS.—To be sold by Obadiah Wells, living in the Sloot behind Mr. Henry Cruger's, Window-Glass of all Sizes with large Ball-Eyes for Sky lights, or small one for Dores; with Putty, Paints, and Oyl, drawn Lead, Chalk fine or corse, where Colours are made fine by the 100 or less Quantity, as also glazing or painting Work is done, and ready Mony for Hogs Bristles: A Parcel of good smook-dryed Bass to be sold.—*The New-York Evening Post,* March 31, 1746.

OBADIAH WELLS.—To be Sold, by Obadia Wells in the Sloat, window Glass, Glaizers Lead, Barrled, Sheatlead, Paints dry or Ground in Oyl, by the Cask. Hundred or less Quantity, such as White lead, Red-lead, Indian red, spanish Brown, Oaker, Yellow, &c. Also Coperas & Rossin, by the Cask or Hundred, Vermillion, Prutian-blue, Umber, Spruce-Oaker, an excellent Glazirs Vice, which draws two sorts of Lead; also a Band Vice with many things necessary for the Business mentioned.

Where all sorts of glazing and painting and Glazing Work is done and Glass Lantorns made and mended at reasonable Rates. N.B. Ready Money for Hogs Bristles. —*The New-York Evening Post*, January 11, 1748.

JOSEPH WOODRUFF.—All Persons that have any Demands on the Estate of Joseph Woodruff, Painter, deceas'd, are desired to pay their Accounts, . . .—*The New-York Gazette and the Weekly Post-Boy*, September 9, 1762.

FREDERICK WOTSES.—The Estate of Frederick Wotses, painter and glazier late of this city, to be settled.—*The New-York Gazette or the Weekly Mercury*, February 12, 1776.

WINDOW GLASS AND PAINTS

WINDOW GLASS.—Anne Vanderspiegel, Widow gives her shop to her son John Vanderspiegel where all sorts of Window Glass is sold.—*The New-York Gazette*, February 17-22, 1737.

WINDOW GLASS.—John Vanderspiegel moves out of New-York City and wishes his debts cleared . . . customers that use to buy window glass from him to apply to Raphael Goelet.—*The New-York Weekly Post-Boy*, February 3, 1746.

DIAMOND GLASS.—Just imported, and to be Sold by Raphael Goelet in Maiden-Lane, near the late Mr.

Anthony Rutgers, a New Supply of Window Crown-Glass of different Sizes, and Crates of Diamond Glass, also Barr and White Lead, Oyl, and all Sorts of Painting Colours.—*The New-York Gazette Revived in the Weekly Post-Boy*, June 8, 1747.

CROWN WINDOW GLASS.—To be sold by John Humble, Painter and Glazier, in Crown-Street, in one of Mr. Hayne's new Houses, near the New Dutch-Church, viz. Paints of all colours, and best Linseed Oyl, also best Crown Window Glass, viz. 6 by 4, 7 by 5, 6 by 8, 7 by 9, 8 by 10, 9 by 11, 10 by 12, 11 by 13, 12 by 14, 13 by 17, 17 by 20, and Sheet Glass. Also a fine Glazier's Vise and several other Things belonging to the Business.—*The New-York Gazette Revived in the Weekly Post-Boy*, April 30, 1750.

GLASS LAMPS.—At the last Session of Assembly, an Act was passed, to prevent the Breaking or injuring of Glass Lamps in the City of New-York; upon which several Gentlemen and others, have since put up Lamps in the Streets, at their Houses and many more design to do the same, to the great Ornament of the City, and Benefit of the Inhabitants.—News item in *The New-York Gazette Revived in the Weekly Post-Boy*, December 23, 1751.

GLASS LAMPS.—Last Monday night several of the Glass-Lamps put up About this City, were taken down by Persons unknown, and left whole in the Meal-Market, all together: It is thought to be done by some daring Rakes in order to Convince the Owners, how easy those Lamps might be demolished without Discovery; but they would do well to reflect, that if the tastless Satisfaction and Meaness of such Action be not enough to deter them, yet that, however often the Pitcher may go safe to the Well, it comes home broke at last: And in particular in a Case, thought to be so much for the Good of the Pub-lick, as to engage the immediate Attention of the Legis-

lature; they would meet with little Mercy; besides stig-
matized, with what ought to be the most odious of Names
viz. Enemies of their Country.—News item in *The New-
York Gazette Revived in the Weekly Post-Boy*, February
3, 1752.

PAINTS.—Just imported in the last Ships from Lon-
don by G. Duyckinck, at his House on the Dock, next
Door to the Sign of the Prince of Orange, near the Old-
Slip. White-Lead, Red-Lead, Spanish Brown, English,
French, Spruce and Stone Oker, Indian and Venetian
Red, Ivory, Frankford and Lamp-Black, Umber Cullin's
Earth, Smalt's Prusian Blue, Vermillion, Verdigrase, the
whole ground in Powder or in Oil, Limner's and Japan-
ner's Colours, Gold, Silver and Brass Leaf, Painters
Brushes and Pensils, Varnish of all sorts, cold drawing
Oil, Linseed ditto, boilt ditto, Rape Seed ditto, Nut
ditto, and Lamp Oil, Window Glass of all Sizes, Pictures
glaz'd of sundry sorts, and sundry other Things too
tedious to mention.

N.B. If any Gentleman inclines to have their own
Colours in Powder, or ground in Oil, may have it done
at a moderate Price, he having a convenient Mill for that
Purpose.—*The New-York Gazette or the Weekly Post-
Boy*, November 18, 1754.

OYL OF TURPENTINE, aetherial spirit of turpentine, best
varnish for chair-makers, and the finest amber-coloured
rosin, are made and sold by John Braser, living back of
Trinity-Church burying ground, near the North-River,
either large or small quantities; He assures those that
may have occasion for any of the above articles, that he
will afford them as cheap and good as any that have
formerly been imported from the neighbouring colonies;
and he hopes an encouragement will be given to our
own manufactory.

N.B. The spirit of turpentine applied to bed-steads
and those places where bugs breed, and lodge, effectually
destroys them, and prevents them from harbouring those

places where it is applied; especially if they should be fresh drawn, and a few drops will effectually take out greasy spots from cloaths, or on floor.—Also the best Pot-Ash.—*The New-York Mercury*, February 23, 1756.

AMERICAN WINDOW GLASS.—Any quantity of American Window Glass of different Sizes, to be sold at a lower Rate than can be imported from Europe. Enquire of Caspar Wistar, at his Still-House near the Ship-Yards, where any Person may be supplied with York Distilled Rum.—*The New-York Journal or the General Advertiser*, September 28, 1769.

IMPORTED WINDOW GLASS AND PAINTS.—Imported in the last vessels from Europe, and to be sold by John I. Roosevelt, in Maiden-Lane, Furniture paper, white lead ground in oil, in powder do. Spanish brown ground in oil, in powder do. yellow oaker ground in oil, in powder do. verdigrease ground in oil, red lead, vermilion, Prussian blue, linseed oil, spirits of turpentine, painting brushes, whiting, blacking, 6 by 8, 7 by 9, 8 by 10, 11 by 9, 10 by 12, 11 by 13, 10 by 14, 13 by 16, best crown Window Glass, looking glasses, decanters of different sorts and sizes, wine glasses, ale glasses, salts, mustard pots, crewits, tumblers, cans, Bristol pipes, &c.—*The New-York Gazette and the Weekly Mercury*, April 15, 1771.

PAINT STORE.—L. Kilburn's Paint Store, At the White Hall, New York Hath for Sale,

White Lead	Vermillion
Spanish brown	Prussian blue
Yellow oaker	White vitriol
Verdigrise	Spanish whiting
Red lead	Paint brushes
Linseed oil	Window glass 6 by 8, 7 by 9, 8 by 10,
White varnish	9 by 11, 10 by 12, 11 by 13, &c. &c.
Spirit of turpentine	

All as cheap as anybody sells in the place.—*The New-York Journal or the General Advertiser*, June 11, 1772.

COACH MAKERS

NICHOLAS BAILY.—Shaes and Chears made and Repear'd by Nicholas Baily, in Duke Street, near the Long Bridge in New York:—*The New-York Weekly Journal,* March 10, 1740.

ROBERT BOYD.—To be Sold, by Robert Boyd, Blacksmith, at his Shop near the Old English Church, A Very neat Curricle with a Chaise Top, that has never been in use. N.B. Said Boyd contracts for Chairs and Chaises of all Kinds. Any Gentlemen who will favour him with their Custom, may depend upon being well used, and supplied at the most reasonable Rates.—*The New-York Gazette or the Weekly Post-Boy,* December 24, 1760.

JONATHAN BROWN, From Boston, Coach and Coach-Harness maker, having set up his Business at Hartford, in Connecticut, makes and repairs all Sorts of Harness, of every Kind, and in the neatest and newest Taste, all Sorts of Coaches, Chariots, Landaus, Phaetons, Post Chariots, Post Chaises, Curricles, Chairs, &c. and has provided himself with the best of Leather and Trimmings, of the newest and genteelest Sorts. Any Gentlemen and Ladies that will please to favour him with their Custom, may depend on being used in the best Manner, and they will much oblige their humble Servant, JONATHAN BROWN. By the Bridge in Hartford.—*The New-York Gazette or the Weekly Post-Boy,* May 5, 1763.

WILLIAM COOPER, from Long Acre, London, (Brother to Doct. Robert Cooper, of Hatton Garden) Coach and Coach Harness Maker, Having set up his Business in Elizabeth Town, in New-Jersey, Makes and repairs all Sorts of Harness Work of every kind, now used in England, in the neatest and genteelest Manner; finishes and trims, in the newest Taste now used in England, all Sorts of Coaches, Chariots, Landeaus, Landeaulets, Phaetons, Post Chariots, Post Chaises, Curricles, Chairs, and new fashioned light Waggons; and has provided himself with the best of Leather, and Trimmings of the newest Fashions. . . .—*The New-York Gazette or the Weekly Post-Boy*, April 21, 1763.

GABRIEL Cox, Coach-Maker, Begs leave to acquaint his friends, and the public in general, that he hath now by him the very best of materials for carrying on the said business in the most extensive manner, at his shop opposite Trinity Church, in Great-George-Street, where coaches, landaus, chariots, phaetons, chairs, sulkeys, sedans &c. are made, and finished in the most neat and elegant manner, with the greatest expedition, and on the most reasonable charges, warranted equal in goodness to any imported: Also carriages of every sort with their harness, &c. compleatly repaired, painted, &c. . . .—*Rivington's New-York Gazetteer*, April 14, 1774.

ELKANAH DEANE.—The Coach-making Business is carried on in all its' Branches, in the most complete Manner, by Elkanah Deane, from Dublin, Who has opened Shop, next Door to Mr. William Gilliland, in Broad-Street, New-York, and proposes to make, trim, paint, gild and finish, in the most genteel and elegant Taste, all kinds of Coaches, Chariots, Landaus, Phaetons, Post Chaises, Curricles, Chairs, Sedans, and Sleighs, with their Harness; and as he is determined to make such Work as will give Satisfaction in every Particular, and to charge on the very lowest Terms, he hopes for the Favour and Encouragement of the Publick. Gentlemen residing in the Country, writing to him, may depend on having their Orders executed with punctuality.—*The New-York Gazette or the Weekly Post-Boy*, February 23, 1764.

ELKANAH AND WILLIAM DEANE.—To the Publick. We the Subscribers being determined to give all the Satisfaction in our Power to those Gentlemen and Ladies, who have or may employ us, for the Time to come, that they shall have their Work done in the best Manner, for the following Prices, Viz.

A Plain Coach, and Harness for two horses,............£ 165 0 0
Ditto, with Livery Lace, and fringed Seat,
    Cloth and richly painted and finished,...............£ 200 0 0
Chariots in Proportion, according to the Patron given.
A Set of Coach Wheels, finished with iron Work,
    and painted,..£ 13 0 0
Chariot, or Post-Chaise, ditto,........................£ 11 10 0
A Chaise with Steel Springs, and Iron Axletree,
    compleatly finished,.................................£ 65 0 0
Ditto, with Wood Spring, Axletree, finished plain,......£ 55 0 0
A new Chair, with Steel Springs, and Iron Axletree,
    finished in the best Manner,........................£ 45 0 0
One plain, ditto,......................................£ 35 0 0
A Pair of Chaise, or Chair Wheels compleatly finished,..£   6 0 0
A new Chaise Harness,...................................£   6 0 0
A pair of Coach Wheel Harness, plain,..................£ 13 0 0
Chariot, or Post Chaise, ditto,........................£ 12 0 0
The best hunting Saddle, wilted, with a Girth, Stirrups,
    and Cruper,..£   3 5 0
Plain ditto,..................................£ 2 12 0
Pellam Bit Bridle,.............................   8 0
Snaffle do...................................   4 6

And all other Work relative to the Coach making or Saddlers Business on the most reasonable Terms, by ELKANAH and WILLIAM DEANE, . . .—The New-York Mercury, September 28, 1767.

WILLIAM DEANE, Coach-maker, Informs the public in general and his customers in particular, that he carries on his business as usual in Broad-street where he makes all sorts of coaches, landaus, phætons, curricles, chairs and chaises; likewise all sorts of harness and saddlers work, as also painting, guilding and japanning, in the neatest and most elegant manner. And as he finishes all carriages whatever in his own shop without applying to any other, He is likewise determined to make them as good, sell them as cheap, and be as expeditious as there is a posibility. And to convince the public of the truth of what he asserts, he will make any piece of work that is required, equal to any imported from England, and will sell it at the prime cost of that imported, by which means those who are pleased to favour him with their custom will save the freight, insurance, and expences naturally attending in putting the carriages to rights after they arrive. And as a further inducement, he will engage his work for a year after it is delivered, that is, if any part gives way or fails by fair usage, he will make it good at his own expence. Those advantages cannot be obtained on carriages imported. He has now a considerable stock of the best of all materials fit for making carriages. For the above reasons, he most humbly requests the encouragement of the public, which will be most gratefully acknowledged by him.

Said Deane paints and repairs all manner of old work very reasonably, and has for sale just finished, a new phaeton, and four new chairs.—*The New-York Journal or the General Advertiser*, June 4, 1772.

JAMES HALLETT.—Chaise-Boxes, Chair and Kittereen-Boxes, with all sorts of Wheels and Carriages for the same, are made by James Hallett, on Golden-Hill, at the Sign of the Chair-Wheel; at the most reasonable Rates, with all Expedition.—*The New-York Gazette Revived in the Weekly Post-Boy*, January 22, 1750.

JAMES LAWRENCE, living in the Broad-Way, at the Sign of the Riding Chair, between Oswego-Market and the Old English Church opposite the Province Arms; Makes and Mends all Sorts of Carriages, such as Coaches, Chariots, Chaises, Chairs, Kittereens, Four-Wheel Chaise, Waggons, Carts, Sleds of all Sorts, and Wheels of all Sorts, likewise chair-Boxes and Kittereen-Boxes of any Form or Shape, after the best and neatest Manner, and newest Fashion, where all Gentlemen may depend on the best Usage, and quickest Dispatch.—*The New-York Ga-zette or the Weekly Post-Boy,* March 1, 1756.

ROBERT MANLY, Coach and Chaise-Maker, almost opposite the Old English Church, in the Broad-Way; Makes, mends and repairs all sorts of carriages, in the best and most genteel manner. Gentlemen that chuse to employ me, may depend on having their work done with great care and expedition, by their humble servant, ROBERT MANLY.—*The New-York Gazette and the Weekly Mercury,* June 6, 1768.

NOAH NOBLE, Coach-Harness-Maker, from London; At the Lower End of the Broad-Way, near the Bowling-green: Begs Leave to acquaint the Public, That he makes and repairs all Kinds of Harness for Coaches, Chairs, Bridles, &c. Likewise Gears for Carts; Sleighs, after a much neater and better Manner than has ever been executed in this Country. Any Gentlemen who will be pleased to employ him, shall be served faithfully, and at the very lowest prices, and the favour of their Commands most gratefully acknowledge, by Their most humble Servant, NOAH NOBLE.—*The New-York Journal or the General Advertiser,* May 12, 1768

STEPHEN STEEL.—To be Sold, a second Hand Curricle with Harness complete, also a new Wiskey Chair with Harness for one Horse; inquire of Stephen Steel, Coach-Maker in King's-Street, New-York.—*The New-York Journal,* September 5, 1771.

COACHES

COL. MORRIS's COACH.—Mr. Zenger; Passing the other Day down the Broad Way I saw a Coach, upon which being a particular Coat of Arms, Crest and Motto, my Curiosity led me to enquire its Owner, which I found to be Coll. Morris, now in England. . . . The Crest is a spacious Stone Castle, with

several Divisions and Appartments, alluding as (I con-
jecture) to a Combination of Power and Strength; the
little Turrets, Battlements, &c. may serve to illustrate
the vain Attempts his Power has made use of, to have
established it self triumphant; the Flames within seem
to discover a Disunion of Councils, and their Bursting
forth at Top, an Indication that their Chiefs or Heads,
venting their unruly Passions, are accomplishing their
own Destruction. The Motto being, Tandem vincitur,
seems to declare the Virtue, Perseverance, Magnanimity
and Success of the Morris Family, against all such com-
bined Force; . . .—Letter to the printer in *The New-
York Weekly Journal*, February 23, 1736.

CHARIOT.—To be Sold, A Chariot, constructed in the
best manner, little worse for wear, with stell springs,
fore and side glasses, blinds, and all appurtenances, the
most compleat of their kind. The coach-box takes off,
shafts fixes on, and it then becomes a genteel, light, easy,
and strong post chaise. It cost originally 74 guineas;
but being not now wanted by the owner, it is to be sold,
and to prevent fraud and trouble, the lowest price that
will be taken is £110 currency. A set of harness will be
given in, and a good coach horse may be had with or
without the chariot. Mr. Field, coach maker, or Mr.
Scot, Stabler, will shew the chariot, and receive the
money, or a good bill, for it, at six months date.—*The
New-York Mercury*, October 11, 1762.

COACH.—To be Sold, A Second Hand Coach in very
good Order, having an extraordinary front Glass. Enquire
of James Hallet, at the Sign of the Coach in the Broad
Way, opposite Battoe-Street.—*New-York Gazette*, March
12, 1764 (*Supplement*).

A POST CHAISE, Built by one of the best Makers in
London, in good condition, with Fore and Side Glasses,
and Mahogany Blinds; the Springs as good as new, and
Wheels that have been but little used, with Harness

for two Horses; to be sold. To prevent Trouble, the lowest Price is fixed at £65 Currency. Enquire of Hugh Gaine.—*The New-York Mercury*, November 3, 1766.

A NEW MODEL.—We hear from Burlington, that the new constructed light travelling waggon, contrived by Richard Wells, Esquire, on a full Trial last week, was found to answer its Design, to great Exactness. Among other Improvements, his invention to discharge the Horses, in case of their runing away is particularly worth Attention. This is done, at the expence of about a Pistole, by the Rider (in the Inside of the Carriage) only by pulling a String, when the Horses go off and leave the carriage standing. An Invention that bids fair to be of great Use and Safety to those who ride in close Carriages. —News item from Philadelphia in *The New-York Gazette*, November 16-23, 1767.

PUBLIC COACHES.—They write from New-York, that the roads at the back of that Province, New-England and Virginia, have been so greatly improved, that they had established public caravans and stage-coaches, for the accommodation of passengers.—News item from London, September 25, 1767, in *The New-York Mercury*, January 4, 1768

A CARAVAN, Fit either for two or four horses, to be sold; it is very large, and will hold eight People. Whoever inclines to purchase the same, may apply to Abraham Van Dycke, near Peck's-slip.—*The New-York Gazette and the Weekly Mercury*, March 1, 1773.

COACH AND CHARIOT.—To be Sold, a Coach and Chariot, Two of the most elegant carriages ever imported into America, and equal to any in London; both crane neck'd, and calculated for the climate, having the pannels to let down on all sides; they have their first set of wheels on, and are in high preservation. Enquire of Mr. Johnson, coach-maker in high-street, Philadelphia.—*The New-*

York Gazette and the Weekly Mercury, February 27, 1775.

SADDLERS

THOMAS CHADOCK, From London, Living near the Old English Church in Wall-Street. Makes and sells Italian spring collars travelling collars, &c. to fit any horse whatever in the most compleat and easy manner; likewise thong making, and piece master harness-maker, and trimmer; he hopes by his assiduity and diligence in his business to merit the continuance of the favours of all his customers. N.B. An Apprentice is wanting to the above Business.—*Rivington's New-York Gazetteer*, July 8, 1773.

HENRY CLOPPER.—To be Sold by Henry Clopper, at the Corner of the Meal-Market, Near the Merchants Coffee House, All Sorts of Men's and Women's Saddles, Saddler's Ware, Breed, Fringe, Plush, Brass Furniture Brass Nails & Tacks, and a large Sortment of Horse Whips; He also has several riding Chairs and Kittereens ready made for Sale, after the newest Fashion; He also mends Coaches, Chaises, Chairs and Kittereens after the cheapest and best Manner.—*The New-York Weekly Post-Boy*, March 27, 1749.

JAMES ETTRIDGE.—This is to inform all Gentlemen, Ladies and others, that James Ettridge, Sadler, in the Broad-way, New-York late from London; Makes and sells all sorts of Sadels, bridles, and furniture, as neat as in London, viz. Ladies hunting side saddles, and all other sorts of side saddles, forest saddles without trees, demi peeks, hunter's, with doe skin seats, either welted or plain, portmantuas, leather bags, villeases for bedding. . . .—*The New-York Mercury*, August 29, 1763.

HALSTED AND THOMPSON, Sadlers, Takes this Method to acquaint the Publick, that they have removed to the House of Mrs. Dawrsey, opposite William Walton, Esq;

a few Doors from which they formerly lived, where they carry on their Business as formerly, makes and sells all sorts of Saddles, and Furnitures, in the neatest manner, viz. Ladies Hunting Side-Saddles, Demi Peaks, Kings Hunters, Forrest Saddles, without Trees, but Doe and Hogskin Seats, welted or plain, Portmantuas, Saddlebags, &c. N.B. Large Allowance will be made to any Person buying a Quantity.—*The New-York Gazette,* December 20, 1762.

THOMAS JACKSON, Sadler and Cap-Maker, from London, Has opened a Shop in the Fly, between the Flymarket and Burling's-Slip. He Makes after the neatest Manner, all kinds of Ladies Hunting side Saddles, Men's Hunters, Demy Peeks and Kings Hunters, with all kinds of laced and plain furniture &c. &c. . . .—*The New-York Mercury,* August 23, 1762.

SELBY AND THOMSON Saddlers from London, Opposite the Meal-Market, New-York. Makes and sells all Sorts of Saddles, and Furniture, Viz. Lady's common and Hunting Saddles, Men's Forrest Saddles without Trees, Pistol Saddles, Demy Peaks, King's Hunters with Doe and Hogg Skin Seats, welted and Plain, Port Manteaus, &c. &c. N. B. Good Allowance will be made to Persons taking a Quantity.—*The New-York Gazette or the Weekly Post-Boy,* May 19, 1763.

CORNELIUS & BENJAMIN WYNKOOP.—To be made, mended and Sold, by Cornelius & Benjamin Wynkoop, Saddlers, opposite the Oswego-Market; chaises, chairs, Kittereens, Men's and Women's Saddles, and Bridles, after the best and neatest Manner: Also a neat Assortment of Whips, and two Second-Hand Chairs, &c. at reasonable Rates.—*The New-York Gazette or the Weekly Post-Boy,* March 12, 1753.

MUSIC AND MUSICAL INSTRUMENTS

MUSICAL INSTRUMENT MAKERS

GILBERT ASH.—For the Benefit of a Poor Widow. On Thursday the 18th Instant, will be open'd, at the City-Hall, in the City of New-York, A New Organ, made by Gilbert Ash. . . .—*The New-York Mercury*, March 15, 1756.

FREDERICK HEYER, Organ Builder, in the Broad-Way, in the same House where Mr. George Cook, Saddler lives, near St. Paul's Church, Makes and repairs Harpsichords and Spinets in the neatest Manner, and with Dispatch, Has some new and very neat Harpsichords for Sale. Also a Chamber Organ, which may, in a short Time, be compleatly finished, and enlarged (if tho't necessary) so as to suit a Place of public Worship.—*Rivington's New-York Gazetteer*, November 11, 1773.

ROBERT HORNE, Musical Instrument-Maker, from London, at Mr. Francis Cooley's, on Golden-Hill; Makes and repairs Violins, bass viols, tenor viols, Æolius harps, gauiters, German flutes, Kitts, violin bows, &c. in the neatest and compleatest manner. All orders punctually obey'd, with the quickest dispatch: The favour of Gentlemen and Ladies shall be duly honour'd with their Commands. N.B. Merchants may be supplied with any of the above, cheaper than in London on proper notice given.—*The New-York Mercury*, September 14, 1767.

ROBERT HORNE, Musical Instrument-Maker, from London, on Golden-Hill, near Burling's Slip, Makes and repairs musical instruments, viz. Violins, tennors, violoncellos, guittars, kitts, aeolus harps, spinnets, and spinnets

365

jacks, violin bows, tail-pieces, pins, bridges; bows hair'd, and the best Roman Strings, &c. N.B. Country stores supply'd on the shortest notice.—*The New-York Gazette and the Weekly Mercury*, January 6, 1772.

DANIEL & PHILIP PELTON, Drums Made and sold by Phillip Pelton, upper end of Queen-street, and by Daniel Pelton, in Chappel street, now called Beekman street, equal to any that have been imported for sound or beauty. As said Persons have great variety on hand any gentlemen may be served at the shortest notice, and on the most reasonable terms. The purchaser may depend upon having their Drums tun'd to sound well.—*The New-York Journal or the General Advertiser*, October 5, 1775.

JOHN SHEIUBLE, Organ Builder, from Philadelphia, Makes and repairs all kinds of Organs, Harpsichords, Spinnets, and Piano, in the best Manner, and with the greatest Dispatch. Any Person that has any Thing to be done in the above Way, may depend on having it executed in the best Manner, and at the cheapest Rate. He is to be spoke with at Mr. Samuel Prince's Cabinet Maker, at the Sign of the Chest of Drawers, in New-York.—*The New-York Gazette and the Weekly Mercury*, March 30, 1772.

JOHN SHEIUBLE.[1] . . . N.B. He has now ready for sale, one neat chamber organ, one hammer spinnet, one common spinnet.—*The New-York Gazette and the Weekly Mercury*, October 10, 1774.

JACOB TRIPPELL, Musical Instrument Maker from London, at the House of Mr. John Ent, Watchmaker, op-

[1] In this advertisement the name is spelled *Sheybli*.

posite to, on the West Side of the Old Slip Market, a few Doors below Duyckinck's Corner, makes and repairs all sorts of Violins, Base and Tenor Viols; English and Spanish Guitters, Loutens, Mentelines, Mandores, and Welsh Harps, at reasonable Rates, as neat as in Europe, Having work't at the Business Nine Years, with the best Hands in London, since I left Germany; I shall Endeavour to Give Satisfaction to those Ladies and Gentlemen, that shall favour me with their Custom.—*The New-York Gazette,* August 24, 1767.

DAVID WOLHAUPTER, Takes this method to inform his friends and customers, that he has removed from the place he formerly lived, to the house where Mr. Muller, leather breeches maker, formerly lived, nearly opposite the Flattenbarrack-Hill, in the Broadway; where he makes and mends all sorts of musical instruments, such as basoons, German flutes, Common do. hautboys, clarinets, fifes, bagpipes, &c. also makes and mends all sorts of mathematical instruments, and all sorts of tuning work done by said Wolhaupter. Any gentlemen that will please to favour him with their employ, may depend upon being served at the cheapest rates, by their humble servant.—*The New-York Gazette and the Weekly Mercury,* June 18, 1770.

DAVID WOOLHAUPTER Instrument-Maker, In Fair street, opposite St. Paul's Church, New York, Makes and sells all sorts of Drums and Fifes. Drums made of Mahogany, curled maple, and Beech wood, in the best and neatest manner, and has now a quantity ready made for sale. He also makes Clarinets, Hautboys, German and common Flutes, and all sorts of Instruments &c.—*The New-York Journal or the General Advertiser,* June 8, 1775.

GOTTLIEB WOLHAUPTER, living at the Sign of the Musical instrument-Maker, opposite Mr. Adam Vanderberg's has just imported from London, a Choice Parcel of the

best English Box-wood; Where he continues to make
and mend, all Sorts of Musical Instruments, such as
German Flutes, Hautboys, Clareonets, Flageolets, Bas-
soons, Fifes, and also Silver Tea-Pot Handles.—*The New-
York Gazette*, November 16, 1761.

MUSIC TEACHERS

NICHOLAS BIFERI.[2]—Music. Mr. Biferi, Musician of
Naples, being determined to stay in this city, informs
the public, that he now teaches singing after the Italian
way, also the harpsichord, and the composition of music,
at one Guinea for twelve lessons, and one Guinea entrance, which entrance is to be paid only by those who
never had a master before. Enquire of said Mr. Biferi,
at Mr. Wilmot's Peck's-Slip—*Rivington's New-York
Gazetteer*, June 30, 1774.

ALEXANDER DIENVAL.—This is to give Notice, That
the Violin and German Flute, are taught in the Space
of two or three Months each, by Alexander V. Dienval,
at Mr. Elphinstone's House in the Slott.—*The New York
Mercury*, September 18, 1758.

WILLIAM CHARLES HULET.—This is to Give Notice,
That the Violin is taught in so plain and easy a Method
(that young Gentlemen of eight or nine years old may
be capable of learning in a short Time) by W. C. Hulet,
at the House of Robert Wallace, joiner, in the Broad-
street, near the Corner of the Old-Dutch Church-street.
Mr. Hulet takes this Method to acquaint the Gentlemen
and Ladies of this City, that he cannot get a Room for a
Dancing School this Winter, but will attend them at their
own Houses if they honour him Commands.—*The New-
York Gazette*, September 24, 1759 (*Supplement*).

---

[2] A notice in *Rivington's New-York Gazetteer*, May 5, 1774, stated
that Mr. Biferi taught music at the New Academy for teaching music,
dancing and the Italian and French languages.

WILLIAM CHARLES HULET. The Guitar, Taught by W. C. Hulet, Dancing-Master, who has opened his Public Dancing-School, at his House in Broad-Street, near the Corner of Beaver-Street, at Three o'Clock in the Afternoon; and an Evening School for such Ladies and Gentlemen, who cannot attend in Day-time. Likewise Hours set apart for such as would chuse to be taught in private. He flatters himself, that the Performance of several of his Scholars, has convinced the judicious and impartial, of his Abilites as a Master.

He teaches the Minuet and Country Dances, by the Whole, by the Month, or Quarter: And likewise the Violin, German-Flute, and Use of the Small-Sword.

N.B. The great Advantage that many Gentlemen have over others (that have not learn'd the Hornpipe) in Country Dancing, has induced Mr. Hulett to open a private School for such Gentlemen, who may chuse to attend.—*The New-York Gazette and the Weekly Post-Boy,* October 15, 1770.

JAMES LEADBETTER, Takes this method to acquaint the ladies and gentlemen, that he intends teaching the Organ and Harpsichord. He may be spoke with at the Widow Vandusen's, in Bayard-street.—*The New-York Gazette and the Weekly Mercury,* April 16, 1770.

JAMES LEADBETTER, Begs leave to acquaint the ladies and gentlemen of this city, that he intends teaching the Organ, Harpsichord, and Spinnet. Any person inclining to be instructed by him, by leaving a line at Mr. Rivington's will be waited upon.—*Rivington's New-York Gazetteer,* May 6, 1773.

CHARLES LOVE, Musician, from London, at his lodgings at the house of Mrs. George, in the first lane from the Bowling-Green, that leads to the North-River, proposes teaching gentlemen musick on the following instruments, Viz. Violin, Hautboy, German and Common Flutes, Bassoon, French Horn, Tenor, and Base Violin, if desired.

N.B. Said Love may be spoke with any time of the day, at his lodgings, where gentlemen who have a mind to be instructed on any of the above mentoned instruments, will be acquainted with his Conditions.—*The New York Mercury,* July 2, 1753.

D. PROPERT,[3] Professor of Musick, Takes this method of acquainting the ladies and gentlemen of this city, that he teaches the organ, harpsichord, guittar, German flute, &c. and has a variety of new musick, Roman strings for violins, and musical instruments, among which is a very fine tone harpsichord and a forte piano, all which he disposes of at Mr. Philip Kissick's wine merchant, the upper end of Queen-street. The above D. Propert gives out plans for organs, from 35 1. to 500 1. and every business in the musical way done with the greatest honour and expedition.—*The New-York Gazette and Weekly Mercury,* September 17, 1770.

——WALL, Comedian, Engages to teach Ladies and Gentlemen to Play on the Guitar to prevent Trouble, his terms are to such as chuse to be waited on at the Houses; One Guinea Entrance, and the same per Month for which he pays Attendance, Three Times a Week. Ladies and Gentlemen, who may think proper to honour him with their Commands, by sending to his lodgings, at Mr. Sproul's, in Depyster's-Street, will be immediately waited on.—*The New-York Mercury,* January 11, 1768.

——WINTER.—This is to give Notice, that Mr. Winter keeps a Singing School of Psalmody, near the lower End of the Broad Way, and waits upon any at their own Houses at seasonable Hours.—*The New-York Weekly Journal,* January 7, 1740.

HERMAN ZEDTWITZ.—The Subscriber intending to settle in this city, proposes to teach a certain number of

[3] For *The New-York Journal,* of October 4, 1770, Mr. Propert wrote an essay on the beauty and meaning of music.

Gentlemen the Violin, in the present taste, Having been a pupil of several of the most eminent masters now in London and Germany. For further particulars, please to inquire of the subscriber at Mr. Buskerk's, nearly opposite the old Presbyterian Meeting. Herman Zedtwitz. —*The New-York Journal*, April 8, 1773.

MUSIC AND MUSICAL INSTRUMENTS

MUSIC.—Just Published, and to be Sold by the Printer hereof. Divine Songs, Attempted in Easy Language for the Use of Children. By I. Watts, D. D. Author of the Lyrick Poems.—*The New-York Evening Post*, March 30, 1747.

MUSIC.—Just reprinted, and to be sold by the Printer hereof, Price 10 d. Or, cheaper by the Dozen; All the Twenty-four Songs of the famous English Archer, Bold Robin Hood.—*The New-York Gazette Revived in the Weekly Post-Boy*, November 5, 1750.

ORGAN.—An Organ with three Stops, to be sold for 40 l. enquire of the Printer.—*The New-York Mercury*, December 4, 1758.

IMPORTED MUSICAL INSTRUMENTS.—To be sold by a Gentleman who lodges at Widow Darcey's nigh the Ship-Yards, opposite to William Walton's, Esq; and who is to go soon out of Town; exceeding good German Flutes, for three Dollars each; likewise others with 2, 3, 4 or 5 middle Pieces to change the Tones and Voice, do. likewise Base Viol Strings of all Sizes, and silvered Ones for Basses, Violins and Tenors. A great Collection of wrote and printed Musick from Italy and England. The newest Sets of Scotch and Irish Tunes, and Airs in Score, Bass Viol and Fiddle Bridges, rulled Musick Paper in Sheets and in Books, German Flute Concertos, Sonatas, Duets and Solos, and a great many other Things in the musical Way, imported by himself from Naples and Lon-

don. Likewise, two fine Violins, a Girls six-stringed Bass
Viole, and a foreign Pocket Gun.—*The New-York Mercury,* August 13, 1759.

Music.—Just published, neatly Printed on fine Paper,
and to be Sold by A. Throne, next Door to the Green-
Dragon, near the Moravian Meeting-House, in New
York, The Mock Bird; or New American Songster: Be-
ing a Collection of all the newest and most approved
Songs. Designed for the Entertainment of the Ladies
and Gentlemen of New-York, and other Parts of North-
America.—*The New-York Gazette or the Weekly Post-
Boy,* March 19, 1761.

Imported Musical Instruments.—Thomas Harrison,
Organist of Trinity-Church, New York, At his House in
King-Street, near Mr. Reade's Church Warden, has imported in the Harriot Packet; Capt. Brayly, Spinnets,
Violins, German Flutes, Musick Books, ruled Paper, Fiddle Strings, Bridges, Pins, Jacks for Spinnets, Hautboys
and Hautboy Reeds at lowest Price.—*The New-York Gazette,* March 30, 1761 (*Supplement*).

Organ in Trinity Church.—To be Sold by the
Church-Wardens, the Organ in Trinity-Church. The
Instrument is large, consisting of 26 Stops, 10 in the
Great Organ, 10 in the Choir Organ and 6 in the Swell,
three Sets of Keys; with a Frontispiece of gilt Pipes, and
otherwise neatly adorned. It may be inspected; will be
sold cheap, and the Purchaser may remove it immediately, (another being expected from England next
Spring) but if not disposed of, is, on the Arrival of the
new Organ, intended to be shipt to England.—*The New-
York Gazette,* November 15, 1762.

Chamber Organ.—To be Sold on Saturday next, for
the want of Money, by James Fuller, Lately from London, at his House joining to Mr. Brazier's Lot, at the
upper End of Cart and Horse-Street, Golden-Hill, A

Very good and handsome Chamber Organ, which, with a few Minutes Instruction, any Person may play on: It has 6 Stops, 15 Mute Gilt Pipes in the Front, and a Set of Drawers at the Bottom; and will be sold cheap.—*The New-York Journal or General Advertiser*, November 13, 1766.

IMPORTED MUSICAL INSTRUMENTS.—Simeon Coley imported among other things . . . The best Lind violins, German Flutes, tipt and plain, Fifes, Tabors and Pipes, with books of Instructions, Violin Bows, the Best Roman Strings, Pins Bridges, &c.—*The New-York Gazette*, June 8-15, 1767.

HARPSICHORD.—To be Sold, a Harpsichord, completely fitted, Maker's Name (Mahoon, London:) For Particulars inquire of W. Rice, Organist.—*The New-York Journal or General Advertiser*, March 2, 1769.

IMPORTED MUSICAL INSTRUMENTS.—Peter Goelet at the Sign of the Golden-Key has to sell among other things . . . The best Roman and Common strings for Violins, and Sets of Strings for Base Violins, Guitar Strings, Harpsicord Wires, Violins, German and common Flutes, Violin Bridges and Bows . . .—*The New-York Gazette and the Weekly Mercury*, January 2, 1769

HARPSICHORD.—To be disposed of, a fine ton'd double key'd Harpsichord, with four Stops, as good as new, made by Hitchcock. Enquire of the Printer.—*The New-York Gazette and the Weekly Mercury*, September 18, 1769.

DRUMS of the best Quality manufactured in America, to be sold by the Printer.—*The New-York Journal or General Advertiser*, October 19, 1775.

MOVING PICTURES, WAX WORKS, AND OTHER NOVELTIES

Moving Pictures and Other Novelties

ORRERY.—At Boston, N England, they having procured that wonderful Machine or Instrument called the Orrery, Mr. Greenwood proposes to illustrate and confirm the Elements of Astronomy there from, by certain explanatory Lectures, which he has composed on the Orrery. The Orrery is a Machine of wonderful Contrivance brought to Perfection by that ingenious Mathematician and Artificer Mr. John Rowley, which Machine illustrates the Motion of the Sun, Moon and Earth to the meanest Capacity. That which is so difficult for many People to apprehend or believe (I mean the Motion of the Earth) and would have taken up a years study to come to a familar apprehension of it by this Machine is communicated in an hour.[1] . . . And therefore it is Hoped that in time not only each Province, but each principal Town in these parts will think it as necessary to have an Orrery, as a publick Town Clock, the one gives the Time of the Day and Night, the other presents to our View the Wonder Works of the Deity.—*The New-York Gazette*, July 1-8, 1734.

MUSICAL MACHINE.—To be Seen, at Mr. Pacheco's Ware-House, in Market field-Street, commonly known by the Name of Petticoat-Lane, opposite the Cross Guns, near the Fort.

A curious Musical Machine, arriv'd from England, the third Day of May last, which performs several strange and diverting Motions to the Admiration of the Spectators, viz. The Doors fly open of their own accord, and

---

[1] A detailed description of the machine follows.

there appears six Ringers in white Shirts all busy pulling
Bell-Ropes, and playing several Tunes, Chimes, and
changes; They first appear with black caps and black
Beards at one Corner there is a Barbers Shop and a
Barbers Pole hung out, and at the Shop Door stands
the Barber's Boy, who, at the word of Command, gives
three knocks at his Masters Door, out comes the Barber
with his Rasor and Bason to shave the Ringers, then the
Doors shut themselves whilst the Barber is Shaving
them, then the Doors open themselves the second Time,
and the Ringers appear all clean shaved and clean Caps
put on; afterwards they ring a long Peal of Changes,
and then fall the Bells to Admiration, after that the
Barber walks into his Shop again, his Boy standing ready
to open the Door for his Master and then shuts it
after him; last of all the great Doors shut themselves
again.   All being performed entirely by Clock-Work in
imitation of St. Brides Bells in London.   There will be
a small Entertainment of Slight of Hand, before the
Clock-Work is seen.   The Proprietor of it will wait on
any Gentlemen or Ladies, at their own Houses.

The same will be shewn every Day in the Week, Sun-
days excepted at 4 o'clock in the Afternoon, and at 7 in
the Evening.   The Price for Grown Person's 1s and for
Children 9 pence.—*The New-York Weekly Journal*, July
18, 1743.

MAGIC LANTERN.—After the announcement of a performance of the Musical Machine is added the following
notice: Where is also to be Seen, the Curious and Surprizing Magick Lanthorn, by which Friar Bacon, Doctor
Faustus, and others, perform such wonderful Curiosities,
representing upwards of 30 humourous and entertaining
Figures, larger than Men or Women; as the Rising Sun,
the Friendly Travellers, the Pot Companions, the blind
Beggar of Gednal Green and his Boy, the merry Piper
dancing a Jigg to his own dumb Musick, the courageous
Fencing Master, the Italian Mountebank or famous in-
fallible Quack, the Man riding on a Pig with his Face

towards the Tail, the Dutchman scating on the Ice in the midst of Summer; with a great Variety of other Figures equally diverting and curious, too tedious here to mention.

N.B. To begin at 7 o'clock in the Evening.—*The New-York Evening Post,* September 8, 1746.

MOVING MACHINE.—To all Gentlemen, Ladies and others, of Curiosity. This is to give Notice, that at the House of Mr. John Hays at the Sign of St. Andrew's Cross, near the Fly-Market, is to be seen a large moving Mashene or Land and Water Skip, representing many Things moving nearly imitating Nature, beginning at Half an Hour after Six in the Evening precisely, Price 1s 6d.

N.B. If any Gentlemen or Ladies, hath a Mind to have a private View of the same, they may, by giving two Hours Warning before hand.—*The New-York Evening Post,* December 29, 1746.

ELECTRICAL EXPERIMENTS.—For the Entertainment of the Curious. To Be Shown, The most surprising Effects or Phenominas on Electricity of Attracting, Repelling, & Flemmies Force, particular the New Way of Electrifing several Persons at the same Time, so that Fire shall Dart from all Parts of their Bodies; as has been Exhibited to the Satisfaction of the Curious, in all Parts of Europe: Electricity became all the subject in Vogue, Princes were will to see this New Fire which a Man produced from himself. And it's tho't to be of Service to many Ailments.

To be seen at any Time of the Day, from 8 o'clock in the Morning till 9 at Night provided the Weather proves Dry and no Damp Air, (a Company presenting) at the House of Mrs. Willson, near the Way House, in New York; where due Attendance is given by Mr. Richard Brickell.

As the stay of this Machine is but a short Time in this Town, those whose Curiosities excites them to behold those wonders, are desired to give their speedy Attendance.—*The New-York Weekly Journal*, May 9, 1748.

PHILOSOPHICAL OPTICAL MACHINE.—To the Publick in general here and hereabouts. Ladies, Gentlemen and every Body else, I am well enough know to all of you, for I am a New-Yorker. I don't pretend to be a fine Scribe; far from it. I have been otherwise employed all my Days, than to have any Time to learn a knack of writing well; but yet I think I am not quite so unlearned, but that I can write so as to be understood; and as I find myself under a Necessity of making my address to you, I hope you will make an Allowance for my manner and Stile.

You all know I lately purchased, and many of you have seen my Philosophical Optical Machine, lately invented in, and imported from London. I have hitherto shewed (out of near 100 Prospects) only two Setts, 8 in each of English Palaces, grand Building, and Gardens, &c. Every one who has seen them, has paid me Four Shillings a Piece for each Set; and I must say, they have gone from me well satisfied; their repeated Visits and constant Recommendations of the Machine, convince me of what I assert.

But tho' all my Customers seem well pleased (except a very few who can approve of Nothing they see others do, or with any Thing but what they say themselves or have a Hand in) yet as I understood, there were great Numbers who think much of Four Shillings, and knowing that there are others who really can't afford it, I began last week to show for Two Shillings only, the first eight English Prospects; and determined to have shewn them no more here. But last Week having been so bad weather, for the most Part, that few People cared to stir Abroad, I hereby give Notice, that none may miss an Opportunity of seeing the English Prospects, that every Morning this Week I will continue to shew the first 8, and every Afternoon and Evening, the other 8 of them, to no less than 6 Persons at a Time; but if a

lesser Number should come, I will leave it to their own
Generosity, according to the Satisfaction they think they
receive. The next Monday I will begin to show, on
the same easy Terms, nine of the French King's Palaces,
and so every succeeding Week different Ones, in different
Parts of the World, till the whole be gone through.
After that, I intend to go to Philadelphia. . . . Jo.
BONNIN.

P. S. Any Body who has once paid for seeing a set, is
always welcome to see the same again gratis, provided
they bring, or come along with a new Company, or when
I am showing what they have seen before. Tickets at
Two Shillings a Piece to be had, as usual, at Mr. Campbell's shop, at the Meal Market, The Tickets always
mention the Prospects to be seen by them.—*The New-
York Gazette Revived in the Weekly Post-Boy*, December 19, 1748.

PHILOSOPHICAL OPTICAL MACHINE.—To be Shewn all
this Week at Mr. John Bonnin's, nine French Prospects,
viz. 1. Veue du Chateau Roial de Seause; A Prospect
of the Palace of Seause; 2. Veue du Chateau de Chantilli; A Prospect of the Palace of Chantilli. 3. Veue du
Thuilleries; A Prospect of the Royal Thuilleries 4. Veue
du Chateau de Medon; A Prospect of the Palace of
Medon. 5. Veue du Chateau de Luxembourg; A Prospect
of the Palace of Luxembourg. 6. A View of the Flower
Gardens, and Part of the Fountains of Fountain-Bleau.
7. A View of one Wing of Fountain-Bleau, taken from
the Court of Fountains. 8. A View of the Canal of
Fountain-Bleau, seven Miles long. 9. The Visto, between
Chestnut Groves in the Gardens of Versailles, justly
esteemed one of the most pleasant Parts in the Garden,
because of its Serenity and Coolness in the most sultry
Heats of Summer. The Groves are inclosed on each
Side by a magnificent Net-Work, adorned with Bustos
of Porphiry, and Statues of White Marble.

N.B. Six Persons comming at a Time together, to be
admitted at Two Shillings each, (without Tickets;) but

if a lesser Number the Overplus to be left to their own
Generosity. Any Body who pays once, may come again
with a new Company, as often as they please gratis.—
The New-York Gazette Revived in the Weekly Post-Boy,
December 26, 1748.

PHILOSOPHICAL OPTICAL MACHINE.—Mr. Bonnin intended to have gone to-day to Long Island, with his
Perspective Machine, according to a former Advertisement; but the People of all Ranks and Ages, having
taken the Alarm, crouded so fast to him, that he had
more Company to visit him last Week, than he has had
for any three Weeks together since he began to show,
and which Encouragement, together with the Cries, Tears
and Prayers of the Populace, as he passes along the
Streets, to continue another Week longer in Town, have
at last prevailed upon him to defer his Removal till next
Week. Now this curious Show, is about leaving this
City, it may with the strictest Justice be said, that there
never was any Entertainment in it, of so pleasing or of
so instructive a Nature; nor which met with so general
an Approbation. There are such vast Varieties of delightful Prospects, that let a Man or Woman's Taste
be what it will, they cannot help meeting with something or another fitted to give them the most delightful
Sensation.—News item in *The New-York Gazette Revived in the Weekly Post-Boy,* January 30, 1749.

PHILOSOPHICAL OPTICAL MACHINE.—Jamaica on Long
Island, March 8th, 1748/9. The common Topicks of
Discourse in this Place, since the coming of Mr. Bonnin,
are entirely changed; instead of the common Chat, there
is nothing scarce mentioned now, but the most entertaining Parts of Europe, which are so lively represented in Mr. Bonnin's curious Prospects, who proposed
to tarry here but one Week when he first came; but
those several Prospects have been so universally satisfactory, that crowded Concourses of People are daily
Spectators, whose Expectations have been so far ex-

ceeded, that he has been prevailed on to tarry here another Week, but designs for Flushing on Saturday next, and Hempsted the Saturday after.—*The New-York Gazette Revived in the Weekly Post-Boy*, March 13, 1749.

PHILOSOPHICAL OPTICAL MACHINE.—This is to inform the Curious of either Sex, That this Day John Bonnin begins to exhibit his Philosophical Optical Machine, which has given so much Satisfaction to all those that have already favoured him with their Company: He has sundry new Additions, which he designs to shew all the Winter Season; to begin at 8 o'clock in the Morning, and continue showing till 9 at night. To be seen at the House of Mr. Victor Becker, opposite to Mr. Haynes's New-Buildings, in Crown-Street. N.B. Price One Shilling for grown Persons, and Six Pence for children.—*The New-York Gazette Revived in the Weekly Post-Boy*, December 11, 1749.

PHILOSOPHICAL OPTICAL MACHINE.—John Bonin, [*sic*] Hereby gives Notice to his Friends and Well wishers, That, After having tried many different Ways to support himself and Family, tho' with the utmost Honesty and Care, yet not being attended with desired Success, has now, by the Assistance of some Merchants, opened a Shop in Crown-Street, in the House where Capt. Hewit lately lived, near Mr. Abraham Lott's; where may be had, Rum, Sugar, and most kinds of European Goods usually sold in Shops. As his Creditors, he is fully persuaded, are such from a sincere and hearty Disposition to serve him, and as therefore he has his Goods at the most easy Rates, his kind Customers may depend on buying of him at the lowest Prices; and for their Encouragement, they shall be wellcome to view his famous Optical Machine Gratis.—*The New-York Gazette Revived in the Weekly Post-Boy*, May 14, 1750.

DIAGONAL MIRROR.—Just imported in the Dover, from London, and to be shewn by James Shaw, at William Willson's on the Dock, near the Old Slip, Diagonal Mirrour, representing the following Prints, being a greater Variety than any Thing of the kind that has ever yet been exhibited to publick View, viz.

16 Perspective Views in and about London.	6 Views of France Palaces.
	7 Inside Cathedrals.
24 Curious Views in and about Venice.	12 Views of Naples and Rome.
	12 Views on the Canal at Venice.
12 Sea Prospects of Ships at Sea, &c.	1 Inside St. Paul's Church in London,
4 Views of Fontainbleau.	1 Inside St. Peter's at Rome.

A View of the great Fire Works on Account of the General Peace: exhibiting the curious Piece of Architecture erected on that Occassion. The three Fire Suns; the middlemost 22 Feet, the other 10 Feet in Diameter; 12 Fire Trees, and that particular grand Scene of the Fire Works, called the Girandola, which is firing at once 6000 Rockets of half a Pound of Powder each.

N.B. This elegant Piece of Architecture is 410 Foot high, is imbellish'd with the Statues of Justice, Prudence, Fortitude, Clemency, Vigilance and Piety, on the Front; on the Top of the Building are 6 Statues, representing Jupiter, Bacchus, Cerres, Pomona, Vesta and Fidelity. Under the great Arch on a peddestal, is the Statue of Peace holding the Olive Branch over Neptune's Head. Over the Arch is painted in Basso Relievo, His Majesty presenting Peace to Britannia; the Basso Relievos on each Side of the Arch; one represents Neptune drawn by Sea Horses, the other the Triumph of Mars. This grand Fire Work will last about 3 Hours, and it is computed Twenty five Tons Weight of Gun powder and Combustibles, will be consumed.

All, or any Part of the above curious Prints, will be shewn at very reasonable Rates, at any Hour of the Day; and in order that no Person's Curiosity may be disappointed, it will be shewn by Candle Light, to oblige those who cannot attend in the Day-Time.

Note, Any Ladies, or particular Family, that have a Mind to see it at their own Houses, by applying to said Shaw, shall be waited on immediately.—*The New-York Weekly Journal*, June 19, 1749.

ATHENIAN TEMPLE OF ARTS AND SCIENCES.—To Be Seen At A large Theatrical Room, next to the Sign of the Dolphin (built on Purpose) near the Work-House, in New-York, for the Entertainment of Gentlemen, Ladies, and Others, to-morrow Evening, and to continue with different Plays ever Week. Punch's Company Of Comedians . . . Likewise. The Athenien Temple of Arts and Sciences. This admirable Piece of Mechanism is entirely of a new Invention, and is now finish'd by some of the best Artists, after several Years and Study Application. It is embellish'd with Variety of Painting, Carving and Gilding, and is acknowledg'd by the Curious, to be one of the most accurate Pieces of Art ever exhibited to publick View There are sundry Histories beautifully represented by moving Figures, in a grand and magnificent Manner and adorn'd with all the Ornaments and Decorations that can fill the Mind with pleasing Ideas, and charm a judicious and curious Spectator.

Note, That the Doors are to be open'd at 6 and begin at 7 o'Clock. Price. Front Seats, two shillings. Middle Seats, one Shilling and six Pence. Back Seats, one Shilling.—*The New-York Weekly Journal*, August 28, 1749.

ROCK AND SHELL WORK.—To be Seen, next Door to the Play House. A most curious Piece of Rock and Shell-Work, superior to any Thing of the Kind in America; a lively Prospect of the memorable Battle of Culloden; with Views of several of the grandest Cities, Palaces, Hospitals, Water Works, &c. in Europe. The Rock and Shell Work, to be seen at One Shilling each Person, and the Prospects at One Shilling per Dozen; Children at half Price.—*The New-York Gazette Revived in the Weekly Post-Boy*, June 25, 1750.

A Course of Natural Philosophy and Mechanics. —To be exhibited, at the House of the Rev. Mr. Ebenezer Pemberton in the Broad-way, in New-York. A Course of Natural Philosophy, and Mechanics, illustrated by Experiments, By Lewis Evans. This Course consists of 13 Lectures, treating of the nature of this World and its Parts. The Solar System is explained by a most curious Orrery, which represents the annual and diurnal Motions of all the Planets primary and secundary, the Causes of Day and Night, Winter and Summer Eclipses of the Sun and Moon, &c.

The Mathematical Terms, Figures and Proportions, necessary for the Understanding of these Lectures, are explained for the Sake of the Ladies and Gentlemen un-skill'd in the Mathematics.

The Properties of Water, Air, Fire, Light, the Electrical Fluid, and Magnetism, are explained by the Help of the best Machines and Instruments hitherto invented; and the Methods of applying them to the Conveniencies and Ornaments of Life, shall be directed on every Occasion.

The Light, that the late Discoveries in Electricity have thrown on Natural Philosophy, enables us to explain the Nature of Attraction and Repulsion, and of several other grand Phaenomena beyond any Thing heretofore im-agined.

The Laws of the Electrical Fluid shall be expressly handled, and this we are enabled now to do, as we are become acquainted with more of its Laws than have yet been discovered of Air. . . .—*The New-York Gazette Revived in the Weekly Post-Boy*, July 29, 1751.

Musical Machine.—Now to be seen by the Curious, at the house of Mr. Adam Vandenbergh, in the Broad-way, to be seen any hour, a curious musical Machine, which represents the tragedy of Bateman, viz. First, Two folding doors fly open, a curtain draws itself up, and exhibits a company of gentlemen and ladies, with knives and forks in motion, sat down to a wedding-dinner. The bride having promised marriage to young Batemen prov-

ing false, and marrying old Jermain, Bateman hangs himself on her wedding day. Four cupids fly down, and carry
Bateman away. The bride still enjoying herself at din-
ner, she at last falls from the table, dead and her rosy
colour changes to a deadly paleness: After which the
devil comes up, and carries her away. Here the curtain
falls, and ends the first act. The curtain drawing up
a Second time, instead of the wedding, exhibits young
Bateman laid in state, with the mourners about him;
dressed in black cloaks and white hatbands; the room
hung with escutcheons, and six ringers, in their shirts;
ringing the bells. The representation of a carpenters
yard, with people at work, with several other moving
figures. The whole represented by clock-work, per
RICHARD BRECKELL.

Who mends and cleans all sorts of clocks, reasonably.
N.B. Gentlemen and ladies will be waited upon at their
houses, on timely notice given. Price One shilling, and
for boys, six pence.—*The New-York Mercury*, December
29, 1755.

MICROCOSM.—We hear, That that elaborate and celebrated Piece of Mechanism, the Microcosm, now at Philadelphia, will speedily be here, and for a short Time exhibited to publick View. As this Piece is deservingly the
Admiration of its Spectators, and universally esteem'd,
as superior to any Thing of the Kind, 'twill doubtless
meet in this, the same Applause, as it has, in every other
Place where exhibited. N.B. This is that Machine
which the late Prince of Wales offer'd the Author Three
Thousand Giuneas for, and Two Hundred Pound per
Annum during his Life.—News item in *The New-York
Gazette or the Weekly Post-Boy*, February 2, 1756.

MICROCOSM.—This Day arrived here from Philadelphia, the inimitable Piece of Mechansim the Microcosm,
or, the World in Miniature, made by the late ingenious
Henry Bridges, of London. This piece for the Magnifi-
cence of its structure, the Beauty of its Painting and

Sculpture, the Excellency of its Music, with just Proportion of the Celestial Phaenomina, and the Variety of moving Figures, is esteem'd as the most instructive as well as entertaining Work of its kind that ever appear'd. We further hear, 'twill be exhibited in this City for a short time.—News item in *The New-York Gazette or the Weekly Post-Boy*, February 9, 1756.

MICROCOSM.[2]—To be seen at the New-Exchange, That Elaborate and Celebrated Piece of Mechanism, called Microcosm, or, the World in Miniature, Built in the Form of a Roman Temple, after twenty-two Years close Study and Application, by the late ingenious Mr. Henry Bridges, of London; who, having received the Approbation and Applause of the Royal Society, &c. afterwards made considerable Additions and Improvements; so that the Whole, being now completely finished, is humbly offered to the curious of this City, as a Performance which has been the Admiration of every Spectator, and proved itself by its singular Perfections the most instructive as well as entertaining Piece of Work in Europe.

A Piece of such complicated Workmanship, and that affords such a Variety of Representation (tho' all upon the most simple Principle) can but very imperfectly be described in Words the best chosen; Therefore 'tis desired, what little is said in this Advertisement may not pass for an Account of the Microscosm, but only what is thought meerly necessary in the Title of such an Account, &c.

Its outward Structure is a most beautiful Composition of Architecture, Sculpture, and Painting. The inward Contents are as judiciously adapted to gratify the Ear, the Eye, and the Understanding; for it plays with great Exactness several Pieces of Music, and exhibits, by an amazing Variety of moving Figures, Scenes diversified with Natural Beauties, Operations of Art, of human

[2] A poem describing the wonders of the microcosm was printed in the *New-York Mercury*, March 1, 1756.

Employments and Diversions of passing as in real
life, &c.

1 Shews all the celestial phaenomena.........................
2 Nine Muses playing in concert............................
3 Orpheus in Forest...
4 Carpenter's Yard...
5 A delightful Grove.......................................
6 A fine Landskip, with a Prospect of the Sea,.................
7 And lastly, is shewn the whole Machine in Motion, when upwards of twelve Hundred Wheels and Pinnions are in Motion
at once...

—*The New-York Mercury*, February 16, 1756.

MICROCOSM.—We, the proprietors of the Microcosm,
beg leave to acquaint the publick, that it will be shewn
at the New-Exchange, (as usual) till Tuesday the 23
instant, and positively no longer, as a further grant cannot be obtained for the use of the Assembly-Room, it
being engaged for that purpose: Therefore 'tis hoped,
all who may be desirous of seeing a piece so much
superior to any thing of its kind, and so worthy the notice
of the most judicious, will be as expeditious as convenient.

N.B. Tickets for Monday, Wednesday and Friday
nights, to be had at the above place.—*The New-York
Mercury*, March 8, 1756.

A WORK IN MINIATURE.—This is to inform the Curious, that at the House of Mr. Provost, Gun-Smith,
opposite the Old-Slip, there is a most beautiful Piece of
Work in Miniature, representing one Part of the City
of Mallaga, Which is commodiously and regularly built;
the Churches and other publick Edifices adorned with
lofty Spires, which adds a great Grandeur to the whole.
A large and well finished Monastry, with its Gardens
decorated with flowers and Fruit Trees; A View of the
Fryars Abess, and Nuns, inclosed within the Walls; Also
a Battery of 12 Guns, well mounted, the Centinals properly placed and compleatly armed; the Streets paved

and populated, with several other Embelishments, particularly a Prospect of green Mountains behind it, with
a View of Creatures on them; a Water Scene, with a
man'd Barge, a rural Spot, with a Sheepherd and Sheep-
erdess, their Dogs and Flock. To be disposed of by Way
of drawing Billets; Any Gentleman or Lady, not inclining to adventure, may satisfy their Curiosity by paying
one Shilling. It is expected it will be disposed of in
about 10 Days.—*The New-York Mercury*, August 29,
1763.

ELECTRICITY.—For the Entertainment of the Curious,
At the Assembly Room, at the City Arms, in the Broad-
Way, will be exhibited, A Course of Experiment in that
curious and entertaining Branch of Natural Philosophy,
called Electricity. To be accompanied with Lectures on
the Nature and Properties of the Electric Fire, By
William Johnson.

The Course to consist of Two Lectures: The first of
which is generally taken up in explaining the Nature
and Properties of that subtle Element, . . .

In the second Lecture, the Electric Fire is shewn to be
the same with Lightning, the Cause and Effects of which
are amply explained. . . .—*The New-York Gazette*,
October 31, 1763.

JERUSALEM, A View of that famous City after the Work
of 7 Years, To be seen at the House of Tho. Evans, Clock
& Watch Maker (opposite the Honourable John Watts,
Esq; and near the Exchange,) from Eight in the Morn-
ing till Seven in the Evening; and from Eight till ten at
Night. One Shilling each person.

It represents Jerusalem, the Temple of Solomon, his
Royal Throne, the noted Houses, Towers and Hills; likewise the Sufferings of our Saviour from the Garden of
Gethsemane to the Cross on the Hill of Golgotha; an
artful piece of Statuary, in which every Thing is exhibited in the most natural Manner, and worthy to be
seen by the Curious. N.B. It will be in New-York three

Months.—*The New-York Gazette or the Weekly Post-Boy*, May 10, 1764.

A CURIOUS MACHINE, in Resemblance of a Boat, (to be taken out of a Man's Pocket, and exhibited to public View) that will carry one Person across a small River, as will be demonstrated at Mr. William Bull's, near Mr. Lispenard's Brewery, on Monday the 19th Day of October last at 3 o'Clock in the Afternoon, for the small Sum of Eighteen Pence for each Person. By JAMES FOSTER.

Those who choose to see this curious Exhibition, will please attend at the above Place. Mr. Foster intends soon to set out for Virginia.—*The New-York Gazette and the Weekly Mercury*, October 19, 1772.

FIRE WORKS.—By Permission of his Excellency the Governor. On Saturday, July the 17, (If the Weather permits.) In the Bowery-Lane, will be exhibited a grand and curious Fire-Work, Divided into three Parts, consisting of the following Variation, Viz.

Part I

A Grand Pyramid turning with a Flower Pot on the Top, and two moving Globes on each Side.

A beautiful Prospect of a Sea-Fight, in which two Men of War will engage, and fire at each other in every Position of a real Battle.

Two capricious Wheels of a new Construction with great Variations of Fire.

Part II

A large Tree illuminated, with several Birds flying out, and coming in again. A Piece representing a Wind-Mill. Two Perpendicular Wheels with Maroons.

Part III

Two Swarm Boxes; Chinese Fountains, and great variations of Fire.

Two Boxes, in which will be represented the Arms of this Province, in brilliant Fire, and several changes.

A fixed Sun of Brilliant, with a Piece representing the Sun and Moon in great Motion.

Two Girondoles, with several Sky Rockets, and Hand Grenadoes.

Also, a large Variety of Fire not mention in this Advertisement.

To prevent Confusion, it is hoped none will take amiss, their not being admitted without a Ticket, which may be had of Mr. James Rivington, and at the Bull's-Head in the Bowery, the Place of Performance, at Five Shillings for the Front Part, and Two and Six-pence for the Yard.

Proper Seats will be made for Ladies and Gentlemen, and the greatest Care will be taken to render the Entertainment agreeable, by Their most obedient Servant, PETER DUMONT.—*Rivington's New-York Gazetteer*, July 15, 1773.

WAX WORKS

EFFIGIES OF THE ROYAL FAMILY OF ENGLAND.—This is to acquaint the Curious. That there is just arriv'd from England and to be seen for a short Time in this Town, at The Sign of the Dolphin Privateer, near the Work-House, New-York. The Effigies of the Royal Family of England. In a Composition of Wax, exactly as big as Life.

I. His Majesty King George the Second.

II. His Royal Highness Frederick, Prince of Wales.

N.B. Both these Effigies are dressed in Royal Robes in the same Manner as when sitting in the Parliament-House.

III. Her Royal Highness Augusta, Princess of Wales.

IV. His Royal Highness William, Duke of Cumberland, in his Regimentals, as he appeared at the Head of the English Arms.

Likewise,

V. The Effigy of the Empress Queen of Hungary and Bohemia.

VI The Arch Duke, Joseph, her Son.

VII A Pandour mounting Guard.

N.B. These three Effigies are dressed in Hungarian Habits. With four curious Effigies, of the four Seasons of the Year,
Likewise,
A Fryar and a Nun in their proper Habits.
The Effigy of Miss Peggy Warfington the present Famous Actress now in England.
With a curious Philosophical, Optical Machine, properly adapted to the Philosophical System of Sir Isaac Newton's Opticks.
Constant Attendance is given from Seven in the Morning, till Six in the Evening; and to be seen by two or more, without loss of Times.
Likewise,
A curious Piece of Ordnance, Which Charges and Discharges both at one Time, and times in a Minute. All the above shewn, by, Gentlemen & Ladies Your most humb. Servt. JAMES WYATT.—*The New-York Weekly Journal*, July 3, 1749.

WAX WORK.—. . . N.B. On Thursday next I design to give a Benefit Night, and likewise the Day to see the Wax Work, for to relieve some of the poor Prisoners in the City Hall; Those Gentlemen and Ladies that will be so charitable to favour me with their good Company, will much oblige their humble Servant, JAMES WYATT. Tickets to be had at Mr. Ramsay's, at Mr. Lepper's, and at Mr. Griswold's, Price Two Shillings each Ticket.—*The New-York Gazette Revived in the Weekly Post-Boy*, October 30, 1749.

WAX FIGURES.—Vaux-Hall Gardens. Mr. Francis begs Leave to acquaint the Ladies and Gentlemen of this City, and the Public in general; that from 8 in the Morning 'till 10 at Night, (at Four Shillings each Person) may be seen at the Gardens, in a large Commodious Room, genteelly fitted for the Purpose, a Group of magnificent Wax Figures, "Ten in Number," rich and elegantly dressed, according to the ancient Roman, and present Mode;

which Figures, bear the most striking Resemblance of real Life, and represent the great Roman General Publius Scipio, who conquered the City of Carthage, standing by his Tent pitch'd in a Grove of Trees, (among which are some of different Fruits, very natural) attended by his Guards; with the King, the young Prince, and Princess, and other great Personages brought before the General, who were taken Prisoners in the City. Also there are several very masterly Pieces of Grotto-Work, and Flowers, composed of various Shells, &c. The Whole affording a very agreeable Entertainment, and are declared by those who have seen Figures of the like kind, much admired in London and Paris, to be no Way inferior.

P. S. A more particular Description, will be ready on Monday to be delivered at the Gardens. Tea, Coffee, Mead, &c. as usual.—*The New-York Gazette and the Weekly Mercury*, July 25, 1768.

WAX WORK ARTIST.—On Monday Evening about 8 o'Clock, a Fire was discover'd in the House of Mrs. Wright, the ingenious Artist in Wax-Work, and Proprietor of Figures so nearly resembling the Life, which have for some Time past been exhibited in this City to general Satisfaction . . . tho' most of the Wax-Work was destroyed, together with some New Pieces which Mrs. Wells (Sister of Mrs. Wright) had lately brought from Charlestown: the whole amounting it is said to the Value of several Hundred Pounds; yet she was so fortunate as to save the curious Piece of the Rev. Mr. Whitefield, the Pennsylvania-Farmer and some others, which she continues to exhibit, and we hear that she proposes to repair the loss sustained by this Fire, as soon as possible, by making some new and curious Pieces.— News item in *The New-York Gazette or the Weekly Post-Boy*, June 10, 1771.

KING GEORGE AND QUEEN CHARLOTTE.—Vaux Hall, Mr. Francis takes this method to acquaint the public, that he has just compleated a number of Wax Figures as large as life, drest in the newest and most elegant manner, representing their present Majesties, King George and Queen Charlotte, sitting on the throne, with their usual attendants, several of the nobility, &c. properly disposed in a large appartment genteely fitted for the purpose, and proper persons to shew the same, from eight in the morning till ten in the evening.—*The New-York Gazette and the Weekly Mercury*, July 6, 1772.

BANQUET IN MACBETH.—To the Encouragers of Ingenuity, and the Public in general. At Vaux-Hall in this City, there are to be seen at any Hour of the Day, a very great Variety of Wax Figures as large as Life, also entirely new dressed, and that in the most elegant as well as genteel Taste. Amongst other curious Representations, one Room contains that of the Banquet in Macbeth, with the Appearance of Banquo's Ghost, and a large Gallery filled with Spectators. Also Harlequin and Columbine, are finished in a very pleasing Manner, and have attracted much Notice; in fine, no Representation of the like Kind has ever been in this City, by any Means equal to the Grandeur and agreeable Entertainment of the present, which have been compleated with very great Trouble and Expence.—*The New-York Gazette and the Weekly Mercury*, August 17, 1772.

WAX WORK ARTIST.—To the Printer, We hear from England, that the ingenious Mrs. Wright, whose surprising Imitations of Nature, in Wax Work, have been so much admired in America, by a diligent Application and Improvement in the same Employment, has recommended herself to the general Notice and Encouragement of Persons of the first Distinction in England, who have honoured her with peculiar Marks of their Favour; and as several eminent Personages, and even his Majesty himself, have condescended to sit several Times, for her to take their Likeness; it is probable she will enrich her

Collection, and oblige her Friends in America, with a View of the most remarkable Persons of the present Age, among which will be the immortal, inimitable Garrick, whom she had began; she has already compleated, and sent over to her House in this City, where they may be seen, the most striking Likeness of the celebrated Doctor Benjamin Franklin, of Philadelphia, now in London, and of Mrs. Catharine M'Cauley, so much admired for her great Learning, Writing and amiable Character.— Letter to the printer in *The New-York Gazette and the Weekly Mercury*, November 9, 1772.

WAX WORK ARTIST.—We hear the ingenious Mrs. Wright from America, at No. 30, Great Suffolk-street, Strand, has lately sent over to New-York, two of her inimitable Wax Figures, representing Dr. Franklin and Mrs. Mackauley; and that she is now making, (to go by Capt. All for Philadelphia), another of a well known character in America, as a present to the America Philosophical Society.—News item from London, December 1, 1772, in *The New-York Gazette and the Weekly Mercury*, February 15, 1773.

WAX AND SHELL WORK.—This is to inform the Public, That at the House of Mr. M'Neill, at the Corner of Chapel-Street, opposite the new Brick Meeting-House, is to be seen, gratis, and disposed of publickly, by the 20th of May next; a most elegant Piece of Wax and Shell Work; the Scheme taken from Homer's Illiad. The Scene Hector and Andromache, with several other beautiful Figures, at the City Gate; the whole judged to be completely finished. The proprietors of this Work, beg leave to acquaint the Ladies, that as they intend continuing in New-York a few Months they propose teaching, on the most reasonable Terms; the Wax and Shell in all its different Branches; and any Ladies inclining to be taught, by applying speedily, may have Time to be perfectly instructed, before their Departure from this

Place.　N.B. Ladies from the Country may be accomo-
dated with Board at a moderate Price.—*The New-York
Journal or the General Advertiser*, May 13, 1773 (*Supplement*).

A REPRESENTATIVE LIST OF WOODCUTS AND ENGRAVINGS ILLUSTRATING NEW YORK NEWSPAPERS, 1726-1776

CHAIRMAKERS

Thomas Ash. *Rivington's New-York Gazetteer,* February 24, 1774

Thomas Burling. *Rivington's New-York Gazetteer,* September 2, 1774

Andrew Gautier. *The New-York Gazette and the Weekly Post-Boy,* April 18, 1765

Adam Galer. *Rivington's New-York Gazetteer,* August 25, 1774

Jonathan Hampton. *The New-York Journal or the General Advertiser,* May 19, 1768

John Kelso. *The New-York Gazette and the Weekly Mercury,* September 5, 1774 (*Supplement*)

SILVERSMITH

Charles Oliver Bruff. *The New-York Gazette and the Weekly Mercury,* March 27, 1775

MAPS

Quebec. *The New-York Gazette,* December 10, 1759

Harbour of Louisbourg. *The New-York Weekly Journal,* December 24, 1733

Plan of the Town and Harbour of Louisburg. *The New-York Weekly Post-Boy,* June 10, 1745

CUTLERS

Richard Sause. *The New-York Gazette and the Weekly Mercury,* April 8, 1771

J. Bailey. *The New-York Gazette and the Weekly Mercury,* October 19, 1772

James Youle. *The New-York Gazette and the Weekly Mercury,* May 18, 1772

Lucas & Shepard. *The New-York Gazette and the Weekly Mercury,* May 13, 1771 (*Supplement*)

COSTUME

Furrier (John Siemon). *The New-York Journal,*
December 19, 1771

Hatter (Nesbitt Deane). *The New-York Gazette
or the Weekly Post-Boy,* August 26, 1771

Leather dressers and breeches-makers: Cornelius
Ryan, At the Sign of the Sun and Breeches, *The
New-York Gazette and the Weekly Mercury,*
March 21, 1774 (*Supplement*); Ethan Sickels,
Rivington's New-York Gazetteer, March 31, 1774

Peruke-maker and hairdresser (James Douglas).
The New-York Gazette and the Weekly Post-Boy,
December 16, 1771

Shoe store (John Milligan's Woman's Shoe Store).
The New-York Gazette, October 31, 1771

Stay-makers: John Burchett, At the Sign of the
Crown and Stays, *Rivington's New-York Gazet-
teer,* July 8, 1773; Peter Hulick, *Rivington's New-
York Gazetteer,* August 4, 1774

ORGAN BUILDER

John Sheybil. *The New-York Gazette and the
Weekly Mercury,* October 10, 1774

BULL-BAITING. *Rivington's New-York Gazetteer,* July,
28, 1774

MICROCOSM. *The New-York Gazette,* March 15, 1756

CHEMIST (Richard Speaight). *Rivington's New-York
Gazetteer,* May 12, 1774

GUN MAKER (Gilbert Forbes, At the Sign of the Sportsman). *The New-York Journal or the General
Advertiser,* March 16, 1775

IRON FURNACE (William Hawxhurst's Sterling Iron
Works). *The New-York Mercury,* July 9, 1764

GRATES (William Bayley's Stove Grate Warehouse). *The
New-York Gazette and the Weekly Mercury,* June
13, 1774

FRENCH BURR MILLSTONES (James Webb). *Rivington's
New-York Gazetteer,* June 16, 1774

INDEX

INDEX

Abbets, James, watchmaker, 143.
Abeel, John, advertisements of, 203, 213, 219; agent for Vesuvius furnace, 219.
Abeel & Neil, auction house of, 270.
Abrahams, Abraham, house of, 173.
Abrahams, I., house of, 277.
Abram, Benjamin, entertainer, 289-290.
Acquakanonk (Acquakanank), N. J., 309; Acquackanung Landing, 210.
Actors, 118, 286-287, 313-314, 370. *See also* Amusements.
Adems, Dunlap, engraver and schoolmaster, 8.
Airey, Mary, silver stolen from, 80-81.
Air-Furnaces: New York Air-Furnace, 188, 189, 213-215; Vesuvius Air-Furnace, Newark, N. J., 188, 189, 219-220. *See also* Forges and Furnaces.
Albany, N. Y., engraved view of, 14; map of road from, 19; craftsmen, etc., in, 105, 143, 146, 147, 248; lumber from, 183, 184, 185; post-rider of, 309-310; mentioned, 4-5, 36.
Albany Pier, 219.
Alcoholic beverages, 123, 239, 296, 299; beer, 290; rum, 91, 92, 105, 121, 123, 183, 212, 219, 270, 296, 299, 355, 380. *See also* Breweries; Distilleries; Punch bowls; Wine.
Aldermen, of N. Y. City, 183, 187, 232 *note*, 237, 267, 282, 292.
Alexander, William (Lord Stirling), proprietor of Hibernia Furnace, 211; house of, 247.
All, Capt., 393.
Allen, J., 125.
Allen, Jacob, gunsmith, 197.
Allen, Moses, schoolmaster, 311-312.
Allentown, 61.
Almanacs, for sale, 247; *Freeman's New-York Almanack for 1770*, 250.

Alsop, John, forge for sale by, 209.
American Colonies, independent of Great Britain as to millstones and semi-precious stones, 78; balance of trade of, 115, 234; civilian action in N. Y. for infraction of non-importation agreement, 37-39; advertisement of conformity with non-importation agreement, 165; decision against imported gloves, 331; tea given up by, 261; Continental Congress of, 16, 58, 152, 215. *See also* American Revolution; Manufactures.
American Company, iron works of, 207.
American Flint Glass Manufactory (Stiegel's), 94-95.
American Manufactures. *See* Manufactures.
American Philosophical Society, 393.
American Revolution, arrival of British fleet in N. Y., 8; map of battlefields of, 27; military companies being organized, 35; advertisement for swords decorated with heads of Pitt, and Wilkes, 35; differences between England and her colonies mentioned, 132; Rivington hanged in effigy, 240; Rivington's printing press destroyed, 241. *See also* American Colonies.
Amory, John, whip maker, 321.
Amsterdam, Holland, 96.
Amusements: plays, 118 *note*, 122, 286; theatres in N. Y. City, 122, 286, 299, 382; theatre in Charleston, S. C., 287; actors, 118, 286-287, 313-314, 370; pantomime, 313; puppet shows, 144, 313, 382; balancing, 289, 290; acrobat, 313; sleight of hand, 312-313, 375; negro impersonator, 314; lectures, 177, 374, 383, 387; electrical experiments, 376-377; concerts, 109, 177, 286, 289, 313,

399

serters from British regiments, 52-53, 115, 128; spatterdashes worn by English soldiers, 331; hooks and eyes for uniforms, 254; tents and marquees, 134, 137, 138-139, 140, 141; field and tent bedsteads, 110, 120, 124, 136, 137, 138, 139; haversacks, 139; colors (flags), 137, 139. *See also* Guns; Swords.

Miller, ——, house of, 78.

Miller, ——, house of, 289.

Miller, Aaron, of New Jersey, clock maker, 154.

Miller, Christopher, 126.

Miller, Eleazer, Jr., 273.

Miller, John, gardener, 132.

Miller, Philip, shop of, robbed, 154.

Miller, [Thomas], ship captain, 3.

Miller, Thomas, Captain, ship built for, 292.

Milligan, ——, shop of, 267.

Milligan, David, secretary of St. Andrew's Society, 258.

Milligan, John, importer, 273; Woman's Shoe Store of, 396.

Milliner, William, house of, 245.

Milliners, 271, 324, 331; millinery taught, 278.

Mills, James, dentist, 299.

Mills, James, tavern keeper, silver stolen from, 62.

Mills, Nathaniel, of Mills, Hicks & Howe, printers, 242-243.

Mills, Hicks & Howe, printers and stationers, 242-243.

Mills, cider, 222; lapidary's, 34; warping and twisting, 262; windmills, 179, 321; metal work for, 194, 197, 202, 210, 225, 226, 227; in Connecticut, 50, 85; in N. Y., 246; makers of, 181-182, 321. *See also* Flour and grist mills; Paper mills; Sawmills.

Millstone, N. J., 149.

Millstones, 78, 209; N. Y. manufactory of, 190-191; American, 78; imported from France, 190, 396.

Millwrights, 181-182, 321.

Milne, Edmond, goldsmith, of Philadelphia, 52.

Milne, John, & Sons, of Manchester, England, 309.

Milworth, Thomas, portrait painter, 6.

Mineral waters, 304.

Miners, 211, 218.

Mines, engine to pump water from, 182, 321; Hibernia iron, N. J., 208, 211; Ringwood Iron, 210; lead, Dutchess Co., N. Y., 211-212.

Miniature painters, 3, 4, 6.

Miniatures, for rings and bracelets, 6.

Minifie, Richard, shop keeper, 255, 269.

Minnett (Minnitt), ——, of Davies & Minnett, 88-89, 98.

Minshull (Minshall), ——, carver and gilder, 128; looking-glass store of, 16, 132-133.

Mirrors (looking-glasses), to be auctioned, 106, 122, 124-125, 126, 133; for sale, 123, 124, 126-127, 129-131, 132-133, 139, 265, 298, 355; broken, bought, 291; frames for, 127, 128, 129, 130, 132, 139; polishing of, 130, 131, 133; silvering of, 130, 131, 132, 349; dressing glasses, 125, 127, 130, 133, 139; pier glasses, 125, 126, 130, 139; looking-glass stores, 16, 129, 130, 132.

Mississippi River, maps of, 17, 25.

Mitchell, Dr. John, death of, 25.

Mock Bird, or New American Songster (1761), 372.

Mohair, 264, 266; buttons, 338.

Molasses, 92, 212.

Molds for iron castings, 208; molding and casting of iron ware, 219.

Money, counterfeit, 47, 49.

Monograms. *See* Ciphers.

Montgomerie, George, deceased, 132.

Montgomerie, [John], Gov. of N. Y., auction of estate of, 120-121.

Montgomery, Alexander, shoe store of, 329.

Montgomery, Alexander, tavern keeper, 30.

Montreal, Canada, on map, 24; furs from, 332.

Monuments, tombs and gravestones, 186, 228, 229, 230.

Moore, ——, Capt., deceased, 328.

Moore, Benjamin, sail maker, house of, 278.

Moore, Blaze, tobacconist, 317.

Moore, Sir Henry, Ratzer map dedicated to, 25.

Moore & Collins, dyers, 282.